SEX, VIOLENCE, AND THE AVANT-GARDE

RICHARD D. SONN

Anarchism in Interwar France

The Pennsylvania State University Press
University Park, Pennsylvania

Material in chapter 5 was first published as the article
"'Your Body Is Yours': Anarchism, Birth Control, and
Eugenics in Interwar France," by Richard Sonn, in *Journal of
the History of Sexuality* 14, no. 4: 415–32. Copyright © 2005
by the University of Texas Press. All rights reserved.

Library of Congress Cataloging-in-Publication Data

Sonn, Richard David.
Sex, violence, and the avant-garde : anarchism in interwar
France / Richard D. Sonn.
    p.   cm.
Includes bibliographical references and index.
Summary: "A study of anarchism in twentieth-century
France during the interwar years. Focuses on anarchist
demands for personal autonomy and sexual liberation.
Argues that these ideals, as well as anarchist hatred of the
government, found favor with members of the artistic
avant-garde, especially the surrealists"—Provided by
publisher.
    ISBN 978-0-271-03663-2 (cloth : alk. paper)
    ISBN 978-0-271-03664-9 (pbk. : alk. paper)
    1. Anarchism—France—History—20th century.
2. Politics and culture—France—History—20th century.
3. Sexual freedom—France—History—20th century.
4. Avant garde (Aesthetics)—France—History—20th century.
    5. Art, French—20th century.
    I. Title.

HX893.S59 2010
335'.83094409042—dc22
2009044136

The Pennsylvania State University Press is a member of the
Association of American University Presses.

for MARY

Contents

Acknowledgments

I would like to thank the University of Arkansas for granting me a leave of absence, which made it possible to spend spring 2004 in Paris doing much of the research for this book. I would also like to thank the National Endowment for the Humanities and Maria DiBattista and Suzanne Nash of Princeton University for including me in the summer 2006 seminar "Modernist Paris." That stay allowed me more time for research and provided stimulating readings and discussions, followed sometimes by sojourns to the iconic Montparnasse establishments frequented by the people whose books we were reading. Thanks are due to the helpful staffs of the Bibliothèque Nationale de France, the Archives Nationales, and the archives of the Prefecture of Police, Department of the Seine. The Internationaal Instituut voor Sociale Geschiedenis (International Institute for Social History) in Amsterdam made it possible for me to read the neo-Malthusian correspondence of Jeanne and Eugène Humbert.

I owe a debt of gratitude to my colleague Evan Bukey for helping me with the German text of Yvan Goll's book *Germaine Berton, die rote Jungfrau.* My colleague Alessandro Brogi made useful critical comments on the chapter "Facing West: American Heroes." Elinor Accampo provided a helpful reading of my gender analysis in chapter 1. Robin Walz read the manuscript and suggested that I add an epilogue focusing on connections between interwar anarchism and the 1960s. He also alerted me to the anarchist and crime novelist Léo Malet. Many of the chapters have been presented as papers over the last few years, especially at the meetings of the Western Society for French History. Thanks also are due to the *Journal of the History of Sexuality* and its editor, Matthew Kueffler, for allowing me to use the material previously published in that journal. Chapter 5, somewhat modified here, was first presented at the 2005 meeting of the Society for French Historical Studies Conference in Palo Alto, California, and subsequently published as the article "'Your Body Is Yours': Anarchism, Birth Control, and Eugenics in Interwar France," *Journal of the History of Sexuality* 14, no. 4: 415–32. The readers of my manuscript for Penn State University Press provided helpful feedback. Thanks, too, to my editor at Penn State, Eleanor Goodman, for taking an interest in my project and helping shepherd it to completion. Amanda Kirsten assisted in the copyediting phase of production. I have had the good fortune to receive continuing support from the chair of the University of Arkansas history department, Dr. Lynda Coon, and from the department office staff, especially Jane Rone. I assume full responsibility for any errors of fact or interpretation.

I am grateful to my daughter, Julia, for helping me prepare the bibliography while she was busy applying to graduate schools. My son, Xan, was applying to colleges while I was in Paris researching this project, which made it harder for me to help him decide which college to attend. Now that the book is done, he is too and is out in the world trying to harness energy from the sun. Both of my children are trying to do their part to save the natural world through science—a goal of which most anarchists would surely have approved. My wife Mary helped me in preparing the index. As a historian who is no longer young, I am fortunate to enjoy multigenerational support and encouragement not only from my children but from my parents and from my uncle, Al Sonnenstein. My father and uncle were born during the Great War, my mother in the year the French occupied the Ruhr. Like them, I too was born in Chicago. We have all lived through tumultuous times.

Introduction:
French Anarchism in the Interwar Era: Decline or Renewal?

Anarchists in interwar France knew that their movement had seen better days. Back in the 1890s they had been at the forefront of the revolutionary struggle, feared by the authorities for their penchant for violence and admired by the masses for their temerity. Their main rivals on the left, the socialists, were preoccupied with the parliamentary politics disdained by the anarchists; communists did not yet exist. While the wave of terrorism that swept the movement in the early 1890s may have been counterproductive, bringing down government repression on their heads and sending many militants into exile, to prison, or to the scaffold, the anarchists responded by reinventing themselves as anarcho-syndicalists. Instead of blowing up the Chamber of Deputies they began organizing workers into revolutionary unions. The main French labor union, the Confédération Générale du Travail (CGT), was anarchist led and dedicated to direct action against the capitalists and the government. For thirty years, from the mid-1880s until the First World War, the anarchists and revolutionary syndicalists had threatened the stability of the Third Republic. The cartons of documents devoted to them in the police and national archives attest to governmental concern for their activities.

Yet by the 1920s and 1930s anarchists could only look back nostalgically at a prewar era remembered as the heroic age of anarchism. As early as 1925, the major newspaper of interwar anarchism, *Le Libertaire*, already featured articles titled "The Crisis of Anarchism." Anarchists were being jailed by Bolsheviks in Russia, fascists in Italy, and the dictator of Spain. In France the movement was beset by polemics and division. In what would become a familiar lament, the author said some anarchists still sought to prepare for the next revolution while others saw it as a philosophical or ethical force and spent too much energy exploring vegetarianism and sexual pluralism.[1] The following month *Le Libertaire* published a response by the foremost proponent of the individualist strain of anarchism, E. Armand, who first denied that there was a crisis because the anarchist press had more readers than in prewar times, and then defended what we would now call "lifestyle" issues such as sexuality and diet by arguing that alcoholics or sexual exclusivists would never destroy political systems of domination.[2]

Yet several years later, in 1931, Armand shared his own gloomy reflections on the problems of anarchism in the pages of another anarchist paper, *La Voix Libertaire*. Armand looked back at thirty years of effort as having accomplished little, since four or five anarchist papers, including his own paper *L'En Dehors*, vied for the same ten to fifteen thousand readers who constituted the base of anarchist support in France. The situation was even worse in the English-speaking countries, Armand wrote, with a mere five thousand subscribers to anarchist papers among 170 million English speakers. He concluded that their papers would only appeal to those already convinced of the truth of anarchist doctrines, and dreamed of a periodical that would not have to breathe a word of ideology but rather would treat daily events in such a way that readers would emerge with a distrust of the state. In fact he guessed that the satirical daily *Le Canard Enchaîné* did more to promote anarchist ideas in the masses than a hundred papers for initiates.[3]

Another anarchist paper, *Plus Loin*, published a series of articles in 1932 that contrasted the heyday of anarchism with the lamentable present state of the movement. The author cited a number of reasons for its decline, starting with the bloodshed of the Great War. Postwar prosperity and increasing access to petit-bourgeois comforts had further diminished its popularity among the workers, and of course there was competition from the *camelots du roi* on the far right and Bolsheviks on the left. He ruefully recognized that some of the most dedicated anarchist revolutionaries had turned to communism as more efficacious and realistic. He also blamed anarchists of the individualist tendency for discrediting the movement by focusing almost exclusively on sexuality, while the revolutionary syndicalists of thirty years ago were now risk-averse bureaucrats. As recession and class antagonism worsened, he hoped that a new generation would be mobilized, and concluded his series of articles on the unduly optimistic note that aspirations for liberty were imperishable.[4] The fact that this writer could recall the glory days of anarchism forty years before suggests his advanced age, and in fact the editorial staff of *Plus Loin* noted wryly that they were known as the "under eighties" by other anarchists due to their redoubtable maturity. They were clearly out of the mainstream of interwar anarchism, being supporters of the ideas of Jean Grave, the major prewar anarchist-communist editor who had supported the French war effort in 1914 and had signed the Manifesto of Sixteen calling on anarchists to support the allied side. This had made Grave and his followers extremely unpopular after the war, when anarchists and many others were filled with revulsion against war as the ultimate murderous expression of nationalism.

Yet as we have seen, the writer for *Plus Loin* was hardly alone in perceiving the hard times upon which the anarchist movement had fallen. A similar discussion took place in the pages of *La Voix Libertaire*, a paper run by Sébastien Faure, the single most important figure in the anarchist movement throughout the Third Republic. Faure's paper was open to anarchists of all persuasions, from individualists to syndicalists to anarchist-communists, since it had been founded in 1928 explicitly to unify the fractured movement. In the opening issues of *La Voix Libertaire*, Faure himself recognized that "Le mouvement anarchiste subit un temps d'arrêt. Il faut y mettre fin" [The anarchist movement has come to a halt. We must end that state]. Faure attributed the state of weakness first to the defection of such recognized leaders as Peter Kropotkin, Jean Grave, and Charles Malato to the war effort in 1914, and second the moral debacle of the unions, which had either become moderate and reformist or had gone over to the communists. Third he blamed the anarchists' own mistakes, principally the divisions between the three major tendencies—individualist, syndicalist, and communist—which rendered the movement weak.[5]

Linert, Faure, and Armand were older men (Armand was nearly sixty in 1932 and the others were even older), but their public declarations of disillusionment with the state of anarchism were more than nostalgic longings for their lost youth. Their statements reinforce the sense that anarchism thrived in the more individualist atmosphere of the turn of the century but was no longer relevant in an era of increasingly centralized and powerful states. The war itself had given vast new powers to governments on all sides, and the workers of those states largely acquiesced in that power, as shown by the spirit of 1914, called in France the *union sacrée* (sacred union). In the aftermath of war a new revolutionary movement arose in Russia that succeeded in seizing state power, and through its success fired the imaginations of revolutionaries everywhere. Even the anarchists were initially seized with enthusiasm for Bolshevism, until by the end of the Russian civil war they could see that far from being a government of workers councils, as the Soviets proclaimed, the Bolsheviks had created a centralized and repressive one-party state. No sooner had the anarchists decided that they would not follow the communist path after all than Mussolini had seized power in Italy and a new all-powerful ideology called fascism claimed the allegiance of the masses. Spain too succumbed to dictatorship and repression in the early 1920s, and libertarian aspirations retracted further as fascism spread to central and eastern Europe in the 1930s. The one bright spot in the international anarchist movement, the Spanish Civil War and the empowering of anarchists in eastern Spain in July 1936, would lead to a renewed sense of betrayal as Stalin's forces crushed the anarchist movement in Barcelona and Valencia in May 1937 and ended the anarchists' influence in the Popular Front government.

To make matters even bleaker for French anarchists, the main hope for the creation of an alternative anarchist society, revolutionary unions, had also been lost by the early 1920s. The principal union, the CGT, had already begun to move away from anarchist control before the war, and its leader in 1914, Léon Jouhaux, had declared labor's support for the French war effort. After the war the CGT split between a moderate majority and a revolutionary minority, the CGTU, or Unitaire; several months later, in 1922, this minority affiliated itself with the French Communist Party. Such party affiliation was anathema to the anarchists, who stood by their Declaration of Amiens of 1906 that the unions should remain independent of all political affiliations. Eventually a third variant of the CGT was born and called itself the CGT-SR, appending "revolutionary syndicalist" to proclaim its anarcho-syndicalist loyalties, but it remained so numerically insignificant that anarchists joked that the s.r. stood for "sans rien," without anything.[6] French anarchists thus faced the specter of the rise of totalitarianism abroad and marginalization at home, as the communists displaced them as keepers of the revolutionary flame. Even as their comrades were being persecuted in the Soviet Union, some French anarchists were nevertheless beguiled by the red star shining from the east. While communists sang in unison, anarchist voices seemed more disunited than ever. Libertarian ideals seemed more than ever as unrealizable dreams out of step with the cruel realities of the modern world. The interwar era was not a period in which to be sanguine about ideals of stateless liberty. What was an anarchist to do? What is a historian of anarchism to do with them?

Interwar Anarchism and the Historians

Some indication of the diminished place of anarchism after World War I in the historical canon can be gleaned from perusing the classic study of French anarchism by Jean Maitron, *Le mouvement anarchiste en France*. First published in 1951 as Maitron's doctoral dissertation, it was expanded and re-edited in two volumes in 1975. The first volume, covering the movement from its nineteenth-century origins to World War I, is nearly five hundred pages long; the second volume contains two hundred pages of text and an additional two hundred of appendices and bibliography. Eighty pages are devoted to the period from 1914 to 1939. Since Maitron (1910–1987) was himself active in the anarchist movement in the 1930s, it cannot be said he was either biased against or ignorant of that period. More general histories of anarchism also concentrate on the 1880 to 1914 period, and coverage of the interwar era focuses on Russia and Spain, with a glance at the Sacco and Vanzetti case in the United States, and barely a mention of France.[7] Perhaps the most dismissive treatment of interwar French anarchism is that of Peter Marshall. In his seven-hundred-page magnum opus, *Demanding the Impossible: A History of Anarchism,* he summarizes: "Outside the syndicalist movement, a small band of ageing militants kept the anarchist message alive in a few papers with declining readership. Their international connections were maintained by the increasing number of anarchist refugees from the Soviet Union, Italy, Germany and Spain to seek asylum in France."[8]

Even the recent study by David Berry devoted to *The History of the French Anarchist Movement, 1917–1945* focuses on the French anarchists' response to the two great revolutionary movements of the era, the Russian Revolution and the Spanish Civil War.[9] Berry generally follows Maitron's interpretation and approach, offering a political and ideological history of the anarchist movement, and like Maitron he is thorough and conversant with the sources. He accepts the division of interwar anarchism into anarchist-communists, individualists, and syndicalists, and argues that the former element dominated in the interwar era as syndicalism declined; individualists such as Armand are portrayed as marginal to the movement.[10] He provides little social or cultural analysis of anarchism, confining his comments on the social and gender makeup of anarchism to a concluding chapter, in which he argues that anarchists did not differ from communists sociologically but only doctrinally. This suggests that they were no longer drawn primarily from the artisanal classes of printers and cobblers, as they had been at the turn of the century. My own research has revealed one especially popular occupational category for Parisian anarchists: a remarkable number worked as proofreaders for various newspapers and controlled the proofreaders' union. This suggests that anarchists had adapted to the modern economy while not entirely discarding their artisanal and print-shop heritage.

The only other major study of interwar French anarchism is the 1993 study by Claire Auzias, *Mémoires libertaires, Lyon, 1919–1939*. As her title indicates, she focuses almost entirely on anarchist activity in the city of Lyon, and her study is based on, and enriched by, oral interviews with eighteen anarchists, men and women, active in Lyon between the wars. In contrast to Berry's near-fixation on organization and ideology, Auzias conveys a fuller sense of anarchism as a way of life. She is particularly sensitive to gender and cultural implications mostly missing from Berry's account. Her Lyonnais anarchists admit that by their time anarchism sometimes resembled a group of friends more than a mass political movement, but their recollections underscore the importance of sociability as well as ideology. Anarchism was lived as much in daily life as it involved planning a utopian future.

Varieties of Anarchism

If anarchists in the 1920s and 1930s were weak and divided, outflanked on the left by communism and proffering a vision of the liberated individual in a world increasingly dedicated to the masses and the state, and if anarchists in France most notably served as a reception committee for immigrants from the real revolutionary hotspots, why devote another study to them? As this brief historiographical discussion suggests, no one has specifically explored the social and cultural contexts of French, and specifically Parisian, anarchism in the interwar era. Many more texts could be cited concerning French anarchism in the Belle Epoque, but due to the perception of anarchist decline, similar attention has not been paid to the interwar era. Such attention reveals that the anarchists responded to the crisis afflicting their movement in innovative and even startling ways. They were not content to accept their own irrelevance; in fact they were convinced that their libertarian ideals were vital to civilization if it was to be saved from the scourge of war and from totalitarian regimes seeking to enslave the individual. In the rest of this introductory chapter I would like to advance three interrelated propositions. With the decline of the era of individual violence known as propaganda by the deed of the late nineteenth century, and of revolutionary syndicalism in the Belle Epoque, anarchists of the interwar era evolved both by preference and necessity toward a form of praxis that can be called ethical anarchism. This approach, which emphasized the positive contribution of anarchism to social thought rather than the negative and destructive aspects, ensured the continuing relevance of the individualist anarchists, the most philosophically oriented of the three main tendencies. Further, it led anarchists into moral campaigns or crusades that required their cooperation with other progressive groups and with each other. It also led to an increasing preoccupation with sexuality and gender relations, another area that the individualists dominated and that connected them to international movements addressing the repression of the body and the psyche. This interpretation implies that while divisions within anarchism were real enough, both anarchist divisiveness and marginality have been overdrawn.

Far from acquiescing in their marginal status, anarchists in the 1920s and 1930s excelled at focusing attention on issues dear to them and enlisting the support of other like-minded people who did not necessarily subscribe to anarchism *tout court*. One of the best examples of this in the 1920s is the six-year-long campaign to save the Italian-American anarchists Nicola Sacco and Bartolomeo Vanzetti from the electric chair. By the summer of 1927 thousands of people were turning out for mass meetings and demonstrations in favor of the anarchist martyrs. Communists, socialists, members of the League of the Rights of Man, and sympathetic citizens joined the anarchists in campaigning for their pardon.[11] The Sacco-Vanzetti committee was led by Louis Lecoin, an anarchist-communist closely associated with Sébastien Faure and *Le Libertaire*. The plight of the two anarchists, universally considered to have been unjustly condemned to death, humanized the movement while attributing violence to the U.S. government and judiciary. Lecoin used similar tactics in the 1930s as he linked anarchists with other left-leaning groups supporting the Spanish republican government against Franco. Lecoin was one of many anarchist pacifists and antimilitarists who campaigned tirelessly to halt the move toward war. Some anarchist purists derided these efforts of "committees for social defense" as reformist. In fact they garnered far more support for anarchist goals than could more narrowly partisan positions, while placing the movement in a constructive and positive light. The principal anarchist movement in support of the Spanish Revolution, Solidarité International Antifasciste (SIA), on which Lecoin served as secretary, raised more than two hundred thousand francs and had forty-five thousand members by 1939.[12]

Anarchists always had to contend with an image problem. Ever since the "heroic" era of assassinations and bombings of the fin de siècle, anarchism had been associated with violence. Anarchists were widely derided as negative destroyers. Anarchy then as now was taken to signify disorder, and no amount of protest by anarchist thinkers such as Elisée Reclus that anarchism was a higher or more natural form of order could shake the association of anarchism with chaos. Anarchists themselves were always reluctant to condemn any revolutionary or even antisocial, criminal activity. Yet as their actual ability to foment revolution diminished, they were able to organize mass movements in favor of peace, or argue for conscientious-objector status for military inductees (which did not exist in France), or broadcast the plight of political prisoners in Russia, and so put their ideals in a positive light. Fervently antibourgeois and opposed to the centralized state, anarchists stood for peace and freedom, for the individual conscience and control of the self, and also for the harmonious balance of man with nature. Anarchism increasingly was redefined as an ethical force (many disliked the word "morality," associating it with repressive religious teachings, and so preferred its synonym). Some individualist anarchists, most notably Han Ryner, condemned all violence, including revolutionary violence, though this position was still hotly debated within the movement in the 1920s, as were the nonviolent tactics of Gandhi. There was no consensus on these controversial issues, but anarchists increasingly portrayed themselves as the moral antidote to a violent and exploitive world.

To argue that ethical issues were gradually supplanting economic and political ones suggests that individualist anarchism was not as marginal to the anarchist movement as commentators such as David Berry maintain. Nor were libertarian communists as removed from the individualists as their own rhetoric sometimes suggests. Frequently frustrated by the individualists' lack of interest in the working classes and the long-awaited revolution, the mainstream anarchist-communists would seem to have had more in common with the syndicalists. Since they rejected political parties, the only mechanism for effecting the revolutionary transition to a stateless society was the labor union, which would regulate production and along with consumer unions would theoretically replace the parliamentary system. The problem with revolutionary syndicalism was that anarchists had lost control of the unions, and the CGT-SR and its leader Pierre Besnard were so jealous of its autonomy as to distrust control by anarchist ideologues. When one prominent anarchist, André Colomer, wrote in the mid-1920s that the union was like a body to which anarchism supplied the soul, Besnard replied furiously that he didn't see it that way at all. Characterized as doctrinaire and rigid, Besnard jealously guarded the autonomy of his diminishing movement from the communists on the one hand and the anarchists on the other.[13]

Colomer, whom I will discuss at length in chapter 8, had passed through all the varieties of anarchism. A Nietzschean individualist in the years before the war, he entered a syndicalist phase early in the postwar era, organizing a union of entertainers, before accepting the editorship of the principal organ of the anarchist-communists, *Le Libertaire*. His paper made the leap from weekly to daily newspaper late in 1923 under his aegis and under circumstances that will be discussed in chapter 3. Yet by March 1925, *Le Libertaire* was unable to maintain the expense of running a daily paper and returned to weekly status; by the late 1920s it wasn't always regularly appearing on a weekly basis and was increasingly precarious financially until the Popular Front era briefly boosted its circulation. The discussion of the "crisis of anarchism" cited above took place in 1925 in *Le Libertaire*, for not only were their hopes for a daily paper dashed but it had become clear that no revolution was in the offing and the moderate left Cartel des Gauches further weakened the anarchist appeal among the masses. Colomer left *Le Libertaire* early in 1925 to found another, more individualist-oriented paper, *L'Insurgé*, which proved to be yet another stepping stone on his path toward communist affiliation. That the biggest issue of these years was the Sacco and Vanzetti campaign, which had nothing to do with unions or general strikes and was tangential to France, reveals the weakness of mainstream anarchism. Into this vacuum stepped the individualists.

Individualist anarchism appealed more to middle-class anarchists such as teachers, journalists, and intellectuals than it did to the workers. Just as fervently opposed to the constraints imposed by the government as any other anarchists, they were less sanguine about the prospects of violent revolution overthrowing it. Arguing that individuals must free themselves from all authoritarian tendencies before any revolution could succeed, they now had the Russian Revolution as an example of the necessary outcome of a revolution that claimed to embody the "dictatorship of the proletariat." The rise of fascism and communism reinforced the individualists' suspicion of power. If the only hope lay in the ethical reconfiguration of the individual, sole reality confronting those fictions called society and nation, then education and self-cultivation rather than unions and insurrections, were more likely to transform society from within. Individualists were as likely to cite the works of Max Stirner, the Young Hegelian author of *The Ego and its Own*, or Friedrich Nietzsche, or the Anglo-American current represented by Henry David Thoreau and Benjamin Tucker, as they were to invoke Mikhail Bakunin and Kropotkin.

Because individualists tended to be better educated than the typical anarchist militant, they played a disproportionate role in the world of anarchist propaganda. Even those publications most identified with the anarchist-communist Union Anarchiste, *Le Libertaire* and the monthly *La Revue Anarchiste*, relied on individualists to supply some of their articles. In 1925

Sébastien Faure announced the grand project of the creation of an *Anarchist Encyclopedia*, to be issued in monthly installments over the next several years. Finally completed in 1934 in four large volumes totaling three thousand pages in small print, most of the contributors were necessarily from the individualist wing of the movement. All of this suggests that the sometimes real animosity between tendencies has been overstated. As the possibility of revolution dimmed, and as anarchism itself was marginalized, individualist ethical concerns became more, not less, central to the movement as a whole. In an increasingly bellicose era, pacifism and antimilitarism, the claims of the individual conscience against the military and imperialist demands of the state, supplanted calls for insurrection (general strikes were called at the beginning and end of this period, in 1920 and 1938, and failed miserably).

Interwar anarchists were particularly beholden to the past. A glance at the major thinkers and leaders of interwar anarchism reveals that nearly all of them were active well before World War I, and often long before. Born in 1858, Sébastien Faure's career spanned the three major periods of propaganda by the deed, syndicalism, and the interwar era. In the late 1920s he was estranged from *Le Libertaire,* which he had founded in 1895, and created instead the appropriately titled *La Voix Libertaire* (Faure was renowned as the outstanding orator of the movement) to advocate synthesis of anarchist factions. At the same time he proceeded with his grandiose project of an anarchist encyclopedia, published by himself on his own printing press. A beloved and respected figure in anarchist circles, Faure served as a living link to the heroic era of Louise Michel and Peter Kropotkin. Unlike Jean Grave, who also survived throughout the interwar era, Faure had not compromised his anarchist credentials by supporting the French war effort, which is why *Le Libertaire* could be reborn after the war while Grave's *Les Temps Nouveaux* died unmourned. Faure died at eighty-four in 1942.

Stoicism and Sexuality

The two preeminent individualist anarchist thinkers and propagandists also came of age during the fin de siècle. Henri Ner, born in 1861, redivided the syllables of his short name so as to become Han Ryner, perhaps in evocation of one of Henrik Ibsen's antisocial heroes, probably also to separate his anarchist writings from his respectable life as a professor at the Lycée Charlemagne in Paris. Beginning in the 1890s and continuing into the 1930s (he died in 1938), Han Ryner published dozens of novels and frequently spoke at lectures and "contradictory" meetings (involving debates over current issues), where he voiced his uncompromising version of anarchist individualism. Ryner was immersed in ancient Greek and Roman thought and was a thoroughgoing Stoic who saw freedom as coming from the renunciation of desires and attachments. While opposed to cooperation with the state, he was also opposed to all violence, even in the service of revolution. By the 1920s he looked every bit the bohemian sage, with a long, flowing, white beard and otherworldly demeanor. So admired was he in the 1920s that the regional anarchist weekly *Le Semeur de Normandie* devoted a special issue to him, the only contemporary figure to receive such an honor. Other special issues were devoted to Beethoven (the esteemed novelist Romain Rolland wrote on how Beethoven defied authority) and Tolstoy, putting Ryner in illustrious company, which his admirers felt he deserved, sure that he would go down in history as a revered writer and thinker. If Han Ryner's reputation has not kept pace with these other artists, it may be because his peculiar fusion of antique and anarchist values did not survive his own lifetime. The anarchist quality of Stoicism lay first in its pagan, pre-Christian orientation, and second in its ideal of a self-regulating individual freed from material desires, and thus autonomous to the highest degree.

The other major individualist propounded an interpretation of anarchism even more controversial than Ryner's pagan pacifism. This was E. Armand, born in 1872 to a communard father. Armand, whose real name was Ernest Juin, especially provoked the ire of the anarchist-communist mainstream. Armand was not an anarchist during the "heroic" era of the 1890s but rather worked for the Salvation Army. He made the unlikely transition toward an uncompromising version of individualist anarchism via Tolstoy's Christian anarchism. He was deeply influenced by Albert Libertad, the radical individualist who founded the journal *L'Anarchie* and died at thirty-three in 1908. Libertad was the embodiment of the "lifestyle" anarchist who saw anarchism more as a way of life than as an ideology. For Armand it was both. Active as an anarchist polemicist before and during the war, Armand spent five years in jail during and after World War I for supposedly aiding a deserter. Almost immediately after he was freed in 1922 he published a major book on the ideology of individualist anarchism and then founded a journal, *L'En Dehors* (Outside), which would last until 1939. The title echoed one edited by another intransigent individualist, Zo d'Axa, in the 1890s. The first *L'En Dehors* epitomized the bohemian union of anarchists and symbolist writers; the second emphasized Armand's peculiar sexual ideas.

Several times in the debate on the crisis of anarchism in the interwar years, the anarchist-communists complained that the individualists were preoccupied by questions of sexuality and the body, or as Ferandel put it in 1925, by "too many polemics on the art of making love in common . . . [and] the nutritive qualities of certain vegetables."[14] The increasingly obsessive focus of Armand's paper on sexual issues reinforced some anarchists' opinion that this individualism was an aberrant branch of the mainstream. Ideals of free love had held sway in anarchist circles since the 1890s since many anarchists had refused to allow either state or church to sanction their unions. Free love had not meant promiscuity but rather serial monogamy; yet promiscuity is just what Armand had in mind. His conception of what he called *camaraderie amoureuse* (loving fellowship or friendship) was intended to lead to a sort of group sex collective. Since Armand was also extremely interested in establishing anarchist colonies in France, Central America, or the South Seas, and was an expert on the history of utopian communities, he along with the naturists and vegetarians seemed to be purposely removing themselves from the urban anarchist mainstream, if not from the modern world entirely. Armand saw colonies and free love as related in that both were posed as alternatives to the nuclear family—an institution he viewed as the foundation of antisocial egoism in the modern world. Though both Ryner and Armand were individualist anarchists, Armand's vision of an apolitical and nonlegal society included voluntary social formations lacking in Ryner's antique formulation.

If propaganda and proselytizing were central to fin de siècle anarchism (the era of "propaganda by the deed") and unions and labor dominated the era of anarcho-syndicalism from 1895 to 1914 (the slogan was "direct action"), then the body and sexuality were central to anarchist discourse of the interwar era. The operative slogan of the era could be borrowed from a novel by Victor Margueritte, not an anarchist but closely in league with them from the mid-twenties to mid-thirties. In 1927 he published a short novel called *Ton corps est à toi* (your body is yours), which helped popularize anarchist neo-Malthusian ideals that sought to limit population growth and provide women with the means for effective birth control. Neo-Malthusianism, or birth control, was already underway in the two decades preceding World War I but was tremendously reinforced by the carnage of war. While the left argued that no one should be compelled to provide cannon fodder for the militaristic state, the government passed laws in 1920 forbidding not only abortion but all propaganda in favor of birth control, in hopes of replenishing the French population sapped by the war. As the state put its weight behind procreation, anarchists played a central role in the movement that sought to limit births. The anarchist and conscientious objector Manuel Devaldès summarized the argument in the title of his 1933 book, *Croître et multiplier, c'est la guerre* (To increase and multiply means war). Armand, along with Eugène and Jeanne Humbert, Madeleine Pelletier, Victor Margueritte, and many others, campaigned for more enlightened attitudes regarding sex and procreation. The free disposition of one's body, of one's being, placed individualist anarchism at the heart of the move toward sexual freedom as the negation of the militarized state, whether republican or fascist. As memory of the recent war and fear of impending war in the near future thrust issues of life and death to the forefront, (control over) reproduction displaced production as the central concern of many anarchists.

"Your body is yours" focused overtly on female bodies exploited sexually by men and the patriarchal state but related equally well to male bodies facing military service. All anarchists were conscious, as well as conscientious (the French *conscience* implied both meanings at once), objectors. The state demanded women's bodies as reproducers and men's as soldiers; only a heightened state of consciousness, a state of anarchist awareness, could make one realize that one's body was one's own and not at the state's disposal. Once in corporeal control, many anarchists became partisans of vegetarianism and of the broader social hygiene movement, which attacked alcoholism and tobacco, and also the health of the body through nudism, swimming and sunbathing, and gymnastics. Han Ryner's ethic of self-control and self-knowledge complemented Armand's rejection of any moral or legal restrictions on the free disposition of one's body. The state could have no domain over men or women, as warriors or procreators. Both Ryner and Armand also blamed the Catholic Church for inculcating many of the values—obedience to the state, sexual repression, hostility to birth control—they found inimical to free exercise of the self.

The synopsis outlined above has said little about gender issues. In the era of the New Woman and the redefinition of women's roles following their large-scale entry into the workplace during the war, anarchists could scarcely be unconcerned with women's role in society. While they frequently asserted their support for female emancipation, we will see that their attitudes toward the social and political roles of women were considerably more ambiguous than were their attitudes toward sexuality. Feminists had put considerable effort into campaigning for women's suffrage, and their efforts were rewarded in much of Europe and America, though thanks to the conservative French senate, not in France. Yet anarchists placed no stock whatsoever in electoral politics and perceived feminists as both misguided and overly bourgeois. They were trying to buy into the system rather than overthrow it. Women themselves were often blamed for their subordinate social status because they were widely seen as more religious than men. While there were a few prominent women in and around the anarchist movement, that movement was, and was perceived as being, predominantly male. Given their revolutionary credentials, the anarchists were surprisingly retrograde in sharing the biases of most other men of their day regarding women. Anarchist women, for their part, were critical of schemes for plural love and sexual emancipation; their lack of enthusiasm further separated anarchist men and women. At the other extreme from Armand, Dr. Madeleine Pelletier counseled complete celibacy as the best guarantee for a woman wishing to preserve her independence. Yet both Armand and Pelletier were hostile to the nuclear family as the fount of jealousy, patriarchal authority, the domination of women and children, and the source of social egoism. Anarchists went much further than communists in their critique of the family.

Purity and Danger

Discourses concerned with sexuality and gender roles took a central place in interwar anarchism, but physicality was expressed in other ways as well. Anarchist individualists were already infamous for their dietary concerns in the years before the war. In her memoir of her anarchist years that was serialized in *Le Matin* in 1913, Rirette Maîtrejean made much of the strange food regimens of some of the *compagnons*. She made light of André Lorulot, who for a time thought oil was a panacea that should be imbibed in large quantities, while proscribing salt and pepper. She described the "tragic bandits" of the Bonnot gang as refusing to eat meat or drink wine, preferring plain water.[15] Her humorous comments reflected the practices of the "naturist" wing of individualist anarchists who favored a simpler, more "natural" lifestyle centered on a vegetarian diet. In the 1920s, this wing was expressed by the journal *Le Néo-Naturien, Revue des Idées Philosophiques et Naturiennes*. Contributors condemned the fashion of smoking cigarettes, especially by young women; a long article of 1927 actually connected cigarette smoking with cancer! Others distinguished between vegetarians, who foreswore the eating of meat, from the stricter "vegetalians," who ate nothing but vegetables. An anarchist named G. Butaud, who made this distinction, opened a restaurant called the Foyer Végétalien in the nineteenth arrondissement in 1923. Other issues of the journal included vegetarian recipes.[16] In 1925, when the young anarchist and future detective novelist Léo Malet arrived in Paris from Montpellier, he initially lodged with anarchists who operated another vegetarian restaurant that served only vegetables, with neither fish nor eggs.[17] Nutritional concerns coincided with other means of encouraging health bodies, such as nudism and gymnastics. For a while in the 1920s, after they were released from jail for antiwar and birth-control activities, Jeanne and Eugène Humbert retreated to the relative safety of the "integral living" movement that promoted nude sunbathing and physical fitness, which were seen as integral aspects of health in the Greek sense of *gymnos,* meaning nude. This back-to-nature, primitivist current was not a monopoly of the left; the same interests were echoed by right-wing Germans in the interwar era. In France, however, these proclivities were mostly associated with anarchists, insofar as they suggested an ideal of self-control and the rejection of social taboos and prejudices.

The other tendency widely associated with anarchists was violence. The same anarchists who practiced nude sunbathing and vegetarianism were more likely to be pacifists than terrorists. Nevertheless, attacks with bombs and pistols called attention to the bodies of others, bodies that were vulnerable to attack in a way that institutions were not. As they attacked figures of authority, these young anarchists put their own bodies on the line for the cause. A series of notorious trials punctuated the 1920s, from the trial of Emile Cottin, the would-be assassin of prime minister Georges Clemenceau in 1919, to that of the Jewish anarchist Sholom Schwartzbard in the fall of 1927.[18] Cottin was quickly forgotten, but when a twenty-year-old woman killed a leading figure—and war hero—of the Action Française in 1923, her trial was widely publicized and politicized, with a variety of leftist luminaries testifying for the defense. Other anarchists' own bodies were vulnerable either to violence perpetrated by themselves or by the state. Most famous were the Italian-American anarchists Nicola Sacco and Bartolomeo Vanzetti, whose execution in August 1927 occasioned riots in the streets of Paris; others attempted suicide out of some combination of personal instability and political despair. Notorious deeds had the effect of personalizing abstract ideological issues. The frail body of young Germaine Berton, the tormented body of the even younger would-be anarchist Philippe Daudet, the Jewish body of Sholom Schwartzbard, the electrocuted bodies of Sacco and Vanzetti, all were paraded before the public as exemplars of sacrifice and martyrdom.

Anarchist bodies always existed in relation to the mass violence perpetrated on bodies in World War I. Cottin tried to assassinate the war premier, Clemenceau, during the Paris Peace Conference; Berton sought to avenge the murder of Jaurès, the martyr to war; Schwartzbard killed a nationalist leader who emerged in the dual context of war and civil war in Russia. Armand spent five years in prison for encouraging desertion, while Eugène Humbert fled France for neutral Spain to avoid military service and then was jailed on his return. The anarchist schoolteacher Maurice Wullens lost a hand in the conflict and became fervently pacifistic. His ally, the neo-Malthusian Manuel Devaldès, fled to England during the war because France lacked conscientious objector status, and remained in exile for over a decade. The war was the supreme example of disorder and corporeal dissolution; anarchists countered the deadly power of state and military hierarchy directly, through violence or flight, and symbolically, through self-purification.

Vegetarian diets and sudden outbursts of violence each sought to purify and reorder the anarchist community. By divesting themselves of intoxicants and foods deemed unhealthy, the naturists were setting themselves apart from the unredeemed members of the population. Anarchist assailants seemed to be sowing disorder, yet they too were attempting to remove sources of disorder from the body politic, thereby restoring it to health. That both Berton and Schwartzbard would be acquitted suggests that sympathetic juries could be convinced that the victims rather than the perpetrators were the genuine sources of disorder. Berton claimed she was avenging the murder of Jean Jaurès, the prewar socialist spokesman for peace, by attacking the rightists who had called for his death. She carried out her deed as French troops were again on the march, guaranteeing German compliance with the terms of the Treaty of Versailles by occupying the Ruhr. She was therefore restoring order rather than sowing disorder. The same can be said for Schwartzbard's killing of the former hetman of the Ukraine, Simon Petliura, whom he held responsible for the murder of tens of thousands of Jews during the Russian civil war. The fact that neither assassin tried to escape, but instead was willing to sacrifice him or herself in order that justice should prevail, attests to the ritualized, reciprocal quality of these particular attacks.

One other current of interwar anarchism also hints at this affirmation of purity. The neo-Malthusian advocates of birth control were also supporters of negative eugenics, who commonly referred to portions of the population as tainted or defective (taré) and advocated voluntary sterilization for tubercular, syphilitic, alcoholic, and feeble-minded people. One would not expect to find anarchists advocating eugenic solutions, yet so committed were they to these ideas that even after they realized that the Nazis were fervent eugenicists they refused to dispense with eugenic solutions to social problems. The desire to purify society, positively by healthy living and negatively by limiting the population through eugenics and violence, reinforced anarchist emphasis on sound bodies and natural balance that was seen as a necessary corrective to the seriously imbalanced society in which they lived.[19]

Armand also supported conscientious reproduction but placed more emphasis on sexual freedom. He was not so much affirming anarchist purity as violating societal taboos. In most societies, no area is as fraught with moral strictures and ritual punishments as that of sexual fidelity and norms of chastity. By transgressing these norms in the name of freedom, pleasure, and new forms of sociability, Armand was intent on demonstrating that society could be transformed more thoroughly by revolutionizing private relations than by overthrowing public institutions. Get rid of monogamy and patriarchy, of jealousy and possessiveness, he argued, and other superstructures of authority would collapse. What other anarchists perceived as an irrelevant obsession Armand saw as a fundamental inversion that would necessitate the overturning of all other hierarchies. The eroticized body, shared openly and equally, was the promiscuous portal through which he imagined that marriage, family, and ultimately the state would be overturned.[20]

Anarchists may have been trying to reorder and purify society, yet most outsiders saw them as sowing disorder. Anarchist individualists who engaged in violence or vegetarianism, who counseled free love or contraception, may have been socially peripheral figures, yet in the age of Sigmund Freud and *La Garçonne* (the popular and controversial gender-bending 1922 novel by Victor Margueritte) they were symbolically and ideologically central in a way their syndicalist and anarchist-communist brethren were not.[21] This peculiar linkage between social marginality and symbolic valence helps explain the appeal of anarchism in the early 1920s to figures active in the artistic avant-garde—Germaine Berton above all. Yet that appeal was not necessarily requited.

Anarchism and Culture

One implication of perceiving the body and sexuality as central to interwar anarchist concerns is that, compared with the 1890s, cultural issues were relatively displaced. This doesn't mean that anarchists no longer appreciated literature and art, but rather that they paid little attention to the artistic avant-garde. Anarchists could look back nostalgically at the symbolists and postimpressionists who were partisans of anarchism in the 1890s while showing little corresponding interest in dada or surrealist artists, or any other modernists. In part this lack of interest reflects anarchist distrust of literary politics, as of all politics. Artistic movements adorned with manifestos were always suspected of being self-serving devices to advance the artistic careers of young bourgeois intellectuals. Coining a new "ism" appeared as a means of garnering publicity. Anarchists respected more mainstream writers such as Romain Rolland and Victor Margueritte who did not innovate stylistically but were committed to the causes of pacifism and emancipated sexuality. While some avant-garde artists shared anarchist ideals, the lack of reciprocity certainly dampened their fervor and may have pushed them into the arms of the communists.

The year in which complaints about a crisis of anarchism began to be voiced, 1925, was also the year that the surrealists announced in the communist journal *Clarté* their intention of dedicating themselves to the triumph of communism. That most prominent anarchists were older than the young surrealists (who were mostly born between 1895 and 1905) may have further distanced these writers from the libertarian movement. Communism appeared more youthful and contemporary, anarchism more rooted in the prewar past. By joining with the communists, Breton and the other surrealists were rejecting their own marginality. Communism was of course not in the political mainstream of the Third Republic, but as a party with representation in the Chamber of Deputies, with the successful Russian Revolution constantly before their eyes, and an infrastructure that included a daily newspaper and intellectual journals, communism further marginalized the fragmented anarchist movement.

If anarchists had little use for the high culture of the artistic avant-garde, perhaps they preferred the down-to-earth popular culture of cabarets, anarchist singers, and poets of the people. Anarchist bards such as Charles D'Avray, Louis Loréal, and Eugène Bizeau still sang in Montmartre bistros like the Grenier de Gringoire on the rue des Abbesses; they and others also enlivened the Grands Fêtes Artistiques that various anarchist groups held to raise funds and spirits. There is no need to minimize this popular culture, though since it has been thoroughly documented by Robert Brécy, there is also less need to dwell on it.[22] Yet working-class popular culture was already declining in the age of American jazz and movie palaces compared to its heyday of the Montmartre cabaret. Perhaps authenticity always seems to recede into the past; certainly there was more competition from mass culture.

The concerns of individualist (and some communist) anarchists of the interwar era were thus central to anarchist critical discourse on power and authority. This perspective helps distinguish them from the preoccupations of their more famous predecessors of the Belle Epoque. It also makes of interwar anarchism a transitional period between the era when anarchism could claim to be a mass movement and the postwar era when, after suffering a precipitous decline in the 1940s and 1950s, anarchism revived in the 1960s precisely along the ethical lines adumbrated by Armand, the Humberts, and Han Ryner. Anarchists shed a class-based orientation as workers as they emphasized the existential freedom of the individual, sexually no

less than politically, seizing upon identifiers of difference such as sexual orientation as means of self-definition. In this they followed the path-breaking
example of their interwar forebears, who were highly aware of the work of
Freud, Reich, and Magnus Hirschfeld in Germany and Austria and Ellis
and Carpenter in England, all pioneers in new definitions of sexuality (none
of them French; nor were any of the five International Congresses for Sex
Reform convened between 1921 and 1932 held in France).[23]As communism
and syndicalism faded, anarchism as personal politics, as a matter of choices
of life style and behavior, renders figures such as Han Ryner, Madeleine
Pelletier, Jeanne and Eugène Humbert, Manuel Devaldès, and E. Armand
of continuing relevance as forgotten forebears. As the artistic avant-garde
of the interwar period prefigured later experiments with the aleatory and
irrational in art and music, so the anarchists were similarly in the forefront
of radical conceptions of freedom, including sexual freedom.

Their decline meant that interwar anarchists were forced into seeking
alliances with other progressive groups, on the one hand, and into reevalu-
ating what they meant by anarchist contributions to ideals of social liberation. No longer able to envision the apocalyptic overthrow of society and
rejecting the simple overthrow of government, anarchists instead began to
flesh out, literally, a *critique des moeurs* that imagined free individuals and
emancipated interpersonal relations as the precondition for liberation. In
the context of the interwar era, they could justly argue that these aspirations
were neither utopian nor messianic but practical responses to threats to their
personal autonomy. Individualist anarchists confronted the abstractions of
power with the immediate physical reality of autonomous bodies.

The Decentering of Interwar French Anarchism

From 1789 to 1914 France stood at the forefront of the revolutionary tradition. The French Revolution was the model of modern revolution, and it was
followed by a succession of smaller upheavals in the nineteenth century,
culminating in the Paris Commune, the bloodiest of all nineteenth-century
European internecine conflicts and immediately proclaimed by Karl Marx
as the first true socialist revolution. French anarchism, as well as socialism,
was born in this era. Though anarchists were critical of this heritage precisely because each revolution ushered in a new political regime that failed
to match up with revolutionary hopes, they still participated in the utopian
aspirations fostered by the knowledge that radical change was possible. Yet
there had been no further revolutions in France since 1871, despite the

appearance of the mass anarchist movement of the late nineteenth century. In the interwar era, French anarchists faced the challenge posed by the successful Bolshevik Revolution in Russia. Initially beguiled by Lenin's call for soviets of workers and soldiers, the anarchists soon concluded that these councils were only window-dressing for domination by the all-powerful Bolshevik Party, which proceeded to reconstruct rather than tear down the hierarchical authoritarian state. Revolution, anticolonialism, and nationalism convulsed much of the world beyond Soviet borders, yet in France the Third Republic, victorious in war, soldiered on. As already mentioned, David Berry focuses much of his study of interwar anarchism on French responses to the Russian Revolution in the 1920s and to the Spanish Civil War in the 1930s, so there is no need to dwell at length on French response to these two great European crises of the left.

French anarchism may also be envisioned as lying between East and West—the East signifying not only Russia but also Ukraine and Poland and the West as America. Anarchist refugees from the Russian Revolution joined the flood of counterrevolutionary émigrés, many of whom sought new homes in Paris. Sometimes those two disparate groups came into direct conflict, as when the Jewish anarchist Sholom Schwartzbard assassinated Simon Petliura on the left bank of Paris in 1926. The Schwartzbard *attentat* and trial of the following year serves as a focal point from which to examine the impact of the influx of Eastern European Jews on interwar French anarchism. This influx did not begin after the war; Schwartzbard himself had first come to France in 1910, as had many Jews fleeing from tsarist oppression. Many of them came with little money and less French; some came knowing only the phrase "rue des Rosiers," the street in the fourth arrondissement that was the center of the teeming Jewish quarter of Paris. Jewish anarchists played a special role in the interwar anarchist movement. They functioned as the conscience of the movement as they sought to distance their libertarian socialist ideals from the increasingly repressive policies they decried in the Soviet Union. They were less significant, numerically, than anarchist refugees from fascist Italy and authoritarian Spain, yet they played at least as important a role in reasserting the unique perspective of anarchism, highlighting their continuing devotion to individual freedom and hostility to militarism and nationalism—even that nationalism cloaked in red. As antisemitism increased in the 1930s, some anarchists revealed their own anticapitalist Jewish stereotypes, while others debated whether Zionism could be justified. While most saw Zionism as one more expression of hated nationalism, some sympathized with the communal idealism of the kibbutz movement. While the French left looked to the east, more of the French were facing west, gazing at the skies as the *Spirit of St. Louis* landed to the syncopated sounds of jazz.

America had an incontestable hold over 1920s France. From the black jazz music emanating from Montmartre nightclubs to the cocktails served at Jean Cocteau's chic Le Boeuf sur le Toit to the expatriates and artists congregating at La Coupole and La Rotonde in Montparnasse, jazz-age Paris was awash in American culture. The vogue for American popular culture had something to do with the World War I alliance and with the presence of so many doughboys in France, but Great Britain had also been a French ally, yet there was no comparable British influence (as there had been in earlier centuries). By the late twenties, a quarter million American tourists were visiting France each year, while the police estimated that thirty-five thousand Americans resided in the French capital in 1927.[24] Some of those tourists visiting Paris in the summer of 1927 would have had to confront French involvement in the martyrdom of Nicola Sacco and Bartolomeo Vanzetti, whose case dominated headlines throughout the decade. They were no less Roaring Twenties celebrities than that other great hero of this publicity-conscious age—the Lone Eagle, Charles A. Lindbergh. The execution of Sacco and Vanzetti occurred just three months after Lindbergh landed at Le Bourget Airfield after his thirty-three-and-a-half-hour transatlantic flight. All through that summer of 1927 anarchists had been leading enormous protest marches against the impending execution. To the French, Sacco and Vanzetti appeared as the Dreyfusses of the hour. Their cause, I will show, was connected in a number of ways to the visit of Lindbergh earlier that year and played a role in the rise of anti-American sentiments. Their deaths fanned anarchist martyrology while allowing the anarchist movement to recapture the spotlight for a few months on the eve of the tenth anniversary of the Russian Revolution.

Lindbergh, Ford, and Louis Armstrong's jazz on the one hand and the image of the New Soviet Man on the other were the contending symbols of modernity between which the French found themselves. In the 1920s, both ideals—of mass consumption capitalism and egalitarian communism—beckoned; in the 1930s both would darken as the United States was engulfed by the Great Depression (although the left found much to admire in Roosevelt's New Deal), and Russia foundered under Stalin's murderous five-year plans and purge trials. The French for a time felt impervious to the Depression: then economics was overwhelmed by politics as the rise of fascism and war appeared as a more imminent threat. Anarchists were increasingly marginalized in the face of these crises. Year of the Popular Front, 1936, was also the year of the Spanish Civil War, and some French anarchists crossed the Pyrenees to join the anarchist militias defending the Second Spanish Republic from the fascists. Yet by 1937 Stalin had managed to end most anarchist influence, particularly in Catalonia; the communists were particularly eager to obfuscate and destroy all evidence of anarchist revolution from below. From 1936 to 1939 a long nightmare descended on the anarchists, relieved only by brief glimmers of revolutionary hope in Paris in May 1936 and in Barcelona that summer and fall. Anarchism seemed near collapse at the end of the 1930s, yet the seeds for its regeneration in the 1960s and after had already been sown in the social and cultural experiments of the 1920s.

Part I

Anarchist Bodies

Interwar anarchists were both preoccupied with and conflicted about sexuality and gender roles. Some were simply annoyed at the prominence given to sexuality by individualist anarchists, most notably E. Armand, editor of the anarchist newspaper *L'En Dehors*. Syndicalists were the least likely to be sympathetic to Armand's preoccupation with sexual freedom, and quite a few anarchist-communists also found his discussion of sex obsessive. Syndicalists, oriented toward the workplace, saw the body primarily as engaged in production. Individualists conceived of the body as a sensual end in itself; sexual attraction connected liberated individuals while violating monogamous social norms. Armand published his journal throughout the interwar period seemingly undisturbed by criticism from fellow anarchists and displayed increasing awareness of the writings of Sigmund Freud, as well as with the work of Magnus Hirschfeld, Havelock Ellis, and other sexologists of the period. He also debated with fellow individualists such as Han Ryner and Manuel Devaldès, who had their own approaches to the disposition of the body. Anarchists were notoriously contentious, and this included the place of sexuality within the movement. Partisans of sexual freedom such as Armand contended with proponents of birth control, who emphasized women's control of their own bodies rather than sexual pleasure. Armand seemed aware that the body was the most potent metaphor for society and held out the hope that a body signifying openness to sensual pleasure could lay the foundation for a body politic that was no longer hierarchical and devoted to power. Anarchist advocates of birth control and eugenics by contrast directly confronted the demographically obsessed French state.

Followers of Eugéne and Jeanne Humbert, publishers in the 1930s of the anarchist neo-Malthusian (birth control) journal *La Grande Réforme,* favored sexual freedom too but crusaded most vigorously for the availability and knowledge of birth control methods, including abortion. They shared with Armand the belief that scientific rationality had made religious strictures obsolete. As anarchists, they also rejected raison d'état and valued individual rights over the prerogatives of the state. The French government's obsession with population throughout the Third Republic was greatly increased by the losses of World War I. Anarchists played the lead role in seeking to overturn the repressive French laws banning all birth control information, filling the vacuum left by the more moderate French feminists, who were mostly unwilling to address the issue. Where the Humberts and their followers and fellow travelers, such as Devaldès and the popular novelist Victor Margueritte, deviated most radically from the anarchist champions of sexual freedom was in connecting two other issues to birth control: antimilitarism and eugenics. The neo-Malthusians were convinced that overpopulation was the major cause of war; hence, birth limitation was critical if future wars were to be avoided. Since the French government wanted above all to increase the population, all of its focus was on positive eugenics, such as giving rewards and tax benefits to families that produced numerous children. These anarchists followed the Americans and Germans in promoting negative eugenics, arguing that it was important for alcoholics, syphilitics, tubercular types, mental defectives, and other "tainted" sorts to refrain from having children. Being anarchists, they were loath to authorize the centralized state to control reproduction, and instead favored self-control, with doctors playing an advisory role. They nevertheless saw negative eugenics as perfectly compatible with anarchist ethics, even as antithetical authoritarian regimes emphasized the creation of healthy populations through similar means.

Two anarchist views of sexuality were seemingly at odds with each other and yet coexisted in interwar France. At one extreme were proponents of complete sexual freedom, who cited modern sexologists from Richard von Krafft-Ebing and Edward Carpenter to Wilhelm Reich in defense of toleration of sexual deviance and celebration of sexual pleasure. Individualists equated the patriarchal nuclear family with the principle of authority; at their most extreme they sought to replace the family with more sympathetic, egalitarian groupings. On the other side were neo-Malthusian eugenicists, who favored limiting population for the sake of peace and a healthier working class. For them, "free love" meant roughly what it had meant a generation before when the term was first widely used: not sexual license, but rather men and women uniting without benefit of either church or state sanction. That anarchists could simultaneously favor complete individual freedom and the sort of social control reminiscent of the Foucauldian term "bio-power" suggests the power of sexual issues. Sexuality lay at the intersection of freedom and control, of war and peace, of the state and the individual. Anarchists were eager to subvert mainstream morality in the name of individual freedom and rationality, yet they proposed a new ethic that condoned only healthy procreation. The paradox may be more apparent than real since anarchists perceived liberation and self-control as two sides of the same coin. Even the most committed eugenicists refused to cede individual autonomy to the state; Manuel Devaldès, for instance, postulated some transnational League of Nations as the only sort of authority he might recognize that could adjudicate "healthy" procreation.

Anarchists were certainly aware of homosexuality, whether represented in the writings and person of their German colleague Magnus Hirschfeld or in André Gide's novel *Corydon;* nevertheless, there was little discussion of homosexuality beyond a general approbation of all sexual activities that did not depend on constraint or unequal power relations. Most discourse was focused on alternatives to monogamy and marriage. Han Ryner titled a 1920s novel *Plural Love;* E. Armand termed his ideal of multiple sex partners *camaraderie amoureuse* (loving friendship). As is clear from Ryner's novel and Armand's efforts to recruit more women to his sex collectives, most anarchists assumed heterosexual relations between consenting adults. Anarchists were neither pro nor antihomosexual, neither pronormality nor antideviance; they were antibourgeois. They opposed bourgeois marital codes based on property exchange and inheritance, which in turn required (female) chastity and legitimacy. Sexual freedom was meant to subvert bourgeois respectability.

Liberated women were therefore in demand, yet anarchists were conflicted about their role in the movement. While paying lip service to their complete freedom and equality, in practice they remained suspicious of women as inherently conservative and religious. They could accept female anarchists only if they behaved and believed exactly the same as male anarchists. They refused to concede that women might have a unique perspective to bring to bear on the movement. Even such "liberated" women as Jeanne Humbert, partisan of nudism and birth control, believed that women tended to be less rational than men. In any case, women comprised a small percentage of the movement, on the order of 10 percent of active militants. Germaine Berton briefly became a heroine both to anarchists and fellow-traveling avant-garde artists smitten by the lure of the violent woman, but her apparent mental instability reinforced prevailing prejudices against women. Anarchist sex radicals remained conservative with regard to gender roles. In part this was due to anarchists' Rousseauist penchant for appealing to that which was "natural," whether that meant the sex drive or what were assumed to be natural gender relations. Insofar as they believed that natural drives could subvert social institutions, they were closer to their contemporary Sigmund Freud than they were to the later ideas of Michel Foucault.

The surrealists and other members of the artistic avant-garde were attracted to anarchism in part because of its association with sexual freedom, which meshed with their own expressive, bohemian values. Anarchist immediacy, which sanctioned violence and direct action rather than indirect representation, had long appealed to artists; as the term "propaganda by the deed" suggested, anarchist violence had it own expressive potential. In both attacking other bodies and declaring the liberation of their own, anarchists conveyed a sense of physicality lacking in more sober movements of the left. While anarchists prided themselves on their rationality, their notoriety lay more in their bodies (and those of their victims) than in their minds.

At the end of the 1920s, a German sociologist named Karl Mannheim published a book titled *Ideology and Utopia,* in which he argued that modern anarchists such as Gustav Laudauer (killed in the attempt to establish a Munich soviet in 1919) were the latter-day counterparts of the ecstatic, chiliastic movements of the Middle Ages. Three decades later, Norman Cohn made a similar argument in *The Pursuit of the Millennium.* More precisely than Mannheim, Cohn compared anarchists to late medieval millenarian movements such as the Brethren of the Free Spirit, whose partisans believed that they were God's chosen and were free of sin. They thus felt free to return to the Edenic state in which Adam and Eve displayed their naked bodies without shame, in a state of prelapsarian innocence. These "mystical anarchists" preached a doctrine of voluntary poverty, and some decried the institution of private property, claiming that "all things which God created are common."[1] Modern anarchists would likely have dismissed the comparison as incompatible with their vaunted rationality, yet anarchist individualists believed that they too had freed themselves from the shackles of a decadent civilization in which people smoked, drank, and lusted while pretending to adhere to Christian moral standards. Like the medieval Brethren, they preached to all who would listen that a repressive and hierarchical society, not the body, was corrupt and in need of radical change. Like the Brethren of the Free Spirit, anarchists did not believe in awaiting some future millennium to usher in an age of harmony. They called for paradise now and hoped that their example would spur others to liberate themselves from the shackles of an obsolete moral code.

Gender and Political Violence: The Case of Germaine Berton

On January 21, 1923, a group of prominent Action Française monarchists gathered at a Paris church to celebrate the memory of King Louis XVI, beheaded on that date during the French Revolution, 130 years before. Among these men of the far right there hovered a young anarchist of twenty who hoped to assassinate Léon Daudet, editor of the newspaper *L'Action Française* and member of the Chamber of Deputies. Daudet and Charles Maurras were surrounded by their *camelots du roi* shock troops and the deed proved impossible. The following day the anarchist went to the Action Française office at 14 rue du Rome and encountered Marius Plateau, secretary-general of the movement. The young Berton was admitted to his office after claiming to know of an anarchist plot to assassinate Daudet. Berton conversed with Plateau for fifteen minutes but became angry when Plateau refused to take the information seriously. Upon leaving Plateau's office, Berton shot him five times with a revolver, then tried to commit suicide. Plateau was killed instantly; Berton was taken to a hospital and soon recovered from a shoulder wound. At the murder trial that ended on Christmas Eve 1923, the jury listened to eight days of testimony before deliberating for all of thirty-five minutes and acquitting the confessed anarchist assassin on all charges.

Given the usual fate of apprehended anarchist terrorists in France and elsewhere, the hasty acquittal would appear to be nothing short of miraculous. What would cause a Parisian jury to show such extraordinary clemency to a confessed assassin and convinced anarchist revolutionary? This remarkable verdict attests to the fact that in the Third French Republic, the sex of the assailant could make all the difference. The anarchist assassin, Germaine Berton, was a woman.

Germaine Berton thus differed in at least two ways—her sex and her legal fortune—from her anarchist predecessors who, thirty years before, had perpetrated a notorious series of bombings and assassinations that culminated in the death of the president of the republic, Sadi Carnot, at the hands of a young Italian male. In fact, all the attacks of the 1880s and 1890s in France were carried out by young men between the ages of nineteen and thirty-three. Of those who were apprehended, none escaped the guillotine or, at the least, a trip to Devil's Island. Their exploits became legendary and are recounted in all histories of the anarchist movement. Yet despite her remarkable acquittal, Germaine Berton has been accorded little or no mention in histories of the left. The fact that her act was sui generis and was not part of the "era of *attentats*" may explain this neglect. Berton is mentioned briefly in histories of the right, but she killed a relatively minor figure, and the little coverage that exists scarcely even raises gender issues.[1]

Germaine Berton also appears in an entirely different context from that of leftist, rightist, or feminist politics. Her deed excited the admiration of the young surrealists Louis Aragon and André Breton, and she was celebrated in the first issue of their journal, *La Révolution Surréaliste*. The surrealist evocation of the *acte gratuit* (gratuitous or free act) of Germaine Berton further suggests the particular hold over the male imagination exercised by a young female assassin. I will argue in chapter 3 that the surrealists' conversion to Marxism in 1925 was preceded by an intense anarchist phase that peaked during the Germaine Berton affair.

To understand the significance of Berton and her acquittal, she must be situated in an anarchist milieu that was ambivalent about women's role in society, as well as in the larger postwar French society that was also troubled by the threat posed by independent young women. To what degree did gender play a role in Berton's trial and acquittal? Did the jury express hostility toward the Action Française, tolerance for anarchism, or sympathy for a desperate young woman? Had attitudes toward female criminality during the Third Republic played a role in the trial, or were political crimes perceived differently from "crimes of passion"? Did the crime and acquittal of Germaine Berton represent the nihilism of the postwar "lost generation"?

The difference between Berton's fate and that of François Ravachol or Emile Henry thirty years before makes one suspect that the strongly gendered notion of crimes of passion might have been involved. Women who could show that their crime was due to an alleged feminine lack of control were frequently acquitted.[2] This was especially true of cases involving husbands and lovers. If a woman, gripped in a moment of passion, shot a man who had wronged her, juries almost always excused her from culpability. Yet in bringing a loaded gun into a stranger's office, Berton had carried out a clearly political act. She did not act as a wronged woman, nor was this a domestic case of betrayed love or jealousy. She even failed to kill her original target, Daudet.

In one regard, however, Berton's case did resemble acquittals for more conventional *crimes passionnels*. Ann-Louise Shapiro reports that attempted suicide and lack of any effort to conceal the crime were signs to juries that this was a moral crime beyond the bounds of criminal law.[3] Germaine Berton did indeed try to commit suicide after killing Plateau, and made no attempt to disguise her crime. Yet the underlying rationale for her actions was totally at variance with the behavior of a woman supposedly under the grip of extreme emotion. Suicide was supposed to show instant regret for the act; lack of concealment legitimized the deed. Yet Berton killed a man she had never met, and the only regret for her deed that she expressed at her trial was that she had killed Plateau rather than Daudet. Undoubtedly her failed suicide attempt inspired sympathy and projected an image of noble self-sacrifice rather than of a conspiring femme fatale. Berton acted not as a woman behaving in an improper way in her proper—that is, domestic—sphere, but in a seemingly gender-neutral manner in the public, political sphere.

Yet in another sense the anarchist extremist was easily imagined to share psychological characteristics with women who committed excusable crimes of passion. Terrorists were generally seen as fanatics in the grip of an all-consuming if irrational ideology. Removed from normal societal constraints, they also lacked a firm grasp of reality. When the police questioned André Colomer, editor of the anarchist newspaper *Le Libertaire*, he characterized Berton as an *exalté*, or fanatic. This was the same term applied to women who committed *crimes passionnels*.[4] While male anarchists had merited this appellation as well and were nevertheless found guilty, perhaps Berton was able to play on the ambiguity implied in the word *exalté*, suggesting at once political extremism and psychological instability. If Germaine Berton was a self-motivated actor in an ideologically driven crime, she was undeniably guilty; if she was caught in the throes of a quasi-religious passion that pushed her over the edge, she might plausibly argue that she was not responsible for her actions. In fact her prior and subsequent history would support the picture of an unbalanced young woman.

Our Enemy: The Woman

André Colomer might purposely have used such language to exculpate Berton from responsibility, or he might simply have been expressing a more general anarchist distrust of women. Before continuing with Berton's story, it will be useful to see how anarchists constructed gender relations in the years following the First World War. While anarchists always supported the freedom of the individual and paid lip service to the equality of both sexes, underlying that liberated attitude was a profound distrust of women. Nowhere was that distrust more evident than in the public lecture given by André Lorulot on February 21, 1921, less than two years before Berton's *attentat*, provocatively called "Our Enemy: The Woman" (Notre ennemie: La femme).

Lorulot's ploy in using a provocative title to draw a large audience apparently worked, for the Large Hall of the Maison Commune on the rue de Bretagne in Paris's Marais district was filled; Lorulot claimed that two hundred people had to be turned away. The talk also generated articles in a number of left-wing publications, including *La Voix des Femmes* (Voice of women), *Le Libertaire, Le Reveil de l'Esclave,* and so forth. The lecture was subtitled "The woman against individuality, against propaganda, against the logical life; the 'exceptions'; the true feminism." Lorulot (real name: André Roulot, 1885–1963) was a veteran of the prewar individualist milieu. He had worked on Libertad's paper *L'Anarchie,* and just before the war had started his own paper, *L'Idée Libre.* The "free idea" was free thinking, and in the interwar period Lorulot devoted his energies almost entirely to antireligious propaganda.[5] In Sébastien Faure's ambitious interwar volumes called *L'Encyclopédie Anarchiste,* Lorulot contributed a remarkable article on the papacy in which he summarized the misdeeds of each pope over the nearly two-thousand-year span of the papacy.[6] Though feminism was outside of Lorulot's main area of competence, he probably did not see it that way, so entwined was the anarchist perception of the "woman problem" and religion. As his talk progressed, it became clear that his title was chosen only partly tongue in cheek.

True to type, Lorulot began his talk with an exhaustive survey of the history of misogyny from the Bible to Baudelaire. He detailed the subservient status of women in the ancient world, which was responsible for the position of inferiority accorded women from Roman times to the present. He proceeded to the Judeo-Christian bias against women, from Eve seduced by the serpent to the sixth commandment, which treated women as property in demanding that one not covet thy neighbor's wife, his cow, or any of his possessions. The Christian Church preached hatred of the flesh, the beauty of celibacy, and the danger of women as temptresses. He cited Paul as counseling female submission to their husbands. He moved on to modern misogyny, and purposely provoked the crowd by discussing not only Napoleon, Nietzsche, and Schopenhauer but also Pierre-Joseph Proudhon. When he maintained that no one was more misogynist than Proudhon, violent protests erupted in the hall. He responded by quoting Proudhon: "The woman is a sort of middle term between the man and the animal kingdom," and "The woman is inferior from the physical, intellectual, and moral point of view."[7] The father of French anarchism even advised prospective husbands to dominate their wives, to be their masters! Proudhon argued that maternal functions rendered the female brain incapable of serious thought. To bring his history of misogyny up to date, Lorulot cited antifemale statements from George Sand, Gustave Flaubert, and even the contemporary leftist writer Romain Rolland.

He concluded his recitation of the history of misogyny by citing phrases from the much-admired anarchist philosopher Han Ryner. In his *Dialogue du mariage philosophique*, Ryner said women were self-absorbed and imitative rather than creative; he actually said that women and crows imitated sounds.[8] Living with a woman threatened to deprive the anarchist of time for serious discourse with friends and for his studies. Since Ryner was steeped in the classics and considered himself a Stoic, such antifeminine attitudes might be expected, but Lorulot's point was not that Han Ryner was philosophically consistent, but that misogyny was common among contemporary anarchists. Then he proceeded to divulge his own thoughts, saying that if men chattered less than women, it was because they were busy drinking and smoking. As for intellectual stimulation, most men were content with the low intellectual level of the mass daily *Le Petit Parisien*. He cited anthropological studies that found that women's brains were 150 to 200 cubic centimeters smaller than men's but said this meant she was different, not inferior. He detailed some of those differences: women were more nervous, more emotional; if her intelligence was less profound, it was more lively and penetrating, and especially more intuitive. He said that women could master most trades equally well as men and should not be excluded from the workshops. He praised American women for their athleticism and cited Marie Curie as a female scientist who proved that women did not need to be frivolous. Still, he affirmed that "the woman must symbolize charm, beauty, grace, while the man represents force and energy."[9] In separating the achievements of individual women from what each sex represented, the anarchist shared many of the prevailing stereotypes of gender difference. He then arrived at the real heart of his talk.

Despite acknowledging thousands of years of bias against women, Lorulot concluded that at present women were their own greatest enemies. He said:

> She is the enemy of all effort for individual and social emancipation [affranchissement]. She is the enemy of revolt and propaganda. She is the enemy of moral and intellectual perfection, the enemy of education, of a more conscious life. During a strike, rather than raising the morale of their men struggling with the bosses, most women discourage them, weakening them with supplications. If the movement fails, one can attribute the responsibility in good part to the action of the woman, factor of resignation and submission.[10]

The crux of anarchist antifeminism was the belief that women were more conservative than men, more respectful of traditional values, more inherently obedient. The freethinker's critique of religion came into play at this point in the lecture. When Lorulot asked why women were more religious than men, he fell back on stereotypes, going so far as to say that as with primitive peoples, women kneeled before mysterious forces. Once freed from control by priests, she would become more rational and less mystical. He even complained they were at least as patriotic as men, embracing the *poilus* of all countries rather than condemning militarism. He applauded all efforts to liberate women, who must not be the slave of men, and yet in the next breath affirmed that women dominated most households and warned, "a bad union is the amputation of oneself. Comrades, it is a veritable moral suicide! Nearly always, marriage is the shipwreck of the conscious individual."[11] For the sake of happiness and anarchist liberation, women must free themselves; a moment later he maintained that for every ten comrades who gave up the struggle, nine will have done so due to the pernicious influence of women. Lorulot concluded by demanding "the independent man and woman in FREE UNION; conscious and free maternity, the child educated and healthy in the freed family."[12] After he finished, Han Ryner took the floor to explain the thesis set out in *Le Mariage Philosophique;* then Julia Bertrand responded that men were often responsible for the ignorance and inferiority of their companions, whom they neglected to enlighten. A feminist from the paper *La Voix des Femmes* spoke from the floor; Lorulot commented that her violent tone created a tumult in the previously calm meeting, which soon ended.

Lorulot's talk has been summarized in some detail because it represents perfectly anarchists' deep feelings of ambivalence toward women. They declared themselves partisans of female emancipation and equality. Anarchist papers featured columns written by women supporting feminism and pacifism. Yet as the discussion at Lorulot's talk suggests, even anarchist women agreed that women were not yet liberated and in fact posed a major problem for the movement. Anarchists were by definition rational individuals disabused of faith in all traditional values, yet women were viewed as irrational and wed to custom and religious belief. Because their main interest lay in protecting home and family, they discouraged men from risking their family's security for the sake of political ideals.

Male anarchists maintained that it was both possible and necessary for women to emancipate themselves, yet they affirmed sexual differences that made gender equality appear unlikely if not impossible. How were women to accede to the anarchist ideal of the autonomous and rational individual if they were inherently more intuitive and mystical? Anarchists had to hope that biology was not destiny, that women could educate themselves and reject being defined by bourgeois social roles. Yet didn't that mean becoming more like (anarchist) men? What then of the sex-based differences that Lorulot also affirmed? Insofar as anarchists bought into the myth of the eternal feminine, which held that women's nature inclined them toward self-sacrifice, nurturance, and emotionalism, they were unlikely to accord them an equal degree of rationality.[13] Anarchist respect for "nature" thus collided with their idealization of rationality, insofar as human reason implied the subjugation of instincts in the name of progress and science.

Anarchist bias against women was reinforced by the preponderance of anarchist men. The national intelligence service (the Sûreté Générale) kept track of anarchist militants, reporting on their domicile every two weeks, thereby making it possible to establish how many anarchists were women. At the end of 1923, their list of dangerous anarchist militants included 370 names, 21 of whom were women. Two years later the list had shrunk to 232 names, 17 of whom were women. By the end of the decade, there were only 170 names left on the list, of which a mere seven were women (Rirette Maîtrejean was dropped from the list in 1924, Germaine Berton in 1929).[14] These figures pertain only to the Paris region and only include active militants, not the much larger number of supporters who might attend lectures such as Lorulot's or subscribe to Le Libertaire. Still, it indicates a salient fact about anarchism: the movement was not just dominated by men but was so identified with them that women were always considered an exception (a fact on which I played when I purposely withheld Germaine Berton's name in my initial discussion of her deed). When Sébastien Faure assembled a team of a hundred collaborators to contribute articles for the Encyclopédie

Anarchiste, only two women contributed articles: Madeleine Vernet, who concentrated on pacifist rather than feminist issues, and Dr. Madeleine Pelletier, who did write on women's issues but was only loosely connected to the anarchist movement. Since anarchists usually lived together without benefit of marriage, the police typically referred to anarchists and their mistresses rather than to male and female anarchists. Yet the anarchists themselves seemed to concur, while regretting that too few women shared their beliefs.

Anarchist uncertainty about women was reinforced by ambivalence toward feminist ideals. Lorulot attacked women who thought that being modern meant smoking cigarettes and hanging out in bars (he opposed tobacco and alcohol use for both sexes). This echoed a common anarchist critique: conventional markers of modernity did nothing to liberate women. In an article called "La femme se modernise" that appeared in *Le Libertaire* in 1924, Lily Ferrer identified the modern woman as one who assimilated herself to society rather than freeing herself. Ferrer feared that women were being seduced by the attractions of material goods and immediate satisfactions, thus prostituting themselves to fashion. The crux of the antifeminist position, however, was revealed when Ferrer wrote, "Feminist, she wants to take part in politics, to create laws, to become a deputy."[15]Feminism was identified with the movement for female suffrage, which anarchists who advised abstention from all electoral politics generally condemned. Even though female suffrage had been withheld from French women by the conservative senate, anarchists did not see enfranchisement as a significant struggle on the road to female emancipation.

Similar ambivalence was registered in *La Revue Anarchiste*, which featured a regular series called "Les femmes et le féminisme" (strangely, feminism is a masculine noun in French) by Henriette Marc, and "La femme dans le monde" (Woman in the world) by "Une Révoltée (a female rebel)." Marc worried that the battle of the sexes weakened the struggle against bourgeois society, which oppressed men and women without distinction. Une Révoltée attacked emancipated women who sought the right to vote and take part in politics, and seemed to think the proper role for women was to uplift men, to give them an ideal.[16] Several months later, in "La femme et la politique," Une Révoltée called suffrage "the right to choose masters," and said women should reserve their energies for education, union struggles, freemasonry, and other progressive movements. She did conclude proudly that "the emancipation of the woman will only be accomplished by the woman herself."[17] The following year the monthly journal featured an exchange of views on the role of women. Eugénie Casteu took exception to Révoltée's tendency to sacrifice women to the needs of men, quoting her as saying, "When one truly loves, all becomes easy, the greatest sacrifices are accepted with joy." Casteu denied that self-abnegation was an anarchist sentiment and recommended an attitude of strength over sacrifice: "My dear young female comrades, I beg you, do not immolate yourselves on the altar of masculine genius."[18] That women should be debating the attitude of anarchists toward the modern feminist movement in the pages of a major anarchist review (La Revue Anarchiste was the monthly counterpart to Le Libertaire, both under the auspices of the anarchist-communist Union Anarchiste) was a healthy sign that not all women were seen as "enemies" or saw themselves that way. Their critique of feminism echoed the general anarchist assessment of movements that focused on political rather than social change.

When a male anarchist made a similar point, it sounded more sexist. In 1924, Maurice Fister commented on Margaret Bonfield of the British Labour Party, who on becoming secretary to the Minister of Labour was the first woman to attain cabinet status. "Candidate, deputy, minister! What sadness to see the woman, blinded by the same ambitions which devour the masculine professionals of politics, engage in that unhappy path and trample on the best of themselves, lying to their nature and their feelings." Fister worried that Bonfield would deprive herself of her femininity and sounded much like antisuffragists everywhere in fearing "les luttes sales de la lice electorale" (the dirty struggles of the electoral lists).[19] Here distrust of politics was mixed with an essentialist view of woman as being too pure for the Darwinian world of politics. He concluded that real emancipation, what he called integral freedom, had nothing to do with politics but involved changing the church, codes, and customs. This was fundamentally the same point made by Emma Goldman—that mainstream feminism served to make women buy into the system of mass consumption and parliamentary politics.[20] "Red Emma," however, was less likely to offer syrupy bromides about women's true nature.

Anarchist ambivalence regarding feminist demands did not escape censure from left-feminist organizations. The Feminist Group of Laic Teaching published a monthly supplement to the publication L'Ecole Emancipée (The emancipated or free school), which commented on articles appearing in the anarchist press. The large number of educated and independent women who filled the teaching ranks provided a prime constituency for feminism as well as for support for birth control. 1924 was an election year, reminding French women of their electoral irrelevance. Responding to the Libertaire article that bemoaned the appearance of the first female cabinet member in England, Pierrette Rouquet agreed that political power might not solve most problems, but reproved the attitude that such power was antifeminine. She demanded not only female suffrage but protection of children, respect for maternity, abolition of prostitution, and higher women's salaries.[21] The following year, a teacher demanded the end of the double standard, claiming for women equal rights in love, including the right to conceive children outside marriage if they so chose. The act of love should not be considered a fault, wrote Josette Cornec, nor should it be restricted to marriage for purposes of procreation.[22]

Testimony from one more prominent anarchist woman whose life spanned the twentieth century will help capture anarchist ambivalence toward feminist ideals. Jeanne Humbert was the wife of Eugène Humbert, lifelong anarchist and neo-Malthusian. Jeanne published a novel, two books about her prison experiences, and contributed numerous articles to *La Grande Réforme,* the journal that her husband edited in the 1930s. After his death in 1944 she continued her anarchist activism until her own death more than forty years later. Yet in two articles titled "Our Equals," which she published in *La Grande Réforme* in 1933, Jeanne Humbert distanced herself from contemporary feminists.

The excuse for her first article was a review of Victor Margueritte's latest book. Jeanne claimed she found the word "equality" almost meaningless when it came to the sexes and preferred the term "equivalence." She found equality between the sexes to be illusory because she emphasized differences rather than commonalities between men and women. She seemed to accept that women lacked creative genius, that their minds were less inventive than men's. Women's intelligence was "more lively," their tastes more subtle, but she claimed they were not as likely to produce original ideas. Further, women were more conservative than men, and they encouraged men to make cowardly concessions so as to preserve domestic quiet. Psychologically as well as physically, women and men were different; Jeanne Humbert's solution lay in equivalence, or what she termed "integral humanism."[23]

Two months later, Jeanne Humbert returned to her topic and repeated many of the biases common to French men of her era. She admitted that women were governed largely by their instincts, that they feared the unknown and were reluctant to accept new and liberating ideas. All great male spirits, she maintained, had suffered from the incomprehension of their female companions. She even cited the examples of male-eating spiders and praying mantises, a common reference among misogynists of the time. She also complained that feminists forgot that the sexual question was at the base of the movement as of all social questions. In a third installment of "Our Equals," Jeanne Humbert declared that conscious maternity must be a basic right of women; that women had the right to the full expansion of brain, heart, and body; that they must become individuals by practicing altruism rather than egotism.[24] These biological references may suggest why Jeanne Humbert was not fully sympathetic to the women's movement. Aside from absorbing male anarchists' biases against overly religious, conservative women, Jeanne seemed to downplay social conditioning in favor of biology, which led her to exaggerate the differences between men and women. If a woman who had fled France during the First World War so that her companion (the Humberts were not married at the time; in fact they only married to legitimize their daughter and so they could visit each other in prison) could avoid military service, and who had been imprisoned in the 1920s for advocating birth control and abortion rights, could publish such seemingly conservative attitudes toward gender roles, one may conclude that anarchists cannot simply be included among feminism's proponents.

Feminists did not fail to respond to Jeanne Humbert's arguments. Jeanne received a request from Mme Andrée Forny, director of Les Cahiers Féministes, for a copy of her pacifist article "You Will Not Kill." Jeanne sent the article and recommended as well her two books about prison life, La Pourrissoir and Sous la Cagoule. In her response to Mme Forny, she mistakenly referred to Forny's publication as "Les Cahiers Féminins" rather than Féministes, as if she did not want to associate herself with feminists. She defended her own feminist credentials by saying she was one of the first women in France to campaign for jury rights for women; yet though she favored the movement for feminine liberation, she did not believe in hostility toward men, preferring "the union of the two against evil powers."[25] Andrée Forny responded the next day that her campaign for equal civil and political rights was not directed against men, and that they in fact hoped to liberate men as well. She objected to the point of view expressed in Jeanne Humbert's articles, saying she didn't "believe in the real feebleness of women. It is an acquired habit. . . . Woman has need of real life, and there I would meet you, I think."[26] By becoming too used to relying on men's support, women turned their companions into their masters.

Anarchists were thus ambivalent about feminism and feminist goals of gender equality. They were prey to the same assumptions of biological essentialism that shaped the attitudes of many first-wave feminists—attitudes that led them to doubt whether most women could become emancipated anarchists. Their distrust of electoral politics further estranged them from the goal of female suffrage, which they did not perceive to be a meaningful reform and certainly not the culmination of women's freedom. Instead they wished women to become as rational and freethinking as men yet harbored doubts that such a transformation was likely. That such skepticism was expressed by Jeanne Humbert as well as by André Lorulot shows that this masculinist rhetoric was pervasive throughout the interwar era.

The Trial of Germaine Berton

The years following the First World War were ones of great social and economic instability in France as elsewhere in Europe. The transformation of women's roles during the war, along with a burgeoning mass consumer culture, increased job opportunities for middle- and lower-middle-class women, and the liberating values of the jazz age created a climate of excitement and fear over gender relations. Conservative politicians concerned about the low French birthrate and France's great losses in the war passed postwar laws banning abortions and birth control, and equated women's sacrifice of their independence with soldiers' sacrifice of their lives for the *patrie* (giving life versus giving their lives); both were necessary if France was to flourish. Yet returning soldiers who might have hoped to find women ready to return to the domestic sphere were not always so reassured, and furthermore the surplus of several million women in the French population guaranteed that many would have to be self-supporting. Despite the concerns of pronatalists, the birthrate remained low, although the birthrate of 19.7 per 1,000 of 1920–25 was higher than those of the decades immediately before or after.[27]

Given the highly politicized debate over the role of women in French society after the war and fears of androgynous freedom signaled by the radical postwar fashions of cigarette-smoking young women flaunting short hair and skirts, one would expect that a woman who killed a decorated veteran wounded in the war would not be kindly received. At her trial, Germaine Berton appeared thin, boy-like, with bobbed hair, a femme fatale in fact if not in appearance, whose crime and trial occurred just as the mass motion picture medium was popularizing the image of woman as a sexually predating vampire sucking men dry.[28] Revolutionary women were doubly reviled.[29]

A book published the year before Berton's *attentat* might also have influenced how the French public perceived her case. Victor Margueritte's bestselling novel *La Garçonne* described a liberated pleasure-seeking young woman who made men feel emasculated and whose transgressive behavior included engaging in lesbian love affairs and smoking opium. Despite being banned by the Church, it sold more than a million copies by the end of the decade.[30] In an era given to imagining women liberated from domestic roles as either femmes fatales or androgynes, one would guess that the average Parisian would not be sympathetic to Berton or her cause. And yet, Germaine Berton was acquitted. Why?

Though Germaine Berton looked the part of a *femme moderne,* she differed from the fictional evocations of the new independent woman in not being self-indulgent. The fact that Berton sacrificed herself for a cause distanced her from the negative stereotypes of the emancipated woman who sought pleasure on her own terms. If she was a femme fatale, she was also a *sacrificiée.* Berton failed to evoke the fears that La Garçonne portended among the twelve mostly middle-class male jurors, precisely because she was dedicated rather than dissipated.[31] Fears of gender reversal or left-wing violence were not as pronounced as fears of right-wing coups d'état (the trial took place only a year after Mussolini's March on Rome and the same year as the French occupation of the Ruhr). Nevertheless, gender issues were scarcely ignored either in the trial or in the abundant coverage by the press, and Berton's acquittal should at least give pause to historians who overly rely on literary evocations of femmes fatales to make their case that Frenchmen were obsessed by the danger posed by freedom-loving women.

The trial of Germaine Berton played a major role in the fortunes of the principal organ of the anarchist press, *Le Libertaire.* In the March 2–9, 1923, issue of the weekly paper, Brutus Mercereau wrote an impassioned article defending her deed. A few weeks later the paper announced that he had been arrested under the 1894 *loi scélérate* that made the apology of violence culpable. A June 1–8 article titled "Ferocious Repression" listed the several-month prison terms meted out to the author and manager of the paper. As her courtroom date neared, *Le Libertaire* announced that they would provide daily coverage, and in the week preceding the trial, each daily issue counted the days until the trial began. In fact, the Germaine Berton trial and the equally spectacular and interconnected case of Philippe Daudet together made it possible for the long-held dream of a daily anarchist newspaper to become a reality.

Philippe was the teenage son of Léon Daudet, monarchist leader, with Charles Maurras, of the Action Française. Less than a month before Berton's trial, Philippe supposedly committed suicide as the taxi he was riding in passed in front of St. Lazare Prison where Germaine Berton was being held. It was rumored that he had anarchist sympathies, that he was in love with Berton, and that the Sûreté had a hand in his death (see chapter 2). These sensational stories provided a high point for the interwar anarchist media. When a historian conducted oral interviews with eighteen surviving anarchists sixty

Fig. 1 Sketch of Germaine Berton, *Le Figaro,* December 19, 1923.

GERMAINE BERTON

Fig. 2 Sketch of Germaine Berton, *Le Figaro*, December 25, 1923.

years later, they cited the trial of Germaine Berton and the Sacco and Vanzetti Affair as the two issues they recalled best from the period.[32] The Union
Anarchiste was able to sustain the daily paper for fifteen months, after which
Le Libertaire returned to weekly status and contributors began to muse about
the decline of anarchism. For the anarchists, the trial of Germaine Berton
was not a marginal event, while Léon Daudet kept the mysterious death of
his son in the courts and the press for years to come.

The Parisian press gave extensive coverage to the assassination of Plateau
and trial of Berton and included artists' drawings of Berton, the lawyers,
and several of the more prominent witnesses, such as the sixty-seven-year-
old feminist journalist Séverine.[33] Berton was portrayed more as a schoolgirl than a terrorist, wearing a white blouse surmounted by a large bow.
Georges Claretie of *Le Figaro* called Berton "a sort of little made-up and smiling doll." The reporter for *Le Matin* asked if she was "the red Virgin of the
scarlet blouse covered by the folds of her large romantic cape," perhaps referring to Louise Michel, called the Red Virgin of the Commune. But he
answered his rhetorical question in the negative; instead they saw "the dis-
creet silhouette of a little, well-groomed Parisienne."[34] Claretie described her
appearance at the cour d'assises in the following terms: "over-made up but
pretty all the same, with her large black eyes and small trembling nostrils."[35]
One surmises that Berton was encouraged by her lawyer to appear as non-
threatening as possible. Nevertheless, she did not deny her anarchist allegiance or even her satisfaction at having killed a right-wing leader. When
she addressed Léon Daudet directly, expressing her regret that she had killed
Plateau rather than him, the hostile reporter for *Le Figaro* added that "her
expression betrays a horrible smile, one glimpses little pointed teeth which
would like to bite. But Germaine Berton is happy that she has produced her
little effect."[36]

Germaine Berton was in fact something of a schoolgirl since she claimed
she had come to Paris from Tours in order to study law but got involved in
radical politics instead. After receiving her certificate of studies, she had
spent over a year at the *Ecole supérieure professionale*. She had worked on an
anarchist newspaper in Tours, then came to Paris in November 1921 and
joined anarchist groups there. She claimed she left the Union Anarchiste
because she did not approve of its communist tendencies, and joined another
more individualist group. Twice she got into trouble in this fifteen-month
period, once for violence against agents of the police, and again for carrying
a weapon. She received brief prison terms for each offense. She shared a
house with other young anarchists and apparently cohabited with a young
bookstore delivery boy named Armand Gohary. These relations would arouse

suspicion during the trial that her attack was part of a plot. A young woman living in the shared apartment, Marguerite Bary, left for Spain days before the murder of Plateau, and Gohary was questioned by the police and then reportedly committed suicide on February 8, shortly after Berton was incarcerated. The anarchists suspected police complicity in this "suicide."[37] Though she claimed sole responsibility for her *attentat*, the police searched the homes and offices of other Parisian anarchists the day after her attack, including that of *Le Libertaire* and its editor, André Colomer. At least two other female anarchists were questioned, including Mme Germaine Linthault, suspected of involvement in a grenade attack at the Salle Wagram several months before, and Mlle Marie Morand. At the *Libertaire* offices at 69 blvd. de Belleville, officers seized correspondence of Linthault, but apparently nothing came of any of this, for it was not brought up at Berton's trial.[38]

At the trial, the prosecution cited a letter that Germaine Berton had written to her godmother in a previous prison visit admitting that she had had an abortion when two months pregnant. Then they read excerpts from a letter to her employer, M. Coste, during a brief period of employment in the autumn of 1922. They quoted her as writing, "If one day, sooner or later, she whom the police call the Black Virgin commits an act which exposes her to republican condemnation, remember her opinions and her rancor against current institutions." Berton replied that she was not referring to a specific deed but to anarchist doctrines in general.[39] Her self-reference as the metaphorical Black Virgin suggests she imagined herself as the successor to Louise Michel, as a symbolic feminine embodiment of anarchy. The reference to the abortion, which of course was illegal in France, was meant to undermine Berton's pose of noble self-sacrifice and make her appear dissolute. The prosecution also tried to show that she sponged off her fellow anarchists and was unable to hold a job for very long.

The historical figure most cited as paralleling Berton's deed was not Louise Michel but Charlotte Corday. Her lawyer later remarked that while awaiting trial in St. Lazare Prison she read a biography of Charlotte Corday. Several witnesses also connected her with the famous assassin of the Jacobin leader Jean-Paul Marat. Such references to earlier heroines point to Berton's awareness of the uniqueness of her position as a female avenger. Of course there was some confusion as to whether the parallels were appropriate since Charlotte Corday killed a prominent figure of the French Revolution. When defense lawyer Torrès asked Léon Daudet whether he had really called for a Russian Charlotte Corday to assassinate "that Jewish Marat Lenin," Daudet replied that in Russia the Bolsheviks murdered Russian patriots, and that Corday killed a criminal, whereas Berton killed a war hero.[40] The image of

Corday, the self-sacrificing young woman who willingly died to save France from the Reign of Terror, was planted in the jury members' minds by Torrès, who referred to her again in his summation.

So was the example of Henriette Caillaux, the wife of the prominent Third Republic finance minister (and former prime minister) Joseph Caillaux, who assassinated the editor of Le Figaro in March 1914 because he was slandering her husband and, she feared, about to publish salacious documents that would reveal her adulterous relations with Caillaux before his divorce and subsequent remarriage to Henriette. Though she practiced at a rifle range with the pistol she bought just before killing Gaston Calmette and admitted killing him in cold blood, she was acquitted in a spectacular trial held on the eve of the war.[41] At Germaine Berton's trial, Mme Caillaux's acquittal was even linked to the murder of Jaurès just three days later, on July 31, 1914, as if the defense attorney wanted to reinforce the point that Berton's act of vengeance for Jaurès was somehow linked to Mme Caillaux's crime of passion. Just as Mme Caillaux's attorney, Fernand Labori, claimed in his summation that wives of deputies in 1885 and 1898 killed men who had slandered their husbands and were acquitted, and therefore there were precedents for acquitting her as well, so Torrès made the same case for Mlle Berton.[42] She had not killed Marius Plateau because of his war record but because of his political activities, which effectively placed him outside the law.

The similarities and differences in these two cases are both striking and revealing. Henriette Caillaux's case is far more famous. Nothing in her background could allow one to predict that the haute-bourgeois wife of a government minister would engage in such extreme behavior, while the petit-bourgeois anarchist had, by her politics, already placed herself outside the system. Furthermore, if expectations of female incapacity allowed juries to excuse them from judicial culpability during the Belle Epoque, one might expect that the transformation of women's roles during and after the war would have undermined such gender biases. Yet the Caillaux case was cited repeatedly during Berton's trial, and the outcome of the two affairs was the same—acquittal despite all the evidence that these murders were premeditated. Evidently, doubts about female capacity for rational self-control remained in Frenchmen's minds. That the young woman from Tours fit the model of the fanatical extremist cast further doubt on her rationality. While Caillaux's lawyers argued that their client would have been incapable of planning her crime, Berton's defenders sought to exculpate her based on her deprived and unstable childhood.

While gendered allusions echoed through the courtroom, they did not explain Berton's rationale for her deed. She claimed she sought to avenge the death of the great socialist leader Jean Jaurès, and also that of Miguel Almereyda, editor of *Le Bonnet Rouge* who allegedly committed suicide in 1917 after being imprisoned for antiwar activities.[43] Although Jaurès had been murdered nine years before, when Berton was only twelve, she revered the memory of the great orator. Jaurès's assassin was not tried for the crime until 1919, and was then acquitted on the grounds that he had been carried away by the intense nationalism of the moment. Berton said that Maurras was responsible for having inspired Raoul Villain to kill Jaurès, and so she attacked the Action Française in the person of Plateau. The clear implication was that since Villain had been acquitted, she should be as well. A year later, Jaurès's body would be ceremoniously reburied in an event staged by the triumphant Cartel des Gauches (left coalition). In protest, the Action Française organized a march to Plateau's tomb, but the counterdemonstration was not a success.[44] This expression of the reverence in which Jaurès, the martyr for peace, was held on the left, explains the logic of Berton's acquittal. Jaurès died, Plateau died, Villain had been acquitted, and now so was Berton.

What does the Germaine Berton case tell us about gender and violence? First and most obvious, French sentimentality toward women allowed them to be acquitted of crimes for which men would have been convicted. None of the male anarchists a generation earlier were accorded the leniency shown Germaine Berton. More contemporaneous, a young man named Emile Cottin had tried to kill Clemenceau during the Paris Peace Conference proceedings of 1919. Though he failed to accomplish his deed, he was sentenced to death, until Clemenceau commuted the sentence to a prison term of ten years.[45] In fact her acquittal encouraged the anarchists to begin a noisy campaign for a pardon for Cottin, in which Berton herself participated (Cottin later went to Spain to fight with the anarchist militia and was killed in 1936).

Second, while Berton's sex was clearly a factor in her trial, her youth may also have helped her. She was included in the "lost generation" (the defense did not actually use Gertrude Stein's term, but that is what it meant), destabilized by the horrors of the war and its aftermath. For comparison's sake, Emile Henry was nearly as young as Berton when he was guillotined at age twenty-one in 1894, but he was not similarly pitied as part of a generation adrift, even though he was born in the aftermath of the Franco-Prussian War to a family that had been exiled to Spain for their part in the Paris Commune. On the other hand, Cottin was also young and Clemenceau had made a personal appeal for clemency, but his nonlethal attack still merited him a sentence of ten years in prison. Journalists attending the trial invariably commented on Germaine Berton's appearance, remarking on how thin and young she looked. Reporters from the daily papers *Le Petit Parisien* and *Le Quotidien* compared her to Collette's schoolgirl character Claudine, responding to the wide white collar and large black bow that adorned her gray dress. Robert Lazurich of *L'Ere Nouvelle* described her as being "still so young she was barely out of adolescence, one in whom the extreme tendencies of her sex were complicated by an unimpeded outpouring of thoughts."[46] From the witness stand, Mme Séverine called her a child abandoned by her mother. During the trial, when Torrès asked one of the witnesses for the Action Française whether he had been an anarchist in his youth, the witness riposted, "Who is not an anarchist at twenty?" As anarchism was equated with youthful rebelliousness, Berton's age and youthful appearance reinforced her sex as an exculpating factor, the combination making her vulnerable and pitiable, as most young men were not. Philippe Daudet echoed her vulnerability by committing suicide, thereby feminizing himself through an act of self-sacrifice and emotional vulnerability.

Third, after the gender and generational contexts, the juridical heritage of similar acquittals for "justifiable" murders, whether hypocritical or not, helped her case immensely. In her testimony for the defense, Séverine referred to the acquittals of Mesdames Clovis Hugues, Marguerite Steinheil, and Henriette Caillaux, all celebrated women who had killed with the excuse of committing crimes of passion. Whereas these women were motivated by self-interest or love, Germaine Berton sacrificed herself for others. "That abandoned child is an unrecognized Charlotte Corday. She is a poor little thing. One must love her."[47] This touching testimony elicited an emotional response from Berton, who rose from her seat to thank the famous old militant. These acquittals and especially that of Raoul Villain, murderer of Jaurès, provided the precedent Berton's lawyer needed to make his case.[48] These three interlocking contexts help explain why Berton was perceived more as an avenging angel than as some androgynous vampire. Germaine Berton was presented in both public and private terms as a woman deserving of the jury's mercy. Her public guise was that of Charlotte Corday, the avenging angel, or Black Virgin of Anarchy. In terms of her private life, a further exculpating narrative based on her youth and sex focused on the family dynamics of the Berton household. Her mechanic and freemason father (his brother Alfred Berton testified that his brother had been a grand master) had taken her to see Jean Jaurès speak before the war, then had died in 1919, leaving her to the care of her unloving mother, who apparently abandoned her and left her to live with an aunt and uncle. The only family member to appear at her trial was this paternal uncle, Alfred Berton. Testimony was introduced to show that the mother considered her daughter to be hysterical.

An early suicide attempt reinforced the mother's desire to be rid of her. She also reproached her daughter for her political associations back in Tours. Alfred Berton's testimony that Germaine had never known a mother's love was echoed by witnesses such as Séverine and emphasized by Henry Torrès much more than her anarchist beliefs (though she never repudiated these). The overall effect was to portray her as a victim, a confused child rather than a femme fatale.

Surprisingly, Torrès never called psychiatrists to testify about his client's mental state; nevertheless, psychology played a considerable role in the defense. Germaine Berton's act of violence was displaced onto the bad mother and the violent victim, while the good father and freemason was connected in her mind with that father of the French left, Jean Jaurès. Germaine Berton was acting out a "family romance," rebelling against her absent and unloving mother while seeking to honor the memory of her dead father and father figure (Jaurès). A similar family romance took even more explicit form in the case of Germaine Berton's putative lover, Philippe Daudet, son of Léon Daudet, the target of her wrath and embodiment of the bad father. Young Philippe was allegedly seeking to commit an anarchist *attentat* in the days before his death, and one possible target was his own father. He had fled the parental household on at least two previous occasions, and his father did not even alert the authorities about his son's disappearance. If Mme Berton was cast as the cold and neglectful mother, Léon Daudet embodied the domineering father. Politics and personal psychology rather than the sociology of class resentment underlay Germaine's trial and the successive trials over Philippe's death of the next few years.[49]

Immediately after Alfred Berton's testimony, Torrès called to the stand several witnesses who recounted the beatings they had received at the hands of the *camelots du roi*. One man had refused to buy their newspaper; another was holding a copy of the left-wing paper *L'Oeuvre* when he was attacked.[50] Maître Torrès's strategy was to try the Action Française, demonstrating that their habitual violence had justified hers; that those who lived by the sword deserved to perish by it (he actually said as much at the trial). He read excerpts from their right-wing newspaper in which they attacked Jaurès and the moderate left politician Aristide Briand and apologized for the crime of Gregori, who had tried to kill Alfred Dreyfus after his conviction for treason had been overturned. A parade of left-wing luminaries such as the socialist leader Léon Blum, Marcel Cachin, communist deputy from Paris, and Marc Sangnier, left-Catholic deputy, warned that Action Française violence presaged the coming of fascism to France. Blum said that his old friend Jaurès would never have demanded the life of Villain as expiation for taking his own; he would only have asked for his remorse.[51] Torrès had lined up some seventy witnesses in all, most of whom had little or no actual connection with the case. The effect of this parade of witnesses was to marginalize the far right—stigmatized as antirepublican and violent—while assimilating the anarchists into the leftist mainstream.

By the end of the trial, the prosecutor knew he was not going to get a death penalty conviction, and while he praised Plateau, in the name of the victim's most Christian mother he said he would not be opposed to the jury mitigating a verdict of condemnation by a show of pity. The other prosecutor also spoke of extenuating circumstances. In his summation, the defense attorney appealed to the jury on a more emotional basis. Reminding them that Germaine's mother had not even bothered to attend the trial, he called her a child of the tormented generation of the war and postwar era. Torrès recounted portions of his peroration in his memoirs. He cited the case of Mme Paulnier, who went to the office of *La Lanterne* intending to kill the editor, Millerand, but seriously wounded his secretary instead. She was acquitted, just as were Mme Clovis Hugues and Henriette Caillaux. Though these crimes of passion seemed different from this political murder, "these crimes, these dramas, all belong to the same order: the passionate order with simply a difference of motives. They struck because they believed they had the right to seek justice, with the idea that they would sacrifice their own life. And I aver that in the long jurisprudence of acquittals for 'crimes of passion,' there has never been a case more worthy of acquittal."[52] He also made a point of distinguishing her deed from those of the men of 1893–94 who

> did not have the goal of striking a particular man for a particular cause, but to give a striking demonstration of force, of violence; the call of the blood instinct. But Germaine Berton has not done that. She has not done what Orsini did, whose bomb killed 83 victims [in the attempted assassination of Napoleon III]. She has not done what was done in [18]94, throwing bombs no matter where, no matter at whom. She struck a particular man for a determined cause. She struck at him following a process of daily mental excitation. She interpreted a whole tradition of violence, all the tradition not only of these women of whom I have spoken, but more recently, that long series of political attacks: the crime of Villain, the gesture of Conradi in Switzerland, acquitted despite their provocations.[53]

Torrès spoke for two hours, after which the jury withdrew and then returned with a not guilty verdict thirty-five minutes later.

The conservative press was particularly upset by the verdict. Georges Claretie of *Le Figaro* regretted that Mme Caillaux, Raoul Villain, and now Germaine Berton had all been acquitted, writing, "after the crime of passion, the political crime is acquitted. Her acquittal marks a critical date in the history of French political and social customs [*mœurs*]."[54] The artist Jean-Louis Forain produced a cartoon for the conservative paper, showing a woman holding a smoking gun with a caption reading, "Who's next?" ("A quand le prochain?") The poet Louis Aragon called Forain the next day, announced who he was, and said he had the honor of informing the cartoonist that the next one would be him. Forain responded, "To hell with you," to which Aragon replied, "Same to you" ("*Je vous emmerde; c'est bien réciproqué*").[55] The *Action Française* was even more incensed at "The Jury's Crime," in which the writer commented sarcastically that the next time one of them was killed, the assassin would receive a decoration. The writer suspected that the jurors were probably freemasons, one of the categories, along with Jews and aliens, frequently attacked in their pages.[56] The prosecutor feared that other anarchists would carry out similar crimes with impunity. Yet Berton appeared to the jury less as a member of a conspiracy or violent movement than as a troubled individual. Her lawyer skillfully removed her from the damaging context of anarchist *attentats* and placed her instead within the dual heritage of feminine crimes of passion and vengeance for past injustices. Her crime remained sufficiently isolated as neither to call forth similar acts nor to be remembered by anarchist historians.[57] Nevertheless, on May 26, 1925, another right-wing activist and associate of Marius Plateau, Ernest Berger, was shot in the back at the Gare St. Lazare metro station by "an insane woman who harbored an ill-defined grudge against the Action Française."[58]

Germaine Berton emerged from her nearly year-long ordeal a free woman and an anarchist heroine. Though she had left the Union Anarchiste in 1922 to join the individualists, she appeared to return to the anarchist-communist fold after her trial. The following April, *Le Libertaire* announced that she and Jules Chazoff (real name: Jules Chazanoff) would be embarking on a speaking tour beginning in Marseilles on May 4 and concluding in Limoges on May 26. Throughout May the paper printed notices advertising the tour and on May 10, 1924, reported that two thousand people had turned out at Saint-Henri to hear Berton call the proletariat to liberate imprisoned comrades while Chazoff warned of the threat of Italian and Spanish fascism spreading to France. Germaine Berton was a celebrity. Unfortunately, the tour never made it to Limoges. On the night of May 21, 1924, a Bordeaux crowd estimated at fifteen hundred people found the hall where they planned to meet closed by order of the police. They marched out to the suburbs, their numbers growing, and Berton harangued the crowd for about twenty minutes. Then they returned to the Cinéma des Capucines where the lecture had been scheduled, the crowd by now numbering perhaps five thousand. A local anarchist activist named Aristide Lapeyre reported in *Le Libertaire* that "the name of Germaine Berton personified for an instant the Revolt of the free conscience; she appeared to the people as a promise of redemption."[59] The police acted to disperse the crowd, fighting broke out, and Berton was arrested for carrying a loaded revolver, which she later claimed she carried to defend herself against attacks by the *camelots du roi*. In an article sarcastically titled "In the Land of Liberty," Berton wrote of how she led the crowd behind the black flag while wearing a black armband. Two women stayed by her side during the struggle, and she called the police cowards and murderers for beating up an old man who had taken part in the demonstration. She was condemned to four months in prison, a hundred-franc fine, and two years of travel restrictions for carrying a weapon and insulting the authorities. She concluded caustically that this must be what the newly elected Bloc des Gauches stood for.[60] One hundred fifty other demonstrators were also arrested. *Le Libertaire* always referred to her as "our friend" or "our Germaine."

After spending nearly all of 1923 in prison in Paris, she endured an additional four months in the Fortress of Hâ. The next notice of her in the anarchist press, dated November 2, 1924, reported on her renewed attempt to kill herself, after her time spent in prison had given her "black thoughts." The paper then printed the following police report:

> Germaine-Jeanne-Yvonne Berton, born 7 June 1902 in Puteaux, declared in a letter opened by the police commissioner of the Belleville neighborhood of Paris that at 2 A.M. she had gone to the area near Père Lachaise Cemetery with the intention of committing suicide with a revolver, but encountering some passersby, she entered some deserted streets nearby. She decided to shoot herself in the chest, but the firearm jammed. Then she addressed a letter to Mme Alphonse Daudet, mother of Léon Daudet and grandmother of Philippe, explaining the motives of her act of despair. She also composed two letters to her friend André Colomer, editor of *Le Libertaire*, then went to sleep. At 10 A.M. the next morning she returned to Père Lachaise with the intention of kneeling on the tomb of someone who was dear to her, where she took poison and left, making her way to the church of Notre Dame des Lourdes, which she entered and lost consciousness.[61]

André Colomer's wife, Madeleine, visited her in the hospital where she was recovering but appeared to be very depressed.

Le Libertaire also revealed the contents of the letter sent to Mme Daudet. Berton felt that Mme Daudet was not sympathetic with her son Léon's campaign to profit politically from Philippe Daudet's death and wanted her to know that "I am going to die as Philippe died, but I do not regret having held tightly in my arms he whose exact age and family name I did not know. Pardon me, Madame, because if Philippe died for me, today I kill myself for him. Germaine Berton."[62] Despite this feverish confession, the writer for Le Libertaire was far from certain that Berton really had known Philippe Daudet in the months before her attentat of January 1923, when he would have been just fourteen years old (though he looked about eighteen). She was clearly obsessed with him, for she wore a medallion around her neck bearing his features.

The day after Berton's attempted suicide, the anarchist Pierre Mualdès defended the right to commit suicide, but he regretted such attempts among revolutionaries and counseled them to struggle against the ugliness of life instead. He queried, "To kill oneself, is it not to admit being beaten?"[63] He also chastised the communist newspaper L'Humanité for gloating about a rash of suicides among the anarchists. In an odd coincidence, Germaine Berton was not the only young anarchist woman to attempt suicide the weekend of November 1–2, 1924. On November 5, Le Libertaire reported that Simonne Willifak [sic], aged twenty and active in the anarchist youth group, was found in a pool of blood in a room in the Hotel Durantin. Police found two letters, one addressed to Le Libertaire. This time they felt obliged to editorialize that anarchists struggled for life, not death: "The anarchist milieus are healthy, vigorous, combative. They are partisans of action and reprove suicide. They have nothing in common with certain little coteries where one cultivates extravagant theories."[64] Young people especially were counseled to escape morbidity and turn toward action. The young woman who had opened her veins, apparently as the result of an unhappy love affair, was Rachel Willissek. As with Berton, she too survived her suicide attempt and went on to take an active role in the anarchist movement. Under the name Simone Larcher, she and Louis Louvet would edit an individualist paper called L'Anarchie from 1926 to 1929, and for several more years would organize lectures and discussions, whose results they also published in a quarterly journal called Controverse in the 1930s. She also worked as a proofreader, joined the proofreaders' union, the syndicat des correcteurs, and eventually became the first woman to sit on the union's board of directors.[65]

These suicide attempts were embarrassing to the anarchists. They reinforced the impression that anarchists were unbalanced, deviant characters
who revolted against society less for political than psychological reasons. This
is what incensed Mualdès about *L'Humanité*'s treatment. The Union Anarchiste was no longer eager to capitalize on her fame. The police, however,
considered her worthy of remaining on their list of dangerous anarchists,
on whom they reported every two weeks. It is thus possible to track her
movements around Paris. When she returned from Bordeaux in August
1924 she spent some time with the young anarchist poet and militant Georges
Vidal, and they may have been intimate for a short time. The police reported
seeing them together at the Montmartre anarchist cabaret Le Grenier de
Gringoire in late August and commented that their relations were other than
those of mere friendship.[66] By October she was staying with another anarchist in the suburb of Noisy-le-Sec; then after her failed suicide attempt she
stayed with the Colomers. After that she moved between the tenth and
eighteenth arrondissements until June 1926, when for the first time she is
listed in the Sûreté records as "femme Burger." From then until 1929 she
is cited as "Germaine Berton, femme Burger," so apparently she established
a stable relationship with M. Burger, who was not himself on the list of dangerous anarchists. In August 1928, the Sûreté noted that she and Burger had
left for Vienna, Austria, and in May 1929 a note said that she now resided
in Germany. Her name was then dropped from the list and did not return
even in the 1930s, despite the rise of fascism there. Given the name Burger,
it seems possible that she married a German or Austrian. In any case Germaine Berton played no further role in the French anarchist movement.[67]

Germaine Berton's repeated attempts at suicide—as an adolescent in
Tours, after killing Marius Plateau, once again the following year, and then,
finally and successfully, in 1942 at age forty—imply mental instability.[68]
Her brief career as an anarchist celebrity and her numerous run-ins with the
authorities suggest that the self-described "Black Virgin of Anarchy" was
unable to distinguish her political from her personal motivations. The very
ambiguity that allowed her clever defense lawyer to free her despite her evident lack of remorse, by playing on her youthful vulnerability, also ensured
that her career as a militant would be short lived. Her behavior would have
reinforced male anarchists' prejudices against women, who were perceived
as being conservative, impulsive, and above all as irrational pawns of their
priests.[69] Henry Torrès noted in his memoirs that he searched her handbag
for weapons before accompanying Berton into the courtroom but failed to
remove her makeup and so was astounded to see her applying lipstick and
powder shortly after seating herself.[70] He should not have panicked; the

gesture emphasized his client's femininity, making her appear less like an anarchist and more like "Claudine."

The one group not put off by her suicide attempt were the surrealists, who apotheosized her in the first issue of La Révolution Surréaliste, which appeared the month after her suicide attempt, in December 1924. On Monday, November 3, 1924, Louis Aragon and André Breton were busy working on their new creation at the Office of Surrealist Research. Aragon noted in the office records that he excused himself from making any proposals, as his spirit was solely preoccupied with Germaine Berton.[71] Ironically, Breton was just then occupied with preparing a survey on suicide that would appear in the initial issues of the new journal. Breton's notes for that day refer to a letter sent to the printer for the suicide survey.[72] Germaine Berton's renewed attempt at suicide did not cause them to launch this survey, as references to the enquête appear in October, but it certainly shook Aragon. Among the articles and references to suicide that appeared in the first issue was one taken from Le Libertaire titled "Live to Struggle," which referred to the suicide attempt by "Villifak."[73] If the anarchists were put off by the eruption of the irrational in their midst, the surrealists were fascinated by the story of life and death, of eros and thanatos, revolutionary politics and violence, love and suicide, that coalesced around the figure of Germaine Berton.

The literary evocation of anarchist violence had little to do with the judgment of the jurors who so hastily acquitted Germaine Berton on Christmas Eve 1923. Those jurors were lenient in part because her attempted suicide and youthful fanaticism enhanced her femininity, i.e., reinforced traditional perceptions of female emotional fragility and hysteria. Despite her own protestations of responsibility for her actions, Berton was perceived as being incapable of full responsibility. The "feminine" qualities that led to her acquittal were idealized by the surrealists as a liebestod of murder and suicide in the service of a higher and nonfunctional, irrational goal. Germaine Berton briefly inspired young artists, while the anarchists moved on to focus on the ultimately unsuccessful struggle to obtain a reprieve for Sacco and Vanzetti. They, rather than Marius Plateau and Germaine Berton, are remembered as tragic martyrs for their cause.

The Bad Father and the Prodigal Son: The Death of Philippe Daudet

If at twenty one is not an anarchist, he is denuded of soul. He who remains an anarchist past the age of thirty is no less than an imbecile.

—BRUTUS MERCEREAU, "Philippe Daudet," *Le Libertaire*, December 7, 1923

Before Germaine Berton arrived at the rue de Rome for her fateful, and fatal, encounter with Marius Plateau, she had tried to gain entry at the home of Léon Daudet, deputy of Paris and editor-in-chief of the *Action Française* newspaper. Fortunately for Daudet, his doorman turned her away. By the time Berton stood trial eleven months later, Léon Daudet would be implicated with the anarchist movement more than he could possibly have imagined back in January. When he took the witness stand at Berton's trial, he testified that the Action Française had never been particularly concerned with anarchism. Yet for much of the next decade, Daudet would be obsessed by the series of events that took place in late November 1923, which involved his young son Philippe and the anarchists of *Le Libertaire*. The inquests and trials stemming from the mysterious death of Philippe Daudet would last until 1931. In 1924, the young anarchist poet and militant Georges Vidal would produce an entire book titled *Comment mourut Philippe Daudet* (How Philippe Daudet Died), in which he detailed his own role in the affair. At the end of 1924, as we have seen, Germaine Berton would once again attempt suicide in response to that of Philippe Daudet a year earlier. In 1925, André Colomer, editor of *Le Libertaire* and a writer and poet, broke with his fellow anarchists over his role in the Daudet affair and left the paper to found his own more individualist-oriented paper, *L'Insurgé*.

The Philippe Daudet Affair is significant, however, not only for its impact on the interwar anarchist movement, or because of its melodramatic quality as an unresolved mystery involving anarchists, monarchists, an alleged love affair, a famous literary-political family, the police, and either a murder or a suicide.[1] The affair reveals particularly clearly anarchist attitudes toward the family and especially the role of the father. Léon Daudet exemplified the negative image of the authoritarian father, Philippe the oedipal, rebellious son. Philippe's dual rebellion against paternal authority and right-wing politics in running away from his family to join the anarchists, and even possibly to assassinate his own father, encapsulated anarchist critiques of the nuclear family as a primary site of repression that must be overcome if a libertarian future was ever to be achieved. The vindictive and somewhat unhinged figure of Léon Daudet, stand-in for the absent king of France, was the perfect foil against whom the anarchists could demonstrate that all forms of authority—national, religious, familial—threatened the freedom of the individual.

Léon Daudet was the son of the well-known writer Alphonse Daudet, author of psychological novels in the last quarter of the nineteenth century. Léon was born in 1867, making him fifty-six in 1923. His first marriage united two great literary houses, since he married the granddaughter of Victor Hugo. Jeanne Hugo did not remain married to Daudet for long, finding him violent and intemperate. They were divorced in 1895. In 1903 Daudet remarried, this time more successfully, but his choice was a little odd, as Marthe Allard was his first cousin. In fact she was his double first cousin, being daughter of his mother's brother and his father's sister! Of the Daudets' three children, Philippe was born in 1909 and was the eldest son. Daudet's literary success did not match his father's, but starting around 1904 under the aegis of Charles Maurras he made a career in right-wing politics and seemed to thrive on conspiracy theories. In December 1912, he denounced the Société Laitière Magiori as a German espionage organization and composed some fifteen hundred articles laying out his charges. In 1913 the company sued Daudet and the Action Française, and in 1920 a court established that Daudet had never proved his contentions. Meanwhile, in 1917 Daudet alleged that the Minister of the Interior, Malvy, had delivered to the Germans the plans for the battle of Chemin des Dames. He admitted to his fellow nationalist Maurice Barrès that he had no proof, and Barrès concluded that Daudet had a feeble grasp of objective fact.[2]

It is possible that the consanguinity of Léon and Marthe Daudet led to physical problems for their son Philippe, who was a frail child and was rumored to be epileptic. Nevertheless, by the age of fourteen years and ten months, Philippe Daudet looked closer to twenty and was tall for his age.[3] A student at the elite Lycée Louis le Grand, he had repeatedly fled the parental household. At age twelve he had gotten all the way to Marseilles, and had fled twice more for brief periods of time early in 1923. So when Philippe disappeared on Tuesday, November 20, 1923, his father assumed this was one more such escapade and hesitated to notify the police of his son's disappearance. Philippe did not merely flee but left with seventeen hundred francs of his parents' money, apparently intending to make his way to Canada. He took a train to the port of Le Havre that afternoon only to discover that he had insufficient funds and lacked the necessary documents to make it to the New World.[4] He stayed in a hotel, registering under an assumed name, and tried to buy a pistol from a firearms store. The arms dealer refused to sell a gun to the adolescent.

Philippe returned to Paris on Thursday and made his way to the offices of Le Libertaire. Here he met Georges Vidal, a dark, thin, twenty-year-old with long hair who looked every bit the bohemian anarchist poet. Vidal had come to Paris from Marseilles the previous year, after spending two months in prison at age nineteen for a poem he had written and published celebrating Emile Cottin's attempted assassination of Clemenceau.[5] Philippe did not reveal his identity other than his first name but told Vidal that he was a fervent anarchist. In the book Vidal published about him the following March, he quoted young Daudet as telling him: "I am sickened by the present society. I'm ready to do no matter what. I am available to you. If you have someone you want to get rid of, give me his name and, this evening, it will be done. There is one among you above all whom I love—Germaine Berton. And I want to avenge her. At age twenty she has not hesitated to sacrifice herself. I too want to give my life for the Cause."[6] Vidal attempted to calm Philippe down, and that evening he took the adolescent to a Young Anarchist meeting at the Maison Commune, convened at 49 rue de Bretagne in the Third Arrondissement, where Philippe befriended a young man named Jean Gruffy. He stayed with Gruffy that night, and Gruffy later testified that Philippe had said that his father brutalized him and that he wanted to kill his father.[7] Some sources speculate that Gruffy and his mistress Marcelle Weill may have relieved Daudet of most of his money since little remained of the seventeen hundred francs he had taken from his parents.[8]

On Friday, November 23, Philippe left Gruffy about 10 A.M. and made his way to the left bank office of Frédéric Rouquette, a well-known writer on Canada and Alaska. Using the name Pierre Bouchamp, the same alias he had used at Le Havre, Philippe asked Rouquette to take him with him to the New World.[9] This suggests that he was still hoping to escape from Paris and his parents even as he contemplated committing an *attentat* or even killing his father. Rebuffed again, he returned to the office of *Le Libertaire*. He had lunch with the anarchists, then left abruptly at 1 P.M., and was absent for part of the afternoon. Afterward they speculated that he obtained a revolver at this time since he apparently brandished a pistol later that day. Some commentators think he obtained the small Browning automatic from the bookseller Le Flaoutter. That his plans to leave for Canada seemed stymied might have hardened his resolve to commit an anarchist deed. That afternoon, he gave Georges Vidal some poems and a letter for his mother, which he asked him to deliver to her in the appropriate circumstances and when his identity became known. This letter, which Léon Daudet was sure the anarchists had compelled Philippe to write, became a central piece of evidence because in it Philippe told his mother he loved her, asked her to hug his younger siblings (*"les gosses"*), and never mentioned his father at all. He also confessed to holding anarchist convictions and felt compelled to commit a deed for the cause.

Philippe was supposed to meet with Georges Vidal Friday night at the Grenier de Gringoire Cabaret at 6 rue des Abbesses in Montmartre, where the anarchist singer Charles d'Avray performed. The quick rapport established by Vidal and Daudet was typical of anarchist *compagnons*, Vidal wrote, and he admitted that his own bourgeois background probably made it easier for Philippe to relate to him. All this time the young man's true identity remained hidden, and in any case Daudet showed up late and Vidal missed him.[10]

On Saturday, November 24, Philippe Daudet went to a bookstore at 46 boulevard de Beaumarchais, about two blocks from the Place de la Bastille, that was run by a reputed anarchist. He asked for a copy of Baudelaire's *Fleurs du Mal* but apparently did not like the editions offered him by the bookseller, Pierre Le Flaoutter. If Philippe had obtained the Browning pistol from Le Flaoutter, it is possible he really returned for magazines of cartridges—two were found on his person after his death. It is unclear who referred Philippe to the bookstore, but apparently the intemperate young man told Le Flaoutter that he wanted to assault some political figure. He mentioned the president of the republic, the president of the council (prime minister), and Léon Daudet. The bookseller told him to return that afternoon and he would help him arrange something. What the anarchists did not know was that the opportunist bookseller was also a police informer, as well as a pornographer and, apparently, a peddler of illegal contraceptive devices.[11] He quickly informed the national investigative police, the Sûreté Générale, who sent agents to guard the dignitaries, and others to stake out the bookstore for the unknown anarchist's return. Philippe returned to the bookstore that afternoon, at around 4 P.M. At this point the story is contested; one likely scenario suggests that he noticed that the police were watching the store, and instead of entering hurried to the Place de la Bastille, where he hailed a taxi.[12] He asked the middle-aged taxi driver, Charles Bajot, to take him to the Cirque Médrano, presumably because it was located at the top of the rue des Martyrs and so would provide easy access to the anarchists at the Grenier de Gringoire and the *Libertaire* office. As the taxi drove along the boulevard Magenta, at 4:15 P.M., it passed the St. Lazare prison, which housed Germaine Berton, still awaiting trial. Philippe pulled out a pistol and shot himself in the head in front of the prison that confined Berton. At about this time, Philippe's father finally decided to have a detective agency search for his son. Philippe was taken to a nearby hospital, where he soon succumbed to his wound. His death was described in the *fait divers* section of *Le Petit Parisien* the next day. Mme Daudet read about the suicide of the unknown young man, and fearing it might be her missing son, went with her husband to Lariboisière Hospital, where they identified the body.

In his autobiography, the lifelong anarchist militant Louis Lecoin recalled forty years later that the Philippe Daudet Affair struck the anarchists like a bolt of lightning. He wrote that Vidal and Colomer came to him to ask his advice, showing him the letter signed "Philippe" that they were to give to his mother. As with Mme Daudet, they too feared that the self-proclaimed anarchist they knew only as Philippe was the unnamed suicide at the hospital. Lecoin knew the secretary of the nurses' union, who got them into Lariboisière Hospital, where they learned that their impetuous anarchist and Philippe Daudet were indeed one and the same. The anarchists decided that this story—the son of Léon Daudet proclaiming himself to be an anarchist—was a propaganda coup too good to pass up, especially given that the Germaine Berton trial was less than a month away.

On December 2, 1923, *Le Libertaire* issued a special edition of their paper with the headline "The Tragic Death of Philippe Daudet, Anarchist. Léon Daudet, his father, hushes up [*étouffer*] the truth." (*Action Française* had announced on Tuesday that Philippe Daudet had died of an illness.) They recounted how Daudet had come to them two days before his death and quoted him as asking what had happened to the heroic times of Ravachol and Henry, or the Bonnot Gang? Philippe had admired the Russian anarchists who wrapped their bodies in dynamite in order to kill the tsar, calling it a "sublime gesture of renunciation."[13] They reported that Vidal and Colomer had tried to restrain Philippe from acting impulsively and expressed genuine regret that his death had deprived them of a good comrade. In emotional language they wrote, "Adieu my friend. Your gesture will not have been useless . . . all the *compagnons* cry out to you their recognition and their love." They also printed, in facsimile, the letter addressed to Philippe's mother, which told her how much he loved her and pointedly failed to mention his father at all. To Léon Daudet they wrote, "Who could have foreseen that a monster had given the light of day to an apostle," and emphasized that "Philippe Daudet was an anarchist. He died because he did not want to remain among you."[14] This letter from Philippe to his mother would constitute a key part of the evidence of Philippe's estrangement from his father, both personally and politically. That his son would kill himself and not even mention his father in his farewell letter was perceived as a deep stain on Léon Daudet's honor—so deep that Daudet insisted that the anarchists had compelled the young man to write the letter under duress. The anarchists replied that there were numerous intervals in which the unhappy adolescent had been free to come and go, and yet he did not return home.

Responses to this bombshell were not long in coming. Daudet immediately denied that his son had committed suicide and blamed the anarchists for his death. The police reported on a meeting of thirty anarchists at *Le Libertaire*'s office at 9 rue Louis Blanc, where Colomer, Vidal, Lecoin, and Pierre Mualdès, along with a few other left-wing journalists, discussed the repercussions of the affair. The others asked the anarchists how they would respond to Daudet's accusations, and Lecoin replied that Daudet should be thanking them that they restrained his son from killing either him or Maurras. Much of the meeting was occupied with plans to commence immediately with daily publication of *Le Libertaire*, with Lecoin saying that the scandal of Philippe's death would save thousands of francs in publicity costs.[15] Instead, the scandal was sure to generate its own publicity, as it elevated the anarchists to the position of principal adversaries of the Action Française. In his memoirs, Louis Lecoin included a letter dated December 3, 1923, sent to *Le Libertaire* congratulating them on their revelations. The letter was signed by eleven surrealists, including André Breton, Paul Elouard, and Louis Aragon.[16] Already taken with Berton's act of defiance (they brought flowers to her hospital room), they were also moved by this act of filial revolt.

The oedipal theme was heightened in the December 4, 1923, edition of *Le Libertaire*. The anarchists emphasized that Philippe loved both his mother and Germaine Berton, the woman who had wanted to kill his father, and that he had entertained similar thoughts. They reported that Léon Daudet hypothesized that the anarchists had sent Philippe to kill someone and he killed himself out of stress, or that they hypnotized him into killing himself. He even imagined that they executed him, fearing counterespionage. This theme was underscored on December 12, 1923, in an article called "Fathers and Children," in which the author speculated on the need for sensitive young souls to reject the ideas of their fathers and cautioned parents not to attempt to indoctrinate their children with their ideas and values for fear of the backlash that they might incur. The only sincere opinions were those for which one struggled on one's own. Parental antagonism was particularly acute between mothers and daughters and between fathers and sons, and the author cited the French proverb, "*A père avare, fils prodigue*" [to a miserly father, a prodigal or wastrel son]. As a generation of freethinkers was some-times succeeded by one of mystics, so the royalist had produced an anarchist son. The author referred not to Freud but to Dostoyevsky for the most pro-found understanding of such psychological stresses.[17]

The next week a regional anarchist paper published in Caen, Normandy, agreed with *Le Libertaire* that Philippe killed himself to escape from his family but strongly dissented from their attempt to make him a juvenile martyr to anarchy. The language of conversion, martyrdom, and idealism made anarchism seem like some surrogate religion. Certainly if anarchism was an act of faith, then a fifteen-year-old could be an anarchist, but truly to study and understand the works of Kropotkin and Reclus took more than an act of faith. If he had really understood, he would have had more respect for life, including his own. The Norman anarchist A. Barbé thus resisted reducing philosophical anarchism to youthful rebellion against the father.[18]

Nevertheless, much of the appeal of the story of Germaine Berton and Philippe Daudet resides in their striking youthfulness. Georges Vidal, who revealed the Daudet story, was the same age as Berton and, like young Daudet, was an aspiring poet as well as a militant anarchist. When André Colomer first made his appearance on the literary scene around 1906, he too embodied the bohemian image of the poet-rebel. Berton was not a poet, but as a young female anarchist with a penchant for the illegal and violent, her subversive appeal was evident. Across the radical political spectrum, the interwar era was rocked by marching young people who rejected the world of their parents and instead created disasters of their own. Léon Daudet no doubt would have preferred that his son join rightist thugs like his own *camelots du roi*, but that would have been neither rebellious nor a sign of youthful sensitivity. The Philippe Daudet story was later told by another young anarchist who arrived in Paris from Montpellier in 1925. Léo Malet was born the same year as Philippe and was just sixteen when he met Col-omer and the Insurgé circle. Though he never met young Daudet, he ac-corded several pages of his autobiography to the Daudet Affair in the section titled "Chez les anars." He read about the case in the Montpellier papers and felt passionately about it because of the coincidence of their ages and what he termed the "call of destiny" since after a sojourn among the surrealists in the 1930s he made his fame as a crime novelist.[19] The story of young love and rebellion was irresistible.

The oft-repeated phrase "who is not an anarchist at twenty" conveys a sense of French worldliness, toleration, and condescension. Let the young sow their wild oats before they settle down, the phrase implies. In the political context of the era, it could suggest that anarchists would mature into responsible parliamentary socialists or dedicated communists. There is some truth to the adage—Vidal, Colomer, and Malet would all move beyond their youthful libertarian enthusiasm, while Berton's active role in the movement ceased by her mid-twenties. Yet it would be incorrect to characterize interwar anarchism as a youth movement since most of the major activists had careers dating back well before the war. For anarchists such as Eugène and Jeanne Humbert, Louis Lecoin, Sébastien Faure, Manuel Devaldès, and E. Armand, anarchism was not a temporary phase but a lifelong commitment.

In Le Libertaire, and again in his 1924 book on the affair, Georges Vidal published not only Philippe's last letter but also the prose poems he had entrusted to Vidal, called Parfums Maudits (Cursed perfumes). The short collection ended with "Départ," in which Philippe says farewell to his parents and plans to leave in two days, a bird on its first flight. The title suggests that young Daudet cast himself in the mold of Baudelaire, Paul Verlaine, and above all Arthur Rimbaud, youngest of the "cursed poets" of the nineteenth century who revolted against all the norms of their society. In La Revue Anarchiste, Vigné d'Octon praised the poems and cited the bitterness of such lines as "you alone are happy, o death. Nothing can be more removed from you, you don't know loves and tortures and you are so happy that you laugh eternally," commenting that few boys of fifteen could summarize Hamlet so well.[20] The poems, which contained allusions to prostitutes, probably shocked the elder Daudets. Since they were handwritten, it was hard to ascribe them to anyone else. They did not, however, make any overt references to Germaine Berton.

Georges Vidal too expressed his admiration for Philippe's poems, which made him further regret Daudet's premature death. Vidal had just published his own first book of poems, Devant la Vie, and said that despite his own bourgeois background he had become an anarchist at age fifteen, or roughly the same age as Philippe. The Philippe Daudet Affair would make Vidal temporarily celebrated in the anarchist milieu, but his involvement after that would diminish. A police informer noted that other young anarchists were already reproaching Vidal for not showing up at their meetings since the death of Philippe Daudet.[21] In 1927 he left for Costa Rica with five friends who hoped to join Raoul Odin's anarchist colony. When that experiment failed, he settled on his own land, which he called Far Away Farm (in English). He returned to France in 1929 and published an account of this adventure in the journal *Les Humbles*. The story he told has an interesting, if tangential, relation to his involvement with the Daudets. He lived with a native woman, and most of the tale concerned his relations with her, with her relatives, and with the native flora and fauna. For example, he recounted hunting tapirs in the jungle and killing a jaguar that was raiding his livestock. The story ended as his native "wife" gave birth to his child and he decided that his much-prized liberty now seemed like subjection. He slipped away in the night as Socorro gave birth, rejecting the role of fatherhood as inimical to anarchist freedom.[22] As he abandoned his familial responsibilities, Vidal also abandoned the anarchist movement and his poetic youth. In the 1930s Vidal became a successful adventure novelist, writing numerous crime and action-adventure novels from 1936 until his death in 1964 at age sixty-one.[23]

The Daudet Affair was temporarily eclipsed by the trial of Germaine Berton, but in the next year and for many years thereafter, Léon Daudet would not or could not let the case die. To acknowledge that his son may have been a secret anarchist was bad enough; to admit that he killed himself out of love for Germaine Berton and hatred of his father was more than he could bear. Daudet soon arrived at what seemed to him a more plausible explanation for his son's death. He decided that Philippe did indeed return to the bookstore that Saturday afternoon in late November, encountered the police, and when it seemed as if he were reaching for a weapon, was shot in the head. When they examined his pockets and realized whom they had killed, they decided to cover up their crime by making it look like suicide. According to this scenario, they carried his mortally wounded body into Bajot's taxi, placed a gun in his hand, and sent the taxi off to the hospital. Bajot was thus most likely also a Sûreté agent. As to the anarchist role in his son's death, Daudet believed they were generally on the police payroll as well, which is why they sent Philippe off to the bookstore to meet his death. Eventually he came to focus almost exclusively on the Sûreté's responsibility, and in this he found some curious allies in the anarchists themselves.

In February and March 1924, the case was reborn into what *Le Quotidien* was already calling "L'Affaire Daudet." In March appeared Vidal's summary of the case, and while in December 1923 he had accepted the fact of Philippe's suicide, by the following March he thought the murder scenario more credible. So did the editor of *Le Libertaire,* André Colomer, who would actually testify on Daudet's behalf in court in 1925.

Vidal and Colomer were convinced by some of the details Daudet's investigators dredged up. After the cabdriver, Bajot, talked with the police on the evening of Philippe's death, he took the taxi to his usual garage, where it was cleaned. The garage man did not find a bullet or cartridge in the cab, and when a cartridge was eventually located, the police were suspected of planting it. Philippe's overcoat, containing clues to his identity, was missing when he got to the hospital. Above all, Philippe's fingerprints were not found on the revolver, although someone preparing to shoot themselves would presumably have a firm grip on the firearm. The anarchists were of course as likely to distrust the police as was the radical right. Nevertheless, most of the *Libertaire* staff found it bizarre that Colomer would testify in Daudet's favor, so hated was this leader of the Action Française. His decision to do so led to his severing ties with *Le Libertaire,* though this may have been a pretext covering deeper disagreements since Colomer would soon diverge dramatically from his anarchist antecedents.

Léon Daudet's theory depended on the taxi driver being an accomplice, or paid servant, of the police. In 1925, after repeatedly being called a police agent in the pages of *Action Française,* Bajot sued Daudet and the manager of the paper for libel. The case was brought before the Twelfth Correctional Tribunal in the spring of 1925, which ruled that only the cour d'assises was competent to decide the merits of the case. The trial took place in late October and November 1925, two years after the events in question. Bajot was ably defended by Louis Noguères, whose book based on his exhaustive courtroom summary given on November 12 and 13, 1925 (the book runs to three hundred pages), is a useful source of details about the death of young Daudet. He emphasized that before *Le Libertaire* published its exposé of Philippe's anarchist connections, no one had any reason to suspect the cab driver's story of suicide, so it was quite normal for the police to release the cab and allow it to be cleaned. Ballistics tests done in 1925 concluded that the wound was made in the taxi. The autopsy report said that nothing contradicted the verdict of suicide, though they could not irrefutably confirm it.[24] Nor was there any proof that Bajot was colluding with the police or had done anything out of the ordinary after Philippe's death. Above all, the cab driver's lawyer could point to Daudet's motive to exonerate himself and his history of seeking conspiracies. Noguères called Daudet a fanatic given to violence. He also made much of Philippe's hereditary flaws, presumably caused by consanguinity, and established that given his past history of fleeing the parental household, his state of mental instability was consistent with a verdict of suicide. Noguères succeeding in convincing the jury that suicide was more probable than a police murder; it sentenced Daudet to five months in prison, a fifteen-hundred-franc fine, and twenty-five thousand francs in damages.[25] Daudet appealed the verdict, and when a court reaffirmed his condemnation in 1927, he went to the offices of *Action Française* and barricaded himself inside. After three days, the head of the Sûreté, Chiappe, knocked on the door and, backed up by a large number of police, convinced Daudet to avoid an armed confrontation and surrender himself. Daudet's surrender to the police did not end the story, however. A month later, the warden of Santé prison received a call from the minister of the interior ordering him to free Daudet, the manager of the *Action Française*, Delest, and an imprisoned communist as a Bastille Day gesture. The call actually came from the Action Française, and Daudet then fled to Belgium, where he gave lectures on literature, being prohibited by the Belgian government from engaging in any political discussions. He was eventually pardoned and able to return to France at the beginning of 1930.[26]

The trials over the death of Philippe Daudet continued into the 1930s. Léon Daudet, with the help of threats of violence by the *camelots du roi*, was able to produce new witnesses who said they saw the police dragging the body of Philippe out of the bookstore. There also was a mysterious woman, brunette then but now blond, who had been hiding in the subbasement of the bookstore and witnessed the murder. This woman apparently was another mistress of Le Flaoutter and had since married a police functionary. Yet she remained unnamed and never appeared at any trial. Confidential police reports attributed the whole affair to the "colossal, furious vanity of Léon Daudet . . . he needed witnesses, and he would find them if he had to go to night asylums or crazy houses."[27] The police also reported that on the ninth and tenth anniversaries of Philippe Daudet's death, thirty or so members of the *camelots du roi* laid a wreath of white chrysanthemums on Philippe Daudet's grave at Père Lachaise cemetery. The dead boy still served as a martyr for the extreme right; one suspects his memory had been effaced on the left by the martyrdom of Sacco and Vanzetti.

Anarchy, Family, and Patriarchy

In her book *The Family Romance of the French Revolution*, Lynn Hunt theorizes that the men who made the French Revolution replaced the royal family with a band of brothers dedicated to the revolutionary goal of fraternity. She borrows the term "family romance" from Freud, who used it to denote the neurotic fantasy of getting rid of one's parents and more broadly to connect the individual psyche to the social order through the medium of the family. Familial imagery and intrafamilial conflict were an inescapable metaphor for the political order in a patriarchal society.[28] The anarchists of the 1920s did not need to read Freud (though some of them had) to make full use of the Daudet Affair as a means of attacking the tyrannical father as synonymous with the repressive state.[29] The anarchists of Le Libertaire immediately perceived the propaganda value of Philippe Daudet's violent reaction against his father and his stated preference for his father's young female would-be assailant. The anarchist-communists of Le Libertaire were, however, less focused on issues of family and sexuality than were the individualists. No Libertaire editorials generalized from the Daudet experience to condemn the institution of marriage or the domination of parents over their children. Daudet was a bad father because he was reactionary. They would have been reluctant to conclude that one was reactionary because one was a bad father, and even less likely to condemn fatherhood in general. There was no such reluctance on the part of E. Armand.

E. Armand, ideological heir of Libertad and the prewar individualist journal L'Anarchie, was the dominant individualist theorist of French anarchism. Since the Daudet Affair directly concerned the anarchists of Le Libertaire, Armand did not play a central role in the discourse surrounding the affair, though he did occasionally publish articles in the paper. Nevertheless, his wide-ranging critique of the family amplifies the attacks that Vidal, Colomer, and others made on the dynamics of the Daudet family. Armand repeated his criticism of the family so often that he was parodied by his fellow anarchists for his obsession with sexuality and its social implications. What follows is a summary of his major ideas concerning the family.

Armand considered the family as central to the social status quo, and he condemned it unreservedly. He did not want to replace the family with a band of brothers who excluded women from the public sphere, as Hunt suggests was the case in the French Revolution.[30] Nor did he wish to imitate the Jacobins' separation of the public and the private spheres. If the family was the central institution of society, then the anarchist social revolution had to address its role in perpetuating the authoritarian status quo and in their vision of the future society. For Armand, the family, especially the bourgeois French family, enshrined the domination of the father over his wife and children, who were essentially his property. Based on private property relations passed down through the generations, it was fundamentally capitalistic and egoistic. While the institution of the family subjected women to men, it was even worse in accustoming children of both sexes to "know their place" and submit to their "superiors." In admonishing all French children to respect the authority of their elders, it inhibited anarchist ideals of autonomy, equality, and individuality.

Perhaps worst of all from Armand's perspective, the bourgeois family linked property values to sexuality. Since men wanted to pass on their goods and their names to their legitimate heirs, their honor demanded that their wives must be chaste, refraining from sexual relations with all other men. This sexual exclusiveness led to the characteristic psychological state of jealousy, against which Armand inveighed endlessly. One of his sexual freedom groups was even called the League Against Jealousy. Nor did Armand believe that the working-class family was immune from the perversions typical of the bourgeois family. Workers were just as jealous and repressive as the bourgeoisie when it came to family relations. The anarchist solution was to abolish the family and replace it with voluntary social groups—precisely parallel to replacing capitalism and government with self-governing workers' collectives. This is the program Armand called *camaraderie amoureuse,* in which individuals of both sexes (ideally in equal numbers) would share what Armand called "sentimental-sexual relations." Sex would be plural, and all forms of sexual relations among individuals would be tolerated, as long as they were freely consented to by all parties and no constraint was employed. Free love constituted the true social revolution.

Armand's ideas on sexuality will be discussed separately at greater length; what concerns us here is his attack on the family, which he saw as unnaturally limiting sexual freedom and expression, as well as creating an egoistic mindset devoted to private property. In a sense, his conclusions were the opposite of those of the Jacobins (as characterized by Hunt): where they attacked the political order of the Old Regime as based on aristocratic and royal conflation of family and polity, and therefore sought to separate public and private life, he wanted to abolish such distinctions. Monogamy would give way to plural love, children would be raised collectively, and their mothers would neither know nor care about their paternity. Armand's anarchist utopia was thus a world without fathers. If Armand did not entirely carry out his prescriptions in his own life, remaining more or less with the same woman for the last half century of his life, he did demonstrate his rejection of fatherhood. According to the biography of him compiled during World War I by the Ministry of the Interior, he followed the example of Jean-Jacques Rousseau in abandoning his three children.[31]

One immediate by-product of Armand's rejection of paternity would be the disappearance of the distinction between legitimate and illegitimate children. Armand himself does not seem to have suffered from the opprobrium that society still conferred on bastards, but a significant number of anarchists whose biographies are known to us did bear this burden. The model for the illegitimate anarchist was Louise Michel, daughter of a provincial noble and a housekeeper. Perhaps the most prominent illegitimate anarchist in this period was Eugène Humbert, whose biography was written by his wife, Jeanne, after his death in 1944. His working-class mother had two children by different fathers and suffered insults for her status as an unwed mother. Humbert attributed his early encounter with masculine irresponsibility as a major reason why anarchist and neo-Malthusian ideas appealed to him early on, and he said he spoke for many who encountered such prejudice from their childhood.[32]

Another anarchist and sexual reformer who was born out of wedlock was Jean Marestan, author of the leading sex manual of the era, *L'Education Sexuelle,* first published in 1910 and reprinted in numerous editions thereafter, although expurgated after the 1920 law banning information regarding birth control and abortion. Marestan (real name: Gaston Havard) was the illegitimate son of a Belgian doctor and planned to become a doctor himself until his father suffered financial reverses and cut off his funds. Instead he turned toward anarchism and used his medical knowledge to good effect in his best-selling book.[33] Another example is Albert Libertad, who was both crippled and illegitimate and fled his boarding school to come to Paris. Illegitimacy was one reason why young people might feel rejected; the experience of an unhappy childhood such as those of Germaine Berton and Philippe Daudet was another. Familial rejection or marginalization would likely contribute to a sense of injustice and the desire to lash out at both parents and society.

Humbert and Berton kept their own names, though Berton did fashion surrogate identities for herself as Charlotte Corday and the Black Virgin. Philippe Daudet either dropped his family name or used an alias to hide his identity. A great many anarchists, however, did take revolutionary names. The names Lenin, Stalin, and Trotsky remind us that this practice was not confined to anarchist revolutionaries. Nevertheless, it is striking that many anarchists followed E. Armand in divesting themselves of the names of their fathers and taking on new identities on becoming *compagnons* or *compagnes.*

Armand's collaborator Robert Collino called himself Ixigrec (French pronunciation of "XY"); André Roulot became Lorulot; Victor Kibaltchich was known as Le Rétif (the insubordinate one) in his individualist years, then as Victor Serge after 1917, while his companion Rirette Maitrejean was born Anna Estorges (she used the name of her first husband but created a new first name for herself based on her middle name, Henriette); the singer

Charles d'Avray was really Charles-Henri Jean; Rachel Willissek became Suzanne Larcher, Eichenbaum became Volin, Henri Ner transformed himself into Han Ryner, and so on. The list could be extended indefinitely, so common was the practice of removing one's family name. The most obvious reason to change one's name was to conceal one's real identity and so elude the authorities, especially for those who wrote for the anarchist press at a time when prosecutions under the 1893–94 *lois scélérates* were common. Others may have been protecting their careers. As well as shielding one's identity, renaming oneself severed one from one's familial roots and reinscribed him or her within the brother- and sisterhood of anarchy. Since individualists envisioned anarchism precisely as liberating one from the socialized constraints learned in childhood, choosing a new name to accompany one's new identity made perfect sense.

Anarchists of all persuasions used the fraternal *compagnon* (feminine version: *compagne*) as the universal term of address. This meant more than its English cognate companion, or fellow, would suggest. A *compagnon* was also a journeyman, the artisanal worker who had advanced beyond the apprenticeship stage but who was not accorded the guild status of master. Journeymen were not only organized by trade in guilds but also frequently belonged to confraternities of journeymen that crossed guild lines and excluded masters. These associations, called *compagnonnages,* employed secret rituals, feast days, and naming ceremonies that often indicated the hometown and character of the fellow worker. The eighteenth-century glazier Jacques-Louis Ménétra thus became Le Parisien-le-Bienvenu, the name by which he was known during the four-year period in which he traveled and learned his trade on his *tour de France.*[34] These traditions of worker brotherhood and bonding spanned the era of the French Revolution but died out in the mid-nineteenth century, to be gradually replaced by labor unions. The anarchists' common term of address thus signified a nostalgic look back to the age of guilds and worker brotherhoods, and the desire to re-create that spirit of fraternity. As a worker brotherhood, the *compagnonnage* of anarchism signified that no matter how embattled their movement might be, they could rely on one another. Anarchists valued solidarity above all other values, except freedom. One stood with and supported one's comrades. If they were imprisoned, one campaigned for their release and contributed funds toward that end. To violate that bond of brotherhood was the most serious breach of faith. There was no greater term of abuse than *mouchard,* stoolpigeon or informer, applied to those who sold out the bonds of solidarity for money or some personal benefit.

The Mystery of Germaine and Philippe

Whether or not most anarchists supported individual acts of violence, they nearly all admired the avenger for their act of self-sacrifice. Though articles did appear after Germaine Berton's *attentat* condemning such acts as counterproductive and a throwback to the practices of a generation earlier, all applauded the selflessness of such deeds. She was addressed as "Germaine" or *"notre amie"* in the anarchist press. As soon as Philippe Daudet showed up at *Le Libertaire*'s office, proclaiming himself to be an anarchist, he was accepted as one of them and that same night found refuge with another young anarchist. He had found a surrogate family. After his death he was spoken of in quasi-religious tones, as having offered his life for his ideal. Vidal, for example, in his 1924 book, wrote of Philippe: "And alone, as a purifying fire, feeling a violent desire to sacrifice himself, to give himself to the Cause."[35] While regretting his death and his loss to the movement, the anarchists sensed that Philippe had ritually sacrificed himself in front of Germaine Berton's prison cell, dying as a protest against his father and for youthful idealism. None would have counseled his death, but many could appreciate its value as a romantic gesture.

Did Philippe Daudet really commit suicide, either because he realized the impossibility of being the anarchist son of Léon Daudet or because of a hopeless love for Germaine Berton, imprisoned and likely to remain so for a long time (though she would instead be acquitted on Christmas Eve, exactly one month after Philippe's death)? Or was Daudet correct in thinking his death was a police cover-up? In *Philippe Daudet a bel et bien été assassiné* (Philippe was really and truly murdered), René Breval weighed the evidence and found Daudet's arguments unconvincing. The autopsy showed that the pistol had been fired in direct proximity to Philippe's head, and the coroners judged it a suicide. Witnesses on the boulevard Magenta heard a shot just before Bajot stopped his taxi, and Philippe's blood was found all over the cab. No blood, on the other hand, was found in the bookstore. None of the eight Sûreté agents or three regular police ever admitted that he was killed at the bookstore, nor did the other witnesses, which included Le Flaoutter, his wife, and a bookbinder named Duval, who was in the store. Bajot, the taxi driver, successfully sued Daudet for libel. Above all, there was no real motive for a cover-up, for the police could say they were merely doing their job in shooting an armed anarchist who had threatened important political figures. Yet Breval suggested a third alternative to Daudet's murder and suicide. He speculated, a quarter century after the events he described, that having returned to the bookstore that Saturday afternoon, Philippe encountered the agents, who convinced him that he would be sent to a penal colony or even to the guillotine for threatening to kill the president and prime minister, and that he would bring shame to his family. They then offered him the option of walking out of there and sparing himself and his family by killing himself—an option he accepted. The only proof offered by Breval was that the police lifted the surveillance on the heads of state and Daudet at around 8 o'clock that evening—behavior that suggested they knew there was no longer a threat. They therefore knew that Philippe was dead. Also, two high-placed Sûreté agents went to the hospital on Monday to see whether Philippe had said anything before he died, suggesting to Breval some sort of guilty conscience of police complicity.[36] Since accusations of police complicity remain speculations, one may conclude along with the various juries that the unforced suicide of Philippe Daudet was the likeliest scenario.

Another mystery surrounding these events is that concerning the relationship between Germaine Berton and Philippe Daudet. According to Vidal, Philippe declared to the anarchists that "there is one among you whom I love—Germaine Berton." Yet it was not clear whether they had in fact ever met, and Léon Daudet concluded, not unreasonably, that it was improbable that his son, who had just turned fourteen the winter of 1922–23, had had an affair with the twenty-year-old Berton.[37] Yet Maurice Privat wrote in 1931 that Germaine said that she and Philippe had met in the stairway of the Saint-Michel metro station in November 1922. As she was struggling with books and copies of Le Libertaire, a young man bumped into her, causing her to drop what she was carrying. He helped her pick things up and they began talking; he revealed only his first name. They saw each other over the next month and went together to Le Flaoutter's bookstore looking for Russian publications. She also affirmed that he accompanied her to her apartment, though her landlady denied seeing him there. Yet Privat doubted Berton's word, saying she was an *illuminée* (crank or fanatic), unable to distinguish between her own imagination and reality.[38] His suicide in front of her prison cell, and her attempted one over his grave a year later, would make a more satisfying story if they really were young lovers rather than simply disturbed teens who had never actually met. The anarchists construed his death not in terms of adolescent love but as filial rebellion. Neither Germaine Berton nor the police but his father drove him to suicide. They regretted his death but capitalized on its sensationalism while commenting sadly and rather embarrassedly on Berton's suicide attempt the following year.

Léon Daudet was a father of "integral nationalism" as well as of Philippe Daudet. Whether or not the anarchists recognized that *nation* derived from *natio*, "to be born," they certainly knew that *patrie*, commonly used to designate the nation, implied rule of the father. In claiming Philippe Daudet as one of their own, a rebellious son against the oppressive father/nationalist, the anarchists were standing up for the right of revolution in the face of injustice. Léon Daudet's conspiratorial worldview was reinforced by his tragic familial loss, and he spent much of the next decade attacking the Sûreté Générale for killing his son and the anarchists as their mercenary accomplices. His honor was motivation enough, but deeper in his psyche there likely lurked a sense that he was defending the honor of the *patrie* as well. In his 1934 book *La police politique,* Daudet began by describing the February 6, 1934 right-wing riots against the republic, and concluded with yet another lengthy disquisition on his son's death.[39] He labored mightily to make his private drama public and conflated the deaths of the right-wing insurgents of 1934 with that of his son over ten years earlier. Six years later, the gravediggers of the Third Republic agreed with Daudet that the republic had been rotten and replaced the French Revolutionary motto with a new triptych, "work, family, fatherland." The story of Germaine Berton and Philippe Daudet was one small episode in the ongoing saga of family, nation, and authority.

Anarchism and the Avant-Garde

"Transform the world," Marx. "Change life," Rimbaud said. These two watchwords are one for us.

—ANDRÉ BRETON, SPEECH TO THE CONGRESS OF WRITERS (1935) AS CITED BY MARK POLIZZOTTI, *Revolution of the Mind: The Life of André Breton*, 1995

Since Bakunin, Europe has lacked a radical concept of freedom. The Surrealists have one. They are the first to liquidate the sclerotic liberal-moral-humanistic ideal of freedom. . . . But are they successful in welding this experience of freedom to the other revolutionary experience . . . the constructive, dictatorial side of revolution? In short, have they bound revolt to revolution?

—WALTER BENJAMIN, "Surrealism: The Last Snapshot of the European Intelligentsia," 1929

André Breton's succinct declaration to the communist-led convocation of intellectuals called the First International Congress of Writers for the Defense of Culture marked the definitive end to the surrealists' decade-long flirtation with the Communist Party. Breton had little to lose in burning his communist bridges behind him, as he was not even allowed to read his own speech; his friend and fellow surrealist poet Paul Eluard read it for him at a time when few were listening.[1] Breton's reference to Rimbaud was not randomly chosen in this context. Rimbaud participated in the canonical episode of revolution that helped usher in the Third French Republic: the Paris Commune of 1871, which Marx immortalized in *The Civil War in France*.[2] In a speech to Czech surrealists made in Prague shortly before the traumatic events of the Paris Congress of Writers, Breton made it clear that artists may commit themselves to politics, yet "the fact is that art, somewhere during its whole evolution in modern times, is summoned to the realization that its quality resides in imagination alone, independently of the exterior object that brought it to birth. Namely, that *everything depends on the freedom with which this imagination manages to express and assert itself and to portray only itself* " (emphasis in original).[3] Art transcended ideology and circumstance.

Breton had been converted to Marxism back in 1925 after reading Leon Trotsky's biography of Lenin; a decade later he returned to Trotsky as the revolutionary alternative to Stalinism, and in 1938 he met the Russian outcast in Mexico, along with artist-hosts Diego Rivera and Frida Kahlo. It apparently did not occur to Breton to seek support among the anarchists despite their renewed prominence in Republican Spain. What role did anarchists play among the avant-garde in the interwar era? To what degree was the surrealist ideal of a revolution that would transform everyday life inspired by anarchism?

The mutual interaction of anarchism and a variety of modernist artistic movements between 1880 and 1914 has been well documented, both in France and in the United States. During this heyday of the anarchist movement, a significant number of artists and writers were drawn to anarchism because it uniquely offered the promise of a radical change in the social order while valuing the role of the artistic avant-garde in helping determine that change. While some anarchist militants were not immune to the socialist tendency to demand propagandistic art that would advance the cause while being immediately intelligible to the working-class supporters of the movement, generally they recognized that radical art signified a parallel rebelliousness against tradition and offered a model of free creativity to which all people might aspire. Modernist demands for artistic autonomy from didactic or moralistic pronouncements and for constant stylistic renewal were satisfied by anarchist recognition of the dual avant-gardes of art and politics. Bohemian lifestyles also fit comfortably into anarchist cultural politics. From artists such as Camille Pissarro and Paul Signac to a broad array of symbolist and naturalist writers, anarchist cultural politics thrived in the fin de siècle and continued only slightly diminished until World War I.[4] A similar anarchist efflorescence took place in pre–World War I America, only to be savagely repressed during and after World War I.[5]

By contrast, much less has been written about anarchism and modernism in the interwar years. French anarchists themselves were partly to blame since they showed relatively little interest in the modern art of their time. Nevertheless, artists' interest in anarchism did not disappear with the First Battle of the Marne or the Versailles Conference, nor had they forgotten the prewar connection between art and anarchism. Insofar as anarchists condemned war and called for revolt against the nationalist status quo, they identified with it; when anarchism signified internecine division, impotence, and nostalgia for a heroic past, they looked elsewhere for revolutionary enthusiasm.

The Anarchist Phase of Surrealism

The story of the surrealists' tumultuous relationship with the left in the 1930s, in and out of the communist party, moving from Stalin's Third International to Trotsky's Fourth, obscures the equally interesting ideological moves of the 1920s. The twenties are often presented as the hedonistic prelude to the politicized thirties—the "crazy years," as the French called the "Roaring Twenties," followed by the pink or red decade. Since the surrealists announced their communist allegiance in 1925, a full decade before Breton's definitive break with the Stalinist left, contrasting the two decades in this way obscures the degree to which surrealism continuously defined itself as a revolutionary movement rather than simply a literary or artistic one. The surrealist journal was called *La Révolution Surréaliste* from its inception in 1924. That date also predates by a year the surrealists' announced adherence to communism, suggesting that their notion of revolution diverged from that of the Communist Party. In fact the surrealists' politics began with anarchism, an ideology that captivated the young writers from the last years of the prewar era until their conversion in 1925 (and for some beyond that date). Benjamin Péret, Robert Desnos, and André Breton were all strongly influenced by anarchism as adolescents; Louis Aragon identified with individualist anarchism in the early 1920s. Emphasizing this anarchist heritage doesn't contradict the idea that French anarchism was declining in the interwar period, but it dates that decline not in 1914 or 1918 but in 1925. The surrealists abandoned anarchism at about the same time that a number of anarchist militants were themselves questioning the viability of the movement.

The surrealists' anarchist roots have not received nearly as much attention as their communist adherence, but they have not been entirely ignored.[6] While nearly everything pertaining to surrealism has been exhaustively studied by art historians and literary scholars, significant gaps remain in the story of 1920s literary anarchism. One is the response of the anarchists themselves. The anarchists remembered the cross-fertilization between symbolism and anarchism in the fin de siècle as vividly as did the surrealists, yet with some exceptions were unwilling to accord the same close relationship to the contemporary avant-garde of dada and surrealism. The surrealists' fame has also obscured other modernist literary and artistic movements of the immediate post–World War I era that identified with anarchism and were as hostile to dada and surrealism as were the anarchists themselves. In particular, the young war veteran and budding art critic Florent Fels published a journal called *Action* from 1920 to 1922 that was as explicitly anarchistic as its name implied. One of the writers whose poems and articles appeared in Fels's journal was Yvan Goll, the Alsatian who pursued a transnational European ideal that he hoped could supplant bellicose nationalism. In 1924, Goll insolently preempted Breton's project by coming out with a journal titled *Surréalisme* just two months before the first issue of *La Révolution Surréaliste*. These two journals of the early 1920s remind us that Louis Aragon and André Breton held no monopoly on the leftist avant-garde.

Mention of the multilingual writer Yvan Goll, who translated German antiwar poems into French and edited an international anthology of poetry in 1922 called *Cinq Continents* (Five continents), may serve to remind us that one more major artistic movement of the period was linked to anarchism—German expressionism. Writers such as Erich Mühsam and Ernst Toller were more politically active than any comparable French avant-garde writer, just as Germany was in greater political chaos in the postwar era. Goll wrote about these figures and others, but since there was no direct French counterpart to expressionism (apart from the work of some individual artists such as Chaim Soutine), it must remain peripheral to this story. Yet it is worth bearing in mind that 1919 witnessed the council revolution in Munich, Germany, which involved Toller, Mühsam, and Gustav Laudauer. The first two were imprisoned for their role in the uprising and Laudauer was killed shortly after his arrest in May 1919. The other major interwar literary figure who connected these French and German movements of the leftist avant-garde besides Goll was Walter Benjamin, who recognized the surrealists' libertarian ideals as stemming from those of Bakunin.[7]

In an interview that Marguerite Bonnet conducted with André Breton in 1964, two years before his death, the founder of the surrealist movement recalled that as a teenager in 1913 he regularly read André Colomer's journal of aesthetic and individualist anarchism, *L'Action d'Art*. He also read *Le Libertaire* and *L'Anarchie* on an occasional basis.[8] He recalled the demonstrations of 1913 protesting the extension of military service to three years, and the red and black flags waving over the demonstrators. Much later he would write that he never forgot the simple device he saw printed on a tombstone, the anarchist slogan "Ni Dieu Ni Maître (Neither god nor master). He agreed with Bonnet's assessment that prewar anarchism was one of the sources of surrealism.[9] Those sources were at least as much literary as overtly political. In these conversations, Breton cited the classic anarchizing works of the symbolist generation: Tailhade's *Ballade Solness,* Jarry's *Ubu Roi,* Schwob's *Le Livre de Monelle.*[10] The young Breton and his friends followed the exploits of the Bonnot Gang of 1911–12 with admiration, and Bonnet even maintains that Breton was thinking of the 1890s terrorist Emile Henry, who threw a bomb in a train station café, when he suggested in the Second Surrealist Manifesto that the simplest surrealist act would be to fire a revolver in the street in the midst of a crowd. Louis Aragon wrote of the Bonnot Gang's exploits in 1922, and reprinted it in his volume *Libertinage* in 1924.[11]

The nihilist dada movement that emerged in neutral Switzerland in 1916 as a protest to the madness of World War I is frequently linked to anarchism, though more in its German and Swiss than its French incarnations.[12] What Breton and Aragon derived from dada politically was a tone of violent provocation that characterized their actions in the early twenties. They staged a number of literary-political events, from the trial of Maurice Barrès in 1921 (done with the cooperation of the arch-dadaist Tristan Tzara) to the savagely satirical eulogy for Anatole France in 1924, called "A Cadaver," to the Saint-Pol-Roux banquet of July 1925, in which they insulted the writer Rachilde for her anti-German sentiments and generally raised such havoc that the police intervened.[13] Aragon specifically used the death of Anatole France in 1924 to poke fun at well-meaning leftists who eulogized the French writer and idealized "Moscou la gateuse," Moscow the senile old woman.[14]

Dadaist provocations paralleled, and were accompanied by, avowed admiration of the anarchist activists of the 1920s. Most notable, the young surrealists were so impressed by Germaine Berton that a year after her trial they placed her picture among their own as a sort of feminine icon. On December 3, 1923, shortly before Berton's trial and just after Philippe Daudet's death (either by suicide or murder), they wrote to Georges Vidal, congratulating him on the article he had published in *Le Libertaire* titled "The Tragic Death of Philippe Daudet." The collective letter declared that though they were not part of the anarchist milieu, nevertheless "we are of one heart with Germaine Berton and Philippe Daudet, we appreciate the value of all true acts of revolt." Eleven names followed the declaration, including those of Breton (both André and Simone), Aragon, Eluard (both Paul and Gala), Desnos, and Péret.[15] For Louis Aragon in particular, the juxtaposition of Germaine Berton, the twenty-year-old embodiment of revolt, with his reference to Moscow as a senile old lady (made in the fall of 1924 at the same time as they were preparing the first issue of their journal, which celebrated the young anarchist assassin), underscores the quasi-sexual attraction of Berton and by extension of anarchism itself. In idealizing Germaine Berton while lampooning the Russian Revolution as an old woman, Aragon implied that anarchism was young and passionate, communism sclerotic and bureaucratic.

Histories of the literary and artistic movement of surrealism refer briefly to the surrealists' apotheosis of Berton in the first issue of their journal, *La Révolution Surréaliste*. This journal appeared a year after Berton's trial, in December 1924, and included an unflattering mug shot of Berton, surrounded by photos of twenty-four men, mostly young surrealists but also including men whom the surrealists admired, such as Picasso, De Chirico, and Freud. A citation from Charles Baudelaire, chosen by Paul Eluard, accompanied the photos: "Woman is the being who projects the greatest shadow or the greatest light in our dreams."[16] Was Berton being acclaimed as a murderess "projecting the greatest shadow"? No text accompanied the photos, but a short notice earlier in the same issue by Louis Aragon praised Berton for having risen up "against the hideous lie of happiness," by which presumably he meant the complacent hedonism of the jazz age. An "unruly woman" appealed to them as a symbol of revolt against the patriarchal state.

At the time of Berton's trial, in December 1923, Simone Breton, André Breton's wife, wrote to Denise Naville (wife of another surrealist) that André saw Germaine Berton as the incarnation of revolution and love. After Berton's acquittal, Simone, Louis Aragon, and Max Morise brought her a wreath of roses and red carnations with a note that read, "To Germaine Berton, who has done that which we did not know how to do."[17] If Berton represented love as well as violence to Breton, he must have been responding to her reputed connection to Philippe Daudet, for otherwise the troubled young woman scarcely projected an aura of love at her trial. Since Berton had tried to commit suicide by Daudet's grave in early November 1924, just as the first issue was being readied for the printer, they were doubtless thinking of this incident as well as her 1923 deed and trial. That issue would include notice of their intention to hold an inquest on suicide. Germaine Berton represented not merely an anarchist *attentat* carried out by a woman but the conjunction of several powerful surrealist themes: women, violence, love, and suicide.

Germaine Berton's erratic behavior called attention to gender as a relevant category in interpreting her act. Whereas the anarchist militants of *Le Libertaire* spoke out strongly against suicide, the surrealists admired her for repeatedly putting her own life on the line. In appropriating Berton's *attentat* as a surrealist act, they idealized it as the essence of feminine irrationality,

La femme est l'être qui
projette la plus grande
ombre ou la plus grande
lumière dans nos rêves.
Ch. B.

Fig. 3   La Révolution Surréaliste 1, no. 1 (1924): 17.

precisely the kind of stereotype resisted by feminists as well as anarchists. Germaine Berton personified *la révolte,* a feminine noun just as were liberty, equality, and fraternity, embodied in the figure of Marianne during the French Revolution. This benign allegorical figure persisted in the Third Republic, yet at its founding had to contend with real revolutionary women such as Paule Minck and Louise Michel, stigmatized as the *pétroleuses* of the Commune. When Adolphe Thiers and the Versaillaise troops crushed the Commune and its red women, they placed Marianne back on her safely apolitical pedestal, where she could stand for a feminine nation, while power was monopolized by the masculine state.[18] Louise Michel had been known as the "red virgin of the Commune," a mythic identity invoked by Berton, who called herself the Black Virgin of Anarchy. As in 1871, a violent woman threatened to displace Marianne from her pedestal and hence challenge the patriarchal authority of the state.

Did she also personify surrealism? In one sense the fact that her picture was surrounded by theirs in the début issue of the journal suggests at the least they thought of her as a muse if not as a surrealist. Breton's famous definition of surrealism as "pure psychic automatism. . . . Thought's dictation, in the absence of any control exercised by reason, outside of any esthetic or moral concerns" suggests that it was not difficult to assimilate Berton's actions of 1923–24 to dada-surrealist practice.[19] Yet they could have admired her as a violent young woman quite apart from any political context. Germaine was the first of a series of young female killers who fascinated the surrealist group. They joined with many who were captivated by the exemplary violence of the Papin sisters, Léa and Christine, who murdered and mutilated their mistress and her daughter in provincial Le Mans early in 1933 and were immortalized in Jean Genet's play *The Maids.* An entire volume of surrealist poems and drawings was inspired by Violette Nozières, who murdered her father later that same year. The surrealists sent Violette a dozen red roses during her 1934 trial, a gesture reminiscent of their homage to Germaine a decade earlier.[20]

Neither of these female crimes of 1933 was explicitly political, yet all were construed as such, as maids attacked their bourgeois employers and a girl took retribution on the father she claimed had sexually abused her. In his poem dedicated to Violette Nozières, Breton referred to her name as foretelling her father's program for her—rape (*viol* is rape in French). Magritte contributed a drawing of a daughter sitting on her father's lap as he put his hand up her dress. At the same time the anarchists took the opportunity of using the case to condemn the lies underlying the petty bourgeois household, with its ideals of holding on to a job, getting a dowry for one's daughter, making her a good marriage to a reliable civil servant.[21] For Breton and the other poets and artists, killing Marius Plateau, head thug of the fascistic *camelots du roi*, was no different from killing domineering employers or an abusive father. Berton and Nozières were celebrated in surrealist books and journals, while the Papin sisters received less surrealist acclaim despite their more spectacular crime since they killed other women and thus less clearly symbolized revolt against the patriarchal order.

The composite photo of Berton and the artists resembles another published five years later in the very last issue of *La Révolution Surréaliste,* in which the artists' faces surround a nude painted by René Magritte. Whereas they are in some sense watching Berton in the earlier montage, in this picture their eyes are closed, while the caption, "I do not see the [woman] hidden in the forest," suggests that they preferred to dream of women to working with them. This latter photomontage portrays an imagined full-length nude as opposed to Berton's face. The nude is hidden and unseen, while Germaine the woman projects light and shadow in their dreams, according to the contrasting captions. The first photomontage opened the surrealist project, the latter concluded it (though a new journal appeared the next year). Both images suggest how they preferred to transmute women through lenses provided by Baudelaire or Magritte. In 1924 they posed with their eyes wide open, directed outward to an icon of activism who was a real woman; five years later their eyes were closed as if turned inward toward a work of art. Evidently to be a seer in the manner of their predecessor Rimbaud did not require using one's eyes.[22]

The surrealists' celebration of the terrorist has an illustrious heritage that links them to the Russian novelists of the nihilist generation, such as Turgenev and Dostoyevsky, and to the "era of *attentats*" of the 1890s, when their symbolist predecessors praised the deeds of Ravachol and Vaillant. Where symbolists idealized the spectacle of anarchist martyrs, the surrealists perceived Berton's deed as an *acte gratuit,* pure and spontaneous, as an inversion of normal violence. A young woman killed a former soldier and nationalist in the name of freedom; in doing so she disrupted the norms of patriarchal society. The specter of female violence still held sway over male imaginations in the Third Republic from Maxime du Camp's horror at the *pétroleuses* of 1871 to André Breton's iconolatry of Germaine Berton.

In the second issue of their new journal, dated January 1925, Breton opened with an article titled "The Last Strike," in which he regretted the distrust that existed between manual workers and intellectuals and proposed that on the model of the workers' strike, key weapon of anarcho-syndicalism, that intellectuals consider making their own strike. They must strike for complete

Fig. 4   *La Révolution Surréaliste* 5, no. 12 (1929): 73.

liberty of thought and expression and, in the only words italicized for emphasis, "this supposes nothing less extreme than *the abrogation of the indefensi-
ble laws directed at anarchist activities*. It is important that men who, without
vulgar ambition, consecrate their life to assure the triumph of the spirit,
once and for all be sheltered from all persecutions, that they have nothing
to fear from the powerful of the world" (emphasis in original).[23] Breton not

only advocated that intellectuals adopt the workers' weapon of the strike but conflated anarchists and intellectuals as similarly persecuted for their devotion to the life of the spirit. Later in the same issue, a one page manifesto announced "Open the Prisons, Disband the Army" in large type, followed by the phrase, "There are no crimes of common law." The unsigned text begins, "Social constraints have had their time. Nothing, neither the recognition of an accomplished error nor the contribution to national defense should force man to give up liberty."[24]

One more example should suffice to give an adequate sense of the anarchistic spirit animating the first five issues of La Révolution Surréaliste. The third issue appeared three months later in April and contained an article by Robert Desnos called "Description of the Next Revolt." After excoriating bloodthirsty nations full of soldiers and repressive laws, he refers to "Protestant America more imbecilic than ever, by dint of Prohibition, masturbating behind your strong-boxes and the Statue of Liberty." He looked forward to a revolt of the spirit, which would be "that spontaneous revolt, barracks and cathedrals in flames," yet he "always distrusted those revolutionaries who, for having put a tricolor flag in place of a white flag, feel satisfied and live tranquilly, decorated by the new state, given a pension by the new government. No, for a revolutionary, there is only one possible regime: The Revolution means The Terror." He liked to imagine the "grand soir," anarchist term for the revolutionary apocalypse, in which diplomats and politicians, and all priests, would march to the scaffold. He mentioned Léon Daudet and Charles Maurras by name, the Action Française leaders whom Germaine Berton had wanted to dispatch two years before. He even imagined rediscovering the language of the Père Duchesne, the argot-inflected newspaper of the French Revolution, to celebrate this future epoch.[25]

When the surrealists chose to call their new journal La Révolution Surréaliste in 1924, they were more committed to anarchist than to communist models of revolution. Since the previous journal in which they published their work was called Littérature, the title change emphasized their shift to an avant-gardist rather than modernist position. Surrealism was meant to revolutionize one's life. The surrealists condemned both aesthetic autonomy and didactic art in favor of a fusion of art and life. They didn't worship at the altar of art as the symbolists had; their dadaist heritage conditioned them to suspect all pretensions to high art. This was what Breton meant in indicating that the messages of Marx and Rimbaud were one. The overturning of the power structure must be accompanied by the purposeful derangement of the senses called for by the bohemian poet. The revolutionary implications were made clear in the most anarchistic issue of Surrealist

Revolution, number 3, edited by Antonin Artaud in April 1925, in which he proclaimed that "we have nothing to do with literature. . . . Surrealism is a means of total liberation of the mind. . . . we are specialists in revolt."[26] Artaud was an actor as well as a writer, the surrealist who best approximated the postwar concept of a "performance artist." By removing the barriers between conscious and unconscious life, as between art and everyday reality, they would create a "revolution of the mind" (to cite the title of a biography of Breton). Yet less than a year after the first issue of *Surrealist Revolution* appeared, Breton and his followers (though not Artaud) declared publicly in the communist newspaper *L'Humanité* that they had never had a surrealist theory of revolution. They now recognized that the only real revolution was social and economic, as power passed from the hands of the bourgeoisie into those of the proletariat, maintained by the dictatorship of the proletariat.[27] What had happened?

When André Breton wondered the same thing in 1953, his answer was efficacy. The communists had uniquely succeeded in creating a revolutionary society in Russia, while the anarchist movements in Russia, Ukraine, and Germany (especially the revolutionary commune that briefly controlled Munich early in 1919) had all failed. Breton had been reading Trotsky's book on the Russian Revolution (ironically at the very moment that Trotsky was being outmaneuvered by Stalin, on his way to being excluded from the Politburo). Meanwhile France was getting involved in a brutal anticolonial war in Morocco in 1925, and the surrealists made common cause with the communists in protesting the Rif War. The most important fruit of their increasing politicization was the publication of the tract "La Révolution d'abord et toujours," (The revolution first and always), which appeared in the Communist Party newspaper *L'Humanité* in September and in the intellectual communist journal *Clarté* in October.[28] The surrealists were flattered to be courted by the intellectual luminaries of communism and declared themselves willing to subsume their own revolution within that of the proletariat. *Clarté* intellectuals such as Jean Bernier and Victor Crastre welcomed Breton and company while acknowledging that only a few months before they had been engaging in polemics with them over their anarchist opinions.[29] As we have seen, "La Révolution d'abord et toujours" was also printed by André Colomer in his anarchist newspaper, *L'Insurgé,* before it appeared in the communist publications. It might seem as if the surrealists were hedging their bets, still unsure of where they stood; yet since we know that Colomer was himself edging toward communism, the publication of the manifesto in *L'Insurgé* and *Clarté* provides further evidence of the evolution from anarchism to communism occurring in 1925. A year after castigating

Moscow as a senile old hag, Louis Aragon argued that anarchists must forego their obsolete adherence to individualism, which revealed their closet bourgeois sensibilities. Either one recognized the truth of class struggle, or else one was counterrevolutionary.[30]

While Breton, along with most others, undoubtedly viewed communism as more grounded in revolutionary praxis than anarchism, there was another reason for their making what seems in retrospect like an improbable move for an extreme avant-garde group. Breton wanted to be taken seriously. The leader of the surrealists was nothing if not serious, yet the young coterie had developed a reputation as provocateurs who indulged in scandals. As late as 1924, Louis Aragon wrote in the preface to his book *The Libertine,* "I've never looked for anything but scandal."[31] The surrealists staged noisy trials of Maurice Barrès and pilloried Anatole France; as late as the summer of 1925 they created a furor at the banquet honoring the poet Saint-Pol Roux. They disrupted performances of rivals, such as Jean Cocteau, of whose work (and politics) they did not approve. Breton himself indulged in more than one personal assault. The price for these high jinks was that they were not taken seriously by other leftists, from the anarchist staffs of *Action* and *Le Libertaire* to the communist staff of *Clarté.* The anarchists stigmatized them as decadents, the communists as anarchists. Breton decided to replace insouciance with commitment; the result was the declaration "The revolution first and always." When their journal *The Surrealist Revolution* ended, he replaced it with the even more politically committed title *Surrealism in the Service of the Revolution.* And yet in the 1930s all hope of making surrealism the brain or at least the heart of communism came to naught under the combined onslaught of Stalinism and the aesthetic doctrine of socialist realism.

Louis Aragon traveled the farthest from being an admirer of anarchism to becoming a paragon of the communist intellectual, to the extent that in the early 1930s he rejected surrealism entirely as he embraced the new communist literary orthodoxy. Aragon had been chiefly responsible for including the paean to Germaine Berton in the first issue of *The Surrealist Revolution,* and as early as the February/March 1923 issue of *Littérature,* he had praised the young woman's deed. Referring to the death of Marius Plateau as a "work accident," Aragon defended the right of Berton to resort to terrorist means, including murder, to safeguard her liberty if she felt it sufficiently threatened.[32] In the May 1923 issue of *Littérature,* Aragon made a political commentary in which he equated a series of historical events with scandal:

There was a social scandal. Gracchus Babeuf and bolshevism. Respectable, but a little short.

There was the military scandal. The war of 1914, without commentary . . .

There was the anarchist scandal: The Bonnot Affair (that's a little better).

ALL THAT ONLY MAKES NEWSPAPER HEADLINES

SCANDAL FOR SCANDAL'S SAKE[33]

The dadaist provocateur subsumed his aesthetic practice onto the larger world. The notion of scandal implies that publicity is an important component of modern historical events. Aragon's comments seem to fall short of condemning the appeal of media, though the phrase "scandal for scandal's sake" described accurately what critics of dada felt about their noisy movement.

In 1924, Aragon published a collection of short works called collectively *Libertinage* (translated as *The Libertine*), whose preface included references to the fin de siècle anarchist terrorist Ravachol, and the forthright declaration that "if it were up to me everything which is opposed to love would be abolished. That's roughly what I mean when I claim to be an anarchist. This is what makes me so absurdly excited whenever I feel the ideal of *freedom* is threatened for one moment."[34] Aragon's style in this work could not have been further from social realism; one can imagine his play "The Mirror-Wardrobe" illustrated by Marc Chagall. The play included fairies and goatherds as well as mechanics called Gentle, Cotton, and Madness, and was set on a glacier.

The title of the collection and the preface makes it clear that the young Aragon conflated political and sexual freedom, just as Robert Desnos did in his book *Liberty or Love*. The surrealists were known for their provocations, for their celebration of the irrational as it erupted among the detritus of everyday life (the marvelous), and for imagining sensuality as coterminous with liberty. The cults of direct action and sexual freedom, if not irrationality, made them anarchists; their embrace of communism in the autumn of 1925 replaced their bohemian version of direct action with the communist theory of revolution and probably meant that liberty could no longer be associated with anything as subjective as love. That Desnos still did so in 1927 showed his rejection of the path chosen by Breton and Aragon (though he did initially proclaim his revolutionary sympathies in 1925, he refused to join the Communist Party in 1927).[35] Surrealism was not only a revolution of the mind but of the body and of the connections between them. Subjective

Bergsonian Idealism gave way to Freudian libido; then both were (at least temporarily) surrendered before communist claims to revolutionary realism and praxis. Breton's reading of Trotsky appears to have convinced him that materialism and class consciousness was theoretically superior to the anarchist celebration of revolutionary will and individual rebelliousness.

Not all of the surrealists followed Breton and Aragon into the communist camp, just as many anarchists expressed a notable lack of enthusiasm for Colomer's ideological trajectory. Robert Desnos, Philippe Soupault, and Antonin Artaud were summarily dismissed from the fold by the authoritarian Breton. A further split took place in 1929 between Breton and Georges Bataille. When Breton changed the title of his journal to *Surrealism in Service to the Revolution* to underscore his revolutionary convictions, Bataille countered with *Documents,* a neutral title that masked an anarchic and primitivist preoccupation with the body, sexuality, and African culture. This "darker side of surrealism" challenged the very idea of "sur"-realism as a higher realm; Bataille wanted the low road of bodily functions to override (or, maintaining the higher/lower distinction, to undergird) mental processes, even unconscious ones.[36] One of his group projects of the 1930s was even called "Headless" (*Acéphale*), announcing a rejection of reason far more radical than Breton was prepared to accept.

Artaud was the "darkest" of all the surrealists, extending his fascination with the earlier symbolist-anarchist playwright Alfred Jarry into his declaration of a "theater of cruelty" in the 1930s. He also published a book about the third-century teenaged Roman Emperor Heliogabalus that he subtitled "the crowned anarchist." Artaud overtly identified with his subject, writing of this strange work of history, "I do not judge what happened as History might judge it; this anarchy, this debauchery pleases me."[37] Artaud's friend, the writer Anaïs Nin, described Artaud sitting in La Coupole restaurant in Montparnasse declaring that he was the mad emperor, pointing out to the street and declaiming, "The revolution will come soon. All this will be destroyed. The world must be destroyed."[38] Artaud was undoubtedly an extremist, but his was a lonely and tormented voice without much resonance in his own time. As the "crowned anarchist" apparently referred to the terror sowed by the mad emperor, Artaud remained wedded to a conception of anarchism as revolutionary violence.[39] Though he ended his life in an asylum, his theatrical ideas and his anarchism—both intended to eliminate boundaries between actors and audience as between leaders and the crowd, between idea and act—would be renewed in Julian Beck's Living Theater in the 1960s.[40] The violently anarchic sensibility of Antonin Artaud was far removed from André Breton's authoritarian personality, while in Elsa Triollet and the Communist Party, Louis Aragon found comradeship at the price of his surrealist youth, if not his poetic soul. In remaining the outsider, Artaud echoed an anarchist-individualist identity (*L'En Dehors,* or Outside, was the title of an individualist anarchist journal of the 1890s under the arch-bohemian Zo D'Axa and in the interwar era under E. Armand).

Florent Fels's *Action* and Cubist Anarchism

Surrealism grew out of the nihilistic anti-art movement called dada, became the dominant avant-garde movement of the interwar era, and was intensely political. It is therefore easy to assume that dada was the aesthetic corollary of anarchism during and after World War I. The dada artists were after all furiously antibourgeois, antiwar, arch-individualists; some, like Hugo Ball, were fond of quoting Bakunin and Max Stirner.[41] Yet dada and surrealism were not the only avant-garde movements of the period, and dada in partic-ular was contested by rival artists who complained that Tzara and company were not merely nihilistic but opportunistic and exhibitionist. Artists who took anarchism seriously complained that the dadas took nothing seriously and mostly engaged in art-politics. True anarchists were more idealistic, and in the aftermath of the Great War demanded that art serve a greater function than indulging in nonsense and revolt for its own sake. One of these modernist opponents of dada was Florent Fels.

Fels was born in 1893 to a petit-bourgeois family of Jewish origin named Felsenberg. His father was a leftist militant involved with the Socialist Party who retired in 1919 and founded a socialist school for workers. He encour-aged Florent to read Zola and Proudhon and took him to meetings where he heard the preeminent prewar socialists Guesde and Jaurès. Florent Fels began life as a blacksmith and belonged to the syndicat du Nord, the metal union located in his hometown of Lille. He traveled to England, learned English and taught in a London high school, and was exposed to the writ-ings of George Bernard Shaw and the anarcho-individualist literary journal *The Egoist.*[42] Fels returned to France in time to volunteer to join the French army. He participated in the mutinies of 1917; the war and especially the repression of the mutinies created in him a deep hatred of militarism. Many of the comrades most opposed to the war were anarchists, and he gravitated to them. At the same time prominent anarchist communists like Jean Grave supported the war effort, so Fels sided with individualists such as E. Armand, who published an anarchist paper during the war. Fels got to know Armand before the older anarchist militant was sentenced to five years in prison early in 1918 for encouraging desertion and disobedience. He also befriended Maurice Wullens, who introduced him to several antiwar anarchist figures, including Han Ryner, the best known individualist writer. Fels took over Armand's *Par-delà la Mêlée* (Beyond the tumult) and with the collaboration of Maurice Charron (pseudonym Pierre Chardon), renamed it simply *La Mêlée*. This new journal, which was subtitled "libertarian individualist organ," began in April 1918 and continued until the end of 1919, when Fels' colleague Charron died.[43] Fels was still enlisted in the army for much of this period; he was wounded in the spring of 1918 and spent time in the hospital with many Americans. Since he spoke English, he became a liaison agent between the French and American forces.

In July 1919 Fels announced in *La Mêlée* a project for a new intellectual review, which he suggested would be called *Les Cahiers Individualistes* and would be an organ of the "political and literary avant-garde." By October, he proclaimed that the journal would instead be called *Action*. In support of this title change, he quoted a phrase from the esteemed antiwar writer and recent Nobel laureate Romain Rolland: "The most effective action is that which empowers everyone, men and women, and the individual act, from man to man, soul to soul, action by word, [by] the example by all beings."[44] Fels planned to have the premier issue appear in January 1920 and advertised that appearance in the very last issue of *The Egoist,* which the British feminist and individualist anarchist Dora Marsden brought out in December 1919.[45] In fact the notice in *The Egoist* appeared on the last page of the final issue and cited an illustrious list of artistic collaborators, including Gontcharova, Larionoff, Gleizes, Picasso, Picabia, Vlaminck, Leger, and Gris. Marsden announced that her efforts would henceforth be focused on publishing books rather than the journal, especially for authors such as James Joyce whom other publishers had turned down (she had earlier published *Portrait of the Artist as a Young Man* and was serializing *Ulysses* in the final issues of her journal). T. S. Eliot was listed as assistant editor; Marsden had found her way to modernism via feminism and anarchism. Fels had no feminist antecedents other than Marsden, but otherwise conjoined antimilitarism, anarchism, and modernist literature and art more like *The Egoist* than like dada.

Action had to wait until March 1920 to make its appearance because the first issue had been seized by the authorities and censored (Marsden, too, complained of problems publishing Joyce). In that issue, Georges Gabory had written a "Praise of Landru," the serial killer who had promised marriage to a succession of older women before incinerating them. Gabory wondered whether "exceptional men" should be exempt from the law. That first, censored issue also reprinted an article from *The Egoist* on the ballets of Stravinsky.[46] The March issue that did appear featured an article by Jean Cocteau on Eric Satie, poems by Max Jacob, an appreciation of the anarchist philosopher Han Ryner by Renée Dunan, and an article on German expressionism by Yvan Goll. Goll cited the expressionist reviews *Die Aktion* and *Der Sturm,* so aside from the anarchist implications of the journal's title, it is possible that it also referred to the radical artistic movement across the Rhine. Goll defined expressionism as the search for profound interior emotion and as "the response of men caught in the abject machinations of nauseating materialism."[47] He described expressionism as the opposite of cubism since the former was metaphysical and the latter mathematical. Nevertheless, cubist aesthetics predominated in this French avant-garde journal.

An article by Dora Marsden on "Art and Philosophy" led off the next issue, with the British anarchist arguing that artists must be intelligent as well as creative so as to be able to articulate their views. This goal neatly defined what Fels would attempt to do in his journal. Issue number 3 of April 1920 contained two more significant articles that, along with Marsden, helped place *Action* in the avant-garde spectrum. In an inquest on "Opinions on Negro Art," Picasso replied laconically, "L'art nègre? Connais pas" (Negro art? Don't know it). More revealing of the orientation of the review was a powerful critique of dada by the cubist painter Albert Gleizes. In January 1920, the journal *Littérature* had sponsored a poetic afternoon featuring Tristan Tzara, newly arrived from Zurich. Among other provocations, Tzara read a text by the right-wing demagogue Léon Daudet while André Breton and Louis Aragon set off alarms. While such high jinks suggest that dada was in fact political, the irreverent tone sufficiently disturbed Fels that he decided to hold a counterpresentation of modern art to show up this mockery of literature. In February, he had artists from the Odéon and the Comédie Française read poems by Apollinaire, Rimbaud, Baudelaire, Jarry, and Mallarmé; music of Satie was played, and Fels himself spoke on "classics of the new Spirit." Fels declared that art must transmit the highest ideals of humanity.[48] In the April issue of *Action* Gleizes attacked dada as a symptom of a decomposing society. Lacking constructive tendencies, these proponents of the avant-garde made of modern art a mere vogue for the latest scandal. He also complained that they were sexually obsessed, both genitally and anally. The essence of Gleizes's and Fels's critiques was that the dadas were sensation-seekers who sought acclaim without having produced any works worthy of merit. Their pursuit of notoriety was radical only in the context of literary politics; it did nothing to threaten society. Fels and his fellow artists possessed none of the contempt for "art" that marked dada; they were modernists who rejected the demeanor of the avant-garde.

The earnest seriousness of Fels's journal contrasts with the irony and sarcasm of dada. As with the anarchists themselves, so these modernists rejected sterile bohemianism as a pose that destroyed both art and political commitment. For example, in the December 1920 issue, the poet Max Jacob contributed a political poem that remembered the Chevalier de la Barre, Enlightenment martyr to free speech, as a precursor of the rebels of the future. The same issue carried a variety of encomiums to the recently deceased painter Amedeo Modigliani and his mistress Jeanne Hébuterne (who committed suicide), remembering him as a great artist whose talent had been undermined by bohemian dissipation.

Action continued to appear throughout 1921 and into the spring of 1922. It reviewed the work of many new artists called the Ecole de Paris, such as the Jewish immigrant artists Zadkine, Kisling, and Lipschitz. In August 1921, André Salmon published an article on the fin de siècle Jewish anarchist thinker and aesthetician Mécislas Golberg. In his autobiography, Fels said he learned of Golberg from the fauve painter Maurice Vlaminck, who described to him Golberg's book *The Morale of Lines* and called him a Nietzschean genius.[49] As well as poems by Jacob and Apollinaire, *Action* featured poems by lesser known contemporary poets such as Paul Eluard and Benjamin Péret, and even an article by Tzara, suggesting it was open to all schools of modernist art. Florent Fels never abandoned modernism, moving on from *Action* to become an art critic and eventually director of the very mainstream periodical *Voilà*, which is also the title he chose for his memoir. Written in the 1950s, that memoir entirely obfuscates Fels's early radicalism, which nevertheless emerges strongly both in the pages of *Action* and in the letters Fels exchanged with Max Jacob at the end of the war.[50] (Even the mainstream Fels was in touch with his radical youth enough to publish a series of articles in 1931 on the anarchists Eugène and Jeanne Humbert's movement in favor of birth control.) Neither the dada/surrealists nor the cubist-inflected modernists had a monopoly on anarchistic art in the years following World War I. Both groups were radicalized by the war, but the dadas embarked on a project of destruction and search for subconscious meaning, while the cubists were constructivist and still able to respond to humanist ideals. A third revolutionary aesthetic, expressionism, was represented in *Action* by Yvan Goll and also by the critic Carl Einstein, but this current was weak in France and mostly signified the pronounced internationalism of modernism. The mystical element of expressionism was entirely lacking. Together, these currents comprised an anarchist dialectic of idealism and destruction, and an artistic dialectic of modernism and the avant-garde.

An important figure in this movement was Yvan Goll and his Swiss wife, Claire. Goll was born Isaac Lang to an Alsatian father and a mother from Metz in Lorraine. His first contribution to French letters was an anthology of fourteen German antiwar poems that he translated and had published as "The Heart of the Enemy" in Maurice Wullens's journal *Les Humbles* in 1919. His most marked contribution to anarchism was his short book published in 1925 in Germany and titled *Germaine Berton, die rote Jungfrau* (Germaine Berton, the red young female). This was, to my knowledge, the only book ever published about Berton's attack and trial, and it was generally admiring.[51] Reinforcing Goll's connection to Berton may have been his response to the trial of Raoul Villain, the murderer of Jean Jaurès, in 1919. During the trial of Villain, Jaurès was much praised as a French patriot, when in fact, Goll maintained, he was a pacifist internationalist much like Goll.[52] Berton claimed at her trial that she was avenging the murder of Jaurès, whom she had heard speak before the war. Goll was unlikely to be smitten by feminine violence as the surrealists were, but like them he found much to admire in this avenger of Jaurès who also attacked the French occupation of the Ruhr in 1923.

Yvan Goll, Surrealism, and Germaine Berton

The Golls arrived in Paris late in 1919 and, as we have seen, were soon affiliated with the leftist modernists grouped around the journal *Action*. This does not mean that Goll was uniquely affiliated with anarchists, for he was foremost a pacifist internationalist as well as proponent of modernism. Goll spent part of the war in Zurich, where he got to know James Joyce rather than the denizens of the Cabaret Voltaire. One of his literary ambitions was to translate Joyce's novel *Ulysses* into German.[53] In 1920, both Golls published articles and poems in *Clarté*, the intellectual journal that was socialist rather than anarchist, though neither term appeared in the journal's subtitle, which instead announced it as part of the "international of thought."[54] Goll's disdain for the dadaists extended to their successors, the surrealists. In particular Goll became antagonistic to André Breton, in part because Goll's resolute individualism made it impossible for him to follow the dictates of the domineering leader of the surrealists. In this he found himself allied with the painters Robert Delaunay and Francis Picabia. Albert Ronsin describes a meeting with Breton at a dance performance in May 1924 that ended in a fist fight between Goll and Breton and led to a twenty-year-long feud that ended only in 1942 when both were in exile in the United States. This same biographer quotes a letter that Goll sent to Breton on March 15, 1942, that reflects on their relative political attitudes:

> I arrived from Switzerland animated by a revolutionary spirit and tried to inflame your young hearts; at that time, motivated solely by aesthetics, you had only mistrust for "action" and for the spirit of revolt. . . . Five years later, it was you who became more revolutionary than the others, in complete contradiction to your principles formulated in *Littérature*. At that time, having already noted the bankruptcy of European regeneration, of the surrender of the German revolutions, I returned to my ivory tower.[55]

Goll makes it clear in this letter that part of the reason for their former animosity lay in their different degrees of politicization and implies that since he knows that Breton turned leftist after this incident, there was no more need to prolong the dispute.

Politics aside, one can imagine Breton's fury when Goll upstaged him by publishing a journal called *Surrealism* in October 1924, just two months before Breton's own journal was due out. Goll claimed that Breton had not invented surrealism; the true founder was Apollinaire, who used the term "surreality" during the war. While Breton did not deny that Apollinaire had coined the term, Breton claimed, along with Philippe Soupault, to have created the movement in 1918, in homage to Apollinaire. The reason for Goll's stubborn insistence on giving Apollinaire priority was that the author of *The Cubist Painters* was closely associated with the prewar cubists. If surrealism stemmed from them, it suggested modernist continuity between Max Jacob and Apollinaire on the one hand and a variety of writers such as Goll, Pierre Reverdy, Paul Dermée, and others not affiliated with dada and not taking orders from Breton. It also placed priority on literary style rather than outrageous behavior. It did not take sides politically, which is just as well since the young writers of 1924 were probably more akin politically than they realized.

Goll's version of *Surrealism* lasted only one issue and certainly failed to quell Breton's ambitions. Its main importance is as a marker of literary politics in an important period of transition. As with Fels's anarchist-modernist project, Goll's *Surrealism* connects the prewar cubist movement in literature and art with the postwar exploration of the irrational, and by so doing sidelined surrealism's connection to dada. Goll made no overtly political statements in *Surrealism*, yet one wonders what Goll made of the encomium to

Germaine Berton in that first issue of *Surrealist Revolution,* given that he too was taken with the "red young woman." What did Yvan Goll mean by "surrealism"? In the manifesto included in the sole issue of *Surréalisme,* Goll argued rather airily that transposing reality as founded in nature to a superior artistic plane constituted surrealism. He specified that the artist must connect distant elements of reality as directly as possible and that sound in the twentieth century had been surpassed by images in this century of film. Goll was influenced by the advent of silent film, though as we know surrealists such as Man Ray and dadaists such as Duchamp (Anemic Cinema) were equally enamored of the possibilities of film. Goll attacked Breton's dependence on the theories of Freud, which seemed to him to suggest a morbid preoccupation with dreams and psychiatry in preference to life and reality.[56] Goll's manifesto was much vaguer than the one Breton would soon offer, but his focus on the clear image and preference for reality over dreams suggests a connection with the doctrine of imagism propounded by the writers associated with *The Egoist,* such as Ezra Pound and, in America, William Carlos Williams. As with Fels's *Action,* Goll's version of surrealism saw poems as embodying the anarchist doctrines of direct action and experiential immediacy. Williams said it more succinctly than Goll in his famous phrase, "a poem does not mean but be." Goll viewed irrationalist surrealism as escapist and apolitical, in contrast to Apollinarian cubism that transmuted life into images.

It is significant that Florent Fels spent time in prewar England and connected his journal with *The Egoist* of Dora Marsden, while Yvan Goll, supreme internationalist, wanted to translate Joyce's *Ulysses* into German. This current of individualist anarchism was based on such nineteenth-century figures as Stirner and Nietzsche, and in the Anglo tradition was related to pragmatism. It privileged experience over theory, immediacy over planning for the future.[57] While Goll did not refer to these Anglo writers directly, he seems to have perceived them as well as the French cubists as a viable alternative to the "decadent" dada-surrealist tendency. He may have hoped that his new journal would continue the tradition of *The Egoist* and *Action;* instead Breton carried the day and Goll has been mostly forgotten.

Goll's ebbing of political fervor coincides with the decline of the revolutionary movements in Germany and with anarchism in France. Yet his book on Berton marks one last significant political intervention by the poet. *Germaine Berton, die rote Jungfrau* was part of a series of books published by Schmiede of Berlin under the rubric "Outsiders from Society." As with Berton and the anarchists, Goll remained a marginal figure who identified with the opposition, whether to Breton and his surrealist followers, or to the organized left. Breton and Aragon, on the other hand, made a conscious decision in 1925 to abandon their marginality and hoped to make surrealism the literary arm of communism. Not until 1934 when the doctrine of socialist realism made this untenable did Breton give up on this goal. By that time there were branches of surrealism in England, Czechoslovakia, Mexico, and elsewhere; the once-rebellious movement threatened to become mainstream.

In sometimes purple prose, Goll's *Germaine Berton* characterized the Action Française and Léon Daudet in particular as French proto-fascists preparing the way for a seizure of power similar to Mussolini's in Italy. Marianne, he wrote, trembled before this national danger.[58] Goll compared Berton to the nihilists of nineteenth-century Russia, who took on this mission of self-sacrifice to save France from this grave threat to its freedom. Her remarkable persona was amplified by Goll in his description of her imprisonment in St. Lazare while awaiting trial. He told in great detail the story of how she converted a young nun, Sister Claudia, to her own ideals, prompting the nun to throw off her habit; a letter from Claudia to Germaine was included in the text.[59] The young anarchist emerged in Goll's text as a fervent true believer who, because of her sex, could be assimilated to such past heroines as Vera Zasulich and Charlotte Corday.

When Goll arrived at the description of Berton's trial, it became clear that he was not only taken with her as an anarchist heroine or symbol of energy, as was the case with Breton and Aragon, but that he saw her as an apostle of peace. Goll took seriously Berton's claim that she wanted to kill Daudet and Maurras because they had incited the murder of Jean Jaurès and glorified militarism, including the invasion of the Ruhr that just preceded her *attentat*. He reported that she spoke at her trial of her terrible memories of 1914, of soldiers creeping back to Tours accompanied by well-tailored officers, and that these visions triggered her sentiment of revolt.[60]Her persona represented to Goll not a murderess or any other negative image associated with anarchy but rather the struggle for freedom and life as opposed to the will to dictatorship. The connection between Germaine and Philippe Daudet reinforced this generational as well as ideological contrast between freedom and authority. For Yvan Goll as for Maurice Wullens, the memory and prospect of war was inseparable from the anarchist vision of revolution in 1923.

Anarchists and the Avant-Garde

How did interwar anarchists react to the literary avant-garde in the early 1920s? For a relatively brief period in 1923–24, *Le Libertaire* ran series of literary articles called "Vie des lettres" written by the young poet Georges Vidal. In the aftermath of the Berton trial, Vidal was open to surrealism. He knew that the surrealists admired Berton and were sympathetic to Vidal's involvement in the Philippe Daudet affair, which Vidal was just then writing up in his book on the case. On January 2, 1924, Vidal cited an article of Breton in *Littérature;* in July he praised Benjamin Péret, who happened to be one of the most anarchistic surrealists.[61] Yet in large part because of the aftermath of the Daudet Affair, by 1925 Vidal and his mentor André Colomer were distancing themselves from *Le Libertaire,* and that journal moved away from sympathy for the avant-garde. One might think that E. Armand's individualist paper *L'En Dehors* would ally itself with radical artists, yet one would search in vain for any reference to surrealism in its pages. Armand was in his fifties in the 1920s and so perhaps not in touch with new literary currents; his own (mediocre) poems appeared frequently, and they certainly showed no hint of modernist influence. Maurice Wullens was more in touch with contemporary literature and published a great deal of radical literature in *Les Humbles.* He too was not sympathetic to dada, allied as he was with *Action* and Yvan Goll. If any movement engaged his support, it was German expressionism, in particular the work of Mühsam and Toller. The anarchists had a higher standard of engagement than could be contained in the notion of the parallel avant-gardes of literature and politics.

Further clues to the anarchists' attitude toward literature come from the remarkable set of volumes titled *L'Encyclopédie Anarchiste,* published in four volumes between about 1927 and 1934. The editor-in-chief was the venerable propagandist and militant Sébastien Faure, who commissioned his fellow anarchists to write articles on a wide variety of issues that were listed alphabetically. On subjects important to them, the articles could run for many pages, conveying an anarchist worldview on topics ranging from communism to dreams to dance to Darwinism. Under "Modernism," an article dealt with the attempt of the Catholic Church to reconcile itself with the modern world. Modernism as a generic artistic term was not commonly used in France, so this lacuna is not surprising. Yet the *Encyclopédie Anarchiste* also had no heading under surrealism, though the literary reviewer Edouard Rothen contributed a lengthy article under the rubric "Symbolisme." Rothen appreciated the fin de siècle union of literature and anarchy and praised a number of writers by name, including Alfred Jarry, a figure beloved by the surrealists. The anarchist reviewer displayed familiarity with more recent literary figures of the avant-garde, from Apollinaire to Tristan Tzara, but treated them dismissively with words like *loufoqueries,* "looniness." He called surrealism the latest installment in the lineage of futurism and dada, all "craziness become academic in the land of fascism."[62] This comment suggests suspicion of right-wing tendencies in modernism, in that futurists such as Marinetti were vocal supporters of Mussolini. Elsewhere in the encyclopedia, Rothen made clear his preference for realistic and proletarian literature. By the 1930s when these words were published, the anarchists displayed little sympathy for an avant-garde that in any case was more Marxist than anarchist. Another clue as to why the anarchists dismissed surrealism came in the article "Rêve" or Dream. The writer was familiar with Freud and admitted that the unconscious played a critical role in human life, but argued that aesthetic creation required the intervention of reason. Dreams were seen as escapist, playing a role analogous to music for American black slaves or Russian mujiks.[63] Surrealism was not mentioned in this context, but these anarchists appeared skeptical of surrealist methods employing chance, dreams, and automatism.

What then became of anarchist modernism? A professor of comparative literature has advanced the provocative proposition that anarchism did not simply disappear in the interwar era, but instead was transmuted into modernist culture. Accepting the close affiliation of anarchism and modernism before the war, David Weir argues in *Anarchy and Culture: The Aesthetic Politics of Modernism* that "the libertarian lessons of anarchism were taken to heart by artists: they were free from all external authority, including the political avant-garde. For many artists the only way to advance anarchism was through culture, not politics, and then only by means of an aesthetic individualism so radical that it could hardly be recognized as specific to anarchism. The irony is that anarchism encouraged the liberation of culture from the political avant-garde."[64]

Weir admits he cannot prove that anarchism was converted into modernism but claims that the "autonomous, heterogeneous, and fragmentary nature of modernist culture" is "structurally homologous" with anarchist ideology.[65] Just as anarchism began to recede politically, first in the face of its chief rival on the left and soon thereafter when confronted by the supernationalistic forces of fascism (both of which anarchists faced in the Spanish Civil War of the late 1930s), it triumphed aesthetically. Weir identifies anarchist characteristics in the work of James Joyce, among dadaists such as Hugo Ball, and in the films of Luis Buñuel. None of these modernist figures was French, though Buñuel worked in France and was closely allied with the surrealists, and Joyce published *Ulysses* with Sylvia Beach's French-based Shakespeare and Co., after serializing it in the individualist anarchist journal *The Egoist*.

What does it really mean to say that anarchism was transmuted into modernism? Does that imply that anarchism ceased to exist in the interwar era? The Spanish Civil War attests to the fact that anarchism had not died in 1914. In fact in two places, Ukraine in 1918–19 and Catalonia in 1936–37, anarchists actually assumed governmental power, while in the abortive revolution in Munich in 1919, anarchists such as Gustav Landauer briefly governed. The 1920s also witnessed the trial and execution of Sacco and Vanzetti, which occasioned worldwide discussion and protest between 1921 and 1927.[66] If anarchism did not disappear, it's hard to know what to make of this argument except to take it to mean that anarchism became less syndical and political than cultural and ethical during the 1920s. It would certainly have astonished the surrealists busily announcing their communist allegiance and the anarchists who were not particularly receptive to the avant-garde. Furthermore, two of Weir's examples, Ball and Joyce, are taken from the years during and immediately after World War I, at a time when anarchism was still vibrant, so it is more correct to say that their literary pursuits reflected, rather than replaced, anarchist ideals. Buñuel is the exception that proves the rule, as his work in the late twenties and thirties reflects the continuing relevance of Spanish anarchism as a serious political force.

In an important lecture that André Breton delivered in Brussels, Belgium, in 1934 called simply "What Is Surrealism?" the poet looked back over the stormy history of the movement he had founded and distinguished two discrete periods. The first, lasting from 1919 to 1924, he called the purely intuitive or heroic epoch, in which the young poets had advanced the "omnipotence of thought." This position he now called "extremely mistaken," as compared to the "reasoning epoch" that ensued in 1925 with the turn toward revolutionary politics.[67] From his 1930s vantage point, Breton was distinguishing an overly idealist and subjective early phase from a more rational or dialectical later phase and seemed to credit Marxism with turning the surrealists toward radical politics. Yet even after their avowal of Marxism, French communists suspected them of retaining their early anarchist tendencies.

After the surrealists announced their adhesion to Marxism in 1925, they sought to play an active role in the PCF, the Parti communiste français. Yet in 1926, the editor-in-chief of the communist party newspaper, *L'Humanité,* wished the editor of the procommunist paper *Clarté* luck in his attempts to "make a group of anarchistic young writers into communist revolutionaries," and soon thereafter fired the two surrealists who had been allowed to work on *L'Humanité*'s literary page. *Clarté*'s editor, Jean Bernier, had good reason to suspect the devotion of the surrealists to Marxism since, back in the autumn of 1924 during the Germaine Berton affair, Louis Aragon had written a letter to Bernier in which he called the Russian Revolution "a vague ministerial crisis" and went on sarcastically, "it is only by a real abuse of language that this . . . can be characterized as revolutionary."[68] This same Aragon broke with Breton and the surrealists in the 1930s to become the Stalinist paragon.

Nevertheless, when Breton decided to pursue the parallel avant-gardes of art and politics, he threw in his lot with the communists rather than the anarchists. His characterization of the early "heroic" period of surrealism a decade later makes it clear that he considered their anarchistic phase overly subjective, individualistic, and utopian. In the new world of ideological power politics and totalitarian states, anarchist intellectuals appeared passé. An anecdote conveys this sense of anarchist impotence. In December 1940, when Breton and his family were in Marseilles awaiting the visa approvals that would take them to exile in New York in 1941, he was brought before the Vichy authorities and questioned about his political affiliation. The head of state Marshal Pétain was visiting Marseilles the next day and potential subversives were being rounded up. Breton of course was vociferously anti-Stalinist and let them know that. When one detective inquired whether Breton was really a communist, the one examining him said, "No, a parlor anarchist."[69] He was nonetheless held with other troublemakers for a few days and then released after the marshal's visit.

Apparently Breton's subversive views did not hinder his entry into the United States either, though he had spent several months in the company of Leon Trotsky as recently as 1938. For André Breton, being considered a parlor anarchist had its advantages. Victor Serge by contrast was not so lucky. Refused entry into the United States due to his revolutionary past, he followed Leon Trotsky into exile in Mexico and would soon collaborate with Trotsky's widow on his biography. Yvan Goll preceded Breton in American exile, where they discovered they had far more in common than their old literary quarrels indicated. Both would return to France after the war, Goll to die of leukemia in 1950, Breton to return to anarchism and surrealism until his death at age seventy in 1966.

Utopian Bodies: Anarchist Sexual Politics

I think of nothing but love. . . . For me there is no idea that is not eclipsed by love. If it were up to me, everything opposed to love would be abolished. That is roughly what I mean when I claim to be an anarchist.

—LOUIS ARAGON, 1924

The noblest desire is that of combating all obstacles placed by bourgeois society in the path of the realization of the vital desires of man, as much those of his body as those of his imagination.

—PAUL ELUARD, 1932

These statements by two of the leading surrealist poets of interwar France underscore the importance of sexual desire in their project to remake the world.[1] From the beginning, sexuality was not restricted to the personal or even poetic spheres but also had political overtones. The fusion of poetry, love, and liberty that defined the surrealist project was echoed by contemporary anarchists who perceived the liberation of sexuality as a revolutionary goal. The discourse on sexuality in the interwar period was inescapably connected with the burgeoning power of the state, whether republican, communist, or fascist.

The centrality of sexuality to the interwar left, whether artistic or political, contrasts markedly with the era of "heroic anarchism" of the late 1880s and early 1890s, when symbolists and postimpressionists expressed enthusiasm for anarchist ideals of free creativity. When symbolist poets spoke of their dreams, they meant that in the pre-Freudian sense of lofty goals. Anarchism signified a perhaps unattainable social ideal. Though the term *amour libre,* free love, was widely used in the fin de siècle, its practitioners understood it as referring to monogamous unions contracted without benefit of church or state sanction rather than to the acceptance of casual sex. While proponents of free love criticized indissoluble marriage and its institutionalization in the bourgeois family, they did not usually question the heterosexual pair-bond. There was little theorizing among nineteenth-century anarchists about either sexuality or women's roles, despite the prominence of Louise Michel in the movement. Michel's famous sobriquet, "red virgin of the Commune," underscored her reputed lack of sexuality, and while she did contest the misogynist attitudes of the father of French anarchism, Pierre-Joseph Proudhon, she did not develop a coherent feminist argument. Michel called for free marriages in which wives were not subject to male authority, and in her memoirs she spoke of the prejudices against "a woman who dares to conduct her own defense, who dares to think, who rejects the Proudhonian alternative, 'housewife or courtesan.'"[2] After the turn of the century, anarchists left Proudhon behind and began to think seriously about the political implications of sexual relations. Paul Robin, Nelly Roussel, Albert Libertad, E. Armand, Madeleine Vernet, and other feminists and neo-Malthusians all envisioned sexual liberation as fundamental to human freedom and, therefore, as central to anarchist practice. Armand went the furthest in perceiving that to undermine the family structure was simultaneously to undermine the social and political structure.

The European Context

French anarchists were hardly unique in interrogating the politics of sexuality in interwar Europe. Great Britain produced two famous sexologists in Edward Carpenter and Havelock Ellis, and birth control advocates such as Stella Browne and Dr. Mary Stopes were supported by such intellectual luminaries as Bertrand Russell and George Bernard Shaw.[3] Active as the English Malthusians were in overturning Victorian attitudes, the center of the sex reform movement was clearly located in Germany, especially in the Weimar era. In Berlin, Magnus Hirschfeld's Institute for Sexual Science opened in 1919, shortly after the founding of the new Social Democratic government of Weimar Germany, and established a pioneering sex counseling clinic. Hirschfeld had long campaigned for homosexual as well as birth control and abortion rights.[4] He was instrumental in organizing the World League for Sexual Reform, which after a preliminary meeting in 1921 held international congresses from 1928 to 1932. These congresses came at the high point of the sexual reform movement and were dominated by German-speaking doctors and leftist intellectuals. German anarchists and socialists established Associations for Sexual Hygiene and Life-Style Reform in the mid-1920s. The Nazis decisively ended all campaigns for toleration and made the earlier movement for *lebensreform* (life reform), which included nudism, vegetarianism, and clothing reform, conform to their own völkisch ideals.[5] Since many of the supporters of sexual reform in Germany were Jews as well as leftists, the movement was doomed. Hirschfeld, for one, fled to France and died in Nice in 1935.[6]

During the brief tenure of the Weimar Republic, the sexual reform movement was not merely tolerated but even supported by the government and by numerous lay organizations. This was markedly different from the situation in France, where government repression led the anarchists to play a more major role than elsewhere. The other major difference between German (including Austrian) and French sex reformers was the influence of psychoanalysts from Sigmund Freud to Otto Gross and Wilhelm Reich on the movement for toleration of deviant sexualities and for an end to sexual repression. Freud was no leftist, but other early German-speaking founders of psychoanalysis did not hesitate to connect ideals of sexual liberation with radical politics.

The example of Otto Gross in particular demonstrates the close connection among psychology, bohemian behavior, and anarchist politics. Gross belonged to the same generation as Armand (Armand was born in 1872, Gross in 1878) and became involved in sexual politics in Munich around 1907, just as Armand did in France. Armand lacked the charisma of a figure such as Gross, who mingled in bohemian Munich's Schwabing district with numerous artists and writers and ultimately influenced the direction of the German dadaists. Gross was linked to the anarchist Tat Gruppe, founded in 1909 by the poet Erich Mühsam, and as Gross became increasingly revolutionary, his artistic followers committed themselves to his attacks on monogamous marriage and the authoritarian family.

Receptive as many of the bohemian artists and writers were to Gross's belief in unrepressed sexual expression, other anarchists attacked this new influence, much as Armand was attacked in France. Gustav Landauer, the most important German anarchist thinker of his era, attacked Gross personally as being a crazy drug addict (he was in fact addicted to several drugs, which would contribute to his premature death in 1920 at age forty-two) who promoted dissolute theories.[7] Landauer conceived personal relationships as being based on mutual free will, much like French proponents of *amour libre*, but stopped short of dwelling on sexual jealousy as a fundamental flaw in monogamy to the extent that Armand and the Tat Gruppe did.[8] Gross and Mühsam were most influenced, among earlier anarchist thinkers, by the arch-individualist Young Hegelian Max Stirner, author of *The Ego and Its Own*, who promoted a highly subjectivist sense of the self unconstrained by norms or laws. Though Armand's Fourier-influenced communalist tendencies contrasted greatly with the inner-directed ruminations of Otto Gross and his disciples in Schwabing, both Armand and Gross decried the baneful influence of the patriarchal family, fount of repression and conditioner of authoritarian personalities

Though it is unlikely that Armand was aware of Freud at that early date, he would later review translations of Freud's works in his interwar newspaper. Yet Freudian psychological categories never played the role in Armand's thinking or that of other anarchists that they did in Germany. Armand was always more sociologically than psychologically oriented, which distinguished him not only from Gross and Reich but from the French surrealists. Shortly after the war, André Breton made a pilgrimage to Vienna to meet Freud and placed Freud's picture among those of the young artists in the first issue of *La Révolution Surréaliste*. Anarchists by contrast distrusted appeals to irrationalism and the unconscious. Anarchist rationalism would make all rapprochement with the surrealists difficult (the communists were no more hospitable to subjectivist dreamscapes), so that no figure in French anarchism influenced artists as directly as Otto Gross did among German expressionists.[9]

From the fin de siècle to World War II, anarchists played a prominent role in French discourse about sexuality. I will discuss their role in the birth control and abortion movement in a separate chapter and emphasize how they opposed the widely held demographic obsession that gripped almost all political sectors after World War I. Even before the Great War, French republicanism was predicated on profamily policy; it has been argued that the denial of women's suffrage was not accidental but rather an inherent part of the fraternal bonds of republican ideology.[10] The other parties on the left were generally reluctant to criticize the patriarchal family. Though Léon Blum had written a rather libertarian critique of the family in his 1907 book *Du mariage*, he had retreated to a more conventional approach to sexuality and women's roles by the time he took charge of the interwar socialist party.[11] The French Communist Party did support women's equality and contraception rights in the 1920s, but during the Popular Front era it too retreated to a strong profamily position and dropped demands for abortion rights.[12] This family-centered consensus left it to the anarchists and the surrealists to draw out the political implications of monogamous marriage and the patriarchal family.

E. Armand, Fourier, and *Camaraderie amoureuse*

No issues were more contentious in the aftermath of the great bloodletting of World War I than those relating to reproduction and sexuality. The joy in victory over the Germans felt by most French after World War I was tempered by the terrible losses sustained by so many French families. One who felt little joy in the immediate aftermath of the war was Ernest-Lucien Juin, incarcerated during the war and for some years thereafter for supposedly aiding a deserter. As a fervent antimilitarist, his name was inscribed on the Carnet B list of people who could endanger the war effort.[13] Juin emerged from prison in 1922 and immediately took up his anarchist identity as E. Armand and his activities as the most prolific of individualist anarchist publicists. A lengthy book appeared the year following his release, apparently written while in prison, followed by many more books, articles, pamphlets, and a journal, *L'En Dehors*, which spanned the 1920s and 1930s. When the next war broke out, Armand was again imprisoned for spreading antimilitarist propaganda. He was released in 1941, possibly because at age sixty-nine (he was born to a communard only a year after the Paris Commune of 1871) the old anarchist did not appear to threaten national security. He lived on for twenty more years and died in 1962 at the age of ninety. A commemorative volume by his friends that appeared two years later mentioned that he was survived by his widow, Denise Rougeault, to whom he had been married for more than fifty years. Reading the interwar writings of Armand, one is struck by remarkable similarities to the ideas of his predecessor by exactly a century, Charles Fourier (1772–1837). The similarity of ideas is striking enough to suggest an unmistakable influence by the utopian socialist prophet of a nonrepressive society.[14] Further, this Fourierist influence connects Armand with the contemporaneous surrealists, also great proponents of the liberation of desire. André Breton wrote a lengthy *Ode à Fourier* in 1945 and considered him along with Sade as one of the surrealists' forebears. Fourierist influence provides some clues, I believe, about why Armand considered notions of the body, family, and sexuality to be central to his conception of personal freedom. Further, Armand was able to use Fourier as a counter to the misogynist and familist ideas of Proudhon.

Sexuality was not a new issue for Armand as he emerged from prison in 1922. His first pamphlet on the topic, "De la liberté sexuelle," dates from 1907, but in the 1920s the issue became obsessive with him and resulted in a deluge of writings, including a lengthy book titled *La Révolution sexuelle et la camaraderie amoureuse* that appeared in 1934. Armand can be understood as a left-wing opponent of the pronatalist policies of the Third Republic and also as an advocate of sexual freedom in the era of Freud, Reich, Hirsch-feld, and André Gide. While he advocated absolute sexual equality between men and women, he appeared to be less concerned about female subjection than sexual repression. Scrutinizing Armand's conception of sexual libera-tion between the wars reveals a significant change in emphasis from the idealization of *amour libre* that many anarchists shared during the Belle Epoque. As the French state promoted fecund, procreative sexuality, Armand advocated a form of sexuality that transgressed marital relations and sepa-rated procreation from the pursuit of sexual fulfillment.

The shift in emphasis in Armand's writings after the war may have been influenced by the laws passed in the immediate postwar period banning all information regarding birth control and abortion[15]. Since one could not overtly advocate family planning, perhaps Armand found it expedient to em-phasize free, nonprocreative sexuality and let the readers come to their own conclusions. In this sense, Armand's sexual campaign of the 1920s and 1930s may be seen as an extension of prewar anarchist advocacy of neo-Malthusianism. Following the long campaign by the freethinker Paul Robin to provide means for family limitation in the early years of the Third Repub-lic, a host of anarchists joined the fight in the years before the war to resist the imprecations of the Alliance Nationale pour l'Accroissement de la Pop-ulation Française (National Alliance for the Increase of the French Popula-tion) to produce more French citizens for the good of the state. In 1911 Armand joined such figures as Eugène Humbert and Nelly Roussel in the pages of *Le Malthusien* in arguing that sexual needs were not synonymous with reproduction and that women who could not control maternity were enslaved to biology. While some of the principal anarchists of the prewar era, such as Kropotkin, Reclus, and Jean Grave, dismissed Robin and the neo-Malthusians as a distraction (Grave called it "the most reactionary doctrine I know"), some syndicalists joined the individualists in viewing reproduc-tive control as vital for working-class welfare.[16] Armand may have shifted emphases on his release from prison in 1922, but he continued a major anarchist assault on state-sponsored sexual ignorance and repression.

It is possible that Ernest Juin chose his pen name in homage to Fourier. His bibliographers sometimes assume that the first initial of his pen name stands for "Emile," and the principal historian of anarchism in the interwar era calls him "Eugène."[17] Yet to my knowledge he never used any first name at all on his many publications, and his anarchist friends never refer to a first name in their tribute to Armand. Since his actual name was Ernest, that would be a likelier possibility, but there is another. If placed last name first, "Armand, E." sounds suggestively like *"Harmonie,"* Fourier's utopian ideal.[18] In any case, the two utopian thinkers shared a monomaniacal devotion to their own ideas that alternately bemused and exasperated their contemporaries.

Charles Fourier is not usually included in the pantheon of anarchist saints along with his rough contemporaries William Godwin and Pierre Joseph Proudhon. He is typically thought of as the most eccentric among those thinkers Marx and Engels called "utopian socialists." Godwin and Proudhon would have found Fourier's communal phalanstery far too regimented and constraining, and one might expect that the staunchly individualistic Armand would have also. Yet the social implications of Fourier's ideas are both more radical than those of Proudhon, and more congruent with Armand's central ideas. Proudhon deserved Marx's epithet of "petit bourgeois" for his staunch defense of the delights of home and family and of the father's dominant place in it. Proudhon the family man was nostalgic for a pre-industrial way of life. While Fourier set his utopian community in the countryside as well, the lifelong bachelor had no use for the family or marriage since an exclusive couple would disrupt communal relations, inhibiting "the noble expression of free love."[19] Fourier intended to replace married by communal love. He maintained that the Jacobins had not gone nearly far enough in merely legalizing divorce; he would abolish marriage entirely in order to achieve the complete emancipation of women and the maximum in sexual freedom and diversity.

Fourier is often seen as proto-Freudian in seeing modern civilization as fundamentally based on instinctual repression, but unlike Freud he intended to remedy the situation. Viewing love as a powerful force for social solidarity, he proposed to institutionalize free love and group sex in Harmony. He was remarkably tolerant in allowing the maximum of sexual variety, including homosexual liaisons for both sexes, and thought that even fetishists and flagellants should be able to express their sexual needs. In fact he banned monogamy in his polygamous world as the most corrupting influence after capitalism. Given his hatred of politics, Fourier would seem to be a likely anarchist saint, but he also rejected revolution as a solution to social problems, preferring instead environmental and architectural modifications of human behavior.[20]

One problem with connecting the sexual ideals of Fourier and Armand is that Fourier's main writings on sexuality, written in 1818, were not published until after Armand's death in 1962.[21] Yet if Armand could not have read *Le Nouveau monde amoureux* (The new amorous world), the essential outlines of Fourier's dream of instinctual liberation were well known (as his popularity among the surrealists attests), if embarrassing to some of his scandalized disciples. It is striking that Fourier composed his magnum opus on sexual freedom shortly after the end of the Napoleonic Wars, during the early years of the Bourbon Restoration. He was seeking new principles of human solidarity after the decades of turmoil, and perhaps new principles of life and love after the epoch of terror, war, and death. Fourier was entering middle age at this time; he was forty-six in 1818. Armand was fifty when he emerged from prison in 1922, exactly the same age as Fourier when he moved from Besançon to Paris in 1822. Though he, like Fourier, had written about free love before, it was especially after the war that he became obsessed by the theme and made it central to his thought, during the "restoration" of the Third Republic. Freedom of sexual choice was fundamental to Fourier and Armand as the key both to individual happiness and group sociability. By contrast, Armand considered modern marriage to be as mercenary as prostitution (an attitude that seems to have had little impact on his domestic life since he was supported by his schoolteacher wife from the time of their marriage in 1911, allowing him to concentrate on anarchist propaganda).[22]

Armand's friends who compiled the memorial volume to him after his death remembered an erudite man fluent in many languages, more cerebral than libidinal. He went through a religious phase in the 1890s and made the transition to anarchism by way of Tolstoy, hence the fervent pacifism that got him into trouble during both world wars. After his metamorphosis into an anarchist after the turn of the century he entirely discarded his religious faith and vehemently condemned Christian morality. His friend Robert Collino, whose pen name was "Ixigrec," called Armand's wife a saint (possibly for tolerating his unconventional ideas about sex and disdain for marriage) and Armand himself a "lay benedictine," sincere, principled, conscientious.[23] His fellow anarchist "Mauricius" (Maurice Vandamme) was more critical, characterizing Armand as an intellectual who had little taste for crowds, heroic action, or even emotion, and who lacked the intense sensuality of a Rodin or a Hugo. "His eroticism is similar to his work, purely cerebral."[24] Aside from his wife's income, he may have earned some money from his writings. His journal L'En Dehors, which he published from 1922 to 1939, reportedly had a circulation of six thousand in 1933.[25]

The police also tracked Armand's long anarchist career and his frequent and serious confrontations with the law. In 1908, when individualist anarchists were experimenting with various forms of illegality, he had been involved in counterfeiting and was condemned to a five-year sentence. Yet he was active in the movement again by 1911, briefly taking over the direction of the journal L'Anarchie after the arrests of Victor Kibalchich (Serge) and

Rirette Maîtrejean. He also aided his friend Georges Butaud in creating the journal *La Vie Anarchiste* to encourage back-to-nature communal ventures.[26] In 1915, a detailed report for the Minister of the Interior recorded his marriage and said he had fathered three children, whom he had abandoned. The police reported that Armand also published a journal printed in Orléans called *Pendant la Mêlée* (During the struggle), which by mid-1916 was called *Par-delà la Mêlée* (Beyond the struggle). The change in title reflected well Armand's attitude toward the cataclysmic events going on around him, and the police reported that comrades were frustrated by Armand's resolute individualism and refusal to discuss the war.[27] Despite his wish to be above the struggle, he was found guilty in 1917 of aiding a military deserter and given a very stiff five-year sentence, which he served out despite a campaign carried out by his comrades on his behalf.

Armand's central idea, "amorous friendship" (*la camaraderie amoureuse*), was intended to supplant the conjugal unit of the couple, transferring the emotional and sexual bonds uniting a man and a woman to a larger group of like-minded people. Armand's insistence on calling this group "a cooperative of loving production and consumption" parallel to any other cooperative enterprise that might produce or consume food or shoes is highly reminiscent of Fourier. He did not insist that all members of cooperatives should engage in sexual activities, but rather that people should group themselves together for the express purpose of sharing, as he put it, "*sentimentalo-sexuelle*" activities. He also insisted that just as age or the length of one's nose would not be cause for discrimination in a food coop, so it should play no role in his love coop. One qualified for inclusion not because of one's sexual attractiveness but by virtue of one's political ideals. Any anarchist who joined the group deserved sexual satisfaction. He hastened to add that since the cooperative was freely entered, it in no way compromised the anarchist's individual freedom, though one might protest that more or less requiring one to have sex with every other member of the group was a form of constraint. Armand did not go so far as Fourier, who imagined "courts of love" in which a young person could be sentenced to sleep with an older one, but the middle-aged anarchist clearly was worried about his relative sexual appeal.[28]

The collective was meant to provide greater sexual satisfaction and variety but was also idealized as an alternative to the conjugal unit. Armand attacked the bourgeois family for reproducing the forms of domination and control represented by the state. Not only did men lord it over women, but parents assumed it was their natural right to dominate their children. As he wrote in *Subversisme sexuel*, "the family is a state in miniature even when the parents are anarchists."[29] This issue of childhood subordination was more urgent to Armand than female subjection since nearly all people emerged from childhood imbued with attitudes of respect for authority. Anarchists were major proponents of free schools that would encourage independent thinking rather than indoctrinating children with habits of obedience. Armand did not develop this line of thought, and in fact did not discuss children much at all. He simply consigned them to group care or, as he wrote at one point, the problem of children could "be resolved by a simple insurance system."[30] In envisioning new, affective structures to replace the pair-bond, he hoped simultaneously to create a more egalitarian and sexually liberated environment. He echoed Fourier in arguing that the family suppressed not just rebelliousness but sociability, isolating the couple from their *compagnes* and *compagnons*. Armand appeared relatively indifferent to questions of reproduction. Sexuality existed as an end in itself and as a means of extending social relations with like-minded comrades. In his journal *L'En Dehors*, he wrote that without control over maternity, women remained enslaved to both men and nature. Birth control made possible the desirable separation of sex from procreation.[31]

Anarchist women were necessarily far more attuned to the problem of children and questioned Armand's blithe assertions that if men could not tell which of them was the biological parent, they would take a collective interest in child raising. Armand frequently wrote on sexuality in other anarchist publications beside *L'En Dehors,* and these papers occasioned a much livelier response to his ideas. In the summer of 1925, for example, Armand wrote a series of articles titled "Sexualisme révolutionnaire" in André Colomer's new anarchist newspaper *L'Insurgé.* Under the rubric "L'Ephémère Féminin," a woman who called herself "l'Eve future" wanted to know what would become of children if love were free and suggested that if they were raised in common without knowing their biological parents society would resemble a "kid factory" (*l'atelier à gosse*). She concluded rather negatively, "Nothing there of the individualist, nothing which permits, which protects the blossoming of individualities which is the basis of our anarchist principles. And then? Very little for us, women."[32] Armand responded that in the history of societies in which sexual promiscuity was practiced, children were more cherished than in family or patriarchal regimes.[33]

Armand's Fourierist theme of "amorous friendship" differed markedly from the prewar anarchist ideal of free love; in fact, the prewar Armand condemned sex without love, distinguishing free love from promiscuity.[34] As sexuality became increasingly central to his conception of anarchist sociability, Armand disparaged monogamous relationships and favored a greater plurality and variety of sexual relationships. This included deviant forms of sexuality.

In his 1930 text *La camaraderie amoureuse,* Armand showed himself to be familiar with the latest currents in sexology, citing Hirschfeld and Freud; he credited the latter with overturning the widely assumed connection between sexual abstinence and worldly achievements. Armand's most in-depth discussion was reserved for André Gide's *Corydon,* in which the French writer openly affirmed his homosexuality. Armand was quite willing to acknowledge homosexuality as a legitimate form of sexual expression, but protested against Gide's distinction between congenital "inverts" and those who made "Greek love" a matter of choice. In Armand's opinion, the ancient Greeks who practiced homosexual love left their wives in an unfairly inferior position, which he doubted modern women would tolerate. Modern homosexuals should not distinguish, as Gide seemed to be doing, between pure, artistic types and effeminate sodomites.[35] Armand found all forms of sexuality, even sado-masochism, acceptable as long as there was no constraint involved.

Armand was a polymath who exposed the readers of his journal to the whole range of writings on sexuality available in the interwar period. Twice in 1935 he published reviews of the latest works of Wilhelm Reich, and the next year he reviewed a French translation of Freud's *New Lectures on Psychoanalysis.* Armand reported that Freud even mentioned anarchism, calling it sublime as abstract speculation but failing as far as practical life is concerned. At the same time Armand commented on the antihomosexuality campaign in the Third Reich and debated Jean Marestan about sexual liberation in the Soviet Union. Not only was Stalin cracking down on free access to abortions, but homosexuals were also being persecuted in Russia as well as Germany.[36] If dictatorship meant suppression of sexual freedom, then only anarchism could truly stand for free sexual expression.

A more revealing debate in the 1930s took place with Armand's fellow French anarchist Han Ryner. Ryner was a decade older than Armand, having been born back in 1861; he would die in 1938. His real name was Henri Ner; probably inspired by Ibsen's characters, he changed the spelling if not the pronunciation in the 1890s for his pen name. Ryner was a well-educated lycée professor of classics who had written a score of novels and philosophical tracts by the interwar era. Bearer of a huge white beard and usually clad in a beret and clogs, he embodied the bohemian philosopher and was highly thought of in the individualist milieu.[37] Ryner first affirmed his anarchism in a 1900 novel titled *Le crime d'obéir* (The crime of obeying); more recently he had explored the same territory that obsessed Armand in two books,

L'Amour plural (Plural love, 1927) and *Prenez-moi tous!* (Take me, everyone, 1931).[38] Ryner too offered a "fraternity of love" in which procreation would not detract from free sexuality, but he aroused Armand's ire in suggesting that couples should apply to participate in love groupings. Armand argued that experience had shown that all anarchist colonies composed of couples had failed. Ryner also recommended free associations but distinguished these from organizations that implied some sort of centralized direction. His novels seemed to be satirizing the ideas of Fourier and possibly also those of Armand.

The conclusion of *L'Amour plural,* for example, takes place at a meeting of the Club des Insurgés devoted to the issue of plural love. Some anarchists defended *amour unique,* while Armand and Han Ryner were there to argue for differing conceptions of free love. One of the characters in the novel, Marie-Louise, who believed in sexual freedom and had been involved in an affair with the main male figure in the novel, Orpheus, declared that she favored the position of Han Ryner over that of Armand. She argued that anarchists believed above all in freedom, which is why they condemned the constrictions of marriage, yet according to Armand's scheme, once you joined the "compagnons de L'En Dehors" you were required to have sexual relations with all members of the group. When Armand objected that joining the group was an act of free will, Marie-Louise replied that the same was true of marriage or entering a convent.[39] She then reproached Han Ryner for not practicing what he preached. In his speech Ryner condemned both debauchery and egoistic exclusivity. He defended instead his conception of *Eros polyphallique,* which thrived in the open air of the Pantheon as opposed to "single love, poor closed church" (*l'amour unique, pauvre église fermée*).[40] Both Armand and Han Ryner condemned the prevalence of jealousy in contemporary culture, but Ryner found Armand's solutions to be mechanistic and devoid of emotional appeal. Despite these differences, the fact that Han Ryner used the setting of the anarchist discussion club for the conclusion of his 1927 novel suggests how ubiquitous such discussions were at the time. The rest of the novel simply recounted the variety of Orpheus's affairs, often with women of a decidedly mystical bent (as if this was a common problem for male rationalists). The novel ends as Marie-Louise leaves Orpheus and Paris behind to join a colony of Swedenborgians in Costa Rica (where there were in fact anarchist colonies).

The response to this all-too-common criticism of Armand's idea appeared in a review of Ryner penned by Armand's collaborator Ixigrec, who said that lacking organization any social group was doomed to chaos. Armand himself averred that he too favored temporary, voluntary associations of individuals and not some collective mechanism. Still, he argued that conventional notions of romantic love were mostly based on social prejudice and could be changed by communal living arrangements.[41] Ryner was a laughing philosopher whose mocking tone deeply offended the humorless Armand, who was vulnerable precisely on the issue of whether he was trying to politicize that which was most deeply personal and resistant to organization. In the April 1931 issue of *L'En Dehors* Armand announced a public debate between himself and Han Ryner titled "Is it necessary to take seriously *Prenez-moi tous?*"

Armand also advocated nudity as a means of diminishing social and moral distinctions. Modesty he viewed as stemming from shame in the human body, a result of a Christian mentality that must be superseded by joy and pride in the body. Like the Jacobins before them, anarchists tended to value transparency and to disparage dissimulation. Clothing encouraged coquetry and hypocrisy; nudism would forthrightly proclaim the disregard of conventional morality. Yet Armand disparaged advocates of "naturism" who claimed that nudism did not provoke sexual desire but merely allowed a more natural relationship with nature. Since some of the German founders of *Nachtkultur* (nudism) were on the extreme right, Armand was probably wise to distance himself from their conception of the pure body.[42] In any case, Armand saw nothing wrong with stimulating desire. His most interesting rationale for nudism was that it undermined the inequitable hierarchy of different parts of the body. Why should the face or arms be acceptable but not the breasts or buttocks, he asked; why is "the nose . . . considered noble and the virile member ignoble, for example?"[43] Clothes, by exposing some parts of the body and concealing others, encoded social hierarchies written on the body. By transgressing these hierarchies and proclaiming all parts of the body beautiful and noble, anarchists could assail social propriety. The lower would displace the higher; the genitals would become as noble as the face; distinctions would cease; and, as bodily hierarchies collapsed, so analogically would other politically sanctioned hierarchies be revealed as naked as in the tale of "The Emperor's New Clothes."[44]

Armand's unique ideas on sexuality evolved in the 1920s partly through discussions and correspondence with readers of his newspaper *L'En Dehors*. Beginning in 1925, he began to organize various associations to further his ideas of *camaraderie amoureuse*, and for an annual fee announced he would issue membership passports so that "companions" traveling in France or abroad could visit one another. By 1927 he announced he had fifty-three members in France, Germany, the United States, Brazil, Switzerland, Argentina, and Morocco. The following year he announced that the disproportion between male and female membership required that all new male applicants must be accompanied by a female counterpart (seemingly conceding Ryner's point, though Armand was not recruiting couples). In 1926 he founded the International Association of Combat Against Sexual Jealousy and Exclusivity in Love, which had a couple of hundred members by the eve of World War II.[45] While these attempts to realize his ideas were not as elaborately conceived as those of Fourier, with his phalansteries and courts of love, they do indicate that Armand took his ideas as serious means of reforming social practice through new forms of sexual behavior.

Also reminiscent of Fourier, Armand was no less derided by other anarchists for focusing on the body and social relations rather than on labor organizing or fomenting revolution against the state.[46] As we have seen, anarchists in the interwar period were divided among syndicalist proponents of anarchist-led unions, communist-anarchists who favored revolutionary direct action, and individualists such as Armand and Han Ryner who were more likely to favor personal transformation that would embody revolutionary change in their daily lives. In the aftermath of the Russian Revolution, many anarchists were compelled to question the tendency to ignore the seizure of state power, and for several years following 1917 many perceived in the soviets a Russian version of their ideal of worker self-determination. Though their enthusiasm for the Russian Revolution waned after 1921, anarchist participation in the Spanish Popular Front government in 1936–37 led hundreds of French anarchists to volunteer in the struggle against Franco in Spain. The renewed focus on revolutionary armed conflict made changes in lifestyle seem dilettantish in comparison.[47]

In retrospect, and especially in the aftermath of the cultural revolution of the 1960s, it is apparent that Armand's notions of "personal politics" deserve their place alongside more militant forms of politicization that marked these turbulent decades. Just as Fourier doubtless struck many of his contemporaries as comical in his utopian fervor for a nonrepressive society but is now seen as a forerunner of the ideas of Freud and the surrealists, so Armand was derided for replacing politics and economics with sexual panaceas promising personal liberation and the abolition of the nuclear family. Anarchists remained distinct from other leftists in refusing to separate means and ends, the ideals of a future society from the way one lived one's daily life. Armand's determination to connect sexual and political hierarchies was echoed in the late 1960s by the anarchist and gay rights activist Daniel Guérin, who brought out a selection of Fourier's writings on sexuality for a generation that assumed that "free love" was a catchphrase they had invented.[48]

The Surrealist Politics of Desire

André Breton, leader of the surrealists, was also enticed by the eccentric philosopher of passionate attraction, and the circumstances of his own attraction to Fourier may indirectly shed light on both anarchy and utopia. Armand's intellectual involvement with Fourier peaked after World War I and a lengthy prison sentence, when it appeared self-evident that radical new principles of social relations were needed. For Breton, the revelation of Fourier's renewed relevance came at the end of the Second World War, which the poet spent in exile in the United States. In the long *Ode à Charles Fourier* that he composed in the summer of 1945, the poet remembered that he had lived a few yards from the statue of Fourier on the boulevard Clichy yet had not thought seriously about the utopian socialist's system of thought. He did not explain that in the years from 1925 until the outbreak of the war he had been a Marxist and Trotskyist and so immunized to the blandishments of utopian socialism. Now disillusioned with the socialist left he was free to dream again of more libertarian alternatives, and after his return to postwar France Breton would establish political connections with the anarchists he had largely disdained for the previous two decades.

The precise context in which he composed the ode further clarifies the place Fourier's ideas occupied in Breton's, and by extension Armand's, thought. Breton wrote his long poem while on a trip to the American West, to which he refers repeatedly. He even provides one date, August 22, 1945, where he salutes Fourier from the bottom of a Hopi kiva in the desert southwest.[49] Breton was thus sightseeing and imagining Fourier a month after the first atomic bomb was tested in nearby Alamagordo, New Mexico, and within weeks of the dropping of the bomb on Hiroshima and Nagasaki. For both Armand and Breton, Fourier's system of passionate attraction was proffered as an antidote to death and destruction, whether of the mud and trenches of World War I or the death camps and atomic bombs of World War II. The same was true of Fourier himself in the aftermath of a generation of warfare.

That Armand and Breton each found in Fourier an important antecedent suggests how interwar anarchists and surrealists shared a discourse of sexual liberation. Armand emerged from prison in the aftermath of World War I more convinced than ever of the need for utopian, sexualized bodies to overcome both the coquette and the bourgeois. The surrealists, a generation younger than Armand (and Han Ryner), were equally determined to substitute an erotic for a thanatopic ethos. Breton's meditation on Fourier may have been imagined as an antidote to war. Another surrealist, acclaimed at one time by Breton as the greatest of them all, succumbed personally to war in 1945. Robert Desnos died of typhus in a Nazi concentration camp at age forty-five. Back in the 1920s, Desnos too saw eros not only as a way of triumphing over death but as a revolutionary act.

At the founding of surrealism as a movement in 1924, Breton wrote that "there are to my knowledge three fanatics of the first magnitude: Picasso, Freud and Desnos. . . . Symbolism, cubism and dada have long since run their course. Surrealism is the order of the day and Desnos is its prophet."[50] Desnos was acclaimed as the master of the trance who could seemingly fall asleep at will and enter a dream state. His novel *La Liberté ou l'amour!* (Liberty or love!) did not appear until 1927, but in the beginning of the novel Desnos offers a date of composition of December 13, 1924. The dedication reads, "To the Revolution. To Love. To she who is their incarnation."[51] The unnamed woman is said to have been a popular singer for whom Desnos had a crush, but given the timing of *Liberty or Love!* it seems equally likely that Desnos was inspired by the example of Germaine Berton, whose picture appeared in the first issue of *La Révolution Surréaliste,* which appeared that same month. The Parisian chanteuse Yvonne George, who did not return Desnos's love, does not seem like a good candidate to incarnate Revolution.[52] Desnos's title implies, and at the same time renounces, the revolutionary slogan "Liberty or Death" (*La liberté ou la mort*), here transformed into the homophonic but very differently signifying *la liberté ou l'amour.* Desnos was fond of such plays on words; here he went beyond wordplay to equate freedom and erotic love.

Most of *La liberté ou l'amour* is not explicitly political, as it follows the violent and obscene exploits of Corsaire Sanglot (the sobbing pirate ship) and Louise Lame (Louise the Blade, a true femme fatale) across dizzying passages through space and time. Yet in one section toward the end of the "novel," Desnos evokes the memory of the execution of Louis XVI, as Corsaire Sanglot watches the guillotine and sees the executioner hold up the severed heads with the same repeated gesture: "Ridiculous heads of aristocrats, heads of lovers full of their love, heads of women heroically sentenced to death. But, love and hate, can they inspire other acts?"[53] Desnos even mentions the date of Louis's execution, January 21. Germaine Berton commenced her *attentat* by attending a mass meeting of the Action Française on that date in 1923, for the 130th anniversary of the king's execution, reinforcing the possibility that Desnos had her in mind as he imagined the Place de la Révolution. Then he shifts abruptly to an encomium to the Marquis de Sade, who was active in the revolution and "suffered much on behalf of liberty!"[54] Sade was one of the surrealists' heroes for pushing Enlightenment assumptions to such extreme conclusions that the progressive ideals of the philosophes were subverted, and who therefore had to be interned in an insane asylum. For Desnos as for Sade, revolution culminates in the explosion of the repressed. For Fourier, who rejected revolution entirely as a pointless power struggle, the utopian body was substituted for revolutionary violence. For Desnos, the "Marquis de Sade places his face next to that of Robespierre" so that violence and the "labyrinth of desire" are mutually implicated.[55] Robespierre joins de Sade on a medallion imagined by Sanglot or "sobs"; love replaces death in the book's title as a solution to the quandary of revolution. Alongside Robespierre the incorruptible moralist appeared de Sade, willing the anarchy of sexual desire. The Janus face of Robespierre and de Sade is the face of true revolution.

Just as André Breton linked Freud's name with those of Picasso and Desnos, he also connected Freud with two other foundational surrealist figures: the Marquis de Sade and Charles Fourier, calling them "the three great emancipators of desire."[56] Sade was the key figure in the history of atheist libertinage, a revolutionary dissatisfied with politics, or at least not satiated by them, who demanded that men must be free to satisfy their desires. Rather than abstract or metaphysical freedom, he demanded bodily freedom, and ironically was incarcerated for so insisting. Desnos had written as early as 1923 that "all our current aspirations were formulated by Sade. He was the first to posit the integrity of one's sexual being as indispensable to the life both of the senses and of the intellect."[57] Sade the revolutionary, Fourier the utopian, and Freud the modern liberator of the self together made possible the surrealist conjunction of poetry, love, and liberty. All preached the liberation of desire (if Freud didn't preach it, his radical disciples on both sides of the Rhine did). True to their Sadean sensibilities, the surrealists were powerfully attracted throughout the 1920s and 1930s to femmes fatales who violated social norms through love and violence. From Germaine Berton's entwining of love, murder, and suicide to Violette Nozières, who accused her father of incest and killed him, to the Papin sisters, who murdered their employers and carried on as incestuous lesbian lovers, the surrealists were fascinated by women who rebelled against the hypocritical social order.[58]

The surrealists not only idealized libidinal freedom abstractly; the way in which they practiced it brings them closer to Armand's ideals of collective love. While most of the surrealists were married at one time or another (as was Armand), they had numerous and multiple sexual liaisons.[59] They were even more unusual in experimenting with group creativity, as in the famous exquisite corpse sessions of the early 1920s, meant to subvert the controlling rational ego. One is tempted to think, "If only Armand had known," yet Armand was a generation older and no artist (he did contribute poems to his newspaper, but they don't bear reprinting, being ideology dressed in poetic form). Han Ryner was more of an artist, though a novelist more than a poet, but stylistically he was more conventional than the surrealists and explicitly renounced de Sade (as well as Sacher-Masoch—masochism as well as sadism) in *L'Amour plural*.

The French surrealists and anarchists pursued parallel goals in liberating sexuality, but their respective politics of desire never quite met. The surrealists wished to subvert the state through their libidos, via the inherent lawlessness of the unrestrained psyche. This position mirrored that taken by German expressionists before the war; yet anarchists from Landauer to Armand resisted such recourse to irrational subjectivity. Particularly in France, where the irrational was associated with the Catholic faith and emotional women, anarchists proved unwilling to accept the new psychological currents, whether they hailed from Germany and Austria or from the Parisian avant-garde.[60]

"Your Body Is Yours": Anarchism, Birth Control, and Eugenics

Eugenics in the interwar period is generally associated with fascist Italy and Nazi Germany, though interest in preventing the "unfit" from breeding also reached a peak in the United States.[1] Most French leaders, by contrast, evinced much less interest in controlling or limiting births than in increasing the quantity of French people.[2] The Third Republic supported pronatalist policies and a host of organizations rallied to the cause of the large family. While many of these profamily organizations were Catholic, members of the Radical Party and even socialists as well as politicians on the right were generally united in encouraging population growth.[3] There remained the secular extreme left to battle for birth control and to advocate quality over quantity, especially a higher quality of life for the working classes. At the forefront of that struggle were the anarchists, who had been identified with neo-Malthusianism, or birth control, since the 1890s.[4] As a logical extension of this demand for control over reproduction and for quality of life over quantity of children, some anarchists began to advocate negative eugenics in the interwar era, arguing that alcoholics, diseased, and other "unfit" people should refrain from having children (in contrast to positive eugenics, which encouraged allegedly superior people to bear more children). This was to be done not for the good of the state as in fascist regimes but for a healthier and self-regulating working class.

The interwar era has been relatively neglected by historians of the French birth control movement, in part because of the wave of repression visited on the movement in the 1920s, after the Chamber of Deputies overwhelmingly passed the law of July 31, 1920, outlawing all information pertaining to birth control and abortion. In 1923, anti-abortion laws were further strengthened, with four-year sentences for abortionists and six months for women undergoing an abortion. Numerous condemnations followed both laws, with the 1920 law resulting in fifty-nine prison terms already by May 1923. The Cartel des Gauches, voted into power in 1924, did nothing to abrogate these laws, which had passed in 1920 by the commanding margin of 521 to 55.[5] The "politics of motherhood" that identified family and maternity with the good of the nation dominated nearly all political factions.[6] Despite the assumption that the cause of birth control had been defeated or at least put on hold, anarchists remained committed to the ideal and even extended it to improving the fitness of the population through the positive effects of sunshine and outdoor activities as well as the negative ones of family limitation.

All birth control advocates were not anarchists and, as we shall see, not all anarchists were enthusiastic about biological and demographic issues. Yet there were good reasons why anarchists played a leading role in promoting this discourse from the 1890s through the 1930s. The Third French Republic, which lasted from 1870 until 1940, was quite literally defined by three wars with Germany (1870–71, 1914–18, 1940), all of which reinforced the dominant sentiment that France was endangered by its lower population and slower rate of growth vis-à-vis its Teutonic neighbor. On this issue as on few others, liberal republicans and Catholic traditionalists agreed. One striking example of this agreement can be seen in Emile Zola's 1899 novel *Fécondité*. For the sake of the *patrie* (fatherland), the naturalist writer called for family values and motherhood to trump attitudes of selfish pleasure. Earlier in the decade, Zola had written novels satirizing the pilgrimage to Lourdes and imagining anarchists blowing up the new Sacré Coeur cathedral, so he was hardly known for his pro-Catholic bias, yet on the issue of "decadent France" republicans and Catholics could make common cause. The loss of 1.4 million Frenchmen in World War I vastly increased the preoccupation with repopulating France and underscores why the French right was less enthusiastic about eugenics than were Germans and Americans. On the eve of World War II, France had the world's oldest population and lowest birthrate. The German population grew by 36 percent from 1900 to 1939; France's grew by 3 percent.[7] Neither selective breeding nor birth limitation were likely to be popular issues in interwar France. It was left primarily to such anarchists as Eugène and Jeanne Humbert, Manuel Devaldès, and Jean Marestan, along with supporters such as the novelist Victor Margueritte, to argue for the rights of the individual and the welfare of the workers over the demands of the nation.

Eugène Humbert, principal propagandist of the interwar birth control movement, was propelled to a position of leadership among French neo-Malthusians after he fell out with the founder of that movement, Paul Robin, in 1908 and started his own journal, *Génération consciente*. That same year he began a liaison with Jeanne Rigaudin, twenty years his junior, which lasted the rest of his life. Her biography of Humbert, published shortly after World War II (he died in 1944; she lived until 1986) is one of the best sources of information not only on Humbert but on the entire neo-Malthusian milieu.

Eugène Humbert's story reveals clearly how personal marginality led to radical ideology and lifelong commitment to a cause. He was born to an illiterate woman, herself from a family of ten children, in the eastern French town of Metz, on the eve of the Franco-Prussian War. His father was an army officer who promised to return from the war and marry his mother but failed to do so. When Metz was annexed to the new German Reich, his mother moved to Nancy and eventually gave birth to a second illegitimate child. His childhood was marked by taunts for his bastard status and was so impoverished that at one point his mother tried to asphyxiate herself and her two sons.[8] The father of the second child eventually left his mother to marry someone else, and when she did finally marry, Eugène did not get along with his stepfather. His early years were thus traumatized by issues related to sexuality, illegitimacy, and poverty. He also used his mother's name as his own, though the police archives refer to him as Eugène Dedenon, presumably after his stepfather. When he discovered libertarian, feminist, and neo-Malthusian ideas in the early 1890s, he fed on them as a starving person, as he later put it, and was soon a fervent anarchist.

After the turn of the century, Humbert became the first full-time employee of the League for Sexual Regeneration and a disciple of Paul Robin. Robin had imbibed the Malthusian doctrine in England in the 1870s, where he was in exile after the collapse of the Paris Commune. The first neo-Malthusian League was founded in London in 1877 by leftists and freethinkers who put a progressive spin on the Rev. Malthus's dour prophecies. Malthus lived through the dramatic rise in population growth that preceded and accompanied the Industrial Revolution, and concluded that population growth was likely to outstrip the food supply, unless checked by war and famine. He therefore counseled moral restraint as preferable to death from war or starvation. His fin de siècle followers agreed that overpopulation was a principal cause both of war and working-class poverty, but they viewed modern methods of birth control rather than moral restraint as the solution to the Malthusian dilemma. "Moral restraint" was the ideal of the English clergyman, not very appealing to anarchist partisans of free love. Birth control made sexual freedom and female autonomy possible, freeing women from the tyranny of uncontrolled reproduction. Robin summarized his ideals by arguing that the secret of happiness lay in good birth, good education, and good social organization.[9] A good birth was one that was planned and voluntary, hence the title of Humbert's prewar journal, *Conscious Generation*, and of Devaldès's 1927 book, *Conscious Maternity. Consciente* might also be translated as "rational," for these proponents of birth control were not simply advocating useful techniques for the bedroom; they believed that science and rationality must subdue the inexorable demands of blind nature and human instinct. Anarchists accepted the late nineteenth-century positivist assumption that science was progressive socially as well as technologically, and that mastery over nature was good. Despite a Romantic undercurrent, this remained the dominant anarchist ideology from the 1860s through the 1930s.

Not all anarchists were equally enthusiastic concerning issues related to human sexuality. Some of the leading communist-anarchists, such as Peter Kropotkin and his French ally Jean Grave, disdained the neo-Malthusians as advocating a lifestyle issue likely to detract from single-minded focus on the social revolution. The syndicalists' preoccupation with the workplace and the revolutionary tool of the general strike also distanced them from sexual issues. Many anarchists also distrusted feminist causes as too bourgeois and suffrage oriented. Anarchists were also predominantly male and tended to distrust women as irrational, religious, and socially conservative. Most anarchist partisans of birth control were therefore individualists, who favored unconditional autonomy and advanced a nonconformist and ethical vision of human behavior. By the 1920s, the heyday of the anarchist movement was clearly over, but popular speakers, such as Sébastien Faure, could still bring out two thousand people to a lecture, and issues dealing with controversial topics such as sexuality and birth control regularly commanded audiences of several hundred.

Given these splits among French anarchists, it was a major coup when Eugène Humbert managed to convince Sébastien Faure in 1903 of the importance of neo-Malthusianism for the liberation of humanity. Faure (1858–1942) had founded *Le Libertaire* in 1895, and though he and his paper were identified with the communist-anarchist wing of the movement, Faure was always more flexible than Jean Grave and his paper, *Les Temps nouveaux*, and in the 1920s sponsored a campaign to unify the divergent anarchist tendencies in a new synthesis. Faure's multivolume *Encyclopédie Anarchiste* devoted several articles to the history of the neo-Malthusian movement. One contributor noted that Kropotkin believed that the earth could sustain much higher levels of population with more intensive cultivation, and therefore felt there was no need to limit births. Nor would Marx, Bakunin, or Proudhon have supported birth control as a means of social combat.[10] Anarchist interest in family limitation developed during the Belle Epoque, becoming an integral part of an ethical conception of anarchism favoring individual autonomy and rational self-control.

Though abortion of course was illegal, birth control information was still tolerated in prewar France. The only tool that *"le père la pudeur"* (father modesty), Senator René Béranger, could use to prosecute journals such as Humbert's was obscenity, and Humbert spent six months in prison in 1912–13 for offending morality. He emerged from prison saying he refused to be intimidated, and on the eve of the war published his most famous article in *Génération consciente,* "The Example Comes from Above," in which he indicated how few children had been born to the leaders of the Third Republic. He counted fourteen children born to nine illustrious couples. President Carnot had three children, as had Loubet; the rest all had from zero to two children each, which Humbert called a model of parental prudence.[11]

On July 31, 1914, with war looming, Humbert left for Spain; Jeanne joined him in Barcelona in September. When he finally returned to France late in 1920, he was tried for being absent without leave and sentenced to the maximum penalty of five years in jail, even though by then he was fifty-one years old. His real crime, the military prosecutor said, was not his own evasion of service but of denying the French army several battalions of potential recruits through his birth control propaganda.[12] Jeanne Humbert did not explain why the couple returned to France months after the passage of the bill outlawing birth control; they must have known they would be targeted.

In the pronatalist climate of 1920s France, the Humberts became exemplary martyrs to their cause. They also got married in 1924 after sixteen years of companionship, legitimating their nine-year-old daughter and making prison visits easier. Eugène was released that year after serving three years of his five-year sentence. Jeanne had been prosecuted in 1921 for selling an old copy of Jean Marestan's 1910 sex manual, *Sexual Education,* which had not had its discussion of abortion expurgated, to an undercover agent. In 1923 she was again sent to prison for complicity in aiding women to obtain abortions.[13]

Now in his mid-fifties, Eugène Humbert briefly edited a physical culture journal that advocated nudism. At the same time, Jeanne Humbert began her novel *En pleine vie: Roman précurseur* (Full of life: A forerunner novel), which she published in 1930 adorned with photographs taken in German and Scandinavian nudist colonies. The French were latecomers to the nudist movement, and the Humberts enthusiastically endorsed the doctrine of truth and health through sunshine. This interlude in their careers indicates the interrelatedness of health, sexual freedom, and "conscious maternity."

Jeanne Humbert's novel was not a literary triumph, but with advocacy of birth control off limits for the time being, she tried her hand at popularizing a rational approach to the body and sexuality. She contrasted the debauched atmosphere of Parisian music halls with the chaste nudity of sun-swept beaches. Sunbathing and even nude beaches may seem like anodyne aspects of mass culture today, but the 1920s witnessed the dawn of the cult of sun and suntans. Humbert set her novel on Majorca, where a young couple discovers love without marriage, health through nudity and naturalness. A set-piece confrontation with a priest, who considers nudity an inducement to vice, also leads the heroine to affirm her desire to commit suicide when the time comes and her life-force has been spent. Humbert cited Bertrand Russell's *Marriage and Morality* in support of her position, and also referred to Sigmund Freud and a host of contemporary anarchists in support of her arguments for sexual freedom.[14] It is highly probable that Jeanne Humbert's determination to express her political views in this manner was influenced by the example of the muckraking novelist Victor Margueritte.

In the summer of 1926, the sixty-year-old writer Victor Margueritte paid a visit to the modest house of Eugène and Jeanne Humbert in Belleville on the north edge of Paris. He knew that Humbert was a well-known proponent of family planning, and said that he had come for information for his next novel, which he planned to call *Ton corps est à toi* (Your body is yours). Eugène replied, "Speak of my reputation! Lorraine bastard, born at Metz the year of the defeat of 1870, I've tried my hand at all trades from cobbler to journalist. You have before you a dangerous revolutionary, anarchist, pacifist, deserter." After citing his various prison terms, Humbert concluded, "You see, I am not someone one can associate with, my Margueritte!"[15] Humbert warned him that birth control was a dangerous topic for his novel, but Margueritte shrugged off the warning, saying he had little to lose. He had been radicalized earlier in the decade after a previous novel, the infamous *La garçonne* (The bachelor girl), had led the president of France to rescind his membership in the Legion of Honor. Now he identified with Humbert as a fellow renegade. The anarchist put his personal library at Margueritte's disposal. The resulting novel sold 180,000 copies, earning the author money as well as the admiration of the left, while not causing him any immediate legal troubles. The best-selling author and general's son could do with impunity what the self-described "Lorraine bastard" could not. At a Bordeaux anarchist meeting in June 1927, Aristide Lapeyre cited the new novel by Margueritte and suggested that all the *compagnons* should read it. The police informer reporting on this meeting got the author's name right but mistakenly referred to the book title in his report as "Your heart is yours" (*Ton coeur est à toi*).[16] The title that was still a mystery to the police would soon become a virtual catchphrase among the left-wing advocates of birth control.

Margueritte's novel was set among peasants in contemporary Provence. The heroine is an adolescent girl named Spirita Arelli, called Spi in the novel. Her father is absent and her mother is strait laced and old fashioned, but she is fortunate in finding a mentor in her worldly Uncle Paccaud, who has sailed the world and is a neo-Malthusian to boot. He tells her about the facts of life, and then warns her that while there is nothing shameful about the body, "Your body is yours . . . make it worthy of the soul in envelops."[17] He recommends two books to her: Marestan's *Sexual Education* and another called *Means of Avoiding Pregnancy*. Then he counsels her to get an education and succeed in life rather than rush to have children. The uncle's sage advice finds its religious counterpart in that of a priest who tells her to love God rather than boys. Yet all such advice proves insufficient, as Spi is raped and impregnated and finds herself on her own as her mother throws her out of the house. She goes to Marseilles, has the baby and leaves it with Public Assistance, and soon gets into trouble for endeavoring to help a poor pregnant friend arrange for an abortion. When facing the judge, who lectures her about the law of 1920, she responds indignantly that the deputies never spoke to women before promulgating this law. When the judge calls her a little anarchist, she replies, "Anarchist! Because I don't like to see suffering, and stupidity disgusts me?" She didn't know if it was anarchy, she told the judge, but she knew her friend didn't make herself pregnant. Finally Uncle Paccaud comes to the rescue by threatening to blackmail the judge, who some years before had arranged for his own mistress to have an abortion. The judge relents, but not before lecturing them that "France needs children! And all those who try, by word or writing, to limit the fecund mission, are enemies of the state. Abortion is a crime against nature. And birth control propaganda is an attack [*attentat*] on society."[18]

Ton corps est à toi concludes with the hope that someday abortions will be available on demand. Uncle Paccaud tells his niece that women will only be men's equals when, along with the right to vote, they can control their own bodies. "Conscious generation is the sine qua non of your definitive liberation."[19] As Spirita and her uncle are walking home, their path is blocked by a flock of sheep marked for slaughter. Poor beasts, Spi mutters, and Margueritte makes it clear that he is really talking about the poor children of the workers who will furnish material for the barracks, factories, and whorehouses. The next novel in the three volume series begun with *Ton corps est à toi* would be a study of eugenics called *Le bétail humain*, "Human cattle," published the following year.

One of the texts that Victor Margueritte found in the Humberts' library that clearly influenced his novel and even found its way into the text was the popular sex manual by Jean Marestan, *L'Education sexuelle*. Marestan, whose real name was Gaston Havard (1874–1951), was, like Humbert, illegitimate. His mother's family fled to Belgium to escape the repression following the Paris Commune, and there she met his father, a Belgian doctor. Their son tried to pursue a career in medicine as well, but a reversal of family fortunes forced him to quit his medical studies. He was soon frequenting Montmartre bohemian circles and collaborating on *Le Libertaire* and *L'Anarchie,* as well as Humbert's prewar journal, *Génération consciente*. He put his medical knowledge to good use when he published *L'Education sexuelle* in 1910, initially with Editions La Guerre Sociale (Social War), later with commercial publishers. Widely advertised in the anarchist press, it was translated into five languages, went through numerous editions, and sold tens of thousands of copies.[20] While it is impossible to know exactly how many people were influenced by anarchist neo-Malthusian propaganda, the wide circulation of these two books by Marestan and Margueritte suggests a much broader impact than simply among the several thousand anarchist sympathizers.

While Marestan was serving in the French medical corps during World War I, an unexpurgated edition of his book appeared in 1916; later editions would no longer contain the explicit discussions of birth control and abortion. Because he advocated free love, he believed men and women must both take responsibility for contraception. The commonest means of avoiding pregnancy among the poor was coitus interruptus, or withdrawal, a practice that Marestan did not recommend.[21] Instead he suggested a variety of mechanical methods including condoms, pessaries, houppettes, or safety sponges. He described uterine pessaries as circles of rubber, which must fit well and be placed correctly; the houppette he described as a tampon made of silk, which must be washed and dried after each use. He also described, along with illustrations, syringes and douches.[22] Marestan did not hesitate to provide social as well as practical advice. In his final chapter, "Moral and Social Consequences of Neo-Malthusian Practice," Marestan promoted contraception as a panacea. He argued that birth control would equalize the relationship between two people, end the double standard, and connect love more directly to marriage. He promoted free love with the benefit of effective birth control as leading to the elimination of prostitution, masturbation, and even homosexuality, as well as abortion and infanticide.[23] Birth control would save lives of women who should not get pregnant for health reasons; limiting family size would increase the dignity and well-being of the workers. It would even reduce wars, linked to overpopulation, and make colonial empires less necessary.[24]

Marestan engaged in debates with other anarchists in the 1930s over the significance of birth control in the Soviet Union, and after visiting Russia published a book in 1936 extolling the great advances made by the Soviets in sexual reform and women's liberation. Unfortunately for Marestan, his book appeared just as Stalin criminalized abortion. He returned to the anarchist fold, and Jeanne Humbert included a testimonial by Marestan in her 1947 book on her martyr-husband Eugène. Yet in this letter from Marestan, dated March 18, 1945, he highlighted not only Humbert's lifelong libertarian convictions but also his indignation at "defective" people who generated more defectives like themselves, "veritable rubbish in society."[25] Anarchism, birth control, and eugenics went hand in hand.

Victor Margueritte remained closely linked to the Humberts and the anarchist neo-Malthusians until 1933. In 1927 he accepted the title of honorary president of the French section of the World League for Sexual Reform. At the league's fourth international congress in Vienna in 1930, he demanded legalized abortion, forty-five years before the Fifth Republic granted French women that right. In 1933 he wrote the preface to Manuel Devaldès's plea for eugenic and birth control practices, *Croître et multiplier, c'est la guerre* (To increase and multiply means war), and accepted Devaldès's contention that overpopulation in Germany, Italy, and Japan was the major factor contributing to the next war. In December 1932, Jeanne Humbert gave a speech in the provincial Norman town of Vire titled "Against the Coming War," in which she quoted from Margueritte's 1931 book *La patrie humaine* (The human homeland—Margueritte had a knack for choosing catchy titles). The local lord registered a complaint of antinatalist propaganda, and Humbert was eventually tried early in 1934. She was defended by the indomitable leftist lawyer Henry Torrès, who read a statement defending her written by Margueritte, who felt as if he was being tried *in absentia*. The passage in question from his book that the government found actionable was "first have no more children as long as countries have the right to kill them."[26] The trial ended with an acquittal, but on appeal by the Garde des Sceaux, the appeals court of Caen, Normandy, annulled the verdict and recognized her guilty of propaganda against reproduction, sentencing her to three months in prison and a hundred-franc fine.

Margueritte allied himself with the anarchists between 1926 and 1933 because they were the foremost proponents of a set of interconnected causes that he championed in the interwar era: birth control, sexual freedom, pacifism, and antimilitarism. Nonanarchist advocates of birth control and abortion rights, such as the Association d'Etudes Sexologiques, founded by the psychiatrist Edouard Toulouse in 1931, were not similarly concerned with the political implications of these issues.[27] The neo-Malthusian connection between population and war received its definitive expression in the book to which Margueritte contributed the preface, Manuel Devaldès's *Croître et multiplier, c'est la guerre.*

Manuel Devaldès, whose real name was Ernest-Edmond Lohy, born in Normandy in 1875 and nearing sixty when his last major book appeared in 1933, had been active in the anarchist movement for nearly forty years. As an individualist, his major emphasis had been more aesthetic than biological in the prewar years. As editor of the ephemeral *La Revue Rouge* of 1896, he had been associated with Félix Fénéon, Laurent Tailhade, Alexandre Steinlen, and other intellectuals of the symbolist generation. In 1913 he was part of the group led by André Colomer that produced the journal *L'Action d'Art,* inspired by Bergson, Nietzsche, and the exploits of the Bonnot Gang. When war broke out, Colomer fled to Italy to avoid military service; Devaldès made his way to London on a borrowed Spanish passport, though when his ruse was discovered he spent several months in jail. His pacifism led him to Maurice Wullens, whose journal *Les Humbles* would focus particularly on the horrors of war and the need to resist another one. In response to patriotic collections of former combatants' war writings, Devaldès edited an issue of *Les Humbles* dedicated to war resisters such as himself and Colomer. During his time in England, Devaldès mastered English (according to his biographer, the Belgian anarchist Hem Day, he also studied Spanish, German, Italian, and Swedish), and it was there that he came into contact with the work of George Drysdale, founder of the Malthusian League of 1877. After the war, Devaldès was threatened with repatriation to France, which would have resulted in a lengthy prison term for avoiding military service. He discovered that England, unlike France, had a conscientious objector provision, which allowed him to remain in England for several more years, until he was no longer faced with prosecution.[28]

The birth control movement would dominate Devaldès's research and writing in the interwar period, as he decided that limiting births was the surest way to eliminate the threat of war. Devaldès argued that neo-Malthusianism was in fact the scientific approach to pacifism and, hence, superior analytically to the moral arguments against war. In his introduction, Margueritte called the title of Devaldès's book an irrefutable axiom, and for proof cited

Mussolini's cry that Italy must either extend itself or implode. He also cited Herbert Hoover, who as emergency food commissioner after the war had said that there were a hundred million Europeans too many to be adequately fed. At the same time, Margueritte hoped that men would refuse to bear arms in case war was declared, which might lead spontaneously to revolution— a utopian assumption given the example of August 1914.[29] Margueritte appeared uneasy about Devaldès's exclusive focus on population control as the best means of preserving a peaceful Europe; he was in fact to move away from anarchism and neo-Malthusianism soon after the publication of Devaldès' book. The author expressed no such reservations, sure that the biological explanation for war had trumped all others.

Devaldès explicitly contrasted the biological explanation for war with its main competitor on the left, the economic. Devaldès acknowledged that most syndicalists believed that capitalism had caused World War I, while the Americans blamed the militarism of the Central Powers. Yet he argued that corporate profits were more a result than the cause of war and cited Bertrand Russell's comment that there were plenty of wars before there was capitalism. He was even more critical of those he called sentimental pacifists, who blamed war on man's natural aggressiveness or egoism. Behind these explanations lay the Darwinian need for struggle over scarce resources, and underlying this was the true cause of scarcity—overpopulation. Whenever a society outstripped its ability to feed its people, it sought additional resources from its neighbors. It then had recourse to the use of armed combat, but arms themselves were a result, not a cause, and therefore disarmament itself would not prevent war. Identifying the struggle for scarce resources as the real cause of war, with scarcity due to overpopulation, Devaldès argued that birth control and eugenics were the keys to avoiding war. He called his approach "scientific pacifism." People must choose between war and population control; either there would be fewer babies born or the Malthusian solutions of war and famine would assert themselves. Devaldès's conception of the problem had clearly evolved since his 1927 book *La maternité consciente*, in which he approached the issue in more traditional anarchistic terms as the need for women to control their own bodies. By 1933, facing depression and war, Devaldès seemed willing to countenance government control to impose eugenic controls over the population, which would seem to enhance the power of the state. He was able to avoid this conclusion, anathema to anarchists, by placing his hope in international organizations such as the League of Nations. He envisaged a worldwide movement and said that politicians would only act when the intellectual elite showed them the way. War was a national measure, peace an international one.[30]

In his conclusion, Manuel Devaldès identified the principal enemy of his ideas, which one might guess would be nationalism and the bellicose nation-state, to be religion. It was the church that issued the injunction to increase and multiply since it saw design in nature created by God. He thus saw Christian pacifism as contradictory, since war must also be part of God's plan, and cited the conservative Joseph de Maistre, who argued that war was part of the divine order.[31] Asian religions were also condemned for pro-ducing a fatalistic mindset that ascribed natural or human disasters to the will of heaven. The anarchist asserted that Malthusians must be atheists. Though he wore the mantle of science, he knew that attaining universal peace would require a moral and intellectual revolution. An international Malthu-sian perspective must replace a nationalist and religious one.

How did contemporary anarchists respond to this demographic fixation? Devaldès's book received a lengthy review by Ixigrec (pen name of Robert Collino) in several issues of the individualist paper L'En Dehors in 1935. He agreed that individualist anarchists opposed overpopulation both on ethical and aesthetic grounds. Yet he questioned the rigid infallibility of the neo-Malthusians. He suggested that perhaps the fascists desired conquest and saw a higher birthrate as a means to that end. He asked whether there really was a clear correlation between overpopulation and warlike countries and doubted if this really was the Italians' and Germans' prime motivation. Furthermore, Devaldès defined overpopulation as population exceeding the productive power of the land, but in a world where resources were imported and exported, people were no longer restricted to their own territory's pro-duction. In a later issue, Ixigrec produced a chart of population density show-ing that Paraguay had only three people per square kilometer, while the densest places were Japan, Holland, Belgium, and Java. The United States and Russia were among the least dense but had been involved in several wars, while the Swiss and Chinese were much denser but also less bellicose. The Dutch were crowded and pacific, the Italians bellicose. He concluded, "Overpopulation is at once a cause and effect of warmongering [bellecisme]. A social transformation will only be possible by a modification of economic conditions, and a modification of human ethics in the individual sense."[32] The anarchist critic was not willing to jettison ethical and economic ap-proaches for a simplistic biological explanation of war. Malthusianism was an important aspect of the anarchist critique but did not subsume it.

Individualists were particularly skeptical of the claims of eugenics. It is troubling to read the Humberts or Devaldès casually referring to the need to prevent defectives (tarés) from reproducing. They meant that syphilitics, alcoholics, and the mentally unfit should refrain from having children, but the unanswered question was who was to prevent them from doing so? They implied that doctors should counsel such people not to reproduce, without clarifying how they could be prevented without state authority to back up such an order. In December 1928, the individualist anarchist E. Armand, editor of *L'En Dehors,* contributed "some critiques of eugenics." Referring to the Fifth Genetics Congress held in Berlin the previous year, and also to the works of Davenport and Pearson, he was skeptical though not entirely dismissive, acknowledging that heredity contributed a great deal to the person. He didn't know what criteria would be selected for by eugenicists, or whether this would be a method of human emancipation or subjection. Genius could appear among criminals and vagabonds; would there be room in a eugenic paradise for bohemians and artists? Forced sterilization, such as was being practiced in Switzerland and the United States, might have prevented the birth of Beethoven, Keats, or Blake.[33] Armand's musings would be amplified a few years later by Aldous Huxley in *Brave New World,* where the scientific eugenic paradise became a dystopian vision of control from above. Meanwhile, voluntary sterilization became another tool in the neo-Malthusians' arsenal.

Interwar anarchists actually engaged in voluntary sterilization. In the spring of 1935, an Austrian doctor named Norbert Bartosek came to France to perform a new male contraceptive practice recently developed by his brother in Graz—vasectomy. The police reported that the anarchist Pierre Ramus had made a specialty of the practice and had sterilized an estimated six thousand men in Vienna. Ramus and twenty accomplices had been acquitted by an Austrian court in 1933, occasioning much rejoicing in the French anarchist press. On arriving in France, Bartosek spent several months in Lyon, where he performed the simple twenty-minute operation at the back of a café on Sundays. Then the libertarian doctor moved on to Bordeaux, where he was assisted by Aristide Lapeyre, individualist and neo-Malthusian who submitted to the operation himself. All patients reported that they suffered no sexual ill effects; the main objection was that the operation was non-reversible. In Bordeaux, most volunteers were Italians and Spaniards. An article in *Le Matin* on April 1, 1935, reported on the case in Bordeaux, with the people implicated in running the operation saying that Lapeyre had convinced them to turn a bedroom into an operating room. Bartosek fled to Belgium, from which the French government was trying to extradite him; the Belgian anarchist Hem Day (real name: Marcel Dieu) had formed a committee to defend the doctor.[34] Bartosek was eventually sentenced to three years in prison; his assistants to four months. The anarchist paper *Le Libertaire* discussed the story in a April 5, 1935, article with the familiar title "Ton corps est à toi," saying the formula established by Victor Margueritte was applicable to men as well. That thousands of left-wing and working-class men were willing to undergo this procedure in the 1930s reinforces the impact of neo-Malthusian propaganda on the behavior of both sexes.

In February 1933 the Chamber of Deputies reopened debate on the 1920 law, and the Humberts thought that perhaps the tide had turned. Growing unemployment in the Depression era had benefited those who called for fewer workers. The Fifth Congress of the World League for Sexual Reform that met in Brno in 1932 had received positive publicity, and that winter the popular magazine *Voilà* had run a series of articles on the international birth control movement that featured a visit to the Humberts' home and an interview with them. Their own neo-Malthusian journal, *La Grande Réforme,* had been appearing since 1931 and had not been prosecuted (though Jeanne Humbert was still having legal troubles). Yet in the legislature, supporters of the 1920 law called neo-Malthusianism a deadly doctrine whose proponents profited from the trade in birth control devices. The amendment to overturn the law failed by a wide margin, as did a proposal to amnesty all victims of the law. The best the Chamber of Deputies could do was to pardon those people found guilty of spreading birth control propaganda.[35] Yet the tide would soon turn against the Humberts, despite their attempt to cooperate with progressive, nonanarchist organizations. In 1935, Stalin launched a campaign to increase the Russian birthrate, and abortion there was soon outlawed. The French Communist Party followed suit. Its leader, Maurice Thorez, met with the leader of the National Alliance for the Increase in the French Population in 1936, and the party supported family and morality as part of its newly-found Popular Front nationalism. The communist paper *L'Humanité* ceased running any articles on sexual issues, and the Popular Front government refused to abrogate the 1920 law. On the eve of the next war, a new Family Code of July 29, 1939, reinforced laws against abortion and increased incentives for large families. Madeleine Pelletier, the crusading left-wing doctor and feminist, ended her days in 1939 in a mental hospital.[36]

The anarchist left of the 1930s did have to confront the fact that their eugenicist outlook was leading them to associate ideologically with some unsavory bedfellows. Devaldès and Humbert can be seen evaluating Nazi eugenics practices in the course of the year 1934, one year after Devaldès's major work was published. In the May 1934 issue of *La Grande Réforme,* Devaldès faced squarely the Nazi plans to sterilize over four hundred thousand people of both sexes who were deemed unfit. Devaldès refused to condemn German forced sterilizations and praised the Nazis for requiring eugenics to be part of the medical school curriculum. He cited the twenty-seven states in the United States that had passed eugenic legislation and complained that no one had criticized eugenics when practiced in the United States, but now that Hitler was carrying it out it was getting a bad name. Devaldès remained adamant that in this area the Germans were contributing to the progress of civilization. Hitler had proclaimed, reasonably so Devaldès thought, that if the church was willing to care for German defectives, fine, but the German state was tired of spending 350 marks per year for each patient. Devaldès stuck to his anticlerical guns, attacking the church rather than the Nazis for obstructing biological progress and rational sociology.[37]

Praising the Nazis in a French anarchist paper dedicated to birth control was too much for Eugène Humbert. That summer, the editor of *La Grande Réforme* asked, "to what point to have beautiful children, a healthy race, if it is to lead them to the gas, machine guns and slaughterhouse of battles?"[38] Even Humbert acknowledged that the Nazis' eugenic marriage regulations sounded reasonable, but it was all pointless if it served a bellicose state ideology. Later that year, Devaldès seemed to respond to Humbert's somber assessment. In a second article, he agreed that the Nazis were practicing *"bellicisme eugéniste,"* seeking a healthy population so as to provide the state with more cannon fodder. The proof was that the Nazis sought to increase the overall population despite the difficulty of feeding their present population. As well as being warmongers, the Nazis were also deeply antifeminist, making women slaves of the male as of the state. Devaldès quoted Hitler that women's only duty was to produce children. Bachelors and widows were to be taxed to help pay for large family subsidies; new couples were to get a thousand marks on marriage, which they would not have to repay if they produced four children within eight years. Because Germany lacked colonies, its expanding population guaranteed that war was on the horizon.[39] Devaldès barely mentioned eugenics in this article, focusing instead on all the areas in which the Nazis contradicted anarchist ideals of pacifism, feminism, and birth control. Nevertheless, despite the right-wing taint the anarchists refused to jettison eugenics, seeing it as the positive counterpart of the negative practice of family limitation. Everyone should control fecundity; only the best should breed.

The Humberts had been fighting a lifelong battle against war and for birth control. In July 1939, a celebration was held for the hundredth issue of *La Grande Réforme,* whose subtitle was the anarchistic *"culture individuelle, réforme sexuelle, transformation sociale."* The vacationing Victor Margueritte wrote to the gathering of how much he admired the Humberts as fervent partisans of free thought and the emancipation of human beings through conscious generation. Over a hundred people came to the banquet, which was the last public contact Eugène Humbert had with most of them. Then war broke out. Jeanne Humbert noted the death of Margueritte at age seventy-five in March 1942 and of the grand old anarchist militant Sébastien Faure in July. That December, Eugène Humbert was arrested for complicity in aiding an attempt at abortion. At his trial, which lasted all of five hours, Humbert said he favored "amelioration of the race by application of eugenic methods and of child care" (*puériculture*). He opposed alcoholism, sexual per-versions, and all causes of degeneration. He also said he was against clan-destine abortions, preferring legal ones but really favoring birth control to avoid it entirely. Eugène Humbert was sentenced to eighteen months in prison; on appeal the judge thought the sentence too lenient and added six months! Humbert was thus confined in an Amiens prison when he died in a British bombing on June 26, 1944.[40]

Neo-Malthusianism remained controversial within anarchist ranks since biology tended to replace economics as the central historical determinant. If they did not usually say so (though Devaldès did), neo-Malthusians at least implied that controlling fecundity was more important than the strug-gle against capitalism, at least in terms of hindering the next war. This had several implications not fully explored by the anarchist proponents of birth control. Figures such as the Humberts favored eugenics, yet as anarchists they rejected any solutions imposed by the state. This meant that the people they called "defective" would have to renounce voluntarily their own right to procreate. Since this would seem unlikely, neo-Malthusians formed alli-ances with progressive-thinking doctors who shared their concerns and could advise patients on the correct eugenic decisions. For example, at the Club du Faubourg, which regularly sponsored debates on controversial topics, six hundred people in 1932 heard Dr. Madeleine Pelletier praise the Soviet tol-eration of abortion. She said she advocated birth control but wouldn't go into detail for fear of ending up in prison that night. Dr. Jean Dalsace, head of the laboratory at the St. Antoine hospital, reported that more than eight hundred thousand illegal abortions were performed in France each year, and advocated voluntary maternity. Dr. Vachet also spoke in favor of sexual reform.[41]

At a lecture organized by the Humberts' League for Human Regenera-tion in February 1938, Manuel Devaldès explicitly stated that the key problem facing the world was not overproduction but rather overpopulation. Jeanne Humbert argued that 90 percent of all births were involuntary and that women must always consciously consent to becoming pregnant.[42] Anarchist neo-Malthusians believed it was possible for rational individuals to triumph over reproductive instincts and identified religion as the chief obstacle to the realization of their rationalist worldview. In order to succeed, the anarchists believed that women in particular needed to replace a religious with a secular worldview.

The anarchists approached eugenics from an entirely different perspective from right-wing ideologues of state control of reproduction. That the libertarian left and the fascist right could both favor population control and prevention of breeding by the "unfit" suggests the credibility of biological solutions to social problems in the interwar era.[43] The crucial difference was that while republican France, fascist Italy, and Nazi Germany all wanted to enlist biology in service to the state, the anarchists wanted it to serve the individual, or more precisely to allow rational individuals to gain control over their bodies. The negative eugenics advocated by some anarchists was designed both to improve their personal economic prospects and to enhance their ethical lives as individuals who refused to bring unhealthy people into the world. While nationalist eugenics implied that women's bodies should be placed in service to the state (parallel to men's sacrifice of their bodies in war), the neo-Malthusian left believed that equality between the sexes could only transpire when women were in control of their own fecundity. The liberation of women from the veils cast by government and religion implied the liberation of humanity in general. Finally, the pacifist left believed that fewer babies meant less chance of war, an attitude viewed by the right as defeatism. Marshal Pétain famously expressed the pronatalist view on June 20, 1940, when he explained the catastrophic defeat to the French people in the following terms: "The spirit of pleasure has won out over the spirit of sacrifice. Too few babies, too few weapons, too few allies, those are the causes of our defeat."[44] His Vichy government would make abortion a capital offense.

For the anarchists as for the Vichy collaborators, sex, gender, and politics were necessarily interrelated, but in antithetical ways. For the anarchists, free love required birth control, and birth control implied women's control of their bodies. If women were to be autonomous individuals and not be subservient to fathers, husbands, priests, and presidents, then gender roles would need to be radically redefined. Gender issues reinforced the biological imperatives raised by the Humberts and their allies, at a time and in a world marching to the beat of a very different drummer.

Part II

French Anarchists Between East and West

French anarchists were fervent internationalists who were highly aware of revolutionary movements taking place elsewhere. The Russian Revolution was the inescapable fact shaping all leftist activity in the interwar era, whether socialist, communist, or anarchist. In the heyday of anarchism at the turn of the century, the socialist parties of Europe were becoming reformist and parliamentary, leaving the revolutionary terrain open to anarchism and anarcho-syndicalism. The great exception was the Social Democratic Party of Russia, which was forced underground by the Russian autocracy and so remained revolutionary. When the Bolsheviks succeeded in overthrowing the Kerensky government in the October Revolution, they immediately became a paragon of revolutionary realism. Anarchists by contrast were cast more than ever in the role of utopian dreamers.

Initially hopeful that the new Soviet Union would be shaped along anarchist lines, anarchists would soon become disillusioned by the authoritarian tendencies of the Bolshevik Party and the gradual disappearance of the soldiers and workers councils, called soviets, which had seemed to promise democratic, decentralized control. By 1921, as the Red Army crushed both the autonomous and heavily anarchist-inspired forces in Ukraine and the rebellious sailors at the Kronstadt Naval Base outside Petrograd, most anarchists lost their enthusiasm for the socialist revolution. Nevertheless, the success of the Russian Revolution presented a constant temptation for anarchists weary of internecine struggles and revolutionary impotence. By the mid-twenties, as hopes for revolution declined in Western Europe, some anarchists would turn toward communism despite their misgivings. As French

anarchists visited the Soviet Union to see for themselves what a social revolution looked like, numerous Russian anarchists made their way to France
to escape Soviet repression.

French anarchists also turned their faces to the west, toward the United
States of America, beacon of technological modernity. Anarchists were likely
to share the prejudices of most French men and women concerning an
America deemed materialistic and dehumanized by the assembly line and
by capitalist greed, yet they were inspired by the anarchist movement in the
United States that emerged bloody but unbowed from the repression visited
on the left during and after World War I. After the U.S. government deported
hundreds of foreign-born leftists, including the anarchists Emma Goldman and Alexander Berkman, to Russia in 1919, anarchists responded with
a wave of terror that culminated in the September 16, 1920, bomb set in a
horse-drawn carriage parked in front of J. P. Morgan's Wall St. headquarters, which killed forty people and wounded hundreds more (and remained
the worst terrorist attack in U.S. history until the Oklahoma City bombing
of 1995). The bomb that aimed at the heart of American capitalism was
possibly meant as a reprisal to the arrest of Nicola Sacco and Bartolomeo
Vanzetti the previous spring, for allegedly robbing the payroll of a Massachusetts shoe factory and killing guards in the process. It certainly in-
flamed American opinion against anarchists, especially foreign-born ones
who embodied everything alien and "un-American." The trial and fate of
the two Italian-born anarchists became an international *cause célèbre* of the
1920s and served French anarchists as an important element of propaganda
for their cause.

The greatest anarchist movement of the interwar period was neither in
France, Russia, Ukraine, nor America but rather in Spain, which became
engulfed in civil war between 1936 and 1939. Anarchists played a major
role in defending the Spanish Republic against Franco and his allies in the
Catholic Church and the Spanish elites. Especially in the Catalan region of
Barcelona and Valencia and in the neighboring region of Aragon, anarchists and anarcho-syndicalists ran cities, factories, and cooperative farms
from the summer of 1936 to the spring of 1937, and in some cases until the
end of the war in the winter of 1939.[1] The Spanish Civil War does not play
a large part in my narrative, in part because the focus here is mostly on the
1920s, and also because French attention was distracted from events in Spain
by the tumultuous domestic scene associated with the Popular Front government of socialist prime minister Léon Blum. Furthermore, as I noted in
my introduction, French anarchist involvement with the Spanish Civil War
has been discussed elsewhere.[2] What is most significant about the Spanish

revolution for the purposes of this book is that it underscores the internationalism of radical activity in the interwar period, with the International Brigades being one of the most famous elements of the civil war. In order to understand interwar French anarchism, then, one must look beyond French borders.

Facing East: Russians and Jews

In the aftermath of the Bolsheviks' victory in the civil war that raged through the old tsarist empire from 1917 until 1921, many of the losers in that epic struggle ended up in Paris. Most of the Russian émigrés had supported the counterrevolutionary White forces defending the tsarist regime; others were Ukrainian nationalists battling the Bolsheviks in the name of Ukrainian autonomy. By the late 1920s, refugees representing these two anticommunist groups numbered more than one hundred thousand in France; more than fifty thousand Russians resided in Paris and the suburbs.[1] At the other end of the political spectrum, a much smaller group of Russian anarchists trickled into France. They had initially cooperated with the communists in deposing the tsar, but by 1921, their usefulness to the Bolsheviks finished, they were already being persecuted. Kropotkin's funeral that winter was the last time the black flag of anarchism flew openly in Soviet Russia. Anarchist and Ukrainian separatist combined in the person of Nestor Makhno, who led peasant bands that fought both the Bolsheviks and the German-installed hetman regime. Makhno made it to Paris in 1925 and died there, of tuberculosis, nine years later.

The Russian émigré population thus changed as dramatically as events in the Russian homeland. Before the war, the prefecture of police characterized the twenty-five thousand or so Russian émigrés as being composed mostly of "anarchists and Jews"; after the war the vast majority of exiles were Russian nationalists and monarchists, practitioners of the Orthodox faith.[2] The image of the down-at-heels aristocrat forced to drive a taxi became a postwar cliché, popularized in the novels of Joseph Kessel, himself a Russian-Jewish immigrant. Sometimes these émigrés revisited the quarrels of their homeland on the streets of Paris.

One such collision occurred on May 25, 1926, when a Jew and anarchist named Sholom Schwartzbard emptied his pistol into the body of the former hetman Simon Vasilievich Petliura. Petliura had led the Ukrainian National Republic, which had briefly been allied with the anticommunist Polish forces until both were pushed out by the victorious Red Army. He was tried the following year, in a highly publicized court case that earned the sobriquet *le procès des pogromes* (trial of the pogroms).

The Schwartzbard *attentat* and trial highlights the massive immigration of Central and Eastern European Jews into France between 1919 and 1939, which coincided with the arrival of refugees from Russia. As Germaine Berton's trial in 1923 dramatized issues of violence and gender, so the "trial of the pogroms" highlighted violence against Jews and, in Schwartzbard's case, recourse to violence as resistance. Other Russian anarchists, many of them Jewish as well, loudly opposed Bolshevik repression and in so doing influenced the French anarchist movement. Their vocal presence compelled the French anarchists to face the dual threats posed by bolshevism and fascism to individualist ideals of freedom and antistatism. The rapidly growing Jewish population also revealed a strain of latent antisemitism within the anarchist movement. Jewish anarchists were not unique to interwar France, but the tripling of the Parisian Jewish population to one hundred fifty thousand from the turn of the century to the 1930s increased their visibility and influence.[3] The assassination of Simon Petliura provides a dramatic entrée into the tensions of these years.[4]

The issue of immigration into France between the wars is tied to gender relations as well. Millions of immigrants were welcomed into France to rebuild the shattered country and to help replace the missing labor of those men killed during the war. Their presence also meant that French women could go back to their homes and bear the babies that the conservative, pronatalist forces so dearly wished for, rather than taking jobs outside the home and leading independent lives. Without immigrants, the hundreds of thousands of French women who had replaced men in the factories might have had to stay there. When naturalization laws were liberalized in 1927, immigrant men could even become voting French citizens, while women born in France were denied this privilege. Immigrant (largely male) labor thus aided in displacing women from the economy; the absolute number of women in the industrial labor force was slightly less in 1926 than it had been twenty years before.[5]

The Trial of the Pogroms

Sholom (called Samuel in the French press) Schwartzbard, thirty-nine years old at the time of his trial, had left his Ukrainian homeland after being imprisoned by the tsarist government for political activities related to the 1905 revolution. His own pregnant mother had been killed in a pogrom.[6] By 1908 he was a militant anarchist residing in Vienna when he was arrested for theft and served a four-month jail sentence. Moving on to Paris along with his brother Meir in 1910, like many other Jews he ended up in the working-class quarter of Belleville, where he practiced the watchmaker trade that he had learned back in his homeland. He and his brother both enlisted in the French Foreign Legion at the outbreak of war, were seriously wounded, and were awarded the Croix de Guerre.[7] He would eventually, in 1925, become a naturalized French citizen. After the outbreak of the Russian Revolution, he went with his wife back to Russia and made his way to his father's house in Balta, Ukraine. He tried to practice his watchmaker trade in Odessa but ended up joining the Red Army, where he fought both Ukrainian nationalists and Denikin's White Army.[8] He witnessed personally the chaos that the revolution visited on Ukraine, and in particular experienced the pogroms against the Jews during the years 1919 and 1920. Fleeing the antisemitic violence, Schwartzbard returned to Paris with his wife after the civil war while maintaining his anarchist affiliation and nursing hatred for the Ukrainian peasants and nationalists, whom he blamed for the deaths of tens of thousands of Jews.[9]

After the Bolshevik victory, Simon Petliura fled to Poland and brought his family to Paris in October 1924. In December 1925, Schwartzbard learned of Petliura's presence and purchased a pistol. He found a photograph of Petliura and pasted it on a card, which he kept with him. He refused to kill the Ukrainian leader as long as he was in the company of his wife and child. By one account, the day before the assassination, Schwartzbard was dining at a restaurant on the boulevard Belleville with the Russian anarchist émigrés Alexander Berkman, Mollie Steimer, and Senya Fleshin when he spotted

Petliura. If this is true, it suggests that Schwartzbard maintained close rela-tions with other anarchists at the time of his attentat.[10] On May 25, 1926, he found the former hetman dining at the restaurant Chartier at the corner of the boulevard St. Michel and the rue Racine, on the left bank. When the Ukrainian emerged from the restaurant, Schwartzbard asked if he was Pet-liura, at which the general immediately sensed danger and raised his cane. Schwartzbard drew his revolver and fired five shots, and as Petliura fell to the pavement, Schwartzbard continued to fire until out of bullets, shout-ing, "Murderer, this is for the massacres, this is for the pogroms."[11] Shortly before his *attentat* and immediate arrest, Schwartzbard sent a pneumatic message to his wife, alerting her as to what was about to happen. He never expressed any remorse for his premeditated crime, and there was no doubt that he had done it, which did not prevent him from pleading "not guilty" at his trial. There was some debate about whether Schwartzbard continued firing as Petliura lay helpless on the ground, but otherwise no one contested the facts of the case. This incontrovertible evidence may have deterred most defense attorneys, but not the fiery leftist lawyer Henry Torrès.

Torrès applied the same techniques that had won him the acquittal of Germaine Berton four years earlier. In the face of defendants who admitted their crimes and showed no remorse, Torrès shifted the burden of guilt to the victim, justifying the crime as an act of revenge against someone who had placed themselves outside the pale. In Berton's case, he managed to marginalize the Action Française as a right-wing, antirepublican movement committed to violence. In some ways, his defense of Schwartzbard was eas-ier than it was for Berton since she had never personally been attacked by Marius Plateau or the Action Française, while Schwartzbard had personally suffered from Ukrainian antisemitism, losing many relatives in the pogroms. Schwartzbard convincingly played the role of avenger of his race, while Ber-ton strained credulity as the self-appointed avenger of Jean Jaurès. Another contrast concerns the two anarchists' parental relations. Berton elicited sym-pathy for having a mother who rejected her, while Schwartzbard was ever the dutiful son. In a letter from prison to his wife, Anna, he wrote that he wanted his father's tomb inscribed with the statement "our son Sholom has avenged the sacred blood of your brother Israel and the martyrdom of the whole people of Israel."[12]

Schwartzbard was praised for standing up for his people, who, it was alleged, too often faced oppression with silent resignation. The Eastern Jew had been transformed by his wartime service to France. Torrès in effect asked the jury how they could condemn someone who heroically defended his people. The crux of the case was to show that Petliura did indeed deserve his fate. This meant shedding light on what took place in Ukraine seven and eight years before, and so the case drew considerable international attention for highlighting the egregious antisemitism that afflicted Eastern Europe after 1880, and especially during the collapse of the tsarist regime. Torrès portrayed Schwartzbard not as an anarchist terrorist, a partisan of direct action, but as a man imbued with French values of justice.

Torrès apparently traveled with Bernard Lecache to Ukraine to collect evidence for the trial.[13] Lecache cited the Schwartzbard case in the preface to his book *Au pays des pogromes; quand Israël meurt* (In the land of pogroms; when Israel dies), published after Schwartzbard's arrest and shortly before the trial. Lecache traveled around Ukraine collecting stories of atrocities, and the book contained numerous photographs and figures alleging murder on a large scale. The evidence of violence was incontrovertible; what was less clear was Petliura's responsibility for the massacres. His defenders pointed to orders he issued on August 26–27, 1919, forbidding pogroms, and argued that attacks were carried out by local commanders in a chaotic situation over which the hetman had little control. Torrès and a number of Jewish witnesses, some brought from Ukraine with financial support from the American Jewish community, retorted that Petliura did nothing to rein in the violence, and never punished a single renegade commander. Torrès contrasted Petliura's toleration of mass murder with the behavior of French commanders at the front who ordered soldiers shot for theft.[14] The next day's headline in the left-leaning newspaper *L'Oeuvre* was titled "Me. Henry Torrès fait le procès de l'hetman Petliura (Mr. Torrès tries the Hetman Petliura)." The reporter noted that a witness for the prosecution, Colonel Boutahoff, played into Torrès's hands when he asserted that a massacre was not premeditated but rather was "spontaneous as an inspiration of a divine will." On hearing this, Torrès jumped to his feet to note that the witness had just admitted that old men, women and children had been killed in order to obey divine will, referring to the death of fifteen hundred Jews at Proskuriv (as many as three thousand may have died in February 1919 at the hands of Hetman Semesenko, who ordered that all strikes and meetings end and that the people "cease its anarchistic outbursts because I have adequate forces with which to combat you, and I especially call this to the attention of the Jews").[15] When the prosecutor, Campinchi, demanded to see an order from Petliura that showed he intended to kill Jews, Torrès responded that it was his responsibility to stop the pogroms and control his army.

The prosecution also tried to argue that Schwartzbard was an agent of the Cheka, the Soviet secret police, but could adduce no proof. The Soviet ambassador to France denied that Schwartzbard was in their pay. Torrès

launched into a disquisition on the differences between bolshevism and anarchism, and said that after the Bolshevik victory the anarchists were immediately targeted for repression. Yet after admitting Schwartzbard's anarchist
affiliation, he tried to mitigate it by calling him "an ideological, idealistic,
theoretical anarchist, what one might term, on the whole, a Tolstoyan. . . .
An anarchist, but not a terrorist of direct action. On the contrary, he led the
calmest, the most peaceful life."[16] This was patently disingenuous of Torrès
since Tolstoy was a Christian pacifist whose ideal of peaceful noncoopera-
tion would influence Gandhi, whereas Schwartzbard was a former soldier
who did not hesitate to kill for a greater cause. Campinchi was probably more
accurate when he said that if Schwartzbard was an idealistic anarchist, his
"idealism started with burglary and ended with assassination."[17] During the
trial, Schwartzbard tried to argue that his arrest in Vienna concerned his
anarchist beliefs, not petty burglary. Similarly, the defense attorney tried to
connect the assassination to Schwartzbard's war experience (manliness versus "eastern" or Jewish resignation), while Campinchi connected it to anarchist terrorist practice.

Schwartzbard testified on his own behalf in front of the crowded courtroom. The reporter for *L'Oeuvre* described him as having the face and bright,
shining eyes of an apostle or a fanatic—exactly as one would expect of an
anarchist willing to sacrifice himself for his cause. In a calm but accented
voice he told how a friend told him he had overheard two officers of the
White army admit to raping numerous Jewish women and to killing fifteen

Fig. 5   Sholom Schwartzbard testifying at his trial, October 1927. From the
Archives of the YIVO Institute for Jewish Research, New York.

Jews in one day. From the day Petliura took power, massacres occurred with ever greater frequency, while his soldiers wore armbands that said "kill the Jews and save Ukraine." He proudly claimed responsibility for his deed, and the reporter felt moved to comment that though the act might be odious one could not deny his sincerity or courage.[18] Other Jewish witnesses described the pogroms as systematic violence, not just an occasional outburst. Mlle Greenburg, a medical student, described the pogroms in detail and claimed that the least word from Petliura would have stopped them. The reporter noted that on the last day of the trial, rarely had such a dense crowd filled Paris's Palace of Justice. Torrès evoked the martyrdom of a whole people; the Jewish lawyer went so far as to appeal to the religious sentiments of the jury by saying, "I come here carrying the cross of suffering, asking of you a verdict of redemption."[19] He also proclaimed, prophetically, that to condemn the pogroms of the past would help prevent those of the future.

The jury took even less time to acquit Schwartzbard—less than half an hour—than the one that had acquitted Germaine Berton on Christmas Eve 1923. The similarity between the two trials of confessed yet acquitted anarchist assassins was not lost on the right-wing press. *Action Française* said it had foreseen this verdict and commented that "the new era opened by the acquittal of [Finance Minister Joseph] Caillaux's wife [in July 1914] is not closed."[20] Schwartzbard for his part could not return to his trade and feared reprisals by the large Ukrainian community. He tried to emigrate to Palestine, but the British would not let him in. Instead he seems to have become a full-time writer and propagandist. Even before his attack on Petliura he had sent articles to the New York–based Yiddish-language anarchist newspaper *Die Fraye Arbeiter Shtimme,* The Free Workers' Voice. Two weeks after the assassination, he wrote them to explain his deed:

> Dear Comrades of The Workers' Voice: I am writing you from my cell and cordially greet all of you. After having served the idea of the revolution and class struggle with devotion, like a faithful soldier, for numerous years, when my life and thoughts clung to a single goal— how to ameliorate the dolorous condition of the poor and oppressed masses of humanity—I have become convinced that before being able to emancipate all mankind, one must first liberate himself, liberate the Jewish people from all persecutions and calumnies which never cease to strike this people which has been abandoned by everyone and is oppressed everywhere.[21]

Schwartzbard embodied the anarchist autodidact, an independent artisan who also wrote articles, poetry, and eventually two volumes of his autobiography.

This statement suggests that he divorced his deed from his anarchist ideals. He may have felt that the particularistic defense of his people took priority over the long-term, universal ideals of anarchism, or else that anarchist violence was restricted to serving the revolutionary interests of the working class. While the prosecutors and the conservative press connected his attack to those of other acquitted French murderers, such as Mme Caillaux and Germaine Berton, his defense attorney preferred to place Schwartzbard in the context of other avengers of persecuted minorities. During the trial, Torrès cited the case of Teilerian, who was acquitted by a German jury in 1924 for killing Talaat Bey as revenge for the Turkish massacre of Armenians during World War I.[22] This comparison made sense given Torrès's successful defense strategy, and it seems as if Schwartzbard agreed that he had acted as a Jew rather than as an anarchist. The leftist and Jewish-run Club du Faubourg sponsored a debate on the Schwartzbard Affair in March 1928 featuring the Russian-Jewish émigré novelist Joseph Kessel and an antisemitic journalist. Despite being held at the very large Salle de Wagram, the debate was sold out and people had to be turned away, suggesting that the case was closely followed by French Jews.[23]

The anarchist man of action buttressed the resolve of the Jew. While Eastern European Jews were perceived as passive victims who failed to defend themselves, Schwartzbard was a veteran and anarchist who refused to accept the affront to the honor of his people represented by the presence in Paris of Petliura. While his acquittal was due primarily to his attorney's equating vengeance with justice, Schwartzbard was also presented as a Gallicized, Westernized Jew who acted less like a terrorist than simply like a man. By way of contrast, when Herschel Grynszpan killed the German Embassy official vom Rath in Paris in 1938, setting off the Kristallnacht pogrom in Germany, Maître Torrès was again called to the defense, though the trial never took place and the teenaged defendant was eventually handed over to the Nazis. Yet Grynszpan was compromised by rumors of homosexual relations with his victim and, unlike Schwartzbard, the Jewish community hastened to distance itself from his violent deed. Between 1927 and 1938 antisemitism increased markedly in France and it is unlikely that Grynszpan would have been treated as tolerantly by a French jury as Schwartzbard, but neither could he have been portrayed as the manly and rational figure of the 1927 trial.[24]

In his book *The Image of Man: The Creation of Modern Masculinity*, George Mosse argues that people in modern societies need a "countertype" against which to define themselves, and that Jews as outsiders functioned admirably as such countertypes. The example Mosse gives to illustrate the desire to deprecate Jewish masculinity is taken from a French book published in 1924. He quotes Camille Spiess as characterizing Jews as "half men, half women."[25] Nationalism provided the opportunity for true men to demonstrate their virility; antisemites argued that Jews, as the prototypical people without a country, could not be true men. The tendency to deprecate Jewish manhood was reinforced, it has been argued, by the favored self-image of Jews as otherworldly Talmudic scholars, the "yeshiva bochar." There was no cultural sanction for the Jewish male as knight or warrior.[26] The Jews' lack of martial élan must have been reinforced by the widespread practice of young Jewish males to flee Russia rather than have to serve in the Russian army and encounter antisemitism. Yet in 1927 Schwartzbard represented the thirty-six thousand Jewish immigrants to France who had volunteered to fight for their adopted homeland. He wore his Croix de Guerre prominently at his trial to emphasize this fact.[27] Schwartzbard was neither scholar nor crafty, money-grubbing merchant—the equally unmanly antisemitic profile of the Jew—but a warrior and self-styled avenger of his people. If Germaine Berton was acquitted in part because she was a woman, hence absolved of full responsibility for her actions, Schwartzbard was acquitted on the opposite ground that he fulfilled his responsibilities as a man of action.

In the 1930s, Schwartzbard would make speaking tours of the United States (presumably in the Ashkenazi lingua franca, Yiddish). In 1936, Schwartzbard addressed a gathering of the League Against Antisemitism in the working-class Paris suburb of Montreuil. His topic was the assassination the previous month of a Nazi official in Davos, Switzerland, by a young Jewish Yugoslav named David Frankfurter.[28] A decade after his *attentat*, Schwartzbard was still associated with Jewish violence against their persecutors. He died in 1938 while on a journalistic assignment in Capetown, South Africa. Later that year, another immigrant Jew, Herschel Grynzspan, committed a deed similar to Schwartzbard's and Frankfurter's, killing a Nazi official at the German Embassy in Paris. Schwartzbard acted in reprisal for pogroms carried out seven years earlier; Grynszpan's deed was the pretext for Hitler to unleash the German pogrom called Kristallnacht. As it happened, Schwartzbard benefited from better timing. 1927 proved to be the high point of benign French attitudes toward immigrants and Jews. Shortly before Schwartzbard's trial, French naturalization laws were relaxed, making it possible for many more immigrants to become French citizens, including fifty thousand Jews between 1927 and 1940.[29] (Vichy would later roll back the citizenship of all Jews naturalized after 1927.) By the late 1930s, many French appeasers blamed the Jews for wanting to provoke a war with

Germany, and even Torrès's considerable legal skills were not enough to free the teenaged assassin, who was handed over by Vichy to the Germans and died during the war.[30]

In the epilogue to her famous book on the trial of Adolf Eichmann, Hannah Arendt compared his 1961 trial to that of Schwartzbard, as well as to the trial of the Armenian Teilerian who assassinated Talaat Bey. Both assassins gave themselves up so that they could use their trials to publicize for the world the crimes committed against their peoples. Schwartzbard's trial was delayed until well over a year after his attack so that documentation of the Ukrainian pogroms could be assembled and published. Arendt was not comparing the Nazi agent of the Holocaust to the Jewish avenger of his people (in that case she might have compared Eichmann to Petliura), but rather connected *le procès des pogromes* to Eichmann's public trial in Jerusalem. She quotes from a letter Schwartzbard sent from his prison cell to the Jews of Odessa, Russia, in which he wanted it known throughout the region that "Jewish anger has worked in vengeance! The blood of the murderer Petliura, which spurted out in the world city, in Paris . . . redeemed the savage crime . . . committed against the poor and abandoned Jewish people."[31] For Arendt, the pogroms were not simply crimes against Jews but, as with Eichmann and the Holocaust, crimes against humanity.

How did French anarchists respond to the killing of Simon Petliura? At a time when *Le Libertaire* was filled with articles condemning the repression of anarchists in Bolshevik Russia, there was only minimal attention paid to the trial of the pogroms. *Le Libertaire* had reverted to being a weekly paper by 1927, so in the issue of October 21 that appeared during the trial it noted Schwartzbard's testimony on why he killed Petliura. A week later, the trial was over, but apparently the next week's issue had gone to press before the verdict was announced. They did publish a letter from the Ukrainian anarchist Nestor Makhno to Henry Torrès protesting the way in which prosecuting attorney Campinchi had attributed antisemitic acts to him and his followers during the civil war. In a long article, he disavowed any contact with Petliura and, as he had done frequently since Petliura's assassination, denied that he had perpetrated any pogroms.[32] There was no mention of the trial in the November 5 issue; instead the anarchist paper devoted most of its space to coverage of the Congress of the Union Anarchiste Communiste. This suggests that the major anarchist-communist paper did not identify Schwartzbard or Yiddish-speaking anarchists as part of their constituency. This minimal coverage contrasts greatly with its near-obsession with Germaine Berton four years earlier.

The individualist-anarchist paper *L'Anarchie* did comment on Schwartz-bard's *attentat* shortly after it occurred, strongly supporting his right to kill Petliura. The article, titled "The End of a Bandit," praised Schwartzbard not only for punishing Petliura but for preventing him from committing further murderous acts.[33] In evaluating the relative detachment of the main organs of Parisian anarchism to Schwartzbard's case, one must remember that until late August 1927, they were preoccupied with the fate of Sacco and Vanzetti. For example, the article in *L'Anarchie* that reported Schwartzbard's *attentat* carried a full-size poster on its center two pages, titled "A Monstrous Crime Is Going to Take Place ("Un crime monstrueux va s'accomplir"). As Louis Lecoin became increasingly involved with the defense committee for Sacco and Vanzetti, *Le Libertaire* became almost single minded in its coverage of the affair, and that coverage did not end with the deaths of the Italian-American anarchists. The riots that broke out in Paris after their executions were a major story, and the commemoration cortege that followed the arrival of their ashes in October was also heavily reported.

The Jews who did enjoy frequent access to the pages of *Le Libertaire* and other anarchist papers rarely discussed their religious origins and certainly did not practice their faith. Their disputes with the Bolsheviks and with each other had nothing to do with their Jewish origins. The only discussion of antisemitism that found a place among anarchists in the 1920s concerned Makhno's frequent denials of any such deeds on the part of his Ukrainian anarchist column during the civil war. Since these denials occurred through-out the years 1926 and 1927, they may be seen as a response to the issues raised by the Schwartzbard trial. Makhno pointed to the many Jews who were part of his contingent as proof that they could not have perpetrated pogroms. While it is clear that the Ukrainian nationalist forces and the counterrevo-lutionary White forces were primarily responsible, the Makhnovists and even the Bolsheviks might not have been entirely innocent of antisemitism.

The Schwartzbard Affair took place in France but reflected animosities of Central and Eastern Europe transferred to Paris. While there was a strong identification between Jews and the socialist and anarchist left east of the Rhine, the Jews of Western Europe were more assimilated and bourgeois. In the United States, Great Britain, and France, it was therefore primarily immigrant Jews from Eastern Europe who transferred the passions of their homelands to their new locales. A rare exception to this incursion of "Yid-dishland" into Western European anarchism was Bernard Lazare, who grad-uated from anarchism to Zionism in the 1890s after playing a key role in exposing the injustice done to Captain Alfred Dreyfus. Lazare died prema-turely shortly after the turn of the century, and so had little influence on the direction anarchism took in later years. The two attorneys who defended anarchists throughout the interwar period, Henry Torrès and Suzanne Lévy, were French Jews, but though widely respected by the *compagnons*, they were not themselves anarchists (Lévy was a communist, and Torrès became a left-wing deputy in the 1930s and a senator after the war). The French anarchists were aware of the tragic Jewish anarchists Gustav Landauer and Erich Mühsam in Germany; they were probably not familiar with the Jewish messianism of such intellectual luminaries as Gershon Scholem, Martin Buber, and Walter Benjamin.[34] Because of their extreme rationalist distrust of religion, very few French anarchists would have been sympathetic to this current of thought. Nor for that matter would most of the Russian or Polish Jewish anarchist émigrés who fled Bolshevik persecution. Nevertheless, they may well have shared a messianic hope in a future era of peace and justice that transcended the nation-state, even if they saw little correspondence between biblical theocracy and modern anarchy.[35] Whether as sociological outsiders or as ideological utopians, German and Yiddish-speaking Jews were particularly susceptible to the internationalist, liberating appeal of socialism and anarchism.

Radical Immigrants from the East

The interwar period witnessed a decline in the Yiddish-speaking population of London, compared to a vibrant presence in the East End from the 1890s to 1914. No such decline took place in Paris given the renewed immigration into that city's east end. From the Marais, centering on the rue des Rosiers, the Jewish immigrants expanded north into Belleville and the place de la République, which became known as the *pletzl*. Parisian Jewish anarchists would organize a youth group, the Fraye Sotsialistn (Free socialists) in 1924, and also reconstitute the Yiddish anarchist newspaper the *Arbayter-fraynt* (Free worker), which had ceased publication in London in 1922.[36] At the turn of the century, the French police estimated eleven thousand Russian immigrants had come to France, which swelled to twenty-five thousand after the pogroms and repression following the 1905 revolution; they guessed that three-quarters were Jewish. Politically, while "all are not partisans of violence . . . all are partisans of revolutionary acts in a more general sense."[37] In the police breakdown of this immigrant population, they estimated that there were one hundred individualist anarchists and four hundred fifty communist anarchists, not all of whom were Jews. They also estimated that three hundred members belonged to the socialist Jewish Bund.[38] The Jewish anarchist communist group was led by a hatter named Kasavielski, which included Jewish workers of the fourth and eighteenth arrondissements. The Agitator group led by Grinstein included both Jews and Orthodox Christians. The American-Jewish anarchist Emma Goldman spoke to them in September 1907 and recommended greater contact with French anarchists, saying, "The revolution will come in five hundred years if the anarchists of all nationalities persist in not putting their forces in common."[39] The police appeared to be concerned about just such an eventuality. They also reported that the previous Yom Kippur, more than four hundred people gathered for a banquet and dance organized by the Russian Jews (unusual behavior for this solemn high holy day) and added that "nearly all were followers of anarchy."[40] In May 1909, a short-lived federation of Jewish anarchist groups in Paris was formed to create a library and establish relations with non-Jewish anarchist groups.[41] This was the active anarchist context that Sholom Schwartbard and many other Jewish émigrés encountered when they arrived in Paris.

One such revolutionary Jewish emigrant to France, Hersh Mendel Sztokfisz, survived revolutions, wars, and the Holocaust, and wrote his autobiography in 1959 at the age of seventy-nine. Written in Yiddish and published initially in Tel Aviv, it was translated into French after the author's death. Though born in Warsaw in 1880 rather than Ukraine in 1888 like Sholom Schwartzbard, in other respects Hersh Mendel's life parallels Schwartzbard's closely. Both fled the Russian Empire after the Revolution of 1905, both came to Paris and became anarchists, and both returned to Russia after the outbreak of the February 1917 revolution. The preface by Isaac Deutscher, the notable biographer of Trotsky, written in 1958, called Mendel's story an exceptional and rare example of a working-class autobiography. It is even rarer as a record of a vanished leftist Yiddish culture and shows both how a Jewish immigrant decided to become an anarchist and how that affiliation was mutable in the context of the tumultuous events he experienced.

Mendel says he was projected out of the slums of his Polish *shtetl* by the Russian Revolution of 1905. He'd read in Maxim Gorky that all revolutionaries must visit the Place de la Bastille, so he arrived in Paris with half a franc and knowing a single French phrase, "rue des Rosiers!"[42] There in the Marais he could communicate with everyone since they were all Jewish. He spoke of meeting a variety of socialist émigrés, including Trotsky, Plekhanov, and Lunacharsky, but felt his ideals betrayed in August 1914, when the French socialists supported the war. Then he heard Plekhanov tell them to go to war and wait to settle their accounts with the tsar. Yet at the Jewish socialist Bund, the majority opposed the war. Foreigners were being sent out of Paris, so he left for a village near Tours. Of the twenty Jews there, all were anarchists except for him. His description of these comrades borders on the satirical: some were back-to-nature types who grew their hair and nails long, others were Nietzscheans who wanted to be supermen, one thought people read Marx's *Capital* in order to learn how to make a fortune, another was an aesthete who admired Oscar Wilde. Many were bohemians who liberally imbibed poetry, philosophy, and wine. One of these was a real painter, Avram Reizen, who became a celebrated artist later in life.[43] Yet despite Mendel's reservations concerning anarchist eccentricities, he concluded that the failure of socialism led him to believe in the superiority of anarchism. Anarchist rejection of all discipline meant it necessarily was antimilitarist and antiwar. (In fact the war split the anarchists as well, with Jean Grave and Peter Kropotkin favoring the allied cause against German militarism. Nor did it hinder Schwartzbard from volunteering to fight for France.) Whereas socialism was based on economics, anarchists followed humanist moral principles, and military discipline was the antithesis of human dignity. With that entree, he began to read Kropotkin, Reclus, and Malatesta, and then the anarchizing nineteenth-century writers: Tolstoy, Wilde, and Ibsen. After returning to Paris in 1916, he and three other Jewish immigrants planned to attack the Russian ambassador, Isvolsky; they would have attempted his assassination if the Russian Revolution hadn't intervened. With news of the February revolution, the whole rue des Rosiers was flying red flags and the people burst out in revolutionary songs.[44]

As with Sholom Schwartzbard, so Hersh Mendel headed back to Russia in 1917. Stopping first in London to visit his brother, he then set sail for Norway. Despite his antimilitarism, he joined a regiment that was strongly influenced by the Bolsheviks and fought on the barricades in Moscow during the October Revolution. He felt that no one had experienced such scenes since the fall of the Bastille and the Paris Commune, thereby making explicit the revolutionary connections between France and Russia. Yet when the Kremlin fell and the White soldiers holding it left to join General Kornilov, he took off his uniform as soon as possible, as it didn't accord with his anarchist tastes.[45] He was sent south with his regiment to fight the Whites and was told that his Jewish countenance would endanger him when they met the Cossacks. Before that happened, the anarchists in the regiment were separated out and told to join other anarchists fighting on another front, so he and the other anarchist in the group took a boat for Nijni-Novgorod. Again he criticized the anarchists, who appeared ill disciplined compared to the Bolsheviks. He ended up in Odessa, where he says he met up with old friends from Paris; one wonders if Schwartzbard was among that group.

Mendel also encountered the waves of antisemitism wracking Ukraine, and early in 1919 left for Warsaw, where he hoped to organize anarcho-syndicalist unions on the French model. When he discovered back in Poland that his father had died of hunger in 1915, his mother and sister in 1918, he ceased political activity for a while. At this point, he read Lenin's 1917 book *State and Revolution* and was convinced that the Bolsheviks were pursuing the same essential goals as the anarchists: "The true way was finally found: by the class struggle of the proletariat, in passing through the dictatorship of the proletariat toward a stateless world, without laws or constraints. It is with profound faith and joy that I entered into the communist ranks."[46] Mendel became a communist because he thought they were really anarchists at heart! He subsequently moved between Poland and Russia, finally returning to France in 1934, where he had a two-hour-long conversation with the exiled Leon Trotsky about the situation in Poland. For a while he was a Trotskyist, then broke with the Fourth International, returned to Warsaw in 1936, and then fled back to Paris in 1938. This volume of his autobiography ends here, and according to the translator, Suchecky, he never did write the promised second volume of his memoirs. Mendel died in Israel in 1969, apparently unhappy in his later years trying to balance the competing claims of socialism and Zionist nationalism.

Hersh Mendel's story offers suggestive similarities and interesting contrasts with that of Sholom Schwartzbard. Though both men left their adopted home in France to fight for the Russian Revolution, Mendel became an anarchist while in France whereas Schwartzbard arrived there as one. Both men fought with or for the Red Army, both found that their ethnicity and their politics caused them problems, and both left Russia, Mendel for his native Poland and Schwartzbard for France. Mendel joined the Communist Party, showing how fluid leftist political affiliation could be. Yet his meeting with the apostate Trotsky in the 1930s shows his unwillingness to tolerate the dictatorial regime imposed on the Soviet Union. Mendel was a socialist or Bundist in Warsaw, an anarchist in France, a Red Guard in Ukraine, a communist in Poland, and a Zionist in Tel Aviv. He seems to have been closest ideologically to the anarchists and syndicalists but was swept up by the achievements and greater organizational abilities of the communists. Under Lenin he thought he might have it both ways; Stalin evidently disabused him of that possibility. Both men really did embody the legend of the Wandering Jew, as they moved back and forth across Europe, and even to America and Israel, though Schwartzbard's notoriety kept him out of the latter destination. Revolutionary Jews were doubly stateless.

Anarchists' reluctance to acknowledge their religious background as in any way relevant to their politics helps explain why Schwartzbard divorced his act of revenge from his anarchist ideals, even though the ideology of direct action probably influenced his behavior. An anecdote underscores the extreme anarchist distrust of any vestige of religious practice. Ida Mett arrived in Paris in 1926, having fled the Soviet Union before completing her medical studies due to her anarchist convictions. In Paris, she wrote for the Russian-language anarchist journal *Dielo Trouda*. When she heard that her father, Meyer Gilman, had died back in Russia, she lit a candle in his memory in accordance with Jewish tradition. For this act of filial piety, the young woman was excluded from the newspaper staff in 1928. She apparently faced discrimination both from her fellow anarchists and from the French state since that same year she and her husband, Nicholas Lazarevitch, were expelled from France.[47] Anarchists considered religiosity to be a female attribute, but it is unclear whether this played a role in drumming her out of the group.

Anti-Bolshevik Russian Jews

The biggest issue facing the mostly Jewish Russian anarchist immigrants in the 1920s was the repression of anarchists in Russia. *Le Libertaire* was replete with articles protesting the imprisonment of particular anarchists, which often served as a prelude to condemning the Bolshevik regime as a whole. The second most important issue to preoccupy the anarchist émigrés was that of organization, a perennial problem for anarchists and one that was highlighted by the Russians' experiences in losing out to the better organized Bolsheviks during the Russian Revolution. The organizational debate would precipitate a major split in French anarchist ranks. These debates did not concern Jews as such, though many of those involved were Jewish. The third issue, precipitated by the Schwartzbard affair, concerned antisemitism within the Russian anarchist ranks. Nestor Makhno protested repeatedly that his peasant band was not responsible for any outrages perpetrated against the Ukrainian Jews. Makhno and his ally, Peter Arshinov, who wrote a history of the Makhnovite movement in Ukraine, were the principal defenders of the so-called Platform that advocated more centralized organization, and many of the Jewish anarchists condemned the Platform approach, so the issues may have been related.

Russian anarchists were becoming disenchanted by the Soviet regime as early as 1918. On September 25, 1918, anarchists along with members of the peasant-based Social Revolutionary Party bombed the headquarters of the

Moscow Committee of the Communist Party; both anarchists and social revolutionaries were motivated by the arrest of others in their parties. Twelve communists were killed and fifty-five wounded; among the latter group was Nikolai Bukharin, editor of the communist newspaper *Pravda*.[48] This violent act led to further arrests. Soon anarchist newspapers were being shut down. Still, with the White counterrevolution threatening, quite a few anarchists supported and fought for the Bolsheviks, and were known as "Soviet anarchists."

Many went to Ukraine to join Nestor Makhno's anarchist partisans. Yet when the civil war ended with Trotsky's Red Army victorious, the Bolsheviks turned on the Makhnovites and dispersed them by the end of 1920, with the Cheka (the Soviet secret police) arresting or simply shooting many of the anarchists.[49] The suppression of the Kronstadt uprising in March 1921, in which sailors stationed near Petrograd resisted Bolshevik Party authority in the name of the soviets, led to a new wave of arrests of anarchists throughout Russia. Early in 1922, Lenin decided to release the better-known anarchist prisoners, provided they leave the country at once. Maksimov, Volin, Mrachny, Iarchuk, and some others departed for Berlin. Some who had not been imprisoned but were profoundly dispirited, such as Emma Goldman, Alexander Berkman, and Sanya Schapiro, left soon after.[50] These were the lucky ones; many others ended up in the gulag. Their escaped brethren tirelessly protested their comrades' imprisonment, meanwhile sending them letters and parcels.

In 1925, before most of the tensions between the Russian émigrés rose to the surface, a group of Jewish anarchists wrote a collective letter to *Le Libertaire* protesting Soviet treatment of anarchists. They called themselves the Gustav Landauer group, after the German-Jewish anarchist intellectual who was killed during the abortive attempt to install a soviet government in Bavaria in 1919 (most of the leadership of the utopian revolution in Bavaria was Jewish, including Erich Mühsam and Ernst Toller).[51] In a May Day article, they noted that Maria Spiridonova, long held in tsarist prisons for her revolutionary activities, was now being attacked by the Bolsheviks, that the Cheka was sending people to Solovetsky prison camp in the far north, and that the anarchist comrade Aron Baron had been arrested again. They concluded by demanding the liberation of political prisoners of all countries.[52] This demand was echoed in succeeding years by a plethora of articles contributed by the Russian Jewish émigrés Senya Fleshin, Mollie Steimer, Alexander Berkman, and Volin, pen name of Vsevolod Eichenbaum. Typical was the article of June 1926 titled "Imposteurs et assassins," which urged the anarchist readers to pay attention to the article by Fleshin, Steimer, and

Volin in the same issue that listed the names of anarchists being persecuted by the Bolsheviks. While the communists protested murders of leftists in Italy, Spain, and Hungary, in fact hangmen from all countries must be condemned, so the article said, for there was no difference between Red and White reactionaries: "Bolsheviks are imposters and murderers."[53] The Russian émigrés not only protested their comrades' plight but sent them packages and letters of encouragement and created organizations to protest their persecution. Numerous letters from the prisoners made it back to Western Europe, with postmarks with stamps from Siberia, the White Sea, and other locales of what would become known as the gulag.[54]

Perhaps the most sustained campaign carried out on behalf of an imprisoned comrade in the Soviet Union was that for Nicholas Lazarevitch (1895–1975). Lazarevitch was born not in Russia but in Belgium, and so had particularly strong ties to French-speaking Europe. His parents had fled to Belgium to escape from the tsar after joining in the People's Will terrorist organization of the 1880s. His mother came from a noble family and had been disinherited for marrying a Jew. Lazarevitch became an anarchist while an adolescent, made his way to Russia after the Russian Revolution, and arrived in Moscow in January 1919. He joined the Red Army but soon had doubts about the Bolsheviks. In the 1920s he belonged to a group that read and translated such Western anarchist periodicals as *Le Libertaire*. He was arrested for spreading anarcho-syndicalist propaganda among the workers. After an extensive protest campaign, he was allowed to leave Russia, arrived in Paris in the autumn of 1926, and married Ida Mett. The following year he and Volin wrote *As in the Time of the Tsars: Exile and Prison in Russia*. Lazarevitch made a lecture tour of France to counter pro-Soviet propaganda and debated the French pacifist and left intellectual Romain Rolland, who had helped in his release but who now praised the great strides made by the Soviets.[55] Lazarevitch's story is strikingly similar to that of Victor Kibalchich, who took the revolutionary name Victor Serge. Serge was also born in Belgium of revolutionary émigré parents, five years before Lazarevitch. He also returned to Russia to join the revolution, would end up in Stalin's prisons until a major campaign liberated him in the 1930s, and also benefited from the intervention of the French writer Romain Rolland. Unlike so many of the other émigrés, Serge was not Jewish.

By the mid-1920s, a number of important Russian anarchists had settled in Paris, where they would exert an immediate impact on the native anarchist movement. As well as continually protesting the persecution of anarchists in the Soviet Union, and trying to expose the nature of the police state that had crushed their movement there, they also reacted to the failure of Russian anarchism by trying to reform a movement that seemed to have lost its way. In November 1926, led by Peter Arshinov and Nestor Makhno, a group calling itself the Platform suggested that the failure of anarchism in the real revolutionary context of the Russian Civil War was primarily due to lack of organization. They proposed that the anarchists follow the Bolsheviks in forming a more unified and centralized international to advance their libertarian goals. There was also talk of creating a "black army" of revolutionary self-defense. Arshinov resided in Berlin, but other Russian and Polish émigrés joined Makhno in supporting a conception of anarchism as a party of action, following the example of Bakunin and Malatesta, as opposed to what they termed the "old school" of anarchists such as Sébastien Faure who placed most emphasis on education. One of the most combative was Maxim Ranko, whose real name was Benjamin Goldberg; the police reported that he came to Paris bearing a Polish passport in 1924. In Paris he helped found a Polish anarchist group and played a prominent role in the meeting attended by sixteen foreign-born and eight French anarchists at the Cinema les Roses in Hay-les-Roses outside Paris in March 1927. At that meeting, closely watched by the police, Makhno's speech was translated by Walecki, whose real name was Isaac Gurfinkiel, also active in the Polish Anarchist Group in Paris. Ranko distrusted intellectual theorizing and preferred to focus on organization and action. Several articles on the Platform written by Ranko appeared in *Le Libertaire*.[56]

The Platform group managed temporarily to take over control of the Union Anarchiste and its organ of publicity, *Le Libertaire*. If they hoped to unify and centralize French and other anarchists, their initiative accomplished the reverse. Sébastien Faure, founder of *Le Libertaire* thirty years before, denounced what he termed the bolshevization of anarchism and was joined by a number of Russian Jewish émigrés who found the whole idea to be anathema to anarchist ideals of decentralization and autonomy. Faure was joined by the most important of these émigrés, Volin, who had returned to Paris in 1924. They created an Anarchist Federation to rival the Anarchist Union, and a new paper, *La Voix Libertaire,* as an alternative to Faure's old paper. Faure called for a new synthesis to heal the split between anarchist factions: he wanted individualists, syndicalists, and anarchist communists to join together. Yet just as the Platformists could not unify the fissiparous movement, so the Synthesists also failed to go anywhere. By the end of the 1920s, the police were reporting that *Le Voix Libertaire* had only attracted fifteen hundred readers, as compared to four thousand for *Le Libertaire,* and was only kept alive at all in its headquarters in Limoges because of the presence of the grand old man of anarchism, Sébastien Faure.[57] The police summarized that the Russians were divided between Volin and Fleshin, partisans of synthesis, and Makhno and Arshinov, who sought a World Union of Anarchists. They reported that Makhno was called the "living cadaver" (he was dying of tuberculosis), and also noted that the Italian and Spanish anarchists were most likely to engage in antifascist activities. The factions would eventually reunify in the crisis year of 1936, as workers engaged in mass strikes and Spain erupted in a civil war in which anarchists played a prominent role. By that time, the impact of Russian émigrés on French anarchism was much diminished.

While the majority of Eastern European Jews came to France to escape persecution and pogroms and to find better economic opportunities, many of the anarchist ideologues came in the aftermath of revolutions—first, that of 1905, and then that of October 1917. Volin is a good example of this pattern, as is Sholom Schwartzbard. Volin was exiled to Siberia after the 1905 revolution, and leaving his wife and children behind, made his way to Paris by 1908. It would be a decade before he would see them again, when he returned to Russia after the February 1917 revolution along with so many other exiles. In between, he had fled war-torn France for the United States in 1915. He played a major role in the Russian anarchist movement first in Petrograd and then in Ukraine, where he joined Makhno's military council. When the Red Army routed the Makhnovites, he was arrested and almost executed by Trotsky but was saved by the intervention of Victor Serge and Alexander Berkman. He was not free for long. When he tried to organize an anarchist congress, slated to open on December 25, 1920, he and the entire anarchist leadership were arrested. Ten anarchists went on a hunger strike to protest their status as political prisoners; of these ten, six were Jews: Volin, Mratchny, Yartchouc, Feldman, Gorelik, and Fleshin. Thanks to the intervention of French and Spanish anarcho-syndicalists, they were released and deported.[58] They made their way to Germany, and Volin returned to France in 1924, this time accompanied by his wife and six children. The police report of September 1927 said Volin was working as a proofreader and translator for the journal *Commerce, Industrie et Finances,* where he earned fifteen hundred francs a month. He also translated Makhno's memoirs, which had recently appeared serialized in *Le Libertaire.*[59] Volin also wrote the most important history of the anarchists in the Russian Revolution, *La révolution inconnue* (The unknown revolution).[60] Volin survived the multiple dangers of being a foreigner, an anarchist, and a Jew in Vichy France, only to die at the end of the war in 1945.

The anarchist movement reached a low point in the late 1920s and early 1930s, which left Sébastien Faure time to devote his energies to his ambitious

Encyclopédie anarchiste, the four-volume first (and ultimately only) part of which, the dictionary, was completed by 1934. In that first volume, Faure himself wrote the long description of *anarchie.* It was followed by another quite lengthy discussion of *anti-sémitisme* by Volin, who blamed the phenomenon on nationalism and chauvinism. He explained the upsurge of antisemitism in recent times as nationalist rather than religious as in earlier eras, as governments such as that of the tsar directed mass hatred against an alien "race" rather than at the real sources of social problems. He discussed the pogroms under the tsar and also those in Ukraine during the civil war, and largely blamed the Whites and nationalists for killing thousands and raping every woman over the age of ten. In the Soviet Union all restrictive laws were abolished and there were no more ghettos or Pales of Settlement, but since many resented the Bolsheviks and many of their leaders, such as Trotsky and Zinoviev, were Jews, antisemitism remained strong there. It was an incontestable fact, Volin wrote, that the Jews were still hated by the ignorant masses.[61] Volin feared that if the Bolshevik government fell, a new round of pogroms could easily ensue. He acknowledged that antisemitism existed throughout Europe and America, but that all the caricatures of the greedy Jew would disappear with the end of capitalism. Millions of Jewish workers retained the best qualities of the "race": the spirit of solidarity, fraternity, and idealism. Antisemitism, the anarchist concluded, was the most hideous manifestation of modern nationalism and would only disappear when that nefarious ideology had ceased to captivate people.

Leftist Antisemitism

Notwithstanding Volin's cogent analysis of the sources of modern antisemitism, France was both capitalist and nationalist, and prejudice against Jews was not unknown even within anarchist ranks. The police reported that on March 31, 1926, two hundred fifty people attended the anarchist-organized discussion group Club des Insurgés to hear Albert Letell speak on the topic, "Do we need to fear Jewish imperialism?" Letell admitted that the two hundred forty thousand Jews currently residing in France posed no threat, but argued that one did need to remember the role that Jewish bankers played in financing the war profiteers of 1914. He gave examples of factories that produced war materiel and claimed that Jewish-owned shipping escaped unscathed while sailing in the Black Sea, while most other ships were sunk. The role of Jewish capital in the world war gave them reason to fear their imperialism. In the discussion period after the lecture, André Colomer, founder of the newspaper *L'Insurgé* as well as the club of the same name, said that one must recognize that Jews arrived poor in France but determined to enrich themselves and seize power. "In France, in a short time they will be at the head of the judiciary, of the army and of the large commercial firms; when they attain their goal, from persecuted they will become persecutors, and that will be the reign of Jewish imperialism."[62] These sentiments of the prominent anarchist poet, writer, and publicist André Colomer suggest that he was probably responsible for arranging the topic of that night's talk in the first place. While he may have been expressing resentment at the increasingly prominent place that foreign-born Jews were playing in the anarchist movement, it is more likely that he was simply expressing traditional left-wing antisemitism that stigmatized Jews as capitalists and *arrivistes* who crowded out small artisans from the market.

Clear evidence of French anarchist resentment at Jewish anarchists emerged a few years later, as the rise of the Nazis in Germany and the threat of right-wing leagues in France made the anarchists even more marginal. From 1922 to 1925, the mainstream anarchist-communist newspaper *Le Libertaire* under the auspices of Sébastien Faure and André Colomer had created a monthly review of ideas called *La Revue Anarchiste*. That title was revived in 1929 by another anarchist, Fernand Fortin, and the journal was published irregularly until 1936. Fortin's antisemitism emerged visibly in 1934 in his discussion of the young Dutch anarchist Marinus Van der Lubbe, who was tried that year for having burned down the Reichstag during the German election campaign the previous year. Fortin seemed to accept that Van der Lubbe had indeed started the fire, and argued that he was not an agent provocateur but a dedicated revolutionary who hoped to awaken the workers to engage in the political struggle. Just as with the French terrorists of the 1890s, who were also sincere revolutionaries, the consequences may well have played into Hitler's hands. Fortin also acknowledged that Van der Lubbe may have been homosexual, but was not disturbed by the revelation. What did disturb him was the condemnation of the act by pro-Jewish anarchists in Germany, most notably Rudolph Rocker, whom Fortin called the "Yiddish Lighthouse."[63] While denying that he was antisemitic, he said that everyone knew of Jewish "salon anarchists" who made revolution all their lives, if need be on the backs of their comrades. Leftist Jews were accused of being self-righteous moralists and even nationalists, presumably a reference to Zionism. Fortin defended the individual deed as the most elementary manifestation of the freedom of the individual, and when such a person was condemned by bourgeois justice, the least the left could do would be to maintain a dignified silence. Elsewhere in the same issue,

an advertisement noted that a woman companion of "one of our best German comrades" had chronic bronchitis and was seeking to stay for several
months in a warmer climate. She would give German lessons and help with
household work. The ad reassuringly noted that she had "nothing in common with the Yid way of abusing comrades" (*rien de commun avec façons
youpines d'abuser des camarades*).[64]

Later than same year, Fortin clarified what he meant by using the deroga-
tory term "youpins" to refer to Jews. He reiterated that "we are not anti-
Semites but anti-youpins. Meaning by this term . . . exploiting another. All
in all frankness, without partiality, if pure Aryans exist who are famously
yids, one must acknowledge that the great majority of yids are recruited
among the semites."[65] The self-proclaimed non-antisemite reported a conversation with a friend, who had declared that we should purge our movement of all the "yids" who come to us under ideological pretexts and only
seek to take over by any means whatsoever. He also reported the words of
comrade Rhillon, who said the time of the Dreyfus Affair was over when
the "copains" were in the forefront of the struggle and then found themselves condemned by those they worked so hard to defend. If Fortin and
his individualist comrades were any indication, the anarchists were feeling
embattled and so were closing ranks and attacking those they perceived to
be outsiders. Fearful of the communist left and fascist right, they lashed
out at Jewish fellow travelers as insincere revolutionaries. As a new wave of
Jewish refugees poured into France from across the Rhine, French antisemitism increased, especially in the context of the Depression in which
jobs were scarce. Anarchists were not immune to such feelings, especially
when Jewish animus against the Nazis was feared as pulling France into a
new war. In the late 1930s, die-hard anarchist pacifists such as Maurice
Wullens would prefer appeasement at any price to anything that might
increase the chances of war. While the right stigmatized Jews as cosmopol-
itan internationalists, the left attacked them as nationalists (Zionists) and
capitalists.

Fernand Fortin, editor of *La Revue Anarchiste,* was one of the few contributors to the journal to sign his articles with his own name. Nearly all the
rest used mocking pseudonyms, such as George Withoutname and Nobody
(both in English), or G. Styr-Nair (playing on Stirner, the Young Hegelian
father of anarchist individualists). They had good reason to hide their identities for fear of prosecution. In 1935, Fortin got a six-month prison sentence
for having called people who assaulted stoolpigeons, broke bakery shop windows to get bread if they were hungry, or stole a strongbox and appropri-
ated its contents as "propagandists by the deed." On appeal, his sentence

was reduced to two months. Then in the final, April/June 1936 issue, Fortin published Georges Yvetot's "Manual of a Soldier," which counseled desertion. For this he was condemned to two years in prison and a thousand-franc fine. He was defended by comrade Suzanne Lévy, who was Jewish; presumably Fortin did not consider her to be among the "youpins."[66]

One can get a sense of the ideological diversity within the interwar anarchist movement by contrasting Fortin's individualist rants with the more measured, intellectual discourse of *Plus Loin* (Further). This monthly review was published from 1925 until 1939 by Dr. Marc Pierrot, who was a follower of the anarchist-communist Jean Grave. In March 1934, Dr. Pierrot confided that the staff of *Plus Loin* was nicknamed the Association of the Under-Eighties, referring to their advanced ages. In many ways then, this journal was probably not typical of how most anarchists thought. An interesting feature of the journal was its periodic discussion of current topics, with various anarchists commenting on a topic and the conversation transcribed and printed in the journal. In the 1930s, the journal paid increasing attention to both Zionism and antisemitism and invited leftist Jews such as Bernard Lecache and L. Filderman to join in discussion with Pierrot, Paul Reclus, and other anarchist intellectuals. In 1934, Pierrot wrote that anarchists could appreciate Zionism as an interesting social experiment but remained hostile to it as a form of narrow and separatist nationalism. Yet two years later, Filderman contributed an article on "The Social Innovations in Palestine," in which he discussed the collectivist colonies there, which he called *kvoutsoth* rather than *kibbutzim*. Of one hundred sixty colonies, ninety were based on collective ownership of property, and the peasants who farmed the land were also intellectuals who actively propagated musical and theatrical troupes. The following month, the journal published a discussion based on Filderman's article. In response to questions from Pierrot and the syndicalist leader Pierre Besnard, Filderman reported that the Zionist workers adhered to the international workers movement much as the French CGT did, that commerce between colonies took place on a cooperative basis, and that tools were bought through cooperatives. He also expressed a strong preference for Hebrew over Yiddish, which "for us is the language of slavery."[67] Pierrot pointed out that the eighteen thousand workers in these colonies were still a small fraction of the total Jewish population and feared that their idealism was being counterbalanced by fanatic Jewish nationalists such as Jabotinsky. While these anarchists remained skeptical of Jewish nationalism, they were at least free of any trace of antisemitism and were willing to consider Jewish settlements in Palestine as an interesting social experiment.

Mécislas Golberg and Mécislas Charrier, Jewish Anarchist Father and Son

Modern Zionism was founded as a direct response to the wave of antisemitism that swept France during the Dreyfus Affair of the 1890s. Some anarchists initially responded to the condemnation of Dreyfus with indifference, seeing him as a rich Jew and army officer. Most anarchists eventually took the Dreyfusard position against the church, the military hierarchy, and antisemitism, with Sébastien Faure leading the way.[68] Jewish anarchists had no such hesitation in defending Dreyfus. Bernard Lazare is by far the best-known Jewish anarchist, who played a key role in helping to reopen the case and then became active in the early Zionist movement before dying at only thirty-eight in 1903.[69] Lazare was a French-born Jew from a bourgeois background. By contrast, Mécislas Golberg was a Jewish immigrant from Poland whose anarchism made him more vulnerable to police persecution. He was exiled twice by the French authorities, once to London for his anarchist activities in 1896, then again in January 1898 to Brussels for his Dreyfusard activism. Up until his own premature death in 1907 at the age of thirty-seven, he lived under the threat of expulsion.[70] Golberg was marginal in every way when compared with Lazare (his name does not even appear in Wilson's biography of his fellow Jewish anarchist), and like Lazare he died well before the interwar era. Nevertheless, to conclude this discussion of anarchist Jews, I want to briefly discuss Golberg to establish the connections between him and two other Jewish figures who were involved in the interwar anarchist movement. One of these was Golberg's illegitimate son, Mécislas Charrier; the other was the Alsatian-born writer Yvan Goll. Charrier was directly influenced by the legend that had grown around his anarchist father; Goll is connected to Golberg indirectly, in terms of parallel political and literary themes that expressed both men's sense of displacement and international identity.

Mécislas Golberg also derived from a bourgeois Jewish background and journeyed from his native Poland to Switzerland to pursue his ambitions for higher education. He came to France in 1891, just at the moment that anarchism was achieving a high profile in the avant-gardes of literature, art, and politics. In pursuing a career as a writer and anarchist, Golberg soon jettisoned whatever was left of his bourgeois background and lived a notoriously hand-to-mouth existence for the rest of his brief life. Despite his slender resources, Golberg founded an anarchist journal in 1895 called *Sur le Trimard,* which he described as the "organ of demands of the unemployed."[71] A *trimardeur* was more equivalent to a hobo than merely an unemployed person. Itinerant anarchist *trimardeurs* traveled the countryside spreading the anarchist message through pamphlets, songs, and harangues. He was a figure with whom Golberg could identify. After the explosion of the Dreyfus Affair made Golberg more conscious of his Jewishness, he contributed, along with Lazare, to a Jewish anarchist Zionist paper called *Le Flambeau*. Golberg saw in Zionism the revolutionary emancipation of Judaism, not the failed version of 1791 that had led to Jewish assimilation and antisemitism. He imagined the Jewish vagabond becoming a heroic figure embodying the highest values of the intellect.[72] In a book called *Lazare le ressuscité* (Lazarus raised from the dead) he wrote in 1901, Golberg conjoined anarchism and Judaism as he imagined the wandering Jew as a subversive force in the world.

At the same time as Golberg began publishing his journal *Sur le Trimard,* he also fathered a son with a woman named Berthe Charrier. This son was called Jacques-Mécislas Charrier, and as his name suggests he was raised by his mother and knew of his father only by reputation. After serving in World War I, he spent two years in jail for collecting his demobilization pay six different times. On his release, he became a medical student (his father had done the same in 1893) and also like his father suffered from tuberculosis. On July 25, 1921, Charrier and two other men held up a first-class railroad car on the Paris-Marseille route. During the hold-up, one passenger resisted and was killed. The police found Charrier's accomplices dining at a café a week later and both were killed in a brief gun battle. Charrier had only been the lookout and so might have looked forward to a relatively light sentence when his trial opened in April 1922. He ruined those chances by proclaiming his adherence to anarchist illegality, calling the robbery *"une reprise individuelle,"* or individual appropriation, the term used by the pre-war proponents of the right to theft. He also proudly proclaimed his connection to his anarchist father, though he hardly knew him and Golberg had died when Charrier was just twelve years old. Condemned to death, he signed his last statement "medical student and libertarian militant."[73] As he was marched to the guillotine, he sang the "Internationale and the Carmagnole," probably in imitation of the anarchist terrorist Ravachol thirty years before. Philippe Oriol calls this pathetic, wayward figure the last person to be executed for anarchism.[74] A year later, Germaine Berton would escape such punishment even though she did kill and (like Charrier) failed to express any remorse for her crime. She did benefit from having a better lawyer; in fact Maître Campinchi, who represented Charrier, opposed Henry Torrès in the courtroom at Berton's trial and lost (again). It may not be particularly significant that a young man of Jewish origin was the last anarchist to lose his life for his ideals, if that is indeed why he died. Though his case had little resonance in anarchist circles, it was covered by André Salmon, a writer who had known Charrier's father, in the anarchist literary journal *Action*. Other friends of Golberg, such as the writer André Rouveyre, also wrote about the case and revived the memory of the fin de siècle Jewish *tri-mardeur*. The father and son who shared the name Mécislas suggest the affinity between Jews, particularly displaced ones, and libertarian ideals.

Yvan Goll, Marc Chagall, and Jewish-Leftist Art

The poet and writer Yvan Goll had more in common with Mécislas the father than the son, starting with his name. Golberg's name was actually Goldberg; he dropped the "d" on coming to France (as well as Gallicizing the Polish Mieszyslaw). Goll was born Isaac Lang but used some variant of Yvan Goll throughout his career (his pseudonyms included Iwan Goll, Ivan Goll, and even Gollivan). He was born to Abraham Lang and Rebecca Lazard in 1891 in St. Dié in the Vosges. His father was Alsatian, his mother came from Metz in Lorraine and raised him there after his father died in 1897. That ancestry made him a German citizen, twenty-three years of age when war broke out in 1914. To escape military service, Goll fled to Switzerland, where he joined the literary pacifists including Romain Rolland, Stefan Zweig, and James Joyce. Joyce and Goll remained friends until Joyce's death. In Switzerland, Goll wrote a collection of poems called *Elegies internationaux,* as well as a "Requiem pour les morts de l'Europe, 1916–17." In a poem called "Noémi" from 1917, Goll acknowledged his Jewish heritage, writing, "Hear O Israel, Adonai was your God, Adonai was the only one [*l'Unique*]." Noémi, described as a daughter of the ghetto, is destined to "give to the ancient faith the name of knowledge [Connaissance]."[75] This poetic activity attracted the attention of a young woman who soon became Claire Goll. I emphasize the Jewish themes of Goll's writing because as with most secularized, leftist Jews, Goll rarely refers to his Jewishness. At the end of his life, Goll did emphasize his internationalism, writing, "I leave with a French heart, German spirit, Jewish blood and an American passport."[76]

The Golls arrived in Paris in November 1919, but even before they arrived Goll had contributed a translation of fourteen poems by German antiwar poets to Maurice Wullens's anarchist journal *Les Humbles*. Wullens titled this collection "Le coeur de l'ennemi" (Heart of the enemy). He became a frequent contributor to Florent Fels's literary anarchist journal *Action* beginning in 1920, publishing his own poems (including one called "Les juifs mendiants") as well as articles on German expressionism, on the sculptor

Archipenko, and so forth. Equally fluent in French and German, Goll functioned as an intermediary between the two cultures and translated and edited
a collection of poems from around the world in 1922 called *Cinq continents*
(Five continents). Goll also, however, contributed to Henri Barbusse's leftist journal *Clarté*, which started out as an independent leftist and antiwar
publication but by 1922 was turning into the intellectual organ of the French
Communist Party. Since both *Les Humbles* and *Action* were as strongly pacifist as they were anarchist, it is possible that Goll's connection with them
signified his internationalism rather than an explicitly anarchist orientation.
None of his biographers identify him as an anarchist writer, though one
characterizes his twin ideals as individualism and humanism, the former
suggesting liberation and the latter as his social mission, which is more
congruent with anarchism than socialism.[77] Another calls him a "romantic
nihilist," a sufficiently vague term that also places him closer to anarchism
than communism.[78] None of his critics, however, discuss his most avowedly
anarchist book.

In 1925, Yvan Goll published the only book ever written on the trial of
Germaine Berton. *Germaine Berton, die rote Jungfrau* was published in Berlin
as part of a series of books with a leftist orientation. While it is possible that
Goll wrote the book more as a money-making venture than as a piece of
anarchist propaganda, he vilified Léon Daudet in the book and idealized
Berton, describing her at one point as having "a soul of burning iron." At
the very least he wanted to inform the German public about French anarchism, and specifically about the anarchists' attempts to rebuff the far right.

As Goll later wrote to André Breton, he left his political action phase
behind just as the surrealists were becoming increasing politicized (see page
92). Yet Goll remained acutely aware of the political and social turmoil of
his times and registered its effect on him in several novels written over the
next decade. Later in the 1930s came several volumes of his poetic cycle
Jean Sans Terre, which also conveys the anguish of the era. Yvan and Claire
Goll—who had met in neutral Switzerland, where Yvan avoided the mael-
strom of World War I—took refuge in America only a week after the start
of World War II in Europe in September 1939. Goll's poetry took an increasingly mystical bent, reflecting his studies of alchemy and, especially, the Jewish tradition of cabbala. In 1946, still in the United States, Goll wrote a
short book of six poems in English called *Fruit from Saturn*, which strongly
reflects these influences. Yet the first poem, "Atom Elegy," mixes references
to Maimonides' *Guide to the Perplexed* and the cabbalists' search for the
names of God with references to the neutrons, uranium 235, and "Einstein's
time," and ends with the line "The Infinite raped in Alamagordo." Another

poem in the collection is titled "Lilith," the biblical Jewish femme fatale who lured men by her sensuality and yet also represented the androgynous unity of male and female. Goll addressed her as "Lilith Androgyne" in the poem and prefaced the poem with a woodcut dating from 1635 called "The Birth of the Harpye," which shows a woman with wings and the claws of a bird.[79] The Lilith theme recurs in Goll's later verse, which suggests that his interest in Germaine Berton two decades before may have reflected this ongoing fascination with dangerous women. Goll's mysticizing of the first atomic test in Alamagordo, New Mexico, also bears resemblance to Breton's response to the same event, though unlike the multilingual Goll, Breton never wrote in English

In 1936, Yvan Goll published an epic poem called "La chanson de Jean Sans Terre" or The Song of Homeless John, which reprised the theme of the wandering Jew at a time when the rise of Nazism had made many Jews refugees. Perhaps a play on the name given the medieval Burgundian noble Jean Sans Peur (or alternatively on the English King John Lackland, so called because as the youngest son of Henry II he seemed unlikely to inherit land), Jean Sans Terre was not explicitly anarchist as had been Golberg's *trimardeur*, but rather identified the plight of the Jews as central to the era. The wandering Jew was the principal victim of the age of extreme nationalism; at a time when ethnicity reinforced the power of the state, the Jew was in danger of becoming stateless. More victim than revolutionary, the Jew like the anarchist had been marginalized in the bellicose atmosphere of the late 1930s. It is not surprising that even anarchists could contemplate with equanimity the Zionist option, especially when presented as a social experiment.

Four years after the Golls arrived in Paris, the painter Marc Chagall returned to France after an absence of nine years, accompanied now by his wife, Bella. As early as 1925, Chagall began illustrating Goll's books of poems. After collaborating on the *Poèmes d'amours* of 1925, Chagall contributed illustrations to Goll's volume *La chanson de Jean sans Terre* of 1936, and after the war and Goll's death illustrated his collected works. Judging from a photograph taken in 1924, which shows the Golls and Chagalls together in a rural setting, the two families were on friendly terms.[80] Marc Chagall is probably more identified with the theme of the wandering Jew than any other modern artist. He painted "The Wandering Jew" immediately on returning to Paris, and included a bearded figure with a walking stick and a satchel thrown over his shoulder in many canvases, including the 1937 painting "The Revolution." Chagall identified with the image of the wandering Jew both in terms of his personal travails from 1914 to 1923 and more generally as an artist who served as a witness to history.[81] The earlier painting foregrounds the wandering Jew with only a hint of a Russian village in the background, while the striking canvas portraying the Russian Revolution features an image of Lenin balancing himself on one hand, while seated at the same table supporting Lenin is a rabbi holding the tablets of the law. The wandering Jew passes before them, looking up in their direction, while red flags wave and a crowd of Russian peasants surges forward. Yet Chagall does not portray the wandering Jew as a revolutionary but rather as a spectator. Chagall himself had been actively involved as a revolutionary artist, yet left Soviet Russia discouraged in 1922. In fact, his abandonment of the Russian Revolution combined with his unconventional, nonrealist style led some on the left to suspect him of being an anarchist.[82] Chagall was too identified with Jewish themes to have appealed to the profoundly antireligious anarchists, but it seems likely that both he and Goll were libertarian socialists if not outright anarchists.

Marc Chagall became the most famous of the hundreds of Jewish artists who congregated in the Montparnasse artist colony of Paris between 1905 and 1930.[83] Not surprisingly, the police kept watch on this large group of immigrants and in a report dated June 5, 1924 singled out two female Jewish Russian émigrés for special attention. One was named Olga Gorney, a painter's model; her redheaded friend Marie Laska sold drawings on the street. Both women were called fervent followers of Germaine Berton. The police noted that Gorney's sister Anna had a lover, a Jewish chauffeur, who had been expelled from France for radical activities.[84] Gorney, born in Nijni-Novgorod in 1893, was the mistress of a taxi driver named Chaim Gopp; Laska was born in 1894 and had recently married an artist named Joseph Klein. It was his art that Marie sold in the streets.[85] This latter information came from a report filed two months after the first, suggesting some considerable effort of surveillance. This hardly constitutes evidence of active anarchist activities among the heavily Jewish "Ecole de Paris," but it does signify the authorities' suspicion of radical sympathies among the Jewish immigrant community.

Yvan and Claire Goll and Marc and Bella Chagall all managed to escape from Europe to the United States, in the Chagalls' case on the same boat as André Breton. Goll, for his part, mended fences with André Breton and returned to Europe after the war already stricken with leukemia. He died in Paris in 1950 and was buried in Père Lachaise Cemetery. His tombstone was inscribed with the most poetic of epitaphs, in a melancholy phrase that underscored the ephemeral quality of life as of the homelessness of his people: "I lasted no longer than the froth on the lips of the waves on the sand.

Born under no star on a moonless night, my name was only a perishable sob [*sanglot*]."[86]

Chagall returned to France as well, though without Bella, who died during the war. In March 1952, a confidential dispatch from the American Embassy in Paris to the State Department identified Marc Chagall as the honorary president, since 1949, of a communist front organization called MRAP, the Movement Against Racism, Antisemitism, and for Peace, a predominantly Jewish organization. The Chargé d'Affaires called him a "painter and political crackpot" and said he was only a figurehead, so Chagall was not taken very seriously as a threat. Later that year, after the Soviets executed several Yiddish writers in Moscow, Chagall left the organization.[87] Stalinist antisemitism severed the ideal portrayed by Chagall in 1937 of the rabbi and the hand-standing Lenin. Chagall lived on for another generation, making it nearly to one hundred, and became the beloved artist of the Jewish bourgeoisie. He is best remembered for his evocation of Russian village life before the revolution and for his whimsical, quasi-surrealist style; both style and content qualified him as "petit bourgeois" in communist eyes. The same mixture of premodern nostalgia and modernist antirealism made of Chagall a good candidate for anarchism, if not in the era of the cold war, at least during the years of his rebound from communism in the 1920s.

The quotation that opens this chapter comes from another famous modernist, the poet Max Jacob. Friend of Picasso in his Bateau Lavoir days before the war, Max Jacob contributed poems to Florent Fels's anarchist journal *Action* after the war. Fels was a secular Jew who had shortened his name from Felsenberg; Jacob was a Jewish convert to Christianity who would die in 1943 after being rounded up by the Nazis. In their correspondence, Jacob gently resisted Fels's enthusiasm for radical politics while admitting that despite his monk-like spirituality one could still find traces of both Jew and anarchist. All of the figures cited in this chapter were complex, multilayered personalities like Jacob. Nearly all had buried their Jewishness beneath other identities: Frenchman, anarchist, artist, or even international man-without-a-country; yet history had a way of dredging up these buried selves.

Facing West: American Heroes

At 10:24 P.M. on Saturday, May 21, 1927, Charles A. Lindbergh landed at Le
Bourget Airport and immediately had to be rescued from tens of thousands
of adoring Parisians. Word of his impending arrival had prompted an enormous traffic jam, as Parisians had streamed up the two-lane road to the
airfield to welcome the twenty-five-year-old American. The seventy-three-
year-old American ambassador, Myron Herrick, spirited the gangly, boyish
pilot away to the American Embassy, lent him some pajamas, and put him
to bed. The next day Lindbergh woke up famous, as well as $25,000 richer
from the Orteig prize for being the first person to fly from New York to
Paris. Over the next week, Charles Lindbergh was the news, his every activity and audience recorded by the press. Day after day, French headlines lion-
ized the intrepid flyer, perfect symbol of a technological civilization and a
new era in which the old world and the new suddenly seemed much closer.

Lindbergh's biographers uniformly report that his reception in Paris was
enthusiastic in the extreme. The most recent one, A. Scott Berg, does note
that on the day of his departure, New York papers carried stories about prison
sentences meted out for the Teapot Dome scandal and about "an anarchistic maniac who dynamited a school, killing forty-two children. [Yet] Charles
Augustus Lindbergh seemed the perfect antidote to toxic times."[1] Lindbergh's
sudden fame contrasted pleasingly with his modest, unassuming Midwest
demeanor. Lindbergh undoubtedly was welcomed by most Parisians, but neither his conquest of distance nor his American identity was quite as un-
problematic as his numerous biographers maintain.[2]

Slightly over three months after Lindbergh landed at Le Bourget, on

August 23, 1927, Nicola Sacco and Bartolomeo Vanzetti would be executed at Charlestown State Prison in Massachusetts, as five hundred armed patrolmen stood watch outside and guards were armed with machine guns. The next night riots broke out in Paris, resulting in hundreds of arrests, with more than two hundred policemen injured and several hundred thousand francs' worth of property damage.[3] Lindbergh's journey to Paris had taken 33.5 hours; Sacco and Vanzetti's had taken seven years since their arrest back in 1920 for allegedly having killed two men and stealing the payroll of the Slater and Morrill shoe factories in South Braintree, Massachusetts. Sacco and Vanzetti were heroes of a very different stripe from Lindbergh, more martyrs than men who had accomplished singular deeds. Yet their long calvary and their own modest demeanors and protestations of innocence heroicized them no less than Charles Lindbergh and his famous flight.

There is another context that aids in understanding the impact of Lindbergh's landing in Paris in 1927, one not mentioned by his many biographers. That same momentous year, three books were published in France that sought to explain the young republic across the ocean to the French, to make sense of this new civilization that was bringing to Europe not only aviators but a new style of mass consumption, mass entertainment, seemingly a whole new way of life. It may have been coincidental that these books by André Siegfried, André Tardieu, and Lucien Romier appeared in 1927 since they had all visited the United States well before Lindbergh's flight.[4] These works inaugurated a spate of books published in France over the next few years that would bear titles such as *America: The Menace,* and *The American Cancer.* While the headlines of May 1927 acclaimed the young aviator, French newspapers also carried stories of Ku Klux Klansmen lynching black men while gangsters gunned down people in the streets of American cities. The racist, violent, and xenophobic society that was Roaring Twenties America could not be represented by the straight arrow from Little Falls, Minnesota, and French response to American society was more complex than the acclaim that greeted young Lindbergh. For that matter, Lindbergh himself proved to be more complex and darker than the tall, thin hero who landed in Paris in 1927. From aviator and sympathetic parent of a kidnapped child, Lindbergh's reputation took a different turn in later years, as he flirted with Nazism and antisemitism in the late 1930s, and after the war turned his fame and wealth in the direction of sexual profligacy, also in Germany.[5]

Juxtaposing the most famous American names of the spring and summer of 1927—those of Lindbergh, Sacco, and Vanzetti—makes it possible to grasp more fully the complexity of French attitudes toward America. Sacco and Vanzetti's anarchism raised the profile of this relatively small movement and implicated anarchism in how America was perceived abroad. Because their deaths were widely interpreted as a travesty of justice, their execution diminished the positive feelings generated by Lindbergh. Yet those feelings were already conflicted.

It is difficult eighty years later fully to understand the acclaim that greeted Lindbergh, or the lifelong fame that accrued to him for risking his life to cross the ocean in a day and a half. Certainly he was brave as well as lucky (the nickname that stuck was Lucky Lindy), and yet the hero worship seems overdone for one airplane flight, whose long-distance record was surpassed within two weeks (though not by a solo pilot). The 1920s was an age of burgeoning mass media, which fed on a hunger for heroes, if only for the moment. But a large part of the explanation lies in the "passion for wings" that overwhelmed the public in France and elsewhere in the first decades of the twentieth century.[6] Flying was still new and exciting, as one can easily gauge by comparing the heroism attached to the air aces of World War I with the far more anonymous pilots of World War II, none of whom attained the fame attached to the names von Richthofen or Rickenbacker.

Flying was also dangerous. Both the acclaim that greeted Lindbergh and some of the ambivalence on the part of the French public were due to Lindbergh's triumph over death. Just twelve days earlier, two French World War I veterans, Charles Nungesser and François Coli, had attempted the same feat in the reverse direction, and their plane, the *Oiseau Blanc*, had disappeared somewhere in the ocean. Four Americans also died that spring while competing for the Orteig prize. Lindbergh's chances of making the flight on his own, flying a day and a half with no co-pilot, was viewed as so foolhardy that Lloyd's of London refused to put odds on his chances.[7] After the disappearance of the French pilots earlier that month, Ambassador Herrick was so worried about the negative response to an American success after the French failure that he warned Washington that any such attempt might be misinterpreted. When Lindbergh heard of the ambassador's warning, he expressed his regrets over the French pilots' fate but insisted that it would not alter his plans.[8] According to *La Revue de Paris,* Mme Nungesser left her visiting card with a word of congratulations the morning after Lindbergh's arrival at the American Embassy where he was staying. The ambassador promised that Lindbergh would visit her to express his condolences.[9] Lindbergh visited Mme Nungesser on his first day in France and would later say modestly that he had the benefit of prevailing tailwinds that the Frenchmen, flying from east to west, lacked. While his visit assuaged French bitterness, his success still underscored the dramatic French failure.[10]

Airplanes and Terrorism

Flying had been even more dangerous in the primitive planes of the pre–World War I era; Robert Wohl titles one of the chapters of his cultural history of early flight "A Rendezvous with Death." He notes that the French shared in early air fatalities—of thirty pilots killed in the first six months of 1911, sixteen were French. In May of that year, a pilot lost control of his plane at the start of a race and crashed into the onlookers, killing the French minister of war while severely injuring the prime minister and a major aviation proponent.[11] Such disasters did little to restrain French enthusiasm for aviation and may even have enhanced the daredevil appeal of flight. Aviation above all symbolized modernity, but it also signified danger and could potentially be subverted for nefarious ends. Fears of airplanes' destructive power led prewar French authorities to the anarchists.

Already by 1912, less than a decade since the Wright brothers' first flight and even fewer years since their sojourn in Le Mans, where they spent several months making test flights, there were over a dozen flight schools operating in France. Nor does it appear that flying lessons were prohibitively expensive. Buried in a file in the Archives Nationales called "les menées anarchistes" (anarchist activities or intrigues) is a report dated February 17, 1912, marked confidential, and directed to the special commissioner that warns that "anarchists are seeking to gain admittance to flying schools with the design of utilizing, to the profit of their subversive theories, the advantages of the new means of air-born locomotion."[12] The response from the office of the minister of the interior was to demand reports on all students taking flying lessons throughout the country. Over the next two months, reports came in from all parts of France, as police watched flight schools at St. Omer, Amiens, Montpellier, Boulogne-sur-Mer, and elsewhere. Most agents reported no suspicious activity, but the April 19, 1912, report that summarized the findings said that at Montpellier, they were watching a man named Georges Canossa, while at Crotoy in the Somme certain revolutionaries had indeed sought flight training.

Just why the Sûreté Générale suspected anarchists might want to use airplanes for terrorist activities, or how they imagined they would use airplanes in the interests of "subversion," was not made clear. Presumably an informer overheard some anarchists discussing airplanes, either as getaway vehicles or else as a platform from which to drop bombs. The documents never stated how the anarchists proposed to use airplanes but seemed to take the threat seriously enough to deploy agents throughout the country to check on all flight schools. The fact that a pilot had managed to kill French politicians the previous year might have suggested to the police that such an attack could be done intentionally as well as accidentally, although since the pilot died in the crash this scenario would imply a suicide attack. While the modus operandi remains unclear, the police clearly feared the extension of terrorism into the air. It is particularly striking that airplanes were imagined as potential terrorist tools even before they had been used for military combat purposes.

The context in which this correspondence took place was the Bande à Bonnot, the anarchist criminal gang that had been terrorizing Paris and environs for the past year and whose members were either rounded up or killed in the spring of 1912. The Bonnot Gang had been among the very first to use getaway cars in the robberies, and perhaps the police extrapolated from cars to airplanes. Individualist anarchists before World War I both praised and employed the policy called *"la reprise individuelle,"* or individual recovery—in other words, ideologically motivated theft. This practice was condemned by most communist-anarchists, such as Jean Grave, as conflating anarchism with criminality. Illegality also ensured that individualist anarchists were carefully watched by the authorities. The Bonnot Gang was the most notorious group of anarchist criminals, whose exploits and stand-offs with the police were widely reported in the press. Since anarchists who planted bombs usually exercised great stealth, it seems unlikely they would have considered dropping them from noisy airplanes and, despite their penchant for martyrology, none willingly killed themselves for the cause. Yet the last years before the war witnessed both syndicalist labor violence and anarchist illegalism, which appeared to worry the national police enough to watch flight schools. No similar reports surfaced after the war, but by then the tide of both labor violence and anarchist illegalism had subsided, and the police were more concerned with communists.

Lindbergh and the Anarchists

Yet if anarchists were no longer interested in taking flying lessons, they were interested in one flyer in particular. Louis Lecoin was a leading anarchist militant, a member of the Union Anarchiste, and attached to the newspaper *Le Libertaire* who claimed proudly in his autobiography to have spent more time in prison for crimes of opinion than any Frenchman other than Auguste Blanqui, the nineteenth-century perennial revolutionary who was imprisoned for thirty-sevev years. Lecoin spent twelve years in jail, mostly for opposing France's various wars. Lecoin was in charge of organizing the Sacco and

Vanzetti Committee, a coalition of various left-leaning groups committed to stopping the execution of the two Italian-American anarchists and calling for a new trial. The enterprising Lecoin made the connection between the young American hero who was the toast of Paris and the anarchists sitting on death row in Massachusetts. In his memoirs, he says that a number of anarchists were waiting in a room adjacent to one in which Lindbergh was engaged in business, and that they managed to get a petition in favor of Sacco and Vanzetti in his hands. Lecoin claims that Lindbergh was willing to sign the petition, but that Ambassador Herrick intervened before he could sign.[13] Lecoin wrote this nearly forty years after the fact, and his story is unconfirmed, but it seems plausible that Lecoin would assume that Lindbergh, as so many other Americans, would support the cause of the two anarchist martyrs.

Lindbergh presumably was not politically formed yet and might not have been opposed to Lecoin's cause. His father, Charles August Lindbergh, had been a radical member of Congress who opposed U.S. entry into World War I and railed against the "money trust."[14] On the other hand, Lindbergh did respond to the congratulatory message from the Italian Olympic Committee with a telegram that read, "Thanks for your message. Long live Mussolini and the Youth of Italy."[15] Mussolini was widely regarded as a great aviation enthusiast, so this does not necessarily imply that Lindbergh favored fascism. Furthermore, Mussolini himself did what he could to support Sacco and Vanzetti and still possessed a lingering admiration for anarchists.[16] The same was not true of Myron Herrick. In 1921, after Sacco and Vanzetti had been found guilty and sentenced to death, Ambassador Herrick had telegraphed his observations about a "certain effervescence in communist and anarchist circles" and offered detailed observations of French communist agitation. Herrick cited as his source of information "the Action Française League"—not the most unbiased source.[17] On October 19 of that same year a package-bomb was sent to Herrick in a box labeled "perfume." It was opened by his valet, a veteran of the Great War who recognized the sound of the arming of the bomb, and beat a hasty retreat before the engine detonated. The valet sustained some injuries; the room was wrecked.[18] Myron Herrick had good reasons for being unsympathetic to French anarchists and for enforcing their distance from Lindbergh six years later. After the riots set off by the anarchists' execution, fifty policemen were stationed at the ambassador's residence for months, until the clamor died down.[19]

The anarchist press paid far less heed to Lindbergh than the mainstream French press, absorbed as it was in the Sacco and Vanzetti case. Nor did the United States loom large in the French anarchist imagination; events in the

Soviet Union, Spain, and elsewhere in Europe commanded much more attention. Overall however, *Le Libertaire* in particular presented a negative image of American culture as hypercapitalist and racist. More than one photograph of the Ku Klux Klan engaged in lynching and cross-burnings conveyed in spectacular fashion the image of American racism, while the Massachusetts trial of the two anarchists stood for judicial repression and xenophobic intolerance. American expatriates may have loved Paris, but the French left did not similarly embrace America.

France Looks at Roaring Twenties America

What about mainstream French opinion? Lindbergh's famous flight may be placed in the context of the spate of books that were published in 1927 and the following years, which tried to explicate the phenomenon of the burgeoning republic across the ocean to French readers. The famous flight must have made French readers more curious about the country that produced the young hero, especially since Lindbergh hailed from the same small-town Minnesota background already made famous, or infamous, in the novels of Sinclair Lewis. Beyond New York and the Alleghany Mountains lay a vast continent, of which Lindbergh, much like Wilbur and Orville Wright, was an authentic representative.[20] The new books about America were reviewed in the journals *Europe Nouvelle* and *Revue de Paris* in early June 1927—within two weeks of Lindbergh's arrival, making it likely that readers of the reviews associated the books with the figurative joining of the continents by air.[21]

The most important, because most impartial, book to appear about the United States was probably that of André Siegfried, *Les Etats-Unis aujourd'hui,* though the volume by the conservative politician André Tardieu was considered to be nearly as praiseworthy (he was henceforth nicknamed "Tardieu l'Américain). These were the two most widely cited authorities, and the *Revue Universelle* noted the following year that these two books had allowed "several thousand elite Frenchmen to develop an accurate idea of the United States, based on reason and reflection."[22] Siegfried's book was so well respected that it was immediately translated into English and appeared as *America Comes of Age* the same year that it appeared in France. It sold one hundred thirty thousand copies, so it reached beyond a narrow elite.[23] André Siegfried (1875–1959) was a member of a distinguished Alsatian Protestant family and a long-standing professor of economics at the Ecole Libre des Sciences Politiques in Paris. If his book was one of the first to advance an anti-American argument, it was not because of any narrow partisan political position. Yet despite his seeming impartiality, his reading of American society would have pleased even the anarchists of *Le Libertaire*, for Siegfried contrasted French individualism, artisanship, and artistry with American materialism, standardization, and even collectivism, by which he meant conformity.

America Comes of Age was divided into three sections, explicating the ethnic, the economic, and the political situations. Siegfried spent several months touring America in 1925, and he had visited the United States a number of times before, commencing in 1898. The America he represented to the French public was that of the Scopes Monkey Trial of 1925, of the laws restricting immigration of 1917, 1921, and 1924, of the Yellow Peril on the West Coast, of extreme race consciousness, Jim Crow, eugenic sterilization of the unfit, and prohibition. Everywhere, Siegfried saw fear provoked by the wave of immigrants who had washed ashore in the previous forty years, threatening the hegemony of Anglo-Saxon Protestant America. The spirit of 1920s America was far closer to that of Cromwell's Puritans than to the enlightened founding fathers. John Calvin seemed more present in America than Thomas Jefferson, as a spirit of evangelistic moralism triumphed over liberty and equality. Feeling themselves to be God's elect, Americans had largely lost the spirit of equality, openness, and diversity represented by the "melting pot" ideal. Instead, they were banning the teaching of evolution in the schools, while even Californians voted in favor of prohibition despite their considerable wine industry. Southerners feared black male sexuality, yet the many light-skinned black people testified to the extent to which white men took black mistresses. In the chapter titled "Resistance to Free Thought," in which he discussed anti-evolutionism, Siegfried opined:

We thus have the extraordinary paradox of the descendents of English and Scotch Nonconformists being changed into the narrowest of conformists, and the United States becoming a country where a man who does not fall in line socially and morally runs the risk of not being allowed to express himself freely. In a word, a transformation of the rights of the individual is taking place under our very eyes. The principles of freedom of speech, of the press, and of association . . . are all solemnly guaranteed by the Constitution. . . . Now, however, a new doctrine, vigorous but undefined, is trying to undermine them by teaching that the rights of the community are almost unlimited, if it is defending itself against alien ideas.[24]

Yet if America was founded on Calvinism, this same religious foundation sanctioned success. America's real religion was material wealth, and Siegfried admired the number of telephones, radios, and especially automobiles enjoyed by Americans. Americans owned 81 percent of all the cars in the entire world, and already Californians enjoyed a ratio of one car for every 3.3 people. America was creating a democracy of capitalists through mass production and standardization, which explained the lack of an active left. The cost of high wages and the gospel of productivity was that America was turning into a vast machine, standardizing workers as much as interchangeable parts. Individualism, personality, and artistry had no place where the most "sacred principle" was efficiency. Siegfried termed the sacrifice of individuality and artistry "tragic." In his conclusion he wrote that "modern America has no national art and does not even feel the need of one."[25] One threat Siegfried did not perceive in 1927 was that of Hollywood, for he perceived no culture at all, neither New Orleans jazz nor motion pictures, much less any high culture. This is slightly surprising, given that Josephine Baker and the jazzy Revue Nègre were all the rage in Paris. The America depicted by Siegfried is the same one that the expatriates of Montparnasse were fleeing.

Since the American mania for productivity and success was the product of unique cultural forces, such as Puritanism, that were mostly lacking in France, and since the two cultures were fundamentally at odds ("The truth is that the Americans and the French have great difficulty in understanding one another; they are so totally different"), one might conclude that there was little risk of Americanization taking root in the antithetical French culture.[26] This may have been true for Siegfried, but other French commentators were not so sanguine. The more partisan commentator Georges Duhamel published his perceptions of America, based on a whirlwind three-week tour, in serial form in the Revue de Paris in 1930 as "Scènes de la vie future." These were translated into English the following year and published as America the Menace: Scenes from the Life of the Future. For the leftist Duhamel, America loomed as Europe's future: in twenty years most aspects of this mass industrial ant-heap were likely to be welcomed by the majority of Europeans eager for similar levels of prosperity and production.[27] The acclaim that greeted Lindbergh thus could have been disquieting to intellectuals who feared the same warm reception would be accorded to other aspects of progressive Americanization. While Americans perceived their own society to be highly individualistic, the French saw in America the effacement of the individual and the usurping of liberty by conformity and efficiency. It is unlikely that anarchists would have found much to criticize in this negative assessment of capitalist, industrial America.

French Response to the Deaths of Sacco and Vanzetti

The anarchists for their part were less worried about the long-range prospects for the Americanization of France than the imminent prospect of the electrocution of their fellow anarchists in far-off Massachusetts. The drama unfolding in the spring and summer of 1927 was the culmination of a story that had lasted the entire decade. As early as 1921, *Le Libertaire* was devoting whole pages to the Sacco/Vanzetti case. By 1927, entire issues of various anarchist newspapers were advertising the mass demonstrations scheduled to take place in Paris. By this time, what had preoccupied anarchists now seized the imagination of a wide range of voices on the left, from the communists to the League of the Rights of Man. Why had the case of Italian immigrants become such a cause célèbre in many parts of the globe? Already in the 1920s, commentators were comparing this case to that of Alfred Dreyfus a generation earlier.[28] Both cases were widely perceived to be miscarriages of justice due to evident bias, in Dreyfus's case due to antisemitism, for Sacco and Vanzetti because of xenophobia and red-baiting. The issue was eloquently phrased by Anatole France in a letter addressed to the People of the United States of America and dated October 31, 1921. The Nobel prize–winning author said that the two men had been convicted for a crime of opinion, and people everywhere who valued freedom of thought must stand up for the condemned anarchists, whatever their own beliefs. He warned the Americans not to make martyrs of these men.[29] At the same time anarchists were not shy about resorting to violent reprisals. On October 21, 1921, U.S. Ambassador Myron Herrick was sent a letter bomb; on November 8, 1921, a bomb damaged the American consulate at Marseilles.[30]

The perception that the U. S. government was ready to execute two men because they were outsiders who refused to melt into the American mainstream and who dared to criticize the country that had welcomed them reinforced all the negative impressions of an insular and intolerant American society. Anarchists were everywhere an insignificant minority, yet in martyring Sacco and Vanzetti, the United States made the marginal central symbolically if not socially. As with Dreyfus, intellectuals and the left organized and spoke out, but though Dreyfus returned from Devil's Island and eventually was pardoned by the president of France and reinstated in the army, Sacco and Vanzetti were never accorded a new trial.

Louis Lecoin played a central role in organizing the Comité Sacco-Vanzetti in France. In order to convince the world that "the most monstrous judicial error of the time was about to happen," Lecoin threw aside anarchist distrust of mainstream politics and welcomed all possible allies in the struggle to free the two men.[31] Until October 1926, the anarchists had used the case to stir up revolutionary agitation, but as the execution seemed more imminent, Sébastien Faure, Lecoin, and Ferandel of Le Libertaire staff decided that the first priority was to organize an effective mass movement that might save their lives. Lecoin sought the help of bourgeois liberals, socialists and communists, and the trade union organization, the CGT, in the common struggle. If he had restricted himself to anarchists, he might have mustered a few hundred supporters, but by broadening his focus, he was able to command mass marches and demonstrations of thousands in the streets of Paris. Though the French Communist Party came late to the crusade to save the anarchists, it eagerly exploited the case for its anti-American propaganda value. At a time of extreme anarchist distrust of the communists, who just then were busy jailing anarchists in the Soviet Union, this communist appropriation of their cause aroused some resentment among the anarchists.

The double execution was announced for July 10, but half an hour before the event, Massachusetts Governor Fuller announced a reprieve. The date was advanced to August 10, which led to more protests on the eve of this date. In Paris, a series of huge protest meetings, including a massive one on July 23 at the Cirque de Paris, culminated on Sunday, August 7, with a large march to the Bois de Vincennes led by Luigia Vanzetti, sister of the defendant, who was on her way to America.[32] A general strike was called for the following day.[33] Lecoin reported that the only intellectual who refused to sign his petition in favor of sparing the two anarchists was Paul Valéry. Lecoin was pleased by the response of the League of the Rights of Man as well as by such famous names as Marie Curie, Joseph Caillaux, Séverine, and other nonanarchists on the French left.[34] Mme Séverine presided at the mass meeting he organized; he claimed that ten thousand attended and twenty thousand more were turned away for lack of room.[35]

After a series of legal maneuvers, including attempts to get the U.S. Supreme Court to overturn the verdict, all legal avenues were exhausted and the men were electrocuted shortly after midnight on August 23, 1927. That same day, Tuesday, the banner headline of Le Libertaire read simply "Assassinés!" followed by the exhortation "All to the American Embassy." A map showed exactly where the embassy was located, and called for people to assemble there at 9 P.M., so that "you will mix your voices with ours, so that powerful as a tempest, our cry of hatred for the Yankee assassin hangmen will ring out."[36] Four days later, a special edition of Le Libertaire ran on its masthead a slogan by Sacco, "They can crucify our bodies but they can never destroy our ideas, which will remain for the use of the youth of the future." The paper revealed that the Sacco and Vanzetti Committee had jointly decided to march to the American Embassy, but that on the morning of August 23 the communist newspaper *L'Humanité* announced a demonstration to be held on the grand boulevards, suggesting that the socialists and communists sought to separate their actions from those of the anarchists. The next day the police reported fully on the riots that broke out the previous night.

On the evening of August 23, the anarchists arrived by metro at the embassy but found it cordoned off and heavily guarded. A column of five hundred people headed down the Champs Elysées singing the "Internationale." By 10:25 P.M., eight to nine hundred were gathered at the Place de l'Etoile. A report issued three weeks later said that some damage was reported along the Champs Elysées and at the Arc de Triomphe, where some anarchists spit on the Tomb of the Unknown Soldier. Yet the great majority of rioting and damage took place further to the north in Paris, among the communist demonstrators. There seem to have been two contingents of demonstrators: the largest group was nearer the center of the city, along the boulevard Sébastopol, with a smaller group in lower Montmartre. The police estimated fifteen hundred people rioted with many windows broken around the rue Etienne Marcel. Around 10 P.M. demonstrators surged up the rue des Martyrs, appropriately enough. At the Place Blanche, stones were thrown at the Moulin Rouge; other Montmartre nightclubs were also attacked. More than two hundred arrests were made that night. The police report of August 24 said thirty-six police were wounded, with four taken to hospitals; the report of September 15 listed 210 total injuries to the police. The police suspected that local youths joined the communist and anarchist militants and augmented the level of criminal violence. The northerly marchers were pushed toward the Gare St. Lazare, where they dispersed. Calm was restored around midnight.[37]

Judging by the police damage estimates, the communists were much more violent than the anarchists. The police reported ninety thousand francs' worth of damages in the area of the Champs Elysées, compared with fifty thousand francs on the grand boulevards, five hundred thousand along the boulevard Sébastopol, and two hundred twenty thousand in Montmartre. Of the individuals arrested, only two were called anarchists, though a number of others were called revolutionary syndicalists, who might have been affiliated with the anarchists. Others were listed as young communists or communists. At least twenty-three French and nine foreigners were found guilty, of whom four were Italian and two American, which makes sense given the identity of the men whose deaths they were protesting.

The anarchists' targeting of the American Embassy was logical, and it also made sense to march on the major thoroughfares of the city, but why did a significant number of demonstrators choose to attack Montmartre, long known as an entertainment quarter? Some clues may be found in *L'Humanité*, which published a long article the next day blaming the police for attacking the calm and dignified crowd. It described a virtual police riot, with the crowd counterattacking. Suddenly the crowd cried out, "To Montmartre, capital of the dollar that enjoys life. One doesn't dance, one doesn't celebrate on the day of worldwide mourning."[38] The communist paper went on to specify the sorts of decadent behavior it decried—people dancing to jazz and doing the Charleston while champagne flowed at one hundred francs a bottle. The partiers grinned at the demonstrators behind the plate-glass windows, provoking them, so these sons of the Commune showed the high-lifers whose terrain they were on. The communists were contesting the expropriation of revolutionary Montmartre by celebrants identified as American, as the Butte was overtaken by jazz music and American dollars. Rocks thrown at French cabarets were thus indirectly attacking the growing predominance of American culture. The glow of Lucky Lindy's heroic flight was extinguished by the martyrs of Massachusetts. The lindy hop, symbol of the jazz age cult of instant celebrity and high spirits, was consigned by the communists at least to the debauched realm of "poules de luxe . . . à la Fuller" (kept women of the governor of Massachusetts).

In a strange juxtaposition, Montmartre in the 1920s featured black American jazz musicians rubbing shoulders with White Russian émigrés from the Russian Revolution. The Russian colony lived in Montmartre and many opened restaurants and cabarets that advertised their cultural heritage.[39] No longer the bohemian and revolutionary site proclaimed by its communard history, Montmartre projected a counterrevolutionary ambience where rich American tourists mingled with exotic blacks and supporters of the tsar. It was also frankly decadent, known for drugs and violence as well as sex and liquor. If communists had ever taken the revolutionary credentials of bohemia seriously, which is doubtful, by the 1920s Montmartre appeared to be the very opposite of proletarian popular culture.[40] Further, as the franc dropped to new lows in 1927, American tourists flocked to France to take advantage of the favorable exchange rates. The American journalist William Shirer reported having seen a busload of such tourists stoned by angry Frenchmen on the Place de la Concorde, which he attributed to the threatened execution of Sacco and Vanzetti and American demands that France repay its war debts as well as to the weak status of the franc.[41]

It was unlikely that the presence of twenty thousand U.S. veterans in Paris the following month greatly improved the French tolerance for Americans.

The American Legion commemorated the tenth anniversary of the arrival of American troops in France during World War I with a march down the Champs Elysées on September 19, which happened to coincide with the funeral of the American dancer Isadora Duncan at Père Lachaise Cemetery. For a week Americans had been getting drunk at Montmartre nightclubs, enjoying nightlife and legal liquor forbidden in Prohibition America.[42] That same day, the anarchist Louis Lecoin sneaked into the American Legion meeting and called out, "Vive Sacco et Vanzetti," for which he was promptly arrested.[43] The poet William Carlos Williams recalled widespread feelings of hatred toward Americans around the time of the Legionnaire's visit, compounded by the recent execution and the quarter million Americans who flocked to France each year from 1926 to 1929, taking advantage of the weak franc as well as the abundance of French wines and spirits.[44]

Sacco and Vanzetti were not soon forgotten. In October, a grand cortege was held in which the ashes of Sacco and Vanzetti were paraded along with death masks of the martyrs. The ashes were apparently provided by Vanzetti's sister.[45] Rarely had anarchist commemoration taken on so overtly a quasi-religious tone. The martyrs of Haymarket Square in Chicago were forty years in the past; now anarchists had new martyr-heroes to celebrate. As with Alfred Dreyfus, the Sacco/Vanzetti case had moral as well as political overtones that were enhanced by the integrity and simplicity of the two men. Remembering their martyrdom while trooping behind their images and remains was meant to make the point that the state could dispose of their physical persons but not their "souls," that is, their anarchist ideals. Yet their road to martyrdom had lasted so long that there was little impetus left after the explosion of anger that followed their execution.

Louis Lecoin embodied similar sacrificial qualities. He has been called the finest figure of anarchism and pacifism of his era for his lifetime of dedication to the cause of peace and for the many years spent in prison. Many years later, at the age of seventy-four, he began a hunger strike on June 1, 1962, to protest France's failure to provide conscientious objector status as an option for military draftees. As he drifted into a coma twenty-three days later, the government gave in, President Charles de Gaulle commenting, "I don't want to see Lecoin die."[46] A committee was formed in 1964 to support Lecoin's candidacy for the Nobel Peace Prize, but he withdrew in favor of Martin Luther King Jr.

Lecoin, along with many others around the world, failed to save the lives of Nicola Sacco and Bartolomeo Vanzetti, but he succeeded in mobilizing tens of thousands of people to protest on their behalf. 1927 turned out to be a watershed year for French anarchism. The publicity generated by the Sacco/

Vanzetti case, the Sholom Schwartzbard case that came to trial in October of that year, and the move spearheaded primarily by émigré Russian anarchists to centralize anarchism around a "Platform" all created a sense of excitement, which the anarchists had a hard time recapturing in succeeding years. In the police reports on the movement issued in 1928 and 1929, agents reported a movement in the doldrums, badly split among contending factions and circulation of anarchist publications in decline.[47] Not until 1936, under the dual impact of the Popular Front and the Spanish Civil War, would French anarchism regain a sense of movement and possibility.

Nobody in 1927 compared Charles Lindbergh to Sacco and Vanzetti. The American ambassador cabled President Coolidge that the young Minnesotan was the perfect exemplar of Americanism.[48] By contrast, travelers to the United States were required to declare upon entry whether they were anarchists and whether they were capable of committing acts of violence against the government.[49] Yet death by electricity was in its own way as resolutely modern and American as flying across the Atlantic in an airplane. Lindbergh's flight and the anarchists' deaths were signs of the triumph of technique over ideology, or rather that American technological acumen was the dominant ideology, destined to efface the ideologies of class and revolt imported from Europe. A dozen years later, Charles Lindbergh would lead an isolationist movement called America First. In 1927, Lindbergh's flight and the Italians' deaths already signaled the spirit of America first, which most Americans would have understood as the triumph of mainstream, Protestant America. The fact that French anarchists could agree with assessments on American civilization made by three conservative French commentators (Tardieu became prime minister of France in 1930; Romier was editor of Le Figaro) suggests that anti-Americanism was less about capitalism than about mechanization and mass conformity. In the issue of Le Libertaire published the day after the execution, the last letter of Vanzetti, dated July 10, was printed, as well as a poem by Marcel Dudach titled "Aux Martyrs des Temps Modernes." The poet may have meant simply "modern martyrs," or he may have envisioned Sacco and Vanzetti as martyrs to modernity.

Renegades

The last years of the interwar era were a hard time for communists and their supporters. Intellectuals who became disenchanted with the Communist Party in the late 1930s have become famous as the "God that failed" school of writers.[1] Stalinism, the purge trials, Soviet betrayal of the Spanish Republic, and the Nazi-Soviet Pact made many Western intellectuals rethink their allegiance to the Soviet Union. This disabused mood came after two decades, from the October Revolution of 1917 to the mid-1930s, in which eager new communists and fellow travelers who may not have joined the party supported the ideal of a classless society as embodied in the Soviet Union.

French anarchists in the 1920s felt a similar sense of disillusionment. Though anarchist disenchantment is less well known than that of the communists, it typified an era when French anarchism was a movement in decline, compared with its fin de siècle and Belle Époque heyday. In contrast to the Bolsheviks, who demonstrated that revolution was possible if a revolutionary vanguard was single-mindedly committed to seizing power, anarchism seemed more unrealizable than ever, an ideal both perpetual and ineffectual. Interwar revolutionary aspirations came closest to fruition for anarchists in Ukraine and Spain, yet these movements too ended in failure, in both cases crushed by the competing and better organized communists. The response of a number of leading anarchists was to turn to communism.

As usual with anarchists, it is impossible to quantify how many militants gave up their libertarian ideals and joined the Communist Party. The malaise was real enough, as was the sense that anarchism's best days were behind it. The Russian émigré anarchists made it clear to all who paid attention that anarchists did not fare well in the Soviet Union, already a police state by the mid-1920s. Yet with all of its flaws, Russia exerted a powerful appeal, even to libertarians used to resisting authority. Communist-anarchists were especially tempted to join a movement that had a proven track record, in contrast to one that mostly excelled at producing martyrs. One of the most spectacular apostasies was that of André Colomer, one-time editor of *Le Libertaire* and founder of *L'Insurgé* who joined a group visiting Russia for the tenth anniversary of the Russian Revolution and returned to France a communist. This was at the end of 1927, only a few months after the execution of Sacco and Vanzetti. Colomer was reviled by his former *compagnons* for forsaking their cause, but he preferred to march into the future with the proletariat rather than expend his life tilting at windmills. In fact his life ended soon enough—he died in the Soviet Union in 1931 at the age of forty-five.

Focusing on a few exemplary cases of anarchists who joined the communist bandwagon will personalize the crisis afflicting French anarchism in the 1920s. Was it the failure of anarchism and the relative strength of Soviet communism in the 1920s that led them to change their allegiance, or was it instead the aging process that encouraged them to jettison their youthful enthusiasm for anarchist purity and adopt a more pragmatic acceptance of the possible over the ideal? Did anarchist individualism itself seem passé in the brave new world of the masses? Did they rethink their ideals, or did they seek more effective ways of realizing those ideals? With the exception of Victor Serge and Rirette Maîtrejean, all of these intellectuals broke with anarchism between 1925 and 1927. As European society stabilized and revolutionary hopes waned, anarchism appeared rooted in the past; the Soviet Union seemed to be the only progressive alternative to the American model of capitalist production and mass culture that threatened to engulf the world.

The model for defectors from anarchism was Victor Serge, who played a major role in the individualist faction of anarchism before the war, spent five years in prison for his activities before and during World War I, and then went to Russia to join the revolution. Serge's female companion, Rirette Maîtrejean, also left the anarchist movement behind after being tried in company with Serge and members of the anarchist-criminal Bonnot Gang, but unlike Serge she moved away from radical politics in the 1920s after he left her for the sake of the revolution. Though she never became the important literary or political figure that Victor Serge did, she did publish her *Souvenirs d'Anarchie*. The two most interesting cases of apostates from anarchism in the interwar era are Colomer and Maurice Wullens. Wullens was a schoolteacher who edited his own journal during the war and continued throughout the interwar period. While *Les Humbles* was idiosyncratic and unaffiliated, it remained anarchistic during and after World War I, while Wullens himself contributed to anarchist periodicals until 1925. In that year, Wullens visited the Soviet Union with a delegation of French teachers, and though his break with anarchism was not as definitive as was that of Colomer, he did gravitate toward anti-Stalinist communism. In the 1930s he collaborated with Victor Serge, upon the latter's return from Stalin's prison camps. For Wullens, a wounded veteran of World War I, pacifism overrode any other allegiance, and on the eve of World War II he was even willing to contemplate some sort of compromise with Hitler in the interest of avoiding another war. Wullens's pacifist commitment led to a definitive break with Serge in the pages of *Les Humbles* on the eve of the next war.

One more redoubtable figure on the left who worked with Victor Serge and Maurice Wullens to expose Stalin's perfidy and the circus of the show trials was André Breton. When Breton founded the surrealist movement in 1924, he and Louis Aragon were anarchist sympathizers. In 1925 they began a decade-long flirtation with communism that led to Breton being ejected from the party, while Aragon for his part chose to remain in the party and sever his ties with the surrealists. In the late 1930s Breton became a Trotskyist, and visited the "Old Man" in Mexico in 1938. Upon his return, Breton announced a new organization of artists with the grand name of the International Federation of Independent Revolutionary Artists. Among the original adherents of Breton's group were Victor Margueritte, Victor Serge, and Maurice Wullens. After the trauma of war and exile in America, Breton returned to France and also to anarchism, to which he openly adhered in the late 1940s and the early 1950s. Examining the anarchism of the surrealists in the context of other "renegades" who turned toward communism at the same time will help clarify why they made the commitments they did.

While men such as Sébastien Faure, Louis Lecoin, and E. Armand remained anarchists their whole adult lives, many others viewed anarchism not as an exclusive commitment but as a means of achieving a goal shared with others on the left. When anarchist means appeared ineffectual, they sought other avenues, without ever jettisoning their allegiance to fundamental values of freedom and justice. Unlike members of the Communist Party, who were required to change their ideas in conformity with the party line, these independent leftists generally remained committed to the same values within different institutional frameworks and changing historical contexts. André Colomer even bounced around among all the branches of anarchism—individualist, syndicalist, and communist—before leaving the movement and joining the Communist Party. If he had survived into the late thirties, it is likely that Colomer too would have joined Serge, Wullens, and Breton on the anti-Stalinist left.

Victor Serge is by far the best known of these anarchist militants (Breton is more famous, but for his art rather than his politics), but his time as an anarchist has been overshadowed by his role in the Russian Revolution. Yet his time in France, in the years before World War I and then from 1936 to 1940, coincided with his periods of greatest involvement in anarchism. He also communicated with the anarchists of *Le Libertaire* during the early years of the revolution. Though he never returned to the anarchist fold after 1917, he cooperated with anarchists in the late thirties as a key figure in the anti-Stalinist Left Opposition. Reviewing Serge's anarchism makes it possible to consider the case of Rirette Maîtrejean, to whom he was briefly married and who was one of the rare female anarchists to write about the movement.

Victor Serge

If anyone embodies the French adage "who is not an anarchist at age twenty?" it is Victor Serge. His given name was Victor Kibalchich, born in Brussels in 1890 to Russian émigré parents who had fled the land of the tsar for revolutionary activities. In the spring of 1937, Serge wrote of these early years for Emmanuel Mounier's journal *L'Esprit* in greater detail than he later included in his classic autobiography, *Memoirs of a Revolutionary*, which he wrote in Mexican exile during the war. The life of an émigré intellectual was hard; when he was eleven his younger brother died of anemia, brought on by hunger. Serge himself would know hunger, poverty, and exile all his life. At sixteen he first read Peter Kropotkin's advice to young people; by nineteen he was in Paris and joined the individualist anarchists.

Serge's arrival came a year after the death of Albert Libertad, a crucial and colorful figure in prewar anarchism. Serge accepted Libertad's central doctrine that one should not await the revolution but instead live it in one's daily life. "Make the revolution oneself. Be free men, live in camaraderie."[2] In her *Souvenirs d'Anarchie*, published in 1913, Maîtrejean described Libertad as a cripple who walked with crutches, had the arms of an athlete, an enormous head with long curly hair, and piercing blue eyes. The illegitimate son of a prefect, he fled his *lycée* and founded the journal *L'Anarchie* in 1905. He died in a brawl, which he had engaged in frequently with his ideological opponents. Maîtrejean met young Victor Serge at the *L'Anarchie* offices and was immediately attracted to the handsome young man with piercing black eyes who affected white flannel Russian shirts. Already his intellectualism disquieted other young anarchists.[3] In 1911 the young couple took over control of the journal, and Serge began using the anarchist nom de plume *Le Rétif* (the stubborn or insubordinate one). He would not use the name Serge until 1917, at the moment that he left anarchism behind.

If the individualists associated with *L'Anarchie* had confined themselves to intellectual or lifestyle issues, they might have stayed out of trouble, but unfortunately Serge's anarchist phase coincided with the exploits of the Bonnot Gang, some of whose members were old friends of Serge's from his Belgian childhood. The police reported that the popular talks sponsored by Libertad's journal advocated illegal acts, and 1911–12 was the high point of the practice called *la reprise individuelle,* or individual restitution, otherwise known as theft. The exploits of the "tragic bandits" (as the Bonnot Gang was romantically known), which aroused the admiration of the individualist anarchists, implicated Serge and Maîtrejean in their crimes. The young couple spent the summer of 1911 with some of the bandits in a house in suburban Romainville. The communist-anarchists condemned individual acts of expropriation as detracting from the collective focus on general strikes and insurrection, leaving the individualists to experiment with politically motivated criminality and arousing the scrutiny of the authorities.[4] The Bonnot Gang committed armed robberies in the course of which people were killed, including an officer of the Sûreté in April 1912. Jules Bonnot was killed in a final shootout with the police a few days later, after a nine-hour siege conducted by hundreds of police and even soldiers. Serge and Maîtrejean were arrested, accused of possessing pistols that the gang had acquired in a robbery. Serge later maintained that his real crime was refusing to inform on the bandits; the police evidently saw him as the mastermind behind the gang.[5] When the surviving gang members were tried in 1913, Serge and Maîtrejean were in the docket alongside them. She was eventually acquitted; he received a prison sentence of five years, in the middle of which they got married to allow her visiting rights. Serge's boyhood friend Raymond Callemin was guillotined.

Rirette Maîtrejean, born Anna Destorgues, arrived in Paris around 1904 as a teenager and soon married a saddler named Maîtrejean. He was jailed for counterfeiting, another popular illegal-anarchist activity, and she left with the anarchist Mauricius for Belgium before taking over the editorship of *L'Anarchie* from André Roulot, called Lorulot, in July 1911. With the rest of the Bonnot Gang dead or in prison, Rirette was in a unique position to write about the notorious band of anarchists. Six months after her release from prison in February 1913, at the end of the trial, she published a series of articles in the mainstream daily newspaper *Le Matin* collectively called

"Souvenirs d'Anarchie, Un Bien Curieux Document" (Memoirs of anarchy, a highly curious document). Her overall message was that illegality was a dead end; her rationale for publishing this censorious piece was that her words might spare other bewildered young souls from following such a path. Adopting a tone of bitter humor, she mocked the bizarre, bohemian behavior of her former comrades. She chose the individualist variety of anarchism, she wrote, because the communist anarchists wouldn't talk to a woman at all, though the individualists weren't much better. They excelled mostly at talking, as well as engaging in all manner of clever scams to avoid paying rent and obtain free food. She particularly ridiculed Lorulot's food fads and nudism. The series concluded with a discussion of the trial and included a poignant note from Serge telling her to enjoy the things they had loved together—sunlight, flowers, books—but to promise never to return to the anarchist milieu. She readily agreed, saying her brush with prison and criminality had cured her of any desire for anarchist militancy. This negative assessment of individualist anarchism allowed her memoir to be published in the mainstream press and seemed like a betrayal to the anarchists. Yet at least for Serge, it was less anarchism than its irresponsible, individualist variant that was being rejected.

Rirette Maîtrejean married Victor Serge while he was in prison and briefly followed him to Barcelona in 1917 upon his release, where he resumed anarchist activity. She soon returned to Paris to care for her two children from her first marriage. Victor and Rirette's paths diverged in 1917, and he remarried not long after arriving in Russia in 1919. He embarked on a life of revolution and exile, while she chose work, home, and domesticity. After the war she joined the anarchist-dominated union of proofreaders and practiced that profession for many decades, while occasionally participating in lectures on prewar anarchism. She died in June 1968, shortly after a feature film appeared on *Les Anarchistes, ou La Bande à Bonnot* featuring Bruno Cremer as Bonnot and the singer-songwriter Jacques Brel as Serge's boyhood friend Raymond "la Science." Billed as the French *Bonnie and Clyde*, the film was perfectly timed to benefit from the neo-anarchism of the May 1968 student movement.[6] Her obituaries all included references to the film.

Victor Serge emerged from five years of prison a man without a country. As a foreigner, he was forced to leave France, and he spent several months in Spain, where he became involved with unsuccessful anarchist attempts to foment a general strike. He corresponded extensively with E. Armand, the individualist who during the war edited the journal *Par-delà la Mêlée* (Beyond the battle), and though he distanced himself from his prewar milieu and admitted that he had begged Rirette to leave it behind as well, he remained an anarchist.[7] He increasingly expressed dissatisfaction at the egotism of Armand's individualist approach, especially his obsession with sex, and called Nietzsche a philosopher of violence and authority. By July, Serge told Armand that he and Rirette had separated and that he planned to return to Russia to lend a hand in the revolution. Instead, he was arrested in France in October 1917 for violating his expulsion order. After fifteen more months of detention, during which he studied the writings of Marx, he finally made it to Petrograd in January 1919. "Le Rétif" materialized in Russia as Victor Serge, on the path to becoming a major political figure, ally of Trotsky and organizer of the Comintern. His anarchist years in France had been a preparatory stage in his revolutionary career. Though he was not French like Maîtrejean, Wullens, Colomer, and Breton, his many books were written in that language.

Victor Serge's career as a Bolshevik in Russia did not involve as clear a break with his anarchist antecedents as it might appear. Immediately after his arrival in Petrograd, he began sending back articles to be published in the newly revived anarchist paper Le Libertaire in which he described the Russian Revolution.[8] In a long letter dated October 1920 and signed Victor-Serge Kibaltchiche, he claimed he was as anti-authoritarian as ever, but that in a revolutionary situation one must either choose revolution or reaction. The time was over, he wrote to his former comrades, when one could believe oneself an anarchist because one was a vegetarian. Revolution meant violence; violence meant authority. Anarchist intransigence, he wrote, guaranteed defeat. Le Libertaire's comment on printing this letter written to an unnamed friend was to refer to him familiarly as "Le Rétif, well known to French comrades."[9] In a pamphlet directed at the French anarchists, Serge tried to explain how the anarchists and Bolsheviks could cooperate, as anarchist concern for liberty balanced the Bolshevik sense of discipline and organization. Nevertheless, in this pamphlet, "Les anarchistes et l'expérience de la révolution russe," published in Paris in 1921, he justified the disarming of anarchists in 1918 and the need for terror during the civil war as products of revolutionary necessity. As late as May 1921, Serge still referred to anarchists as "we," though by this time he was a member of the Bolshevik Party.[10]

In 1921, French anarchist attitudes toward the Russian Revolution shifted from cautious approbation to condemnation. With that shift, Victor Serge became persona non grata. In January 1921, an unsigned article castigated Serge, reporting that he had ceased relations with Peter Kropotkin, that he now wore a uniform and was authorized to stay at the Astoria Hotel in Petrograd.[11] The next month, when Le Libertaire announced the death of Kropotkin, it did not mention that Serge was the only Communist Party member to attend his funeral. Serge seemed taken aback by the attitude of the French anarchists and asked his comrades how he merited such attacks. Was it because he said that Kropotkin suffered no persecution in Russia? He reported that the Russian nation was in mourning over the great anarchist's death. The anarchists responded that Serge was the agent of a government that imprisoned and shot their anarchist brethren.[12] Articles on the repression of Russian anarchists would accelerate in 1921.

By the end of 1921, *Le Libertaire* was printing personal attacks on Victor Serge. One such article was signed by Rhillon, who claimed he had known Serge back in Belgium. He called Serge a provocateur of illegalism who never worked but kept the anarchist bandits under his spell. Serge was portrayed as an opportunist—the articles failed to mention the five years in prison Serge had endured—who now worked for the dictatorship of the proletariat while Russian anarchists rotted in Bolshevik prisons.[13] In the next issue, Maurice Wullens, later a close collaborator of Serge, also blackened his reputation; while admitting he didn't know Serge personally, he repeated uncomplimentary stories of his behavior in prison.[14] The anarchists of *Le Libertaire* were particularly likely to attack individualist anarchists and were even less sympathetic to one who had become a Bolshevik, especially after the Kronstadt naval uprising in March 1921 ended any positive relations between anarchism and communism.

As rapprochement between anarchists and communists became increasingly unlikely after 1921, Serge maintained an anarchist-bred distrust for the abuses of power and centralized control. He was one of the first, if not the very first, theorists to apply the term "totalitarian" to the Soviet Union. Though he criticized the anarchists for lacking the political praxis necessary to seize power, he appreciated their critique of political power.[15] Ironically, in the same year that the French anarchists broke with him, Victor Serge was already becoming disillusioned with the path the revolution was taking. In his memoirs, written two decades later while in exile in Mexico City, Serge condemned both the immaturity of the Russian anarchists and the intolerance and bad faith of the Bolsheviks. On the one hand, he concluded that "anarchism was basically a doctrine of far more emotive power than intellectual"; on the other, he still believed that "these impassioned dissidents of the Revolution, crushed and persecuted as they might be, were still right on many points, above all in their demand . . . for freedom of expression and the restoration of liberty in the Soviets."[16] Serge also sympathized with the Kronstadt rebellion against Bolshevik tyranny that broke out in March 1921, a month after Kropotkin's funeral, yet feared at the same time that the Communist Party was all that stood between the revolution on the one hand and chaos and counterrevolution on the other.[17] He remained loyal to the party despite his misgivings.

Serge wrote his memoirs after having spent many more years in prison, this time in the land of revolution itself. He was first imprisoned in 1928, then again from 1933 to 1936. A major campaign back in France led to his release just in time to avoid the purge trials, in which he surely would have been implicated and executed. Serge's arrest and imprisonment east of the Urals was protested in a speech to the pro-Marxist Congress of Writers of 1935 by Magdeleine Paz—the same conference that refused to let André Breton speak. Serge came to believe that Romain Rolland later convinced Stalin to release him.[18] The timing of his release was so fortuitous that shadows of suspicion were cast on him as a Stalinist agent who had been allowed to escape.[19] Serge did not move in anarchist circles on his return to France, yet within a short time he had published two major articles on anarchism. In April 1937, the left-wing Catholic journal *L'Esprit* published his "Méditation sur l'Anarchie." The following January, the mainstream journal *Le Crapouillot* published a special issue on anarchism for which Serge wrote the section on anarchist thought. Neither of these were anarchist journals (which would not have accorded Serge this privilege), yet these articles demonstrate that Serge the anti-Stalinist was still associated with anarchism twenty years after he left the movement.

The "meditation on anarchy" was included in an issue of *L'Esprit* devoted to "Anarchy and Personalism," with the editor, Emmanuel Mounier, drawing connections between his values and those of anarchism. Serge reminisced about his youth, yet when he observed the present he saw the same tendencies of a heroic and doomed movement that he had experienced in prewar France present in contemporary Spain. He contrasted the romanticism of anarchism with the efficacy of Marxism, which he still believed, despite his exile, had a superior command of historical necessity. In the article for *Le Crapouillot*, Serge wrote that there was not a single ideologue operating today who was comparable to the older generation of anarchists—a fact that demonstrated the decline of the movement. He named a variety of militants from Emma Goldman to Sébastien Faure, all of whom had been active before World War I. He was particularly hostile to the individualist strain of anarchism represented by E. Armand. Serge denied Armand's claim that the individual preceded the group in social evolution, arguing that species, family, and clan came first, with the individual being a peculiarly modern idea. Serge praised anarchism as a moral force, which if linked to scientific socialism could provide great benefits. Yet the trajectory of interwar anarchism to Serge was one long tragedy, following a path that led from Russia to Spain to France to the increasingly likely prospect of a new war.[20] To Victor Serge writing in 1938, his own life and times traced the end of idealism, the downfall of the dream of liberty. Jean Bernier, as anti-authoritarian a social-ist as Serge, added an essay on the present situation of anarchism and con-cluded that everywhere the problem of the state, whether capitalist, fascist, or communist, was "imposed on us as in a nightmare." These sober if sym-pathetic assessments of anarchism revealed that by the 1930s, the nineteenth-century revolutionary hopes of Marx, Bakunin, and Proudhon had suffered a drastic decline.[21]

Victor Serge had every reason to be sober about his life's project in 1938, as he watched his old Bolshevik comrades tried and executed in the purge trials. After Trotsky was murdered in 1940, Serge was virtually the only survivor of the Left Opposition who had been close to the Old Bolsheviks, and his own life was in danger. Things turned from bad to worse with the fall of France, as Serge had to worry about the Vichy authorities, the Gestapo, and the Soviet secret police. He managed to make it to Marseilles, where he benefited from help from the American Relief Committee. He stayed for several months at the Villa Air-Bel, along with André Breton, whose pres-ence there was due to Serge's influence. Unlike Breton, as a former Bolshe-vik he could not obtain a visa authorizing entry into the United States, but he eventually made it to Mexico. There in his last years, poor as ever, he wrote his now-classic *Memoirs of a Revolutionary,* a book remarkably free from rancor. Another great disabused leftist, George Orwell, appropriately helped arrange the publication of Serge's memoir after the author's premature death in 1947 at age fifty-seven.

Maurice Wullens

Victor Serge was a true internationalist, nearly a man without a country, expelled from Belgium, France, and Russia, who died penniless in Mexico. Maurice Wullens came from a Flemish peasant background, rooted in the soil of northern France. Five of his eight siblings failed to survive their child-hood, and his mother died when he was nine.[22] Yet his service in World War I turned the Flemish peasant into a lifelong internationalist. He later said that when a German soldier spared his life while in combat, he real-ized it was pointless for men of different countries to fight one another when they shared common working-class interests.[23] Wullens published articles in all of the major anarchist newspapers and journals of the era: *Le Liber-taire, La Revue Anarchiste, L'En Dehors,* and in 1925 after he broke with *Le*

Libertaire, in *L'Insurgé.* Yet he was never an anarchist ideologue and was equally involved with the overlapping movements of syndicalism, pacifism, antimilitarism, anti-Stalinism, and even communism. He represented a Third Republic stereotype in being a leftist schoolteacher whose major contribution was to produce a political/literary journal throughout the interwar period calling *Les Humbles: Journal Littéraire des Primaires* (The humble ones: Literary journal for primary teachers). Wullens's career exemplifies why anarchism in this period must be seen in the broader context of the left, and even beyond the left. Wullens worked closely with Victor Serge in the 1930s. Serge broke with him when he began to publish articles by Moeller van den Bruck in 1938 and accepted national socialism as a revolutionary movement. Serge went into exile; Wullens contributed articles during the war to Pierre Drieu La Rochelle's archcollaborationist journal *Je Suis Partout.* Wullens seemed not to perceive any large gap between feeling positive toward a German soldier in World War I and seeking common grounds with Germans in World War II. His overriding pacifism also explains why he signed the anarchist Louis Lecoin's manifesto demanding "Immediate Peace" in September 1939.

A short encomium to Maurice Wullens appeared at the beginning of 1925 in an article that André Colomer published in *Le Libertaire.* Colomer recalled that this *poilu,* upon leaving the army, tried to restart his journal *Les Humbles* in 1916 (a few issues had preceded the war, when Wullens was barely twenty), but the authorities would not allow him to publish an issue devoted to pacifism. Still he managed to publish the works of the anarchist Han Ryner, the communist Henri Guilbeaux, and above all Romain Rolland, to whom Wullens was especially devoted. Rolland had written the most important French antiwar tract of World War I, *Au-dessus de la mêlée* (Above the tumult), and he stood, much as Wullens himself, for sincerity and intransigence. After the armistice, a number of pacifists, individualists, and internationalists emerged who praised Wullens's courage in resisting the imprecations of nationalism. Colomer called him a moralist who published a special appeal for the communist Guilbeaux, condemned to death, after publishing another in favor of the imprisoned anarchist Armand.[24] With his long beard, shaggy hair, and mangled hand from the war, Maurice Wullens looked the part of the high-minded bohemian anarchist.

Wullens single-handedly produced *Les Humbles* during the war and, except for a brief hiatus in 1920, kept it going continuously until 1939. The unusual title suggested that it was directed at members of his profession, public school teachers who favored left-wing international literature. As a quasi-professional journal it reflected Wullens's strong syndicalist sympathies;

he was also active in the teachers' union. Readers might find selections from the works of Rolland, Henri Barbusse (author of a famous antiwar novel, *Le feu*), the German-Jewish anarchist Ernst Toller, and the Austrian Stefan Zweig (translated by Wullens). Anarchist theory, letters by Jean Marestan, the anarchist proponent of sexual education, might follow articles on Breton nationalism (in which Jean Jaurès was quoted as saying, "A little internationalism distances one from the country, a lot of it leads one back in."). The fact that Wullens was able to transcend the partisan splits between anarchists and interact freely with syndicalists, individualists, and anarchist-communists suggests that his literary focus placed his journal slightly out of the main axes of confrontation among schools of thought. That tone of benign toleration would change in 1925.

In the summer of 1925, several articles appeared in *L'Ecole Emancipée,* the journal of left-wing teachers, advertising subsidized study trips to the Soviet Union. The Pan-Russian Union of Workers in Teaching invited fifty teachers to spend their summer vacation in Russia. If the teachers could find two thousand francs to fund their travel to Russia, the Soviet teachers' union would fund the rest. Wullens couldn't afford to go on the first scheduled trip, but went with a second delegation at the end of August 1925. He wrote an account of his travels in 1926 and self-published it the following year as *Paris, Moscou, Tiflis: Notes et souvenirs d'un voyage à travers la Russie Soviétique.* His exiled communist friend Henri Guilbeaux wrote in the preface, "From rather individualistic tendencies and hostile in principle to all States . . . Maurice Wullens left one fine day for Soviet Russia. . . . Revolutionary spirit and intelligence led him beyond prejudices to question and examine everything. His anti-statism and anti-militarism suffered a rude assault."[25]

Wullens's account of his Russian trip was indeed positive, especially when contrasted with the sordid state of France. As he headed for the Gare du Nord to catch his train, he referred to the old prostitutes along the boulevard Sébastopol as representing the "syphilization" of their rotten old society.[26] He contrasted this departure with being welcomed in Leningrad four days later by teachers singing the "Internationale." He was impressed by the heroic efforts teachers were making to educate a nation of peasants and by his discovery that the teachers, like all other unionized workers, had their own cooperatives, rest houses, and retirement centers. The French delegation met with Lunacharsky, minister of education who admitted that they had tried replacing school superintendents with committees, but when that didn't work they put party men in charge. Upon visiting Lenin's tomb, Wullens praised the Soviet leader for being the first to stop the butchery of the

war, yet he also witnessed maneuvers of the Red Army. Even here the pacifist praised the equal pay for officers and enlisted men, the lack of saluting
and other paraphernalia of rank, and the inculcating of literacy for peasant
recruits.

Upon his return to France, Wullens embarked on a lecture tour to con-
vey his impressions of the Soviet Union and was accused of accepting money
from a foreign government. He denied any pecuniary motives and concluded his text by describing the great efforts of a liberated people: "a people which dethroned MONEY, corrupter of our old civilization, and which
has tried to replace it with WORK. . . . I also saw . . . pedagogical innovations which are truly marvelous."[27] He summarized these innovations: self-
government of the students, suppression of rewards and punishments,
collaboration of masters and students, and enlightened attitudes toward
sexual education. Convinced he had seen the future, Wullens was no longer
willing to participate in anarchist propaganda against the Soviet regime.

Maurice Wullens never joined the French Communist Party, but his praise
of Russia elicited strong comments from anarchists such as E. Armand and
Eugénie Casteu who thought he had been duped by the warm reception
given the teachers. The campaign to free imprisoned Russian anarchists
filled the pages of the French anarchist press. Wullens had himself contributed articles arguing in favor of Nicolas Lazarevitch, sentenced to five
years in Siberia for advocating workers' unions independent of state control.[28] In September 1926, Wullens published a letter in the Communist
Party newspaper L'Humanité arguing that the issue was not as clear as it
seemed and that in any case such repression was a minor issue compared
to more urgent tasks. In the summer of 1927, Wullens's own brother, Marcel, also a schoolteacher and a syndicalist, raised the issue at the congress
of the teachers' federation. This debate led to a total rupture between the two
brothers, accompanied by some public acrimony in the anarchist and syndicalist press.[29] The bitter feud lasted until the following year, when Marcel
Wullens died suddenly from tuberculosis at only twenty-nine years old.

Maurice Wullens's closest flirtation with communism occurred in the relatively liberal, NEP era of the 1920s. In the 1930s, he sided decisively against
the Communist Party line delivered in France by L'Humanité and began to
defend the victims of Stalinist persecution. His was thus one of the first
and strongest voices to demand the release of Victor Serge. A month after
Serge's release and arrival in his natal Belgium in April 1936, Wullens published a letter from Serge in Les Humbles expressing his gratitude: "I understand that in fighting for me you are fighting so that revolutionaries can
breathe in the USSR, in that duel between the working class avant-garde

and the increasingly reactionary government bureaucracy."[30] This was the beginning of a close relationship between the two former anarchists. Wullens devoted an increasing portion of his journal to publicizing the anti-Stalinist opposition. In a combined September/October 1936 issue of *Les Humbles,* Wullens published a lengthy inquest into the first purge trial, with contributions by André Breton, Maurice Parijanine, Magdeleine Paz, Victor Serge, and others. Several of the contributors denied they were Trotskyists but declared that the obsession with stamping out Trotsky signified Stalin's need to destroy whatever remained of the October Revolution. Long excerpts were reprinted from Serge's forthcoming book on the repression in Russia. One surmises that Wullens must have deeply regretted the split with his deceased brother over Soviet repression.

In 1938, Wullens opened his journal with a joint inquiry by himself, Victor Serge, and Alfred Rosmer, longtime syndicalist, on the assassination of Ignace Reiss in Switzerland, presumably by Stalin's henchmen, on September 4, 1937.[31] In October 1938, Wullens published the manifesto of André Breton and Diego Rivera, produced in conjunction with Leon Trotsky in his Mexican exile, "For an Independent Revolutionary Art." It was supported by the anarchist Herbert Read in England, by the *Partisan Review* staff in the United States, and by many French surrealists. Signers in France included Serge, Wullens, Victor Margueritte, Jean Giono, and Henri Poulaille. Belgium was represented by the anarchist Hem Day. The next issue of *Les Humbles* was devoted to the poems of Victor Serge, collectively titled "Resistance."[32]

What were the anarchists doing while Wullens, Serge, and Breton were attacking Stalinism? Anarchists refused to take sides in the battle between Stalin and the Left Opposition led by Leon Trotsky (though Serge refused to join Trotsky's Fourth International and exchanged sometimes acrimonious letters with him). They still reproached Trotsky for using the Red Army to crush the followers of Nestor Makhno in Ukraine and for suppressing the revolt of the Kronstadt sailors in 1921.[33] In August 1936, when the campaign against the purge trials began, most anarchists had their attention focused on events in Spain rather than Russia. Since they had been protesting the repression of anarchists in Russia ever since 1921, they were unlikely to be overly sympathetic to the purge of Bolsheviks by other communists. Wullens's participation in the campaign against Stalin was consistent with his libertarian convictions but nonetheless registered his distance from the libertarian left.

As civil war in Spain and the purge trials faded before the prospect of another world war, Wullens's fundamental allegiance to pacifism and antimilitarism reemerged.[34] In his eagerness to present himself as an internationalist

and a European, he began printing articles by Moeller van den Bruck exposing the Nazi point of view. It wasn't long before he lost the allegiance of
Victor Serge. In his memoirs, Serge wrote, "I had to break off relations with
one small review of the far Left edited by a libertarian veteran, usually a
most sensible man, because it was invoking the principle of free discussion
as an excuse to print apologies for Nazism!"[35] In Wullens's defense, he did
publish Serge's critique. Nor is it surprising that Wullens felt that peace
with Germany was preferable to a second world war. For contributing articles to collaborationist journals during the war, Wullens was reproached by
the Resistance after liberation, but due to his ill health he escaped prosecution and died of a heart attack in February 1945, only fifty-one years old.[36]
Victor Serge similarly died of a heart attack in exile in Mexico two and a half
years later. War was the defining issue of Wullens's life, as revolution was
for Victor Serge.

André Colomer

Serge may have been correct in saying that no notable anarchist thinkers
emerged after World War I; Colomer was born in 1886, four years before
Serge, and became an anarchist in the decade before World War I. On the
eve of the war he was the key figure behind one of anarchism's most original intellectual journals. Yet André Colomer was more than an anarchist
intellectual; he was the nearest thing interwar anarchism had to a star. Of
his generation, none was more flamboyant. Before he left anarchism for
communism in 1927, he had experimented with every variety of anarchism,
beginning with individualism, then moving to syndicalism and anarchist-
communism. He was a philosopher, poet, and orator but also organized a
union for theater performers. His final apotheosis as a communist was cut
short by his death from cancer in Moscow in 1931, aged forty-five. Some of
his anarchist peers called him a *cabotin*, a ham perpetually in search of the
limelight, and he was publicly excoriated after his conversion to communism.
Yet in an obituary published in the anarchist journal *Le Semeur*, A. Barbé
remembered him as "revolt personified," one whose fiery Catalan temperament helped explain his ideological reversals.[37] André Colomer was reviled
for turning communist because, as the most outstanding figure to take center stage in the French anarchist movement between 1913 and 1925, his
apostasy was particularly damaging. Even the right-wing publicist Léon Daudet wrote of the handsome, charismatic Colomer, "What a shame a man of
that caliber is an anarchist. What a Minister of the Interior he would have

made."[38] Colomer's unusual attitude regarding the Philippe Daudet Affair would play a role in distancing him from his anarchist colleagues.

In the summer and fall of 1927, shortly before Colomer's decisive trip to the Soviet Union, Maurice Wullens published a lengthy work edited by Manuel Devaldès called *Anthologie des écrivains réfractaires de langue française* (Anthology of writer-resisters of the French language), which featured writers who had refused induction into the army and expressed their hostility toward war. This was meant as a pacifist rejoinder to the five-volume *Anthologie des écrivains morts à la guerre* (Anthology of writers who died in the war). André Colomer was featured prominently, and because Devaldès had worked with Colomer closely before the war, he included a good brief biography of the poet. Colomer was born at Cerbère in the Pyrenees, on the French-Spanish border. His parents brought him to Montmartre, the Paris artists' colony, at the age of six, but each summer he returned to the south to spend the summer with his uncle, the archbishop of Albi. Montmartre in the early 1890s was suffused with anarchist bohemian culture; one might imagine that something rubbed off on the impressionable child.[39] He benefited from a good *lycée* education and became enamored of the symbolist poets while at the same time becoming politicized by the Dreyfus Affair. During his year of military service in 1906, he joined in the revolt of the vintner workers. After several years as a poet, he founded an anarchist literary journal in 1913 called *L'Action d'Art* in company with Devaldès and Gérard de Lacaze-Duthiers.

This intellectual journal defended the thought of Nietzsche and the deeds of the Bonnot Gang in the same breath. Colomer referred to "Kibaltchiche" in the first issue of *L'Action d'Art,* which appeared during the trial of the tragic bandits; he did not say whether he knew the young Victor Serge personally. Above all, Colomer exalted the intuitionism of Henri Bergson and wrote a series of articles annexing Bergson's ideas to anarchism while rejecting any sort of scientific determinism that limited the freedom and spontaneity of the individual. The title of his articles on Bergson's philosophy summarized the epoch perfectly: "From Bergson to Bonnot: The Sources of Individual Heroism."[40] For Colomer, Bergson demonstrated that each individual life was not predetermined by external forces, but rather contained within itself all it needed to expand and express its intensity. Intuition was the contemporary counterpart to Max Stirner's Unique. Annexing Bergsonism to individualist anarchism was not so surprising, given the popularity of the thought of Nietzsche at the time, but it did suggest an acceptance of irrationalism that was somewhat unusual for anarchists. The war ended this important contribution to anarchist aesthetics and philosophy.

Already in 1911, Devaldès wrote, Colomer had spent twelve days in prison for refusing to fulfill his military obligations, before getting sick and being released. In 1914, he crossed the Italian frontier with his pregnant wife with the intention of reaching Switzerland. His wife, Madeleine, had to stop in Genoa to have her baby, so the Colomers settled there, with André teaching French and lecturing on modern poetry to support his family. After Italy joined the war on the French side, he was no longer safe and tried to cross into neutral Switzerland but failed. Back in Genoa he was subject to police harassment and went on a hunger strike. Eventually he was hidden by leftist comrades in Genoa and while in hiding wrote the novel based on his wartime experiences, *A Nous Deux, Patrie!* (It's just the two of us, my country), which he would publish in 1925. He also wrote a philosophical text, *La Matière, l'Esprit et Moi*, in which he analyzed the ideas of Stirner and Nietzsche.[41] Unlike his fellow draft evader Devaldès, who remained in exile in London for many years after the war, Colomer was able to return to France with his family. He briefly tried to resurrect *L'Action d'Art*, began moving away from individualism, and eventually condemned his prewar flirtation with irrationalism. In the first issue of the new monthly anarchist journal *La Revue Anarchiste*, dated January 1922, Colomer disavowed his earlier enthusiasm for Bergson. The experience of war had discredited the liberating potential of the unconscious; the individual who abandoned his analytical powers was too vulnerable to collective passions.[42] Distrust of irrationalism was typical of most interwar anarchists and would limit their rapprochement with artists who otherwise shared many anarchist goals. A few months later, Colomer would also revise his earlier opinion on Nietzsche's influence on anarchism. He now rejected Nietzsche's analysis of the will to power as encouraging domination for its own sake. For Colomer, the essence of anarchism was neither to command nor obey. He furthered criticized the German philosopher for rejecting revolution and being hypnotized by the genie of force.[43]

In December 1927, after Colomer's defection to the communist ranks, one of his former anarchist colleagues on the staff of *Le Libertaire* summarized Colomer's career in the ironically titled "De l'individualisme heroïque à la dictature du proletariat" (From heroic individualism to the dictatorship of the proletariat). The war having ended their "little group of dilettantes" and their philosophical speculations, Colomer left individualism behind and in 1920 served as a syndicalist delegate at the Congress of Lille. In the early twenties he characteristically merged his newfound interest in syndicalism with his artistic bent by organizing theatrical performers into a new *syndicat des spectacles*. In 1921 he became an editor of *Le Libertaire*, the principal anarchist newspaper in France, and presided over its expansion to a daily paper at the end of 1923. Throughout the early 1920s, Colomer organized, edited, and wrote numerous articles for the anarchist press. Yet he broke with his colleagues at the paper and in the Union Anarchiste over the Philippe Daudet Affair. The anarchist Pierre Le Meillour summarized Colomer's attitude as "with Daudet against the police," which he said was akin to being with cholera against the plague.[44] Colomer became convinced that Léon Daudet was correct in asserting that his son Philippe had been murdered by the police on November 24, 1923, and he testified on Daudet's behalf in the 1925 trial (Daudet had been accused of libeling the cab driver who had picked up Philippe that day and who denied that he was a secret police agent). For Colomer to side with a leader of the Action Française was too much for the anarchists, even if it was due to their mutual antagonism toward the police. They suspected Colomer of being overly fond of the limelight and reported unfavorably on his positive treatment by the mainstream press.[45] In a bitter article titled "Incomprehensible Deviation," Georges Bastien summarized the anarchist position as "with the anarchists against the murderous cops? Always. With Léon Daudet against whomever or whatever? Never." Bastien saw Colomer's mercurial flirtations with rival extremist groups as a threat: "Now you offer carnations to communists after doing so to royalists."[46]

Colomer left *Le Libertaire* to found a new journal, *L'Insurgé* (The insurgent or rebel). As Bastien suggested, Colomer was abandoning leftist sectarianism for broad-based coalitions of all revolutionary elements. In October 1925, under the poetic title "Our Road under the Stars," Colomer affirmed his commitment to individualist anarchism and also to revolution. Since he judged the Communist Party to be at the present time the greatest threat to French nationalism, capitalism, and the bourgeoisie, he supported it. He also supported the communist trade union, the CGTU. Colomer declared that nothing would stop the parallel march of individual culture and revolutionary action along the road that they pursued tirelessly under the stars.[47] The next issue of Colomer's new paper featured an article by Maurice Wullens describing the impressive educational achievements taking place in the Soviet Union. In the same palace where Rasputin was killed, Wullens reported, workers now held union meetings. Factories and regiments provided portable libraries. Everywhere there was feverish change.[48] Wullens and Colomer were on the same page in 1925. Both were banished from the dogmatic *Le Libertaire*, and both refused to condemn the only revolutionary society in the world. They opened the new journal to the archindividualist E. Armand, who proclaimed his "revolutionary sexualism" in the July 25 issue, though not without criticism. Even more significantly, in that same issue there appeared an article titled "Antifrance d'Abord," (AntiFrance First) by the surrealist poet Paul Eluard. Colomer prefaced Eluard's antinationalist remarks by suggesting that "the libertarian ideal arouses a whole generation of young writers who don't hesitate to overturn idols, to knock over the priests. Nothing is sacred for them any longer; they want to affirm life." There followed Eluard's response to *Clarté*'s poll of young writers, in which he hoped France's enemies would triumph: "I only await Liberty! All war supposes a defeat, all defeat a revolution."[49] One month later, on August 29, Colomer published the entire surrealist political manifesto, "La révolution d'abord et toujours!" (Revolution first and always!). This declaration also appeared in *L'Humanité*, though not until September 21, and in *La Révolution Surréaliste* and *Clarté*, though not until October 15.[50] By publishing this document, Colomer demonstrated that like the surrealists he was seeking a broad-based revolutionary movement that would resist French nationalism and imperialism. Such an alliance seemed possible to some on the left in the mid- to late 1920s.

Colomer's new organ was more than a newspaper; from the start it was meant to function as a public forum for new approaches to libertarian communism. Colomer created a group called Friends of *L'Insurgé*, which later became the Club de l'Insurgé. This club was modeled on the well-known Club du Faubourg organized by Léo Poldès, which sponsored debates on a variety of topics of interest to workers and leftists. Poldès considered Colomer's club a direct competitor and would not allow speakers such as Dr. Madeleine Pelletier to participate in the *L'Insurgé* meeings. Orator that he was, Colomer played a major role in the debates organized by his new club and was able to attract between one hundred fifty and seven hundred people for discussions of free love, religion, the Daudet Affair, and many other topics.[51] Occasionally concerts were organized as well. At the end of 1925, André and Madeleine Colomer had to defend themselves in a tumultuous meeting from attacks by former colleagues from *Le Libertaire* regarding his behavior in the Daudet Affair. Six weeks earlier, on November 11, an audience of five hundred heard a debate on whether anarchists should support the Communist Party. Colomer argued that anarchists should be willing to support all revolutionary movements, which was not the same as engaging in electoral action; others argued against him.[52] At another of these meetings, an unnamed delegate from the surrealist group, which other sources identify as Louis Aragon, declared his group's support for the dictatorship of the proletariat.[53] Colomer's disaffection from *Le Libertaire*, ostensibly over his cooperation with forces of the right, also involved his new stance regarding communism. *Le Libertaire* continually criticized the Soviet Union for its treatment of anarchists; any suggestion of cooperation with communists was anathema. Colomer, like Wullens, had participated in this anti-Bolshevik campaign; now he was distancing himself from it. His reorientation would culminate in a visit to Moscow for the tenth anniversary of the Russian Revolution in October 1927.

On his return from Russia, Colomer organized several meetings at the Club de l'Insurgé (the journal had long since folded) to discuss his trip to Russia. Two hundred fifty people paid three francs each to hear him speak on February 23, 1928, with much applause but also cries of traitor, renegade, and sell-out. Colomer called the Russian proletariat the soul of the revolution, alone capable of giving humanity peace and happiness through labor. He concluded by saying that those who saw him as a traitor should instead follow Victor Serge's advice in aiding the Russian people to build a proletarian society whose example would be a torch of world liberation. Other anarchists were allowed to contradict him, one arguing that Colomer was only shown a façade, behind which miserable peasants still suffered.[54] Two weeks later, Colomer described Soviet factories as the living cells of proletarian democracy. He praised factory councils, free daycare facilities, and lodging. In response, a young anarchist woman demanded that he talk about freedom of opinion. Two Russian émigrés spoke against the Soviet Union, but the police informer reporting on the meeting said they were outnumbered by communist sympathizers, who left the hall singing the "Internationale."[55] The next day, March 9, Colomer left for Lyon, where he was met at the station by anarchists, who accosted him with cries of "renegade." He returned to the train until he could be escorted by guards. That night, Nicholas Lazarevitch was the opposing speaker, and while Colomer spoke twenty gunshots went off and fights broke out in the crowd. Though it only lasted a few minutes, the uproar was remembered as the "fusillade de l'Alcazar" and one anarchist was wounded in the foot. Colomer abandoned the rostrum precipitously.[56]

After his tumultuous return from Russia, André Colomer disappeared from the anarchist press. He would die only three years later while in Moscow. He had already endured significant health problems, causing the anarchist press to solicit funds for his medical care in 1926–27. L'Humanité announced his death on October 10, 1931, and Wullens reported it in Les Humbles that same month, saying that "the brusque news of Colomer's death has strangely moved us." Wullens wrote that Colomer had gone to Russia to care for his health, apparently because his poverty kept him from getting good care in France. Wullens commented that "one could differ in opinions with Colomer, poet, romantic revolutionary, and somewhat theatrical

[type]. No one can deny his ardent sincerity."[57] Two months later, Wullens reprinted the eulogy that had been published in the individualist anarchist paper *Le Semeur*, which wrote of Colomer's trajectory from the most ardent individualist to the seemingly opposite pole of communist. They attributed this change to his practical realism and also on his poor health which might have depressed his independent spirit. Others attributed his dramatic sensibility to his southern temperament, so "it would be irrational to reproach this visionary for the evolution of his ideological states" any more than for his long black hair.[58] Though some anarchists suspected that venality was responsible for his change of allegiance, his eulogists denied that the impoverished Colomer sought stipends from the Soviets. Wullens commented cynically that there were two kinds of anarchists: those rare ones such as Colomer who really believed that salvation lay in the social revolution, and the run-of-the-mill losers who used anarchism to mask their vices.[59]

The Surrealists

The surrealists have already made their appearance in this discussion of the evolution of the libertarian left, both in the mid-twenties context of some anarchists' growing allegiance to communism and in the following decade as André Breton made common cause with the anti-Stalinist left around Victor Serge and Maurice Wullens, among many others. The context provided in this chapter suggests that Breton, Aragon, and other writers made the same trajectory at the same time as the other figures discussed here. Until 1925, the surrealists showed strong anarchist affinities, which would rematerialize for André Breton during and after World War II (while Aragon famously broke with surrealism in 1932 and remained loyal to communism). Not only do literary analysts miss this context but they also tend to ignore both the degree of commonality between surrealists and anarchists and the factors limiting such rapprochement. Perhaps they should not be faulted since André Breton himself wondered thirty years later why the evident similarities between surrealism and anarchism had not led them to act more in common.[60]

We have already seen that until the summer of 1925, the young surrealists were closer in ideological allegiance to anarchism than to communism. Though their sympathies for anarchism were not new, they were reaffirmed by the Germaine Berton and Philippe Daudet affairs and pervaded the initial issues of *La Révolution Surréaliste*. The presence of Antonin Artaud, who edited the most anarchistic of these issues, increased this influence. In the summer of 1925, the Rif War in Morocco heightened their anticolonialism, which also signified their contempt for Western culture, which they perceived as overly rationalist and dominating. Breton's reading of Trotsky increased his sympathy for communist ideals. From the publication of "The Revolution First and Always" in the fall of 1925, the surrealists joined the communist intellectuals of the journal *Clarté*, and two years later, in 1927, some of them joined the Communist Party, though in most cases not for long. Some of the surrealists, such as Artaud and Desnos, refused to join the party, a decision that distanced themselves from Breton and his followers. Whatever his adherence, Breton always insisted on the autonomy of art, a position that led to his break with Louis Aragon and later with Paul Eluard, who remained more orthodox party members.

Although André Breton would not return to anarchism until after the Second World War, he recognized long before that that there was no place for avant-garde artists in the Stalinist world of 1930s communism. He had broken with Aragon as early as 1932, and made his famous speech to the communist-led International Congress for the Defense of Culture in June 1935, in which he subversively equated the bohemian search for individual transformation with the Marxist demand to transform society. For a few months in the autumn and winter of 1935–36, Breton and Georges Bataille collaborated in an extracommunist movement called Counter-Attack, which issued pamphlets and organized lectures. Typical of their efforts was "La Patrie et la Famille," (The fatherland and the family), in which "père, patrie, patron" (father, fatherland, boss) were attacked as interlocking elements of the old patriarchal society as well as of fascism.[61] Freed of ties to the Communist Party and its focus on class and economics, the surrealists could reassert their social-psychological critique of the authoritarian state. By March 1936, Breton and Bataille had split again and Counter-Attack was superseded by the short-lived enthusiasms of the Popular Front. Unlike the sudden shift in 1925 from anarchism to communism, there would be no similar reversal in the 1930s, at least for Breton, but rather an evolution toward a left-libertarian perspective. Bataille has been suspected of being attracted to the irrationalist antimodernism of fascism, and it has been argued that Breton's realization of this attraction propelled the dissolution of Counter-Attack.[62]

In the era of the Spanish Civil War and the Stalinist purge trials, Breton and the remaining hard core of surrealists favored Trotsky's Fourth International. Benjamin Péret, Breton's most loyal follower among the surrealists, fought fascism in Spain with the anti-Stalinist Workers' Party of Marxist Unification (POUM). In 1938 Breton spent four months in Mexico to meet his revolutionary idol Trotsky. The "old man" was being sheltered by the

surrealist artist Frida Kahlo and the muralist Diego Rivera. Ever the organizer, Breton returned to France to propose a new group of anti-Stalinist
left-wing artists, called FIARI, the International Federation of Independent
Revolutionary Artists. The manifesto signed by Breton and Rivera in Mexico in July 1938 explicitly acknowledged the need to balance the benefits of
socialism and anarchism: "If for the development of productive material
forces the revolution is held to erect a socialist regime of centralized planning, for intellectual creation it must from the start establish and assure an
anarchist regime of individual liberty. No authority, no constraint, not the
least trace of command!"[63] Anti-Stalinism made possible a rapprochement
of Marxists and anarchists.

The journal *Clé* (Key), the "monthly bulletin of the FIARI," which appeared in January and February 1939, demonstrated this unity. The National
Committee included a broad range of anti-Stalinist leftists, among them
Breton, Marcel Martinet, Henry Poulaille, and Maurice Wullens. Victor Serge
did not join the committee, but in a letter included in the January issue
addressed to "My dear André Breton," Serge agreed that the principles stip-
ulated in Breton and Rivera's document coincided with the views he had
expressed in his 1932 book *Literature and Revolution*. Serge wrote that the
agony of the purges would inevitably lead to a crisis of Marxism and that
Marxists must renounce any attempts to impose some sort of hegemony
over the left.[64] From England, Herbert Read wrote that certain pages of his
recent book *Poetry and Anarchism* were nearly identical with Breton's manifesto and that he was ready to adhere to the federation. From Belgium the
anarchist Hem Day joined the new organization. In the February issue, Leon
Trotsky saluted Breton, Rivera, and the others for being not merely independent spirits but true artists. In capital letters, Trotsky the Marxist praised
"the unshakeable fidelity of the artist to his interior self."[65] The next page
featured a selection from Kropotkin on the need for communes to struggle
against the power of the state as they organized mutual aid. Despite the
good feelings expressed by these contributors, 1939 was not an auspicious
time to begin such a journal, and the proletarian-populist writers such as
Martinet and Poulaille were uncomfortable with the many surrealists in the
new movement.[66]

The following year, after the fall of France, the fifty-year-old Victor Serge
and the forty-four-year-old André Breton would both take refuge at the Villa
Air-Bel outside of Marseilles, waiting for visas for themselves and their families so they could escape to the New World.[67] Serge and Breton were joined
by Marc Chagall. On the boat on which he and Serge fled France in March
1941, Breton met a young Jewish anthropologist named Claude Lévi-Strauss.

Lévi-Strauss later recalled that compared to Breton and Serge, who were housed below decks among the "riff-raff," he was privileged to occupy a cabin with three other men, one of whom was a wealthy Creole "who was felt to be worthy of special treatment since he was the only person on board who could reasonably be presumed to be neither a Jew nor a foreigner nor an anarchist."[68] Lévi-Strauss claimed to be intimidated by Serge as the former comrade of Lenin, but described him in uncomplimentary terms as "a prim and elderly spinster. The clean-shaven, delicate-featured face . . . had an almost asexual quality . . . which is very far removed from the virile and superabundant vitality commonly associated in France with what are called subversive activities."[69] Victor Serge no longer appeared as the dashing anarchist "Le Rétif," and his Soviet years and "man without a country" status must have aged him prematurely. Breton spent the war in the United States and returned to France in 1946. Unable to obtain an American visa, Serge spent the war in Mexico, collaborated on a biography of Trotsky with Trotsky's widow, and wrote his masterful *Memoirs of a Revolutionary.*

The overlapping trajectories of these writers and revolutionaries suggest the ideological intensity and intellectual commonalities that characterized this relatively brief era. All were profoundly affected by the war, by the Russian Revolution and the growing authority of the Communist Party, by the rise of fascism and then of Stalinism. Coming from an anarchist background allowed Victor Serge to warn of the dangers of totalitarianism well before the term was commonly employed. To all of these men (if we exclude Maîtrejean, whose anarchist militancy was confined to the prewar years), anarchism appeared to be an overly individualistic and even self-indulgent philosophy, capable of transforming one's life but not of changing the world. For Serge and Aragon, anarchism was a youthful enthusiasm that each had jettisoned by the time he was thirty. Aragon went on to become the French national poet during the war whose poems were quoted by General de Gaulle, but such radical reversals were at least as dependent on the vicissitudes of history as on personal transformation.[70] Anarchism appealed to the young poets Colomer and Breton as well, but Colomer did not turn to communism until he was past forty, and Breton returned to anarchism in his fifties and sixties. Wullens's brush with collaboration mostly revealed the depths of his pacifist convictions, having renounced war forever after his near-death experience in the trenches of World War I.

All of the figures discussed in this chapter came to realize that anarchism in France was losing political relevance as a viable revolutionary movement. Alone among them, André Breton returned to anarchism after the war, perhaps for lack of alternatives, perhaps because he saw it as the only alternative to the cold war ideologies of communism and capitalism, even if in a utopian guise. Breton and Aragon lived well beyond the Second World War; Louis Aragon is interred among the communist luminaries in Père Lachaise Cemetery. Colomer died in Moscow before the extent of Stalin's perversion of Marxism became clear; Wullens and Serge died at or near the end of the war while still in their fifties, and while Wullens's final years must have been dispiriting, the subtitle of Victor Serge's biography phrases the revolutionary future more optimistically: "The course is set on hope."

Epilogue: The Renewal of Anarchism

The individualist anarchists of the 1920s conflated the personal and the political, the sexual and the social. So did the surrealists, as André Breton's well-known comment equating Rimbaud and Marx made clear. If anarchists and surrealists failed to coalesce in the 1920s, forty years later their mutual influence could be felt among the radical students on the left bank. Of the many slogans that graced the walls of Paris in that revolutionary springtime of 1968, one in particular summarized perfectly the overall mood. The student who scrawled, "The more I make love, the more I feel like making revolution. The more I make revolution, the more I feel like making love," knowingly or not was echoing the ideal of E. Armand as well as A. Breton.[1] Someone else less originally contributed, "Make love not war," in English, to the walls of Paris. The war referred to here was Vietnam, but it could have been World War I for an earlier generation. Love and revolution were equally proffered as alternatives to war.

In the epilogue to his unconventional history of anarchic moments in twentieth-century cultural history, *Lipstick Traces,* the music critic Greil Marcus confesses that his inspiration for the book came from his own student experience at the University of California at Berkeley in 1964, during the Free Speech Movement (FSM). In particular he describes the incident at the open-air Greek Theater, at which the university chancellor spoke soothing and rational words that lulled the students into a sense of complacency. Then Mario Savio, spokesman of the FSM, tried to speak and was dragged away by the campus police. Immediately all the chancellor's words were effaced as the repressive nature of the university power structure stood revealed.[2] Marcus says he never got over the sense that everything had suddenly changed, and he sought similar moments in the past. Marcus experienced such a transformative moment on first hearing the Sex Pistols' song "Anarchy in the U.K." in 1976, which took him further back in time to find precedents in the situationists of the 1950s and 1960s, and then back to their progenitors, the dadaists of the Cabaret Voltaire in Zurich, Switzerland, during World War I.[3]

Although I was only a freshman in high school in 1964, I too may be found guilty of reading back from my sixties experiences (though no one moment stands out as it did for Marcus) to seek precedents in earlier periods of cultural rebellion. My interest in European anarchism helped me comprehend the ideological origins of the New Left, of which I was a part in the late sixties. I was particularly drawn to artistic movements that made common cause with anarchism as a way of further understanding the countercultural manifestations of the sixties. How did artistic movements take on a particular political coloration? Have there always been parallel avant-gardes of art and politics, and how have they interacted? How can this question be clarified by sorting out the overlapping terms "bohemian," "avant-garde," and "modernism"? Beyond these questions involved in establishing connections between radical politics and more or less formal artistic movements, are there more broadly social and cultural manifestations of antinomian ideologies and unconventional, bohemian behavior that have recurred at different periods, as in the 1890s, the 1920s, and the 1960s?

One cannot help but be struck by the number of parallels between the individualist anarchists of France in the period immediately after World War I and the quasi-anarchist New Left that emerged in Europe and America forty years later. The similarities are so striking, in fact, that the reader might be justifiably suspicious that the above confession of personal interest has biased the investigator, so that he has found the parallels he was seeking while ignoring those aspects of the anarchist movement that did not fit the pattern. In one sense, this historian must plead guilty to understanding history as the interplay between the present of one's own life and the past; one can best relate to that which is perceived as most meaningful about the past. Nevertheless, the diligent historian, while aware of his biases, must also be true to his sources and respectful of the differences between past and present. Thus most anarchists of the 1920s were not particularly receptive to such avant-garde artistic movements as dada and surrealism, and their narrowly positivist outlook precluded them from sympathizing with anything they deemed irrational. Similarly, many French anarchists were unable to discard the sexist biases of their time, and even some female anarchists reproduced these biases in their published works. Most would probably not have accepted the label of feminism, though virtually all contemporary anarchists living in the wake of second-wave feminism would do so. Anarchists of the 1920s rejected surrealism as both bourgeois and irrational; their attitude toward feminism was also linked to their distrust of it as a largely bourgeois phenomenon, while most women were deemed to fall short of their rationalist ideals. Above all, what must strike the modern reader, and researcher, as most bizarre about interwar anarchists was their open espousal of negative eugenics. Their position can be clarified and understood within their own context—eugenics was widely accepted as progressive and scientific—while still thinking it strangely coercive for partisans of freedom to be advocating sterilization of the "unfit."

Differences between the two postwar eras, those of the 1920s and of the 1960s, do not need to be minimized; yet the parallels leap to one's attention. If we can see many of the aspirations of 1920s anarchism reawakened two generations later, what does this say about the decline and marginalization of the anarchist movement in the interwar era? Few of the protagonists cited in these pages lived long enough to experience the triumph of their ideals. André Breton died in 1966, just two years before the May Events at which the black flag of anarchism flew again. Breton had once again made common cause with the anarchists of the journal *Le Libertaire* in the 1950s and would no doubt have appreciated the overt recognition of surrealism by radical students who proclaimed their revolutionary goals as living according to their desires and who equated making revolution and making love. Rirette Maîtrejean died in 1968, shortly after the film about the Bonnot Gang premiered in Paris, and enjoyed a brief moment of renewed celebrity to match that which she experienced in 1913 when she published her *Souvenirs d'Anarchie*. Despite this revolutionary nostalgia, she had not been active in the movement for a long time. E. Armand died in 1962 at the age of ninety, before the sexual revolution for which he had longed in the early part of the century took off. Louis Lecoin, born in 1888, lived until 1971, and as late as the early 1960s was still actively protesting. His hunger strike in favor of conscientious objection from the military influenced de Gaulle's decision to grant this option to French citizens. Perhaps the anarchist who would have been most gratified by the changes she witnessed was Jeanne Humbert, born in 1890, who lived until 1986 and thus survived to see birth control and abortion legalized in France. Humbert had spent time in jail for merely advocating birth control in the 1920s. There is no better example of an issue once deemed marginal becoming mainstream in the very different demographic context of the post-WWII era.

Yet Jeanne Humbert must have realized that the issue that had been championed almost exclusively by anarchists fifty years before had become law in part because it was no longer associated with the far left. Is that true of most of the issues championed by individualist, "lifestyle" anarchists of the interwar era? Yes and no. Anarchist propensities toward nudism, vegetarianism and other dietary regimens, and birth control had diffused through the culture mostly shorn of their political associations. It was still an act of collective bravery for several hundred prominent French women to admit that they had had illegal abortions in 1971.[4] Pacifism and antimilitarism, belief in direct action, in utopian dreams of a nonrepressive society composed of small, self-managing groups, the back-to-nature ideal of rural communes, the rejection of bureaucracy and hierarchy, and especially Armand's dream that total sexual freedom constituted a primary form of rebellion against the institution of the patriarchal family all retained their anarchist associations. Their rebirth in the 1960s New Left might signify that these tenets of individualist anarchism had more staying power than orthodox Marxism precisely because they were not associated with the working class. Instead they sanctioned unconventional, bohemian forms of behavior that proved attractive to the newly enlarged cohort of youth born in the decade following World War II. One can imagine people of the 1920s smiling if they could witness the youth movement of the 1960s, as they recalled the familiar saying "Who is not an anarchist at twenty years of age?" In the 1960s a growing cohort of those aged twenty were in college, so that the leading figure in the French revolution of 1968, Daniel Cohn-Bendit, could open his 1968 instant book on the movement by paraphrasing Marx's *Communist Manifesto* of 1848, writing, "A specter is haunting Europe—the specter of student revolt."[5]

Worldwide outrage at the execution of Nicola Sacco and Bartolomeo Vanzetti in 1927 led to a crescendo of anti-Americanism. When demonstrators in Paris were prevented from reaching the American Embassy, some resorted to attacking symbols of American culture such as clubs featuring jazz music and American-style cocktails. Anti-Americanism swelled in interwar France, was temporarily quelled by the American-led liberation of France in 1944, but was soon revived by the French Communist Party as well as by fears of American economic hegemony. In the 1960s, French criticism of the United States was principally related to the war in Vietnam, which fit in nicely with the left's anti-colonialism and Third World orientation. In the 1920s America was portrayed as racist and xenophobic; in the 1960s as racist and imperialist.

We have seen that Jews played a significant role in interwar anarchism. The same could be said of the 1960s student movement in which young

Jews were disproportionately represented among the movement activists. When Daniel Cohn-Bendit was refused reentry into France (he was born in 1945 to German-Jewish parents and carried a German passport), fellow students raised placards declaring, "We are all German Jews." By the 1960s France had the largest Jewish population in Europe outside of the Soviet Union, with the Ashkenazi population of Eastern European immigrants swelled by the influx of Sephardic Jews from Algeria at the close of the Algerian war. A few of the prominent Jewish activists of the May events include, in addition to Cohn-Bendit, Alain Geismar, Pierre Goldman, André Glucksmann, Alain Krivine, Marc Kravitz, Bernard Kouchner, Regine Dekois-Cohen, Michele Firk, Benny Lévy, and Alain Finkielkraut.[6] These young French Jews were probably unaware of such predecessors as Bernard Lazare, Mécislas Golberg, and Yvan Goll, though no doubt they were aware of more famous revolutionaries such as Leon Trotsky and his fellow Jewish Bolsheviks Kamenev and Zinoviev. Sholom Schwartzbard was peripheral to French anarchism in a way that the young rebels of '68 were not, though the Gaullist state tried to marginalize Cohn-Bendit. Many of these names later achieved prominence in the fields of letters and politics, revealing the greater possibilities of assimilation as well as political integration in the postwar era. Whereas radical Jews of the interwar period were mostly drawn from the ghettos of Eastern Europe and were resented by native-born French Jews, such a conflict was scarcely relevant for most postwar youth. When such conflicts of identity or nationality did appear, French youth explicitly negated them.[7]

The disillusionment with Stalin's version of communism that marked the interwar era also had its counterpart in the post-1968 era. Though Daniel Cohn-Bendit identified with the anarchist tradition and pointedly referred to communism as "obsolete" in 1968, many other young leftists still participated in various Marxist groups, especially those calling themselves Maoist and oriented toward third world liberation. Though few belonged to the ossified Parti Communiste Français (which in any case did all it could to discredit the student revolt), they nonetheless felt complicit in Soviet totalitarian practice as revealed most famously by Alexander Solzhenitsyn in *The Gulag Archipelago*. The so-called New Philosophers of the 1970s, most notably the young Jewish intellectuals André Glucksmann and Bernard-Henri Lévy, were often associated with a swing to the right and disavowal of the revolutionary utopianism of the sixties.[8] These disabused leftists portrayed themselves as moralists rather in the vein of Albert Camus, who no longer could accept egalitarian ends that were perverted by such unsavory means as the Russian gulag or the contemporaneous genocidal practices of

Pol Pot in Cambodia.[9] Lévy's 1977 book title, *Barbarism with a Human Face,* is a play on the slogan of Prague Springtime nine years earlier, "Socialism with a Human Face," suggesting once again the disillusionment with socialist ideals.

This weighing of means and ends bears comparison with the campaign by Victor Serge, Maurice Wullens, André Breton, and many other French leftists against Stalin's purge trials in the late 1930s, which placed these earlier critics of totalitarian practices not on the right but rather on the Trotskyite and libertarian left. Another great moralist of the earlier period, George Orwell, unmasked the counterrevolutionary betrayal of the libertarian left in Spain in 1937 by Stalin's commissars in *Homage to Catalonia.* In both periods, radicals who emerged out of the anarchist tradition were particularly cognizant of the danger inherent in dogmatic Marxist appeals to historical necessity to justify inhuman acts. Individualist anarchists had always refused to collapse means and ends; they saw revolution as a process rather than a goal, and a process highly susceptible to abuse by those aspiring to power. Rather than viewing the New Philosophers' critique of Marxism as a neoliberal repudiation of the sixties, then, one may see it as the logical outgrowth of the antinomian and experience-oriented New Left, which itself was based on the earlier critique of the abuse of power and hierarchical party politics called anarchism.

Communism would suffer further collapse between 1989 and 1991. While the most obvious beneficiaries of the end of the Cold War were the apparent victors, the United States and the democracies that comprised the European Union, the triumph of capitalism and nationalism over international socialism was not entirely uncontested. In the late 1990s, protest movements emerged against the power of transnational capitalism that went by the name of globalization, and anarchists were at the forefront of the anti-globalization forces. The letter A with a circle around it appeared on walls in such sites as Seattle, Washington, and Genoa, Italy, as meetings of the World Trade Organization were disrupted by young anarchists intent on keeping alive the direct action tactics of earlier generations. The cultural counterpart to this renewed political activism was alternative rock. The definitive "grunge rock" band of the nineties, Nirvana, fantasized about anarchists taking over the high schools.[10] More avowedly political groups such as Rage Against the Machine perpetuated the conjuncture between radical art and politics, and unlike the still-elitist modernist movements of the interwar era, these artists achieved mass popularity.

Earlier icons of rock rebellion such as Jim Morrison of The Doors and Patti Smith had been inspired by the poetry and example of the *poètes maudits*

Arthur Rimbaud and Paul Verlaine; the rebelliousness of Kurt Cobain was presumably less French derived. Nevertheless, these references to American rock music have relatively little to do with modern France. Much as French anarchism of the interwar era was marginal compared to more momentous movements elsewhere, so the culture of rock and roll spawned only pallid imitations in 1960s France. Somewhat later, French youth were more influenced by American rap and African pop. At a time when the radical right National Front Party was campaigning for the exclusion of North Africans from France, music that was influenced by the Beur music of French-born North Africans took on an automatic political coloration.[11]

Whether represented by the sounds of grunge rock or Beur rap, the phenomenon of generational revolt and cultural transgression has exhibited a staying power not matched by Marxist class-struggle doctrine. To the degree that patriarchal authority is associated with the larger authority of the state, one can expect rebellion to renew itself at the continually flowing fountain of youth. Whether these movements will tether themselves to a renewed anarchist movement, as suggested by the 1999 American film *Fight Club*, or to some other ideology with an equivalent subversive allure, one may expect that the personalist values of individualist anarchism—freedom-as-liberation, direct action, resistance to hierarchy, authenticity and self-expression, community—will live on.

Notes

Introduction

1. S. Ferandel, "Le crise de l'anarchisme," *Le Libertaire*, September 11, 1925.
2. E. Armand, "Le crise de l'anarchisme," *Le Libertaire*, October 2, 1925.
3. E. Armand, "Réflexions," *La Voix Libertaire*, November 28, 1931.
4. Auguste Linert, "Souvenirs des temps d'anarchie, 1885–1895," *Plus Loin*, June 1932. The series of articles ran from April to June.
5. Sébastien Faure, "Le mouvement anarchiste subit un temps d'arrêt. Il faut y mettre fin," *La Voix Libertaire*, June 1, 1928.
6. Jean Maitron, *Le mouvement anarchiste en France*, vol. 2, *De 1914 à nos jours* (Paris: Maspero, 1975), 71n42.
7. See, for example, James Joll, *The Anarchists* (New York: Grosset and Dunlap, 1964), and Richard Sonn, *Anarchism* (New York: Twayne, 1992).
8. Peter Marshall, *Demanding the Impossible: A History of Anarchism* (New York: Harper-Collins, 1992), 445.
9. David Berry, *History of the French Anarchist Movement, 1917–1945* (Westport: Greenwood, 2002). This book originated as a doctoral dissertation with the revealing title "The Response of the French Anarchist Movement to the Russian Revolution (1917–1924) and to the Spanish Revolution and Civil War (1936–1939)" (University of Sussex, 1988).
10. It is telling that Berry refers to "Eugène Armand," when to my knowledge Armand never used that first name. His real name was Ernest Juin, and while some historians refer to him as Emile Armand, I have never seen him refer to himself as anything other than E. Armand.
11. Lisa McGirr, "The Passion of Sacco and Vanzetti: A Global History," *Journal of American History* 93, no. 4 (2007), emphasizes that the human pathos of the case attracted a wide variety of supporters well beyond the anarchist and communist left.
12. Berry, *History of the French Anarchist Movement*, 197.
13. Maitron, *Le mouvement anarchiste en France*, 2:59, 60.
14. Ferandel, "Le crise de l'anarchisme."
15. Rirette Maîtrejean, "Souvenirs d'anarchie, un bien curieux document," *Le Matin*, August 19 and 21, 1913.
16. *Le Néo-Naturien*. See the December 1922/January 1923 issue for definitions of vegetarianism and the announcement of the opening of the Foyer Végétalien at 40 rue Mathis. Another article in this same issue titled "Bistrocratie" attacked alcohol as enslaving the working man. An article in July/August 1922 by Julia Bernard, titled "Aux femmes," criticized young women who smoked. The August/October 1927 issue revealed the connections between smoking and cancer. For background on the vegetarian movement, see Arouna Ouédraogo, "Food and the Purification of Society: Dr. Paul Carton and Vegetarianism in Interwar France," *Social History of Medicine* 14, no. 2 (2001): 241, who suggests that individualist anarchists were the principal followers of this propagandist, despite the fact that Dr. Carton tended toward the Catholic right.
17. Léo Malet, *La vache enragée* (Paris: Hoëbeke, 1998), 43.
18. Maitron, *Le mouvement anarchiste en France*, discusses none of these figures, presumably because they come after the "heroic" era of propaganda by the deed.
19. The terms "purity" and "danger" have been borrowed from Mary Douglas, *Purity and Danger: An Analysis of the Concepts of Pollution and Taboo* (London: Routledge, 1966). I have

not followed her in applying a structural analysis of these concepts, but rather wish to highlight perceptions of order and disorder.

20. Peter Stallybrass and Allon White, *The Politics and Poetics of Transgression* (Ithaca: Cornell University Press, 1986), theorize about the connection between bodily and social hierarchies. In their analysis of the carnivalesque they frequently cite Douglas's *Purity and Danger.*

21. Stallybrass and White, *Politics and Poetics of Transgression*, 3: "What is socially peripheral is so frequently symbolically central."

22. See Robert Brécy, *Autour de la Muse Rouge, 1901–1939* (Paris: Pirot, 1991), and *Florilège de la chanson révolutionnaire, de 1789 au Front Populaire* (Paris: Ed. Ouvrières, 1978).

23. Carolyn Dean, *Sexuality and Modern Western Culture* (New York: Twayne, 1996), 48, lists the five conferences as taking place in Berlin (1921), Copenhagen (1928), London (1929), Vienna (1930), and Brno, Czechoslovakia (1932).

24. Patrice Higonnet, *Paris, Capital of the World,* trans. Arthur Goldhammer (Cambridge: Harvard University Press, 2002), 328.

Introduction to Part I

1. Karl Mannheim, *Ideology and Utopia,* trans. Louis Wirth and Edward Shils (New York: Harcourt, Brace and World, 1936), 225, 244; Norman Cohn, *The Pursuit of the Millennium* (New York: Harper, 1961), 185–94, "the doctrine of mystical anarchism" (194).

Chapter 1

1. The standard, authoritative history of French anarchism is by Jean Maitron, *Le mouvement anarchiste en France* (Paris: Maspero, 1975), two volumes. Berton does not appear in volume 2 of Maitron, nor in the two standard English-language histories of anarchism, Joll, *The Anarchists,* and George Woodcock, *Anarchism* (New York: Meridian, 1962). She does appear briefly in the recent study of interwar French anarchism, Berry's *History of the French Anarchist Movement.* Not only does Berry not discuss the Berton case in any depth but dismisses all individualist acts of violence as throwbacks to the presyndicalist era. On the history of the right, Eugen Weber, *Action Française* (Stanford: Stanford University Press, 1962), does discuss Plateau's murder, but he is not particularly interested in Berton. In his recent book *Surrealism and the Art of Crime* (Ithaca: Cornell University Press, 2008), Jonathan Eburne writes extensively about Berton but never once employs the word "gender."

2. Ann-Louise Shapiro, *Breaking the Codes: Female Criminality in Fin de Siècle Paris* (Stanford: Stanford University Press, 1996), 14, reports that in the 1890s, 50 percent of women tried for crimes in the cour d'assises, the main court for felonies in Paris, were acquitted, compared with a 30 percent acquittal rate for men.

3. Shapiro, *Breaking the Codes,* 138.

4. Shapiro, *Breaking the Codes,* 148.

5. Maitron, *Le mouvement anarchiste en France,* 1:423 and passim.

6. André Lorulot, "The Papacy," *L'encyclopédie anarchiste,* vol. 3 (Paris: Eds., 1934).

7. André Lorulot, "Notre ennemie: La femme," conférence prononcée le 12 février 1921 dans la Grande Salle de la Maison Commune, à Paris (Conflans-Honorine: Editions de L'Idée Libre, 1923), 13, 14.

8. Bram Dijkstra makes much of men animalizing women in the late nineteenth and early twentieth centuries. See his pair of books, *Idols of Perversity: Fantasies of Feminine Evil in Fin-de-Siècle Culture* (Oxford: Oxford University Press, 1986), and *Evil Sisters: The Threat of Female Sexuality in Twentieth-Century Culture* (New York: Henry Holt, 1996).

9. Lorulot, "Notre ennemie: La femme," 21.

10. Lorulot, "Notre ennemie: La femme," 24.

11. Lorulot, "Notre ennemie: La femme," 29.

12. Lorulot, "Notre ennemie: La femme," 30.

13. In her study of the anarchist and feminist Nelly Roussel, *Blessed Motherhood, Bitter Fruit: Nelly Roussel and the Politics of Female Pain* (Baltimore: Johns Hopkins University Press, 2006), Elinor Accampo succinctly phrases leftists' conflicts regarding women's liberation: "Freethinkers' glorification of nature also reified women's place within it. Spellbound by the 'eternal feminine,' most of them believed womanhood could never be free of nature's dictates" (63). Accampo traces antifeminist polemics among anarchists back to the turn of the century; she cites an article in *Le Libertaire* in 1903 that repeated the well-known biases of Proudhon (65). She also demonstrates that Roussel gave a lecture titled "The Woman and Free-Thinking" between 1906 and 1910 that attacked freethinkers' misogynist assumptions (109).

14. Archives Nationales (AN), F7 14790, liste des vérifications des domiciles d'anarchistes, Département de la Seine. It is worth noting that polls taken in France in the 1990s confirmed that this pattern was still the case. *Le Monde Libertaire* polled 294 anarchists and found that only 18 percent were women. A 1992 poll taken in Brussels, Belgium, similarly found that of 261 responses, 21.8 percent came from women. See *La Culture Libertaire*, 405, 406.

15. Lily Ferrer, "La femme se modernise," *Le Libertaire*, October 24, 1924.

16. Henriette Marc, "Les femmes et le féminisme," and Une Révoltée, "La femme dans le monde," *La Revue Anarchiste* 1, January 1, 1922.

17. Une Révoltée, "La femme et la politique," *La Revue Anarchiste*, October 1922.

18. Eugénie Casteu, "Le 'moi' féminin," *La Revue Anarchiste*, February/March 1923.

19. Maurice Fister, "Une défaite du féminisme," *Le Libertaire*, January 26, 1924.

20. Emma Goldman, "La tragédie de l'émancipation féminine," trans. E. Armand, *L'En Dehors*, October 20, 1924. After leaving the Soviet Union in company with Alexander Berkman in 1921, Goldman finally settled in the south of France, where she composed her memoirs, *Living My Life*.

21. Pierrette Rouquet, "Les féministes en période électorale," *Bulletin des Groupes Féministes de L'Enseignement Laïque*, February 1924.

22. Josette Cornec, "Une seule morale pour les deux sexes," *Bulletin des Groupes Féministes*, June 1925.

23. Jeanne Humbert, "Nos égales, la vraie compagne de l'homme—la femme de demain," *La Grande Réforme*, July 27, 1933.

24. Jeanne Humbert, "Nos égales," *La Grande Réforme*, September 29 and November 31, 1933.

25. Jeanne Humbert, letter of March 23, 1934, Humbert Correspondence, International Institute for Social History (IIHS), microfilm reel #479.

26. Andrée Forney, letter of March 24, 1933, to Jeanne Humbert, Humbert Correspondence, IIHS, microfilm reel #479.

27. Mary Louise Roberts, *Civilization Without Sexes: Reconstructing Gender in Postwar France, 1917–1927* (Chicago: University of Chicago Press, 1994), 123.

28. For an extended discussion of the vampire theme in early twentieth-century culture, see Dijkstra, *Evil Sisters*.

29. See, for example, Dijkstra's discussion of the 1926 German film *Metropolis* in *Evil Sisters*, 340–45. Of course France had a long history of anathematizing lower-class and revolutionary women, going back to the French Revolution.

30. Roberts, *Civilization Without Sexes*, 46.

31. *Gazette des Tribunaux*, 188, audience of December 18, 1923, reports the occupations of the jurors. They included bakers, clerks, a foreman, a bookstore owner, and businessmen, including a factory director. The only clearly working-class juror was a carpenter. Roberts, *Civilization Without Sexes*, 46, discusses these stereotypes of the femme fatale and the sacrificial woman at length but does not mention Berton.

32. Claire Auzias, *Mémoires libertaires, Lyon, 1919–1939* (Paris: L'Harmattan, 1993), 298.

33. I consulted *Le Matin* and *Le Figaro*, which covered the Berton affair from January 23 to 25, 1923, and from December 18 to 25, 1923, when the trial took place, for the mainstream press. The *Gazette des Tribuneaux* specialized in judicial proceedings, while *Le Libertaire* covered the

trial in great detail and used the notoriety of the case to become a daily rather than weekly paper.

34. *Le Matin,* December 19, 1923.

35. *Le Figaro,* December 19, 1923.

36. *Le Figaro,* December 20, 1923.

37. *Gazette des Tribunaux,* 188, audience of December 18, 1923, and 191, audience of December 21, 1923. Also see *Action Française,* December 23, 1923, and the memoirs of May Picqueray, *May la réfractaire* (Paris: Jullian, 1979).

38. *Le Matin,* January 24, 1923.

39. *Gazette des Tribunaux,* 188, audience of December 20, 1923.

40. *Gazette des Tribunaux,* 189, audience of December 21, 1923. Of course Lenin was wounded by a young woman assailant, and his premature death early in 1924 was probably hastened by her attack. Unlike France, Russia had a long history of female terrorists dating back to the populists and nihilists of the 1880s. For a comparison between French and Russian terrorism as it relates to gender, see Richard Sonn, "Gender and Political Violence in Nineteenth Century France and Russia," *Proceedings of the Western Society for French History* 28 (2002): 199–206.

41. See Edward Berenson, *The Trial of Madame Caillaux* (Berkeley and Los Angeles: University of California Press, 1992), for an account both of the trial and the gendered contexts in which it took place.

42. Benjamin Martin, *The Hypocrisy of Justice in the Belle Epoque* (Baton Rouge: Louisiana State University Press, 1984), 205.

43. See Martin, *The Hypocrisy of Justice in the Belle Epoque,* 212–14, for Almereyda, whose real name was Eugène Bonaventure Vigo. Martin links the trials of Henriette Caillaux, Joseph Caillaux, and Raoul Villain, assassin of Jaurès, as representative of what he terms the hypocrisy of justice.

44. See Weber, *Action Française,* 154, 155.

45. Robert Wohl, *French Communism in the Making, 1914–1924* (Palo Alto: Stanford University Press, 1966), 128.

46. "Autour du procès," *Le Libertaire,* December 19, 1923, citing comments by Robert Lazurich of *L'Ere Nouvelle,* December 23, 1923, for *Le Quotidien* and *Le Petit Parisien.*

47. Séverine, cited by *Le Libertaire,* December 23, 1923.

48. See Martin, *The Hypocrisy of Justice in the Belle Epoque,* for a good discussion of all of these cases. Martin concludes his discussion of "politics, money, and sex" (233) with a look at the Stavisky scandal of the 1930s. There is no mention of Berton, but money and sex were not major elements in her case.

49. I am only aware of one book that deals with the trial of Germaine Berton: Iwan Goll, *Germaine Berton, die rote Jungfrau* (Berlin: Verlag die Schmiede, 1925), but a number of books appeared concerning the Daudet affair, including ones written by both of his parents. See Léon Daudet, *La police politique, ses moyens et ses crimes* (Paris: Denoël et Steele, 1934), Marthe Allard Daudet, *La vie et la mort de Philippe* (Paris: Arthème Fayard, 1926), Maurice Privat, *L'énigme Philippe Daudet* (Paris-Neuilly: Les Documents Secrets, 1931), Louis Noguères, *Le suicide de Philippe Daudet* (Paris: Librairie du Travail, 1926), and René Breval, *Philippe Daudet a bel et bien été assassiné* (Paris: Scorpion, 1959).

50. *Gazette des Tribunaux,* 189, audience of December 20, 1923.

51. *Gazette des Tribunaux,* 189, audiences of December 21 and 22, 1923.

52. Henry Torrès, *Souvenir, souvenir, que me veux-tu?* (Paris: Ed. Mondiales, 1964), 97, 98.

53. Torrès, *Souvenir,* 102.

54. *Le Figaro,* December 25, 1923.

55. Exchange cited by José Pierre, ed., *Tracts surréalistes et déclarations collectives, 1922–1939* (Paris: Le Terrain Vague, 1980–82), 384.

56. *Action Française,* "Le crime du jury," December 25, 1923.

57. Weber, *Action Française,* 138–40, says that the assassination provoked violent demonstrations by the right-wing shock troops, the *camelots du roi.* This antirepublican street violence probably aided Berton's defense later that year.

58. Weber, *Action Française*, 161. This is all Weber says about this minor incident. The descriptive "insane woman" implies that she was not an anarchist.

59. A. Lapeyre, "Une manifestation révolutionnaire," *Le Libertaire*, May 29, 1924.

60. Germaine Berton, "Au pays de la liberté," *Le Libertaire*, May 27, 1924.

61. "Germaine Berton tenté de se suicider," *Le Libertaire*, November 2, 1924.

62. "Pourquoi Germaine Berton a-t-elle tenté de se suicider?" *Le Libertaire*, November 2, 1924

63. Pierre Mualdès, "Aux hasards du chemin," *Le Libertaire*, November 4, 1924.

64. "Un mal qui répand la terreur," *Le Libertaire*, November 5, 1924.

65. *Dictionnaire biographique du mouvement ouvrier français*, vol. 33, "Larcher, Simone (Willisak, Rachel), 1903–1969," 269, 270.

66. Préfecture de Police (PPo), Dept. de la Seine, Paris, BA 2034, report of August 22, 1924.

67. AN, F/7, 14790, liste des vérifications de domiciles d'anarchistes, Dept. of the Seine.

68. "Germaine Berton a Suicide," *New York Times*, July 7, 1942, 5. A brief obituary dated-lined Vichy incorrectly reports her age of death as thirty-four (which would have made her fourteen at the time of her *attentat*) and also incorrectly claims that she mistook Plateau for Daudet. The most interesting fact reported is that Léon Daudet died the previous Wednesday, and Berton died of a drug overdose in a Paris hospital the following Saturday. That the two deaths were somehow connected is implied, but this appears to be speculation. I owe the location of this obituary to Jonathan Eburne, *Surrealism and the Art of Crime*, who cites the obituary in chapter 3, 284n15.

69. This is not to imply that they suspected Berton of religious affiliation, though in her final suicide attempt she did make her way from Père Lachaise Cemetery to a nearby church. On December 8, 1923, in the build-up to her trial, *Le Libertaire* reported that Berton had befriended a nun while at St. Lazare Prison and had convinced Sister Claudia to leave the order and go out into the world.

70. Henry Torrès, *Accusés hors série* (Paris: Gallimard, 1957), 39.

71. *Bureau de recherches surréaliste: Cahier de la permanence, octobre 1924–avril 1925*, Archives du surréalisme 1 (Paris: Gallimard, 1988), 45.

72. *Bureau de recherches surréaliste*, 45.

73. "Vivons pour lutter," *La Révolution Surréaliste*, December 1, 1924, 21.

Chapter 2

1. Aside from Georges Vidal's instant book on the Daudet affair, a number of other books discuss the death of Philippe Daudet, most written by participants. See chapter 1, note 49. Eugen Weber devotes a chapter to "Philippe" in *Action Française* and tells the story well but strangely never connects it with that of Germaine Berton. Weber sees Philippe as an unbalanced teenager who sought adventure, either by voyaging to Canada or by consorting with anarchists in Paris. He thinks the verdict of suicide to be the most likely explanation of young Daudet's death.

2. PPo, BA 1583, Philippe et Léon Daudet. Biography of Léon Daudet composed July 1929. The police reported that Daudet was born in 1867, while Noguères gives 1868.

3. The first notices of his death in *Le Petit Parisien*, for example, referred to the still-unidentified body as that of "a young man of twenty." Clipping from *Le Petit Parisien*, November 25, 1923, in AN, file "Mort de Philippe Daudet," F/7 12865.

4. Many of these details come from Louis Noguères, *Le suicide de Philippe Daudet*, 167–211. Noguères represented the taxi driver Bajot in his defamation suit against Daudet in 1925.

5. PPo, BA 2034, police file on Georges Vidal, 1903–64, dated November 29, 1926. The poem, "À Cottin," was published in *Terre Libre*.

6. Georges Vidal, *Comment mourut Philippe Daudet* (Paris: Ed. De L'Epi, 1924), 8.

7. Reported in "Le visage vrai de l'anarchiste," *Le Libertaire*, December 9, 1923.

8. Breval suggests the theft in *Philippe Daudet*, 46.

9. Privat, *L'énigme Philippe Daudet*, 72. Interestingly, Rouquette's office where Daudet visited him was on the third floor of 5 rue Las Cases, upstairs of the Musée Social, a small library of social history.

10. These details come from the police report in BA 1583, "Emploi du temps de Philippe Daudet," signed by agent Riboulet, December 23, 1923, and also from Vidal, *Comment mourut Philippe Daudet.*

11. So at least maintains Auzias, *Mémoires libertaires*, 174.

12. 46 boulevard de Beaumarchais is at the corner of the rue de Chemin Vert; the rue Amelot faces the other side of the store just behind. The corner currently houses a pharmacy, with a bank next door. It is a quick two-block walk or run to the Place de la Bastille. On April 18, 2004, when I looked at the site, primarily to establish whether it would have been likely that Philippe would have gone to the Bastille to hail a cab, a poster on the corner advertised a film called *Mémoire d'un tueur* (Memory of a Killer), part of a film series of police dramas. In any case, it was quite feasible for Philippe to return to the Place de la Bastille in order to escape from the police and catch a taxicab.

13. "La mort tragique de Philippe Daudet," *Le Libertaire*, December 2, 1923.

14. "La mort tragique de Philippe Daudet."

15. PPo, BA 1583, December 3, 1923, report. The meeting took place the preceding afternoon.

16. Louis Lecoin, *Le cours d'une vie* (Paris: author, for the journal *La Liberté*, 1965), 113.

17. La Ronce, "Pères et enfants," *Le Libertaire*, December 12, 1923.

18. A. Barbé, "Philippe Daudet," *Le Semeur de Normandie, Organe de Libre Discussion*, December 19, 1923.

19. Malet, *La vache enragée*, 31.

20. P. Vigné d'Octon, review of Georges Vidal, *Comment mourut Philippe Daudet*, *La Revue Anarchiste*, April 1924.

21. PPo, BA 2034, file on Georges Vidal, report dated January 4, 1924.

22. Georges Vidal, "Ma femme et ma forêt: Journal d'un colon," *Les Humbles*, February 1929.

23. Obituary in *Le Monde*, November 23, 1964, included in police file BA 2034.

24. PPo, BA 1583, ballistics report of July 6, 1925.

25. Noguères, *Le suicide de Philippe Daudet*, passim.

26. Breval, *Philippe Daudet*, 93–99.

27. PPo, BA 1583, undated report, probably June 1931, titled "Les dessous d'une palinodie."

28. Lynn Hunt, *The Family Romance of the French Revolution* (Berkeley and Los Angeles: University of California Press, 1992).

29. References to Sigmund Freud appear fairly regularly in the more intellectually oriented anarchist reviews of the interwar era, such as *La Revue Anarchiste*, *Plus Loin*, and especially in E. Armand's *L'En Dehors*. See, for example, the February 1935 issue of *L'En Dehors*, in which Armand reviewed Wilhelm Reich's newest book, called him the chief of the Marxist-Freudian school, and said he agreed with many of Freud's ideas. In a July 1936 review of Freud's *New Lectures on Psychoanalysis*, Armand actually cited Freud's opinion of anarchism as being sublime when applied to abstract speculations but a failure in practical life.

30. Hunt, *Family Romance*, chapter 3, "The Band of Brothers."

31. Report of the Sûreté Générale, AN, F7 13061, November 24, 1915, on Juin, Lucien Ernest, called Armand.

32. Jeanne Humbert, *Eugène Humbert: La vie et l'oeuvre d'un néo-malthusien* (Paris: La Grande Réforme, 1947), 15.

33. On Jean Marestan, 1874–1951 (real name: Gaston Havard), see *Dictionnaire biographique du mouvement ouvrier français*, 14:8. His mother's family had fled to Belgium after the failed Paris Commune.

34. On Ménétra, see Daniel Roche, ed., *Journal of My Life* (New York: Columbia University Press, 1986). On the *compagnonnages*, see Roche, *Journal of My Life*, and also William Sewell Jr., *Work and Revolution in France: The Language of Labor from the Old Regime to 1848* (Cambridge: Cambridge University Press, 1980).

35. Vidal, *Comment mourut Philippe Daudet*, 13.

36. Breval, *Philippe Daudet*, 154, 155. He also suggests that Vidal was in league with the police, that they provided him with the picture of Philippe published in *Le Libertaire* and even gave him five thousand francs to cover the costs of the special issue. None of these assertions are documented.

37. Léon Daudet, *La police politique*, 245.

38. Privat, *L'énigme Philippe Daudet*, 19, 20. Privat goes on to accuse Berton of becoming the mistress of Le Flaoutter, and thus being suspected by other anarchists of also belonging to the police. It must be said that the author provides no evidence for any of his assertions, and his account was published as part of a series called Les documents secrets.

39. Léon Daudet, *La police politique*, chapter 1, "Un régime condamné," chapter 2, "Le 6 février, insurrection de l'honneur français," and chapter 6, "Un secret d'Etat: Comment la Sûreté générale tue un enfant."

Chapter 3

1. Gérard Durozoi, *A History of the Surrealist Movement*, trans. Alison Anderson (Chicago: University of Chicago Press, 2002), 299. Another surrealist poet, René Crevel, committed suicide over his frustration at the split between communists and surrealists. Roger Shattuck discusses Breton's speech in "Having Congress: The Shame of the Thirties," in *The Innocent Eye* (New York: Farrar, Straus and Giroux, 1984), 21. See also Dudley Andrew and Steven Ungar, *Popular Front Paris and the Poetics of Culture* (Cambridge: Harvard University Press, 2005), chapter 10, "Turbulence in the Atmosphere."

2. For Rimbaud's role in the Paris Commune of 1871, see Kristin Ross, *The Conquest of Social Space: Rimbaud and the Commune* (Minneapolis: University of Minnesota Press, 1988).

3. André Breton, *Manifestoes of Surrealism*, trans. Richard Seaver and Helen Lane (Ann Arbor: University of Michigan Press, 1969), 220.

4. A number of books have established the politicization of the symbolist generation of 1885–1900, beginning with Richard Sonn, *Anarchism and Cultural Politics in Fin de Siècle France* (Lincoln: University of Nebraska Press, 1989), and Joan Halperin, *Félix Fénéon: Aesthete and Anarchist in Fin-de-Siècle France* (New Haven: Yale University Press, 1989), while Patricia Leighten sought anarchist connections among the cubists in *Reordering the Universe: Picasso and Anarchism, 1897–1914* (Princeton: Princeton University Press, 1989). Two more books on anarchism and art appeared in the 1990s: John Hutton, *Neo-Impressionism and the Search for Solid Ground: Art, Science, and Anarchism in Fin-de-Siècle France* (Baton Rouge: Louisiana State University Press, 1994), and Alexander Varias, *Paris and the Anarchists: Aesthetes and Subversives During the Fin de Siècle* (New York: Saint Martin's Press, 1996).

5. See Allan Antliff, *Anarchist Modernism: Art, Politics, and the First American Avant-Garde* (Chicago: University of Chicago Press, 2001). There is a large literature on Emma Goldman, who played a considerable cultural role in popularizing the work of writers such as Ibsen but whom one cannot exactly describe as a modernist. For a discussion of Goldman and much else in the New York radical scene, see Christine Stansell, *American Moderns: Bohemian New York and the Creation of a New Century* (New York: Metropolitan Books, 2000).

6. French scholars have been most attentive to this anarchist influence. The best work focusing on surrealist politics is Carole Reynaud Paligot, *Parcours politiques des surréalistes, 1919–1969* (Paris: CNRS Editions, 1995). The most inclusive examination of literary anarchism is Alain Pessin and Patrice Terrone, eds., *Littérature et anarchie* (Toulouse: Presses Universitaires du Mirail, 1998). An earlier work in English that slights this influence is Helena Lewis, *The Politics of Surrealism* (New York: Paragon, 1980). Still, Lewis does state that "surrealism, at least in its early period, was clearly in the anarchist tradition" (27). Since Lewis argues that the French dada movement was apolitical, she confines their anarchist affinities to the brief period in 1923–24 before the turn to communism. In *Surreal Lives: The Surrealists, 1917–1945* (New York: Grove, 1999), Ruth Brandon briefly discusses anarchism in the tellingly titled chapter "Dreams and Commissars." Some discussion of anarchism may be found in Durozoi, *History*

of the Surrealist Movement; the page from *La Révolution Surrealiste* with the picture of Germaine Berton is reproduced on page 62.

7. See Walter Fahnders, "Gustav Landauer, anarchisme, littérature, révolution," in Pessin and Terrone, eds., *Littérature et anarchie*. The artist André Lhote published an article titled "L'expressionisme français" in the *Nouvelle Revue Française*, December 1928, in which he cited artists such as Soutine, Chagall, and Vlaminck as expressionists. He described expressionism as systematic deformation that departed from the Greco-Latin tradition and implied that it was inappropriate for France.

8. Bonnet, *André Breton*, 51.

9. Bonnet, *André Breton*, 50, 51, 55.

10. Bonnet, *André Breton*, 55. For the close connection between literary symbolism and anarchism, see Sonn, *Anarchism and Cultural Politics in Fin de Siècle France*.

11. Bonnet, *André Breton*, 62–65. For Emile Henry, see John Merriman, *The Dynamite Club: How a Bombing in Fin-de-Siècle Paris Ignited the Age of Modern Terror* (Boston: Houghton Mifflin Harcourt, 2009).

12. Hubert van den Berg makes this claim in "Dada et anarchisme," in Pessin and Terrone, eds., *Littérature et anarchie*. As mentioned above, Lewis dismisses dadaist interest in politics in the first chapter of *The Politics of Surrealism*.

13. These "happenings" are widely cited. For the most exhaustive coverage, see Durozoi, *History of the Surrealist Movement*, chapters 1 and 2.

14. Cited by Alain Huraut in *Aragon, prisonnier politique* (Paris: Alain Balland, 1970), 56.

15. Lecoin, *Le cours d'une vie*, 113, 114. Lecoin claims in his autobiography that the surrealists wrote this letter to him, but it seems more likely that they addressed Georges Vidal directly since he was the anarchist most intimately involved with Philippe Daudet. In the book Vidal wrote based on his newspaper articles, *Comment mourut Philippe Daudet*, he includes the surrealists' letter on page 94.

16. *La Révolution Surréaliste*, December 1, 1924, 17.

17. *La femme et le surréalisme* (Nice: Groupe Eluard, 1992), 49.

18. Leora Auslander makes this distinction between maternal nation and paternal state in "The Gendering of Consuming Practices in Nineteenth-Century France," in Victoria de Grazia and Ellen Furlough, eds., *The Sex of Things: Gender and Consumption in Historical Perspective* (Berkeley and Los Angeles: University of California Press, 1996), 101–4.

19. Durozoi, *History of the Surrealist Movement*, 68.

20. José Pierre, ed., *Violette Nozières: Poèmes, dessins, correspondance, documents* (Paris: Le Terrain Vague, 1991), 8. On the Papin sisters, see Gérard Gourmel, *L'ombre double, dits et non dits de l'affaire Papin* (Le Mans: Cénomane, 2000).

21. Bardamu, "Points de vue d'un solitaire: Infortunée Violette Nozières!" *La Revue Anarchiste*, November 1933.

22. The surrealists' closed eyes suggest Martin Jay's argument about the importance of vision in modern French thought. Yet surprisingly he does not mention this photomontage in his chapter on surrealism. See his *Downcast Eyes: The Denigration of Vision in Twentieth-Century French Thought* (Berkeley and Los Angeles: University of California Press, 1993), ch. 4, "The Disenchantment of the Eye: Bataille and the Surrealists."

23. André Breton, "La dernière greve," *La Révolution Surréaliste* 2 (January 15, 1925): 3.

24. "Ouvrez les prisons, licensiez l'armée," *La Révolution Surréaliste* 2 (January 15, 1925): 18.

25. Robert Desnos, "Description d'une Révolte prochaine," *La Révolution Surréaliste* 3 (April 15, 1925): 26.

26. Quoted by Durozoi, *Surrealist Movement*, 86.

27. Huraut, *Aragon, prisonnier politique*, 59.

28. Durozoi, *Surrealist Movement*, 126.

29. See Breton et al., "La revolution d'abord et toujours," *Clarté* 77 (1925): 78.

30. Louis Aragon, "Le proletariat de l'esprit," *Clarté* 78 (1925): 336, 337.

31. Aragon, quoted in Julia Kristeva, *The Sense and Non-Sense of Revolt*, trans. Jeanine Herman (New York: Columbia University Press, 2000), 118.

32. Louis Aragon, untitled paragraph in *Littérature* 9 (February/March 1923): 15.

33. Louis Aragon, "Le manifeste est-il mort?" *Littérature* 11 (May 1923): 11.

34. Louis Aragon, *The Libertine*, trans. Jo Levy (New York: Riverrun, 1987), 11. The reference to Ravachol is on page 24.

35. Durozoi, *Surrealist Movement*, 137.

36. "The Darker Side of Surrealism" is a chapter title dealing with Bataille in Petrine Archer-Shaw, *Negrophilia: Avant-Garde Paris and Black Culture* (London: Thames and Hudson, 2000), 143, 144.

37. Quoted in Stephen Barber, *Antonin Artaud: Blows and Bombs* (London: Faber and Faber, 1993), 61.

38. Quoted in Barber, *Antonin Artaud*, 61.

39. Julia Costich, *Antonin Artaud* (Boston: Twayne, 1978), 59.

40. Costich, *Antonin Artaud*, 69.

41. See Hubert van den Berg, "Dada et anarchisme: Problèmes rencontrés lors de l'étude d'un lien apparemment manifeste," in Pessin and Terrone, eds., *Littérature et anarchie*.

42. Walter Langlois, "Action: Témoignage d'un courant oublié de l'Avant-Garde (1920–1922)," introduction to reprint of *Action: Cahiers de Philosophie d'Art*, March 1920–April 1922 (Paris: Jean-Michel Place, 1999), ix–xi.

43. Langlois, "Action," xiii–xv.

44. Langlois, "Action," xxv.

45. *The Egoist* 6, no. 5 (December 1919): 80.

46. *Action* 1 (February 1920).

47. Yvan Goll, "Expressionism," *Action* 2 (March 1920): 58.

48. Langlois, "Action," xxxiv.

49. Florent Fels, *Voilà* (Paris: Arthème Fayard, 1957), 78.

50. See Max Jacob, *Lettres à Florent Fels* (Paris: Rougerie, 1990).

51. A book in Dutch published in 1924 by Albert de Jong, *De Roode Maagd: Germaine Berton, geweld, gezag en anarchisme* (Amsterdam: De Fakkel), is only nineteen pages long, really a pamphlet; Goll's book numbers seventy-seven pages. The title "The Red Maiden" is strikingly similar to Goll's and highlights Berton's youth and gender.

52. Michel Grunewald, "Yvan Goll, les Français, les Allemands, et les Européens (1918–1934)," in Grunewald and Jean-Marie Valentin, eds., *Yvan Goll (1891–1950): Situations de l'écrivain* (Bern: Peter Lang, 1994), 43.

53. Jean Bertho, preface, "Autour de la revue *Surréalisme*," *Surréalisme* 1 (October 1924) (Paris: Jean-Michel Place, 2004).

54. Yvan Goll published the article "Le Torse de l'Europe," *Clarté* 35, no. 2 (October 1920); Claire Goll published a poem in the same journal two months later.

55. Albert Ronsin, "Yvan Goll and André Breton: Des rélations difficiles," in *Yvan Goll (1891–1950)*, 60, 61.

56. Jean Bertho, ed., "Yvan Goll," *Surréalisme* 1 (October 1924): viii.

57. In *Mosaic Modernism: Anarchism, Pragmatism, Culture* (Baltimore: Johns Hopkins University Press, 2000), David Kadlec makes much of these connections among Marsden, Joyce, Pound, and other modernists.

58. Goll, *Germaine Berton*, 25.

59. Goll, *Germaine Berton*, 35.

60. Goll, *Germaine Berton*, 42.

61. Paligot, *Parcours politiques des surrealistes*, 32.

62. Edouard Rothen, "Symbolisme," *L'encyclopédie anarchiste*, 4:2694.

63. L. Barbedette and M. Pierrot, "Rêve," *L'encyclopédie anarchiste*, 4:2356.

64. David Weir, *Anarchy and Culture: The Aesthetic Politics of Modernism* (Amherst: University of Massachusetts Press, 1997), 162.

65. Weir, *Anarchy and Culture*, 165.

66. In August 2002, anarchists celebrated the seventy-fifth anniversary of the execution of Sacco and Vanzetti in New York at a commemoration in Union Square.

67. Mark Polizzotti, *Revolution of the Mind: The Life of André Breton* (New York: Farrar, Straus and Giroux, 1995), 402.

68. Quoted in Polizzotti, *Revolution of the Mind*, 222. The warning to Bernier about the "anarchistic young writers" is cited on page 255.

69. Quoted in Polizzotti, *Revolution of the Mind*, 492, 493.

Chapter 4

1. Louis Aragon, quoted by Jennifer Mundy, "Letters of Desire," in Jennifer Mundy, ed., *Surrealism: Desire Unbound* (Princeton: Princeton University Press, 2001), 22. The quotation comes from the introduction to Aragon's 1924 book *Le libertinage* (unattributed by Mundy), which the young surrealist dedicated to Pierre Drieu la Rochelle. That Aragon would soon gravitate to communism and Drieu to fascism underscores the degree of ideological mobility possible for avant-garde writers of this era. Paul Eluard's quote is also from Mundy, *Surrealism*, 16.

2. Michel quoted by Marie Marmo Mulvaney, "Sexual Politics in the Career and Legend of Louise Michel," *Signs* 15, no. 2 (1990): 322.

3. Anne-Marie Sohn, "Between the Wars in France and England," in Françoise Thébaud, *A History of Women in the West: V. Toward a Cultural Identity in the Twentieth Century* (Cambridge: Harvard University Press, 1994), 110.

4. See Atina Grossmann, *Reforming Sex: The German Movement for Birth Control and Abortion Reform, 1920–1950* (New York: Oxford University Press, 1995), 16, 17.

5. Grossmann, *Reforming Sex*, 26–31.

6. Grossmann, *Reforming Sex*, 138, reports on the high percentage of Jewish doctors and public health clinic workers. Hirschfeld's fate and that of the Sexual Science Institute is discussed on page 146. Hirschfeld's death and importance to the sexual reform movement were noted in Armand's journal *L'En Dehors*, June 1935.

7. Eugene Lunn, *Prophet of Community: The Romantic Socialism of Gustav Landauer* (Berkeley and Los Angeles: University of California Press, 1973), 3, calls him the most important German anarchist since Max Stirner.

8. Jennifer Michaels, *Anarchy and Eros: Otto Gross' Impact on German Expressionist Writers* (New York: Peter Lang, 1983), 21–23.

9. See Michaels, *Anarchy and Eros*.

10. Charles Sowerwine, "The Sexual Contract(s) of the Third Republic," *French History and Civilization: Papers from the George Rudé Seminar* 14 (2005): 247.

11. Helmut Gruber, "French Women in the Crossfire of Class, Sex, Maternity, and Citizenship," in Helmut Gruber and Pamela Graves, *Women and Socialism, Socialism and Women: Europe Between the Two World Wars* (New York: Berghahn, 1998), 305 and passim. Gruber's bibliography is particularly rich in sources on interwar feminism and leftist attitudes toward women.

12. Christine Bard and Jean-Louis Robert subtitle their chapter, "The French Communist Party and Women, 1920–1939, From Feminism to Familialism," in Gruber and Graves, *Women and Socialism*. They conclude on page 344 that the Parti Communiste Française (PCF) "has maintained . . . conservative positions on the family and sexuality" and their attitude toward the emancipation of women was not much different from that of the Catholic Church!

13. Mauricius, "E. Armand tel que je l'ai connu," in *E. Armand, sa vie, sa pensée, son oeuvre* (Paris: La Ruche Ouvrière, 1964), 121.

14. Gaetano Manfredonia and Francis Ronsin do not discuss the impact of Fourier on Armand, but they do mention that Armand cited Fourier in a defense of pedophilia. E. Armand and la Camaraderie Amoureuse, "Revolutionary Sexualism and the Struggle Against Jealousy," in *Free Love and the Labour Movement*, Internationaal Instituut voor Sociale Geschiedenis Research Paper 40 (Amsterdam: Internationaal Instituut voor Sociale Geschiedenis, 2001), 5.

15. The best book on the topic is Francis Ronsin, *La grève des ventres: Propagande néo-malthusienne et baisse de la natalité Française, 19e–20e siècles* (Paris: Aubier, 1980). For a brief

but cogent review of French laws suppressing birth control, see Charles Sowerwine, *France Since 1870: Culture, Politics, and Society* (New York: Palgrave, 2001), 124–29.

16. See Ronsin, *La grève des ventres*, 166.

17. Berry, *History of the French Anarchist Movement*, 22n2.

18. Technically, *harmonie* would more closely resemble "Armand, Y.," in French pronunciation. Armand was, however, familiar with English, in which the letter "e" may be given a long "e" sound. In any case this is merely speculation.

19. Fourier, quoted in Jonathan Beecher, *Charles Fourier: The Visionary and His World* (Berkeley and Los Angeles: University of California Press, 1986), 311.

20. Pamela Pilbeam, "Fourier and the Fourierists: A Case of Mistaken Identity," *French History and Civilization: Papers from the George Rudé Seminar* 1 (2005): 188, 195.

21. Beecher, *Charles Fourier*, 298.

22. See *Dictionnaire biographique du mouvement ouvrier français*, 10:157.

23. Ixigrec, "L'evolution d'E. Armand," in *E. Armand*, 28.

24. Mauricius, "E. Armand tel que je l'ai connu," 121.

25. Manfredonia and Ronsin, "E. Armand and la camaraderie amoureuse," 7, citing a police report of 1933.

26. Sûreté Générale, AN, F7 13061, November 24, 1915.

27. Sûreté Générale, AN, F7 13061, May 22, 1916, June 17, 1916. Armand was reported leading frequent "promenades champêtres" to pastoral suburbs of Paris.

28. E. Armand, Vera Livinska, and C. de St.-Hélène, *La camaraderie amoureuse* (Paris and Orléans: Ed. De l'En Dehors, 1930), 3–7. This pamphlet bears the same title as the book that would appear four years later.

29. E. Armand, *Subversisme sexuel*, quoted in *E. Armand*, 75.

30. Armand, *La camaraderie amoureuse*, 17.

31. Quoted in *E. Armand*, 368, 369.

32. "L'ephémère féminin," *L'Insurgé*, August 15, 1925.

33. Armand, "Sexualisme révolutionnaire," *L'Insurgé*, July 12, 1925.

34. Armand makes this distinction in one of his earliest writings, *Qu'est-ce qu'un anarchiste?* quoted in *E. Armand*, 51.

35. Armand, *La camaraderie amoureuse*, 28, 29.

36. *L'En Dehors*, February 1936, for homosexuality in Germany; July 1936 for Armand's comments on Freud and Marestan.

37. Manuel Devaldès published a study of Han Ryner as early as 1909; see *Han Ryner* (Nice: La Revue des Lettres et des Arts, 1909); in July 1927, the Norman anarchist paper *Le Semeur* devoted a special issue to Ryner. Previous special issues had been devoted to Beethoven, Tolstoy, and Errico Malatesta, placing Ryner in esteemed company.

38. See Devaldès, *Han Ryner*, 19, for the early novels; see also *Actes du colloque Han Ryner* (Marseilles: CIRA, 2003). The 2002 Marseilles colloquium dates *Prenez-moi tous!* as 1932, but Armand reviewed it in 1931, so unless it was serialized before being published, it seems to have appeared by 1931.

39. Han Ryner, *L'amour plural: Roman d'aujourd'hui et de demain* (Paris: Radot, 1927), 236, 237.

40. Han Ryner, *L'amour plural*, 241.

41. Armand, *L'En Dehors*, March 15, 1931, and Ixigrec and Armand, May 31 and June 15, 1931.

42. Dean, *Sexuality in Modern Western Culture*, 58, 59, refers to Heinrich Pudor as a right-wing promoter of nudism who contrasted decadent corruption with nudist purity. For a full discussion, see Chad Ross, *Naked Germany: Health, Race, and the Nation* (Oxford: Berg, 2005). As Ross's subtitle makes clear, the dominant German ideology of nudism was designed to create "a racially homogeneous, socially united, politically powerful Germany" (158). This nationalist slant was obviously distant from Armand's anarchist ideals.

43. Armand, *La camaraderie amoureuse*, 23.

44. See Stallybrass and White, *Politics and Poetics of Transgression*, for a fuller discussion of transgression of social hierarchies.

45. Manfredonia and Rosin, "E. Armand and *la camaraderie amoureuse*," 7.

46. Beecher, in *Charles Fourier*, 336–37, makes it clear that even Fourier's disciples were embarrassed by some of the master's more extravagant pronouncements, such as the sexual proclivities of the planets. His disciple and first biographer was silent about Fourier's sexual ideas (10). His American disciples were even more distressed by Fourier's sexual ideas, Mrs. Hawthorne calling them "abominable, immoral [and] irreligious," which could be explained by the fact that he wrote shortly after the Revolution, when "the people worshipped a naked woman as the Goddess of Reason" (498).

As noted above, many anarchist communists opposed the individualists' focus on lifestyle issues. Jean Grave was so hostile to Armand that he suspected him of being a *mouchard*, or police agent, which was the worst accusation one could level at a fellow anarchist (and seemingly unjust for one who had spent years in prison for his beliefs). The Russian anarchist Volin of the Fédération Anarchiste Française bitterly attacked Armand's paper *L'En Dehors*. See Berry's Ph.D. dissertation, "The Response of the French Anarchist Movement," 361.

47. For French anarchist reaction to the Russian Revolution and the Spanish Civil War, see Berry, *A History of the French Anarchist Movement*. Berry cites the anarchist Mauricius, who much later contributed to Armand's memorial volume, as one who criticized a prewar anarchist for "contemplating your navel, doing a moonlight flit and practicing free love." Berry, *History of the French Anarchist Movement*, 35, originally in *Ce qu'Il Faut Dire* 76 (November 3, 1917).

48. Charles Fourier, *Vers la liberté en amour*, ed. Daniel Guerin (Paris: Gallimard, 1967, 1975).

49. André Breton, *Ode à Charles Fourier* (Paris: Klincksieck, 1961), 75.

50. Breton quoted by Terry Hale, introduction to Robert Desnos, *Liberty or Love!* trans. Terry Hale (London: Atlas, 1993), 7.

51. Desnos, *Liberty or Love!* 27.

52. The anarchist May Picqueray claimed that Yvonne George and the anarchist singer of the Muse Rouge group Maud Geor were the same person, in which case Desnos's dedication to her makes more sense. Picqueray's claim is not corroborated by any other source, however. See Brécy, *Autour de la Muse Rouge*, 111.

53. Desnos, *Liberty or Love!* 122.

54. Desnos, *Liberty or Love!* 123.

55. Desnos, *Liberty or Love!* 122.

56. Cited by Mundy, "Letters of Desire," 48.

57. Cited by Annie Le Brun, "Desire—A Surrealist Invention," in Mundy, ed., *Surrealism*, 305.

58. Durozoi, *History of the Surrealist Movement*, 238–40. For an extended analysis of the surrealists' debt to the Marquis de Sade, see also Neil Cox, "Critique of Pure Desire," in Mundy, ed., *Surrealism*, 256 and passim.

59. Vincent Gille, "Lives and Loves," in Mundy, ed., *Surrealism*, 163, reports that the "libertine notion of romantic relationships" was opposed by the more traditional Breton.

60. The surrealists shared anarchist hostility to religion and their appreciation for women was limited to the roles of muses and lovers, yet they were able to identify artistic creativity with the powers of the subconscious in a way that did not imply either faith or femininity.

Chapter 5

1. For a comparative survey of eugenic policies, see Maria Sophia Quine, *Population Politics in Twentieth-Century Europe* (London: Routledge, 1996). A popularized account of American eugenics is Edwin Black, *War Against the Weak: Eugenics and America's Campaign to Create a Master Race* (New York: Thunder's Mouth Press, 2003). See also Wendy Kline, *Building a Better Race: Gender, Sexuality, and Eugenics from the Turn of the Century to the Baby Boom* (Berkeley and Los Angeles: University of California Press, 2001).

2. This is not to say that there weren't mainstream proponents of eugenics practices. See, for example, Anne Carol, *Histoire de l'eugénisme en France: Les médecins et la procréation, XIXe–XXe*

siècles (Paris: Seuil, 1995), which cites numerous French doctors who favored eugenic practices. Yet theirs remained a minority movement, as shown by the failure of the initiative by
Deputy Pinard to have the Chamber of Deputies pass a law in 1926 requiring a prenuptial certificate guaranteeing that newlyweds be free of contagious diseases (227). Such a law had to
await the Vichy regime, which passed a prenuptial law in 1942.

3. Richard Tomlinson, "The 'Disappearance' of France, 1896–1940: French Politics and
the Birth Rate," *The Historical Journal* 28, no. 2 (1985): 414; Marie-Monique Huss, "Pronatalism in the Interwar Period in France," *Journal of Contemporary History* 25 (1990): 42. A recent
book on the continuity of pronatalist policies of the Third Republic and Vichy is Kristen Stromberg Childers, *Fathers, Families, and the State in France, 1914–1945* (Ithaca: Cornell University
Press, 2003).

4. The term neo-Malthusian was meant to distinguish anarchists from proponents of
Rev. Thomas Malthus's solution to the problem of overpopulation—moral restraint. Anarchists,
by contrast, favored free love and mechanical methods of contraception.

5. Three notable books that discuss birth control and eugenics seem to conclude with the
passage of the 1920 law, as if this meant that the birth control movement had ended. See
Angus McLaren, *Sexuality and Social Order: The Debate over the Fertility of Women and Workers
in France, 1770–1920* (London: Holmes and Meier, 1983), Ronsin, *La grève des ventres*, and
William Schneider, *Quality and Quantity: The Quest for Biological Regeneration in Twentieth-
Century France* (Cambridge: Cambridge University Press, 1990). Schneider does range beyond
1920 but scarcely mentions the anarchists at all. He does not, for example, cite the name of
Eugène Humbert.

6. So argues Karen Offen in "Body Politics: Women, Work, and the Politics of Motherhood in France, 1920–1950," in Gisela Bock and Pat Thane, eds., *Maternity and Gender Policies:
Women and the Rise of the European Welfare State, 1880s–1950s* (London: Routledge, 1991), 152.

7. Colin Dyer, *Population and Society in Twentieth Century France* (New York: Holmes and
Meier, 1978), 64, 66, 79.

8. Jeanne Humbert, *Eugène Humbert*, 20.

9. Roger-Henri Guerrand and Francis Ronsin, *Jeanne Humbert et la lutte pour le contrôle
des naissances* (Paris: Spartacus, 2001), 19–21.

10. Sébastien Faure, ed., *Encyclopédie anarchiste*, vol. 2, C. Lyon, "Malthusianisme et
néo-malthusianisme."

11. Jeanne Humbert, *Eugène Humbert*, 134.

12. Jeanne Humbert, *Eugène Humbert*, 187–89.

13. PPo, BA 2235, neo-Malthusian file, report of May 18, 1932. Jean Marestan (real name:
Gaston Havard) advertised *Sexual Education* widely in anarchist publications and sold more
than one hundred thousand copies of his book. The book was as much an anarchist and eugenic
tract as it was a sex manual. In chapter 11, "The Necessity for Conscious and Limited Procreation," Marestan argued that it was better to produce higher quality individuals rather than
large numbers and gave statistics about the high infant mortality rates in industrial cities. The
pre-1920 edition had a chapter on abortion, which he recommended be done in the first two
months of pregnancy. See Jean Marestan, *L'éducation sexuelle* (Paris: L. Silvette, 1916).

14. Jeanne Humbert, *En pleine vie: Roman précurseur* (Paris: Ed. Du Lutèce, 1930), 227, 243.

15. Patrick de Villepin, *Victor Margueritte: La vie scandaleuse de l'auteur de La Garçonne*
(Paris: Francis Bourrin, 1991), 212.

16. AN, F7 13059, notes on anarchist-communist activities in Bordeaux and the Gironde,
and in Toulouse and the Haute Garonne, 1926–1932, June 16, 1927.

17. Victor Margueritte, *Ton corps est à toi* (Paris: Flammarion, 1927), 10.

18. Margueritte, *Ton corps est à toi*, 63; Villepin, *Victor Margueritte*, 215.

19. Margueritte, *Ton corps est à toi*, 70.

20. "Jean Marestan," *Dictionnaire biographique du mouvement ouvrier français*, 14:8.

21. Marestan, *L'éducation sexuelle*, 166. Dyer, *Population and Society in Twentieth Century
France*, 145–46, provides figures that confirm that as late as the early 1960s, withdrawal was
still the most common form of birth control in France by a wide margin.

22. Marestan, *L'éducation sexuelle*, 170–71.

23. Marestan, *L'éducation sexuelle*, 210.

24. Marestan, *L'éducation sexuelle*, 215.

25. Jean Marestan, *L'émancipation sexuelle en URSS: Impressions de voyage et documents* (Paris: G. Mignolet et Storz, 1936). Quotation about Humbert from Jean Humbert, *Eugène Humbert*, 302.

26. Villepin, *Victor Margueritte*, 221.

27. For Dr. Toulouse and his organization, see Schneider, *Quality and Quantity*, 177–82.

28. Neither Hem Day nor the biography of Devaldès included in the *Dictionnaire biographique du mouvement ouvrier français* (25:156, 157) make it clear just when he returned to France, but he seems to have spent most or all of the 1920s as a refugee in England. By 1936 he had joined the union of proofreaders in Paris. See Hem Day, ed., *Manuel Devaldès, 1875–1956* (Paris-Brussels, 1957), introduction by Marc Larralde, 6–11.

29. Victor Margueritte, introduction to Manuel Devaldès, *Croître et multiplier, c'est la guerre!* (Paris: Mignolet et Storz, 1933), 7, 8.

30. Devaldès, *Croître et multiplier*, 289, 290.

31. Devaldès, *Croître et multiplier*, 298.

32. Ixigrec, review of Devaldès, *Croître et multiplier, c'est la guerre! L'En Dehors*, July/August 1935. Earlier parts of the review appeared in April and May 1935.

33. E. Armand, "Quelques critiques de l'Eugénicisme," *L'En Dehors* (November/December 1928).

34. Claire Auzias discusses the case in *Mémoires libertaires*, 252. In the neo-Malthusian carton at the PPo, BA 2235, there is a file on Bartosek, including the article from *Le Matin*.

35. Guerrand and Ronsin, *Jeanne Humbert*, 106–8. The Guernut Amendment, sponsored by a radical-socialist, passed by a vote of 310 to 262. The broader communist amendment, which would have pardoned those guilty of encouraging abortions as well, failed by a vote of 402 to 165.

36. Guerrand and Ronsin, *Jeanne Humbert*, 116–23. On the communists, see Tomlinson, "Disappearance of France," 414.

37. Manuel Devaldès, "La stérilization en Allemagne et l'église catholique," *La Grande Réforme* 37 (May 1934).

38. Eugène Humbert, "En Allemagne," *La Grande Réforme* 40 (August/September 1934).

39. Manuel Devaldès, "La surpopulation allemande et la guerre qui vient," *La Grande Réforme* 42 (November 1934).

40. Humbert, *Eugène Humbert*, 292.

41. PPo, BA 2235, report of December 30, 1932, on Pelletier and Dalsace; report of May 18, 1932 on Vachet.

42. PPo, BA 2235, report of February 3, 1938.

43. French anarchists were not unique in focusing on sexuality and women's control over reproduction. For Germany, see Willem Melching, "'A New Morality': Left-Wing Intellectuals on Sexuality in Weimar Germany," *Journal of Contemporary History*, 25 (1990), though eugenics is not mentioned; for Spain, see Richard Clemenson, *Anarchism, Science, and Sex: Eugenics in Eastern Spain, 1900–1937* (Bern: Peter Lang, 2000).

44. Francine Muel-Dreyfus, *Vichy and the Eternal Feminine* (Durham: Duke University Press, 2001), 63.

Introduction to Part II

1. See George Orwell, *Homage to Catalonia* (Boston: Beacon, 1952), for a brilliant analysis by a firsthand observer of anarchist Barcelona. There are of course many recent accounts of anarchist participation in the Spanish Civil War, but none capture better than Orwell the exhilaration of finding "the working class in the saddle," as he put it (4).

2. See Berry, *History of the French Anarchist Movement*.

Chapter 6

1. Robert H. Johnston, *"New Mecca, New Babylon": Paris and the Russian Exiles, 1920–1945* (Kingston: McGill-Queen's University Press, 1988), 25. Johnston admits that estimates range from 60,000 to 400,000 Russian émigrés in France, but he discounts the latter figure as much too high. Howard Sachar, *Dreamland: Europeans and Jews in the Aftermath of the Great War* (New York: Knopf, 2002), 14, cites the figure of 400,000.

2. Johnston, *"New Mecca, New Babylon,"* 17, 18.

3. David Weinberg, *A Community on Trial: The Jews of Paris in the 1930s* (Chicago: University of Chicago Press, 1977), 4, breaks down the 150,000 Jews residing in 1930s Paris into ethnic categories. Of the 90,000 Eastern European immigrant Jews, 50,000 were Polish, 15,000 Russian, 11,000 Hungarian, 10,000 Romanian, 1,500 each Lithuanian and Latvian. This influx made Paris the third most populated Jewish city in the world, behind only New York and Warsaw; with the arrival of North African Jews in the 1960s and the extermination of Eastern European Jews in the Holocaust, Paris now has more than 300,000 Jews, making it the largest Jewish community in Europe.

4. Sachar's principal source for information on the Schwartzbard trial is Saul Friedman, *Pogromchik: The Assassination of Simon Petlura* (New York: Hart, 1976). As the title indicates, while Friedman discusses the trial in great detail, his primary interest lies in the pogroms of the Ukraine and Petliura's responsibility for those pogroms. There is little on Schwartzbard's anarchist affiliation and so little discussion of French or Jewish anarchism that the word "anarchism" does not even earn a place in the index. Friedman cites not only trial transcripts and newspaper coverage but also Schwartzbard's own autobiography, *Inem loif fun yoren*, published in Yiddish in Chicago in 1933.

5. Steven Hause, "More Minerva than Mars: The French Women's Rights Campaign and the First World War," in Margaret Higonnet et al., eds., *Behind the Lines: Gender and the Two World Wars* (New Haven: Yale University Press, 1987), 106.

6. Sachar, *Dreamland*, 3.

7. Friedman, *Pogromchik*, 58.

8. Sachar, *Dreamland*, 4, 5.

9. Paul Magocsi, *A History of Ukraine* (Seattle: University of Washington Press, 1996), says that of 1,236 pogroms that occurred between 1917 and 1921, most were in 1919 and 1920 and estimates between 30,000 and 60,000 deaths. The figure of 60,000 was widely used in France at the time of the trial, although some estimates ranged as high as 300,000. Sachar, *Dreamland*, 18, estimates that up to 150,000 Jews died during the civil war in Ukraine. See also John Reshetar, *The Ukrainian Revolution, 1917–1920: A Study in Nationalism* (Princeton: Princeton University Press, 1952), which discusses the Schwartzbard case on page 315 but never mentions his anarchist affiliation. For newspaper coverage of his trial, see "Samuel Schwartzbard qui tua le Général Simon Petliura comparaîtra demain devant les Assises de la Seine," *L'Oeuvre*, October 17, 1927. Friedman, *Pogromchik*, 62, maintains that Schwartzbard returned to Russia out of enthusiasm for the revolution and that he left out of disgust for the treatment of the Jews, not due to Bolshevik suppression of anarchists.

10. May Picqueray reports this meeting in her memoir, *May la réfractaire*, 126. However, her memory may have been faulty, as she got the date wrong by two years (she claimed it took place in 1924). It's also not clear in her account why, if they were together in Belleville, he was able to track down Petliura the next day in the Latin Quarter. Picqueray later became an assistant to Emma Goldman when she was writing her autobiography in the south of France, and so probably heard this story from Goldman's friends a couple of years after the incident.

11. Henry Torrès, Schwartzbard's lawyer, reports this in *Accusés hors série*, 91.

12. Torrès, *Accusés hors série*, 94. Torrès also recorded his summation of this famous trial the following year in *Le procès des pogromes* (Paris: Ed. Du France, 1928).

13. Sachar, *Dreamland*, 9, says Torrès sent an assistant to Ukraine to interview Jewish survivors. Lecache founded an organization called The League Against Pogroms based on his experience with the Schwartzbard case, which in the 1930s mutated into The League Against

Anti-Semitism. In *French and Jewish: Culture and the Politics of Identity in Early Twentieth-Century France* (Oxford: Littman Library of Jewish Civilization, 2008), 100, Nadia Malinovich maintains that Torrès accompanied Lecache to Ukraine, though she does not indicate when this trip took place. Malinovich also reports that both Lecache and Torrès were expelled from the French Communist Party in 1923, the same year Torrès was defending Germaine Berton. See Malinovich, *French and Jewish*, 208n21.

14. P. Bénard, "Schwartzbard devant assises," *L'Oeuvre*, October 20, 1927.

15. Reshetar, *Ukrainian Revolution*, 254, provides this quotation and cites more than 3,000 deaths at Proskuriv on page 255. The testimony of Col Boutahoff was reported by P. Bénard in *L'Oeuvre*, October 21, 1927.

16. Torrès, *Le procès des pogromes*, 17, translated and quoted in Friedman, *Pogromchik*, 329.

17. Friedman, *Pogromchik*, 314.

18. P. Bénard, "Schwartzbard revendique fierment la responsabilité pour son actê," *L'Oeuvre*, October 19, 1927.

19. P. Bénard, "Schwartzbard est acquitté après une émouvante plaidorie de Me. Torrès," *L'Oeuvre*, October 27, 1927.

20. Charles Maurras, "L'acquittement de Schwartzbard," *L'Action Française*, October 28, 1927.

21. Torrès, *Le procès de pogromes*, 257, translated and reprinted in Friedman, *Pogromchik*, 85.

22. Friedman, *Pogromchik*, 334, 335.

23. See Malinovich, *French and Jewish*, 135.

24. See Richard Sonn, "Jews, Manliness, and Political Violence in Interwar France," *Proceedings of the Western Society for French History* 33 (2006).

25. George Mosse, *The Image of Man: The Creation of Modern Masculinity* (Oxford: Oxford University Press), 73.

26. See Daniel Boyarin, *Unheroic Conduct: The Rise of Heterosexuality and the Invention of the Jewish Man* (Berkeley and Los Angeles: University of California Press, 1997), passim.

27. Deborah Waroff, "When France Embraced a Jewish Avenger," *Forward.com*, October 23, 2008.

28. Jean Laloum, *Les juifs dans la banlieue parisienne des années 20 aux années 50. Montreuil, Bagnolet et Vincennes à l'heure de la "solution finale"* (Paris: CNRS, 1998), 95n7. The working-class suburbs east of Paris contained more than 3,000 Jews on the eve of World War II.

29. Esther Benbassa, *Histoire des juifs en France* (Paris: Seuil, 1997), 231. Jean Bonnet reports in *Les pouvoirs publique française et l'immigration dans l'entre-deux-guerres* (Lyon: Centre d'histoire économique et sociale de la région lyonnaise, 1976), 378, that nearly a million immigrants were naturalized as French citizens during the interwar period. The 1927 law made it possible to achieve French citizenship in only three years, and if one married a French citizen one could also choose to become French (160). Bonnet also notes that in the year before Schwartzbard's trial, nearly 10,000 foreigners were expelled from France, of whom 682 were militant communists (107), suggesting that it was dangerous for foreign nationals to attract political attention.

30. Friedman, *Pogromchik*, 347. Torrès became a deputy from 1932 to 1936 and after the fall of France fled to the United States. He returned after the war and served in the French Senate.

31. Hannah Arendt, *Eichmann in Jerusalem: A Report on the Banality of Evil* (New York: Viking, 1963), 245.

32. Nestor Makhno, "Lettre à Me. Torrès," *Le Libertaire*, October 28, 1927.

33. Tichka, "La fin d'un bandit," *L'Anarchie*, June 9–22, 1926.

34. See Michael Lowy, *Redemption et utopie: Le judaïsme libertaire en Europe Central: Une etude d'affinité elective* (Paris: Presses Universitaires de France, 1988), which in chapter nine calls Lazare the only Western European figure who was at all comparable to the Jews of Central Europe.

35. Lowy, *Redemption et utopie*, 238.

36. Nathan Weinstock, *Le pain de misère, histoire du mouvement ouvrier juif en Europe*, vol. 2, *L'Europe central et occidentale jusqu'en 1945* (Paris: La Découverte, 2002), 270.

37. Michel Lesure, "Les réfugiés révolutionnaires russes à Paris: Rapport du Préfet de

Police au Président du Conseil 16 décembre 1907," *Cahiers du Monde Russe et Soviétique* 6, no. 3 (1965): 427. This article contains a lengthy excerpt from the Sûreté Générale report of 1907 in the Archives Nationales.

38. Lesure, "Les réfugiés révolutionnaires russes à Paris," 431.

39. Lesure, "Les réfugiés révolutionnaires russes à Paris," 434.

40. Lesure, "Les réfugiés révolutionnaires russes à Paris," 423.

41. Nancy Green, *The Pletzl of Paris: Jewish Immigrant Workers in the Belle Epoque* (New York: Holmes and Meier, 1986), 98.

42. Hersh Mendel, *Mémoires d'un révolutionnaire juif,* annotated and translated from Yiddish by Bernard Suchecky (Grenoble: Presses Universitaires de Grenoble, 1982), 133.

43. Mendel, *Mémoires d'un révolutionnaire juif,* 155.

44. Mendel, *Mémoires d'un révolutionnaire juif,* 165.

45. Mendel, *Mémoires d'un révolutionnaire juif,* 184.

46. Mendel, *Mémoires d'un révolutionnaire juif,* 212.

47. Ida Mett, *Souvenirs sur Nestor Makhno* (Paris: Eds. Allia, 1983), 23, 24. Mett, née Gilman, wrote this memoir in 1948.

48. Paul Avrich, *The Russian Anarchists* (Princeton: Princeton University Press, 1967), 188.

49. Avrich, *The Russian Anarchists,* 221.

50. Avrich, *The Russian Anarchists,* 229–33.

51. See Sachar, *Dreamland,* for a discussion of the many German Jews involved in the revolutionary events of 1919.

52. "Groupe anarchiste juif Gustave Landauer," *Le Libertaire,* May 1, 1925.

53. "Imposteurs et assassins," *Le Libertaire,* June 11, 1926.

54. Abe Bluestein, ed., *Fighters for Anarchism: Mollie Steimer and Senya Fleshin* (Libertarian Pub., 1983), 16. Bluestein notes that Steimer and Fleshin's archives at the International Institute for Social History in Amsterdam are filled with such letters from the gulag.

55. Pierre Pascal, *Pages d'amitié, 1921–28* (Paris: Eds. Allia, 1987), 137–42. Pascal first met Lazarevitch in Moscow in 1921.

56. PPo, BA 1709, report of February 28, 1927. The police prepared a lengthy report on the Platform group and the debates between the Russian and French anarchists. On Ranko and the meeting at Hay-les-Roses, see the reports of March 21 and November 1927. The March report broke down the nationalities of the foreign anarchists into two Spaniards, three Russians, two Bulgarians, four Poles, four Italians, and one Chinese. It did not discuss Jews, but it is possible that all of the Russian and Polish anarchists except for Makhno were of Jewish origins.

The divisions within anarchist ranks and the ideas of the Platform group have been discussed recently by Berry, *History of the French Anarchist Movement,* so there is no need to go into detail on this debate. My interest here lies primarily in the impact of Eastern European Jews on the French anarchist movement.

57. BA 1899, "Le mouvement anarchiste," December 27, 1929.

58. Jean-Marc Izrine, *Les libertaires du Yiddishland* (N.p.: Alternative Libertaire/Le Cocquelicot, 1998), 42.

59. BA 1899, September 6, 1927.

60. For brief biographical summaries of Volin and many other Russian Jewish revolutionaries, see Arno Lustiger, *Stalin and the Jews: The Red Book* (New York: Enigma, 2003), 306 for Volin.

61. Volin, "L'antisémitisme," in *L'encyclopédie anarchiste,* ed. Sébastien Faure (Paris: Librairie Internationale, 1934), 11:102.

62. BA 1899, March 31, 1926.

63. Rocker was not actually Jewish, but ever since he had worked with poor Jewish immigrants in the East End of London at the turn of the century, he had been identified with them. He had even learned Yiddish and was highly regarded within the Jewish leftist community.

64. Fernand Fortin, "A propos d'un acte individuel," *La Revue Anarchiste,* March 1934.

65. Fernand Fortin, "De l'unité d'action a l'union sacrée," *La Revue Anarchiste,* August/September 1934.

66. See the last three issues of *La Revue Anarchiste*, which appeared July/September 1935, October/December 1935, and April/June 1936.

67. "Palestine and Zionism," *Plus Loin*, July 1934; L. Filderman, "Les innovations socials en Palestine," *Plus Loin*, March and April 1936 (quotation from the April issue).

68. See Sébastien Faure, *Les anarchistes et l'Affaire Dreyfus* (Paris: Le Fourneau, 1993), one volume in the Collection noire edited by Philippe Oriol.

69. See Nelly Wilson, *Bernard-Lazare: Antisemitism and the Problem of Jewish Identity in Late Nineteenth-Century France* (Cambridge: Cambridge University Press, 1978).

70. Mécislas Golberg, *Morituri: Textes*, ed. Catherine Coquio (Paris: Fourneau, 1994), preface by Coquio, "Mécislas Golberg, écrivain trimardeur," 8. Also, see Catherine Coquio, ed., *Mécislas Golberg, passant de la pensée (1869–1907), une anthropologie politique et poétique au début du siècle* (Paris: Maisonneuve et Larose, 1994), 103.

71. Coquio, "Mécislas Golberg, écrivain trimardeur," 9.

72. Coquio, "La résurrection de Lazare et l'intellectualisme juif," *in Mécislas Golberg, passant de la pensée*, 113–24.

73. Philippe Oriol, "La triste et lamentable histoire de Mécislas Charrier," in *Mécislas Golberg, passant de la pensée*, 455.

74. Oriol, "La triste et lamentable histoire," 456.

75. Yvan Goll, *Oeuvres*, vol. 1, ed. Claire Goll and F. X. Jaujard (Paris: Emile-Paul, 1968), 39.

76. Yvan Goll, *Mélusine* (Clermont-Ferrand: Presses Universitaires Blaise Pascal, n.d.), 7.

77. Grunewald, "Yvan Goll, les Français, les Allemands, et les Européens," 40.

78. Francis Carmody, *The Poetry of Yvan Goll: A Biographical Study* (Paris: Caractères, 1956), 15.

79. Yvan Goll, *Fruit from Saturn* (Brooklyn: Hemispheres, 1946); "Atom Elegy," 12–18; "Lilith," 29–34. For a study of the mystical influences on his work, see Vivien Perkins, *Yvan Goll: An Iconographical Study of His Poetry* (Bonn: H. Bouvier, 1970).

80. See Bertho, "Autour de la revue *Surréalisme*," 37. The caption below the picture reads: "Ivan et Claire Goll avec Marc, Bella et Ida Chagall, Bois-de-Cise, 1924."

81. Richard I. Cohen, "Entre errance et histoire, interpretations juives du mythe de Gottlieb à Kitaj," in *Le juif errant un témoin du temps*, catalog of an exhibition at the Musée d'art et d'histoire du Judaïsme (Paris: Société Nouvelle Adam Biro, 2001), 166–68, 214, 215.

82. Bela Uitz, "A propos de Chagall et de Foujita," *Clarté* 72 (1925): 29–31. The art reviewer for the communist intellectual journal *Clarté* resented Chagall's abandoning of revolutionary Russia, as well as his surrealistic style. He wrote, "He, who had led the combat for Abstraction, for Anarchy, for his Self and his navel, would be a realist? . . . He thought to seize the truth by means of anarchist reality, individualist and egoist. . . . But the revolution demanded just the opposite: not an individualist ideology, but the just comprehension of the collective world problem of the organized proletariat." The reviewer of Chagall's first postwar Paris show concluded that Chagall's productions of 1919–24 couldn't be taken seriously from either a bourgeois or a proletarian point of view, which left him open to the charge of anarchism.

83. Nadine Niezawer, Marie Boye, and Paul Fogel, *Peintres juifs à Paris* (Paris: Denoël, 2000), estimate that five hundred Jewish artists were working in Paris in the interwar period.

84. PPo BA 1709, June 4, 1924, signed "from a correspondent."

85. PPo, BA 1709, August 13, 1924.

86. Quoted by Bertho, "Autour de la revue *Surréalisme*," 55.

87. Benjamin Harshav, *Marc Chagall and His Times: A Documentary Narrative* (Stanford: Stanford University Press, 2004), 785–87.

Chapter 7

1. A. Scott Berg, *Lindbergh* (New York: Putnam, 1998), 114.

2. For a somewhat dated sampling of Lindbergh biographies, see Perry Luckett, *Charles*

A. *Lindbergh: A Bio-Bibliography* (New York: Greenwood Press, 1986). For more recent biographies, as well as the Berg book already cited, see Joyce Milton, *Loss of Eden: A Biography of Charles and Anne Morrow Lindbergh* (New York: HarperCollins, 1993).

3. PPo, BA 1637 file, "Sacco and Vanzetti," reports of August 24 and September 15, 1927.

4. The books were Siegfried's *Les Etats-Unis d'aujourd'hui,* translated by H. H. and Doris Hemming as *America Comes of Age* (New York: Harcourt Brace, 1927), Tardieu, *Devant l'obstacle: l'Amerique et nous,* translated as *France and America: Some Experiences in Cooperation* (New York: Houghton Mifflin, 1927), and Romier, *Qui sera le maître, Europe ou Amérique?* translated by Matthew Josephson as *Who Will Be the Master, Europe or America?* (New York: Macaulay, 1928).

5. The recent novel by Philip Roth, *The Plot Against America* (New York: Houghton Mifflin, 2004), highlights Lindbergh's antisemitism. Roth imagines that Lindbergh defeats Roosevelt in the 1940 presidential election and then allies with Hitler while enacting antisemitic laws. Rudolf Schroeck, *The Double Life of Charles A. Lindbergh* (Munich: Heyne Verlag, 2005), maintains that Lindbergh sired seven illegitimate children in postwar Germany with three different women, two of them sisters. Paternity was confirmed by DNA tests conducted at the University of Munich. The Schroeck book was reviewed by David McHugh, "Book: Lindbergh Had 7 Children with 3 Germans," *Arkansas Democrat Gazette,* June 4, 2005.

6. See Robert Wohl, *A Passion for Wings: Aviation and the Western Imagination, 1908–1918* (New Haven: Yale University Press, 1994).

7. William Shirer, *Twentieth Century Journey* (Boston: Little, Brown, 1976), 1:324.

8. Shirer, *Twentieth Century Journey,* 327, 328.

9. Albert Flament, "Tableaux de Paris: La nuit de Lindbergh," *La Revue de Paris* 34, no. 3 (1927), 929.

10. Mark Heibling, "The Meaning of Lindbergh's Flight in France," *Research Studies* 50, no. 2 (1982), 93, discusses the ambiguities of the French response to Lindbergh, including the sense that he had succeeded where they had failed. Heibling does not, however, raise the issue of the publication of books critical of the United States. He compares French ambivalence to Lindbergh to American fears in the late 1950s and early 1960s that they had been bested by the Soviets in the space race.

11. Wohl, *A Passion for Wings,* 133.

12. AN, series F/7, 13053, *Les menées anarchistes,* February 17, 1912.

13. Lecoin, *Le cours d'une vie,* 135. Moshik Temkin, *The Sacco-Vanzetti Affair: America on Trial* (New Haven: Yale University Press, 2009), 107, repeats this story, saying that Lecoin persuaded a leftist deputy from Marseilles to present the petition to Lindbergh. I only read Temkin's book while copyediting my book, but it parallels my account in a number of ways. In addition to making the connection between Lindbergh and the Sacco-Vanzetti case, Temkin also refers to André Siegfried's *America Comes of Age.* Temkin does an excellent job of placing the case in an international context. The only glaring error I caught occurs on page 106, when he lists among the signers of Lecoin's petition for clemency "the painter and sculptor Amedeo Modigliani." Modigliani died seven years earlier, before the robbery/murder in Massachusetts had even taken place.

14. Berg, *Lindbergh,* 48–50.

15. Milton, *Loss of Eden,* 121.

16. See Vincent Cannistraro, "Mussolini, Sacco-Vanzetti, and the Anarchists: The Transatlantic Context," *Journal of Modern History* 68, no. 1 (1996): 31–62.

17. G. Louis Joughin and Edmund Morgan, *The Legacy of Sacco and Vanzetti* (New York: Harcourt Brace, 1948), 231.

18. T. Bentley Mott, *Myron T. Herrick, Friend of France: An Autobiographical Biography* (Garden City: Doubleday, Doran, 1929), 290. In *The Sacco-Vanzetti Affair,* 103, Temkin identifies the young anarchist May Picqueray as the one who delivered this bomb, citing her memoir.

19. Mott, *Myron T. Herrick,* 291.

20. In Robert Wohl's new book about the early years of airplanes, *The Spectacle of Flight: Aviation and the Western Imagination, 1920–1950* (New Haven: Yale University Press, 2005), 42–43,

the author underscores the similarities in background and persona of Wilbur Wright and Charles Lindbergh. He also acknowledges the "smoldering resentment" (10) in the French populace after the loss of their own heroic aviators and the "smorgasbord of recently published anti-American books" (10) that suggested mixed feelings among the French populace.

21. David Strauss, *Menace in the West: The Rise of French Anti-Americanism in Modern Times* (Westport: Greenwood, 1978), 69 and 78n11.

22. Quoted in Strauss, *Menace in the West*, 68. "Tardieu l'Américain" is cited in Higonnet, *Paris, Capital of the World*, 371.

23. Sales figure from Sean Kennedy, "Situating France: The Career of André Siegfried, 1900–1940," *Historical Reflections* 30, no. 2 (2004): 195.

24. Siegfried, *America Comes of Age*, 68.

25. Siegfried, *America Comes of Age*, 350.

26. Siegfried, *America Comes of Age*, 317.

27. Georges Duhamel, *America the Menace: Scenes from the Life of the Future*, trans. Charles M. Thompson (Boston: Houghton Mifflin, 1931), xiv, for twenty years in the future, and 214 for "the American ant-heap."

28. See Joughin and Morgan, *The Legacy of Sacco and Vanzetti*, 338, 339. Temkin, *The Sacco-Vanzetti Affair*, 111, 112, reports that Dreyfus himself spoke out against the executions shortly before they took place.

29. Joughin and Morgan, *The Legacy of Sacco and Vanzetti*, 233, 234.

30. McGirr, "The Passion of Sacco and Vanzetti," 1091.

31. Lecoin, *Le cours d'une vie*, 117.

32. David Felix, *Protest: Sacco-Vanzetti and the Intellectuals* (Bloomington: Indiana University Press, 1965), 208.

33. Franck Thiriot and Ronald Creagh, *Sacco et Vanzetti* (Paris: Le Monde Libertaire, 2001), 9.

34. Lecoin, *Le cours d'une vie*, 135.

35. Lecoin, *Le cours d'une vie*, 137.

36. "Assassinés! Tous a l'Ambassade américaine," *Le Libertaire*, August 23, 1927.

37. PPo, BA 1637, Sacco and Vanzetti, reports of August 24 and September 15, 1927.

38. *L'Humanité*, August 24, 1927, included in a folder of press clippings in PPo, BA 1637.

39. Tyler Stovall, *Paris Noir: African Americans in the City of Light* (Boston: Houghton Mifflin, 1996), 40.

40. For the revolutionary heritage of Montmartre and the anarchist influence that pervaded the Butte in the 1890s, see Sonn, *Anarchism and Cultural Politics in Fin de Siècle France*, especially 49–94.

41. Shirer, *Twentieth Century Journey*, 328.

42. Shirer, *Twentieth Century Journey*, 318, 319. Shirer was a friend of Duncan's and wanted to attend her funeral, but his editor required him to cover the American Legion march. Temkin, *The Sacco-Vanzetti Affair*, 134, 135, reports that Duncan called the affair a blot on American justice and got involved in an argument with an American judge at the Select café.

43. Jean Preposiet, *Histoire de l'anarchie* (Paris: Tallandier, 2002), 313.

44. See Harvey Levenstein, *Seductive Journey: American Tourists in France from Jefferson to the Jazz Age* (Chicago: University of Chicago Press, 1998), 275. Levenstein also reports on the incident that took place July 23, 1926, in which two thousand Parisians attacked American tourists sightseeing on Paris by Night buses, attacks which *L'Humanité* condemned as chauvinistic. See 269, 270.

45. "Dimanche, tout au grand cortège," *Le Libertaire*, October 7, 1927.

46. Preposiet, *Histoire de l'anarchie*, 318.

47. PPo, BA 1900, July 31, 1928, December 27, 1929, "Mouvement anarchiste."

48. Merrick's cable to Coolidge read, "Had we searched all America we could not have found a better type than young Lindbergh to represent the spirit and high purpose of our people." Quoted by John W. Ward, "The Meaning of Lindbergh's Flight," *American Quarterly* 10, no. 1 (1958): 6

49. The list of thirty-six questions is cited at the beginning of André Lafond, *Impressions of America*, trans. Lawrence Riesner (Paris: Fondation R. B. Strassburger, 1930), 3.

Chapter 8

1. A book titled *The God That Failed*, ed. Richard Crossman (New York: Harper, 1949), included the autobiographies of six former communists, including Koestler, Gide, Richard Wright, and others.

2. Victor Serge, "Méditation sur l'anarchie," *L'Esprit*, April 1937, 37.

3. Rirette Maîtrejean, "Souvenirs d'anarchie," *Le Matin*, August 20, 21, and 22, 1913.

4. AN, F7, 13053, *Les menées anarchistes*, n.d. but evidently 1912.

5. Susan Weissman, *Victor Serge: The Course Is Set on Hope* (London: Verso, 2001), 18.

6. PPo, EA 140, "Bande à Bonnot," newspaper clipping from *France Soir*, June 18, 1968, on Rirette Maîtrejean's death and the film.

7. Jean Maitron, "De Kibaltchiche à Victor Serge. Le Rétif (1909–1919)," *Mouvement Social* 37 (April–June 1964). Maitron included a number of letters from Serge to Armand written in the spring and summer of 1917.

8. The first postwar issue of *Le Libertaire* was dated January 26, 1919; the next issue, February 2, contained an article signed V. S. Le Rétif, showing that he still sometimes used his anarchist nom de plume

9. Victor-Serge Kibaltchiche, "Lettre de Russie," *Le Libertaire*, November 7, 1920.

10. Bill Marshall, *Victor Serge: The Uses of Dissent* (New York: Berg, 1992), 9, 10.

11. "Sur Kropotkine, réponse à Kibaltchiche," *Le Libertaire*, January 21–28, 1921.

12. Victor Serge, "Quelques mots personnels," *Le Libertaire*, March 4–11, 1921.

13. Rhillon, "Un révolutionnaire vertueux: Victor Serge," *Le Libertaire*, October 28 and November 4, 1921.

14. Maurice Wullens, "Kibaltchiche," *Le Libertaire*, November 4–11, 1921.

15. Weissman, *Victor Serge*, 48.

16. Victor Serge, *Memoirs of a Revolutionary*, trans. Peter Sedgwick (Iowa City: University of Iowa Press, 2002), 118, 120.

17. Serge, *Memoirs*, 128, 129.

18. An excellent discussion of Paz's speech in favor of Serge, and on the Congress of Writers more generally, can be found in Shattuck, "Having Congress," 1,18, 25.

19. Weissman, *Victor Serge*, chapter 6, discusses the complex web of betrayals that surrounded the left oppositionists around Serge and Trotsky.

20. Victor Serge, Alexandre Croix, and Jean Bernier, "L'anarchie," *Le Crapouillot* (January 1938): 6–13.

21. Serge, Croix, and Bernier, "L'anarchie,"65.

22. "Maurice Wullens, 1894–1945," *Dictionnaire biographique du mouvement ouvrier français*, 43:392, 393.

23. The only in-depth secondary source I have located on Wullens is a master's thesis published in Paris in the early 1970s: Michele Chevalier, "*Les Humbles*, 1919–39: En marge du syndicalisme révolutionnaire" (Paris I, Centre d'histoire du syndicalisme, 1973–74), 40.

24. André Colomer, "Les lettres vivantes," *Le Libertaire*, January 1, 1925.

25. Henri Guilbeaux, preface to Maurice Wullens, *Paris, Moscou, Tiflis: Notes et souvenirs d'un voyage à travers la Russie soviétique* (Paris: Les Humbles, 1927), 5.

26. Wullens, *Paris, Moscou, Tiflis*, 20.

27. Wullens, *Paris, Moscou, Tiflis*, 222.

28. See, for example, the article by Wullens, "En Russie révolutionnaire," *Le Libertaire*, January 11, 1925.

29. Chevalier, "*Les Humbles*," 85.

30. Letter from Victor Serge to Maurice Wullens, May 6, 1936, *Les Humbles*, May 1936, 27.

31. Alfred Rosmer, Victor Serge, and Maurice Wullens, "L'assassinat d'Ignace Reiss," and "L'assassinat politique et l'URSS," *Les Humbles*, April 1938.

32. "Pour un art révolutionnaire indépendant," *Les Humbles*, October 1938; Victor Serge, "Résistances," *Les Humbles*, November/December 1938.

33. Françoise Vanacker-Frigout, "Le mouvement anarchiste à travers *Le Libertaire*, 1934–1939" (mémoire de maîtrise, Université de Paris I, 1971), 55.

34. In an appendix to his *History of the French Anarchist Movement, 1917–1945* (Westport: Greenwood, 2002), titled "French Anarchist Volunteers in Spain, 1936–1939," David Berry lists Maurice Wullens as one of the French anarchists in Spain. This must have been a brief visit in 1937; whether he still deserved the appellation "anarchist" is questionable.

35. Serge, *Memoirs of a Revolutionary*, 347.

36. "Maurice Wullens," *Dictionnaire biographique du mouvement ouvrier français*, 393.

37. A. Barbé, "André Colomer est mort," *Le Semeur* (October 15, 1931).

38. Daudet quoted by André Salmon, *La terreur noire* (Paris: Pauvert, 1959), 283.

39. See Sonn, *Anarchism and Cultural Politics in Fin de Siècle France*, especially chapter 3, "The Social and Symbolic Space of Parisian Anarchism."

40. Colomer referred to Kibaltchiche in the first issue of *L'Action d'Art* (February 15, 1913). The series "De Bergson à Bonnot: Aux sources de l'heroïsme individualiste" appeared beginning March 1, 1913. Also see Mark Antliff, *Inventing Bergson: Cultural Politics and the Parisian Avant-Garde* (Princeton: Princeton University Press, 1993), which discusses the journal *L'Action d'Art* in chapter 5.

41. Manuel Devaldès, ed., "Anthologie des écrivains réfractaires de langue française," *Les Humbles*, August, September, October 1927.

42. André Colomer, "Henri Bergson, maître à penser de la 3e république," *La Revue Anarchiste* 1, no. 1 (1922).

43. André Colomer, "Réflexions sur Nietzsche et l'anarchie," *La Revue Anarchiste*, June 1922.

44. Pierre Le Meillour, "De l'individualisme heroïque à la dictature du proletariat," *Le Libertaire*, December 2, 1927.

45. Le Meillour, "De l'individualisme heroïque."

46. Georges Bastien, "Déviation incomprehensible," *Le Libertaire*, June 6, 1925.

47. André Colomer, "Notre chemin sous les étoiles," *L'Insurgé*, October 3, 1925.

48. Maurice Wullens, "Il y a, tout de même, quelque chose de change!" *L'Insurgé*, October 10, 1925.

49. Paul Eluard, "Antifrance d'abord," *L'Insurgé*, July 25, 1925. Léo Poldès, whose real name was Léopold Szeszler, was a Parisian-born Jewish journalist and playwright who founded the Club du Faubourg in 1918 and ran it until his death in 1970, with the exception of the war years. Though such Jewish themes as Zionism and antisemitism were debated at the club, so were a variety of controversial issues, which often attracted thousands of participants. See Malinovich, *French and Jewish*, 134.

50. Durozoi, *History of the Surrealist Movement*, 126.

51. Audience estimates come from the police, who reported regularly on these meetings. See PPo, BA 1899. The reports begin in October 1925 and continue into the spring of 1928.

52. PPo, BA 1899, reports of December 30, 1925, and November 11, 1925, of Les Amis de *l'Insurgé*.

53. PPo, BA 1899, report of November 4, 1925, of Les Amis de *l'Insurgé*. In *History of the Surrealist Movement*, 130, Gérard Durozoi discusses briefly a meeting held by the "Club of Rebels," in which Colomer shared the stage with Aragon, a member of the Communist Party and a union leader.

54. PPo, BA 1899, report of February 23, 1928, meeting of Club des Insurgés.

55. PPo, BA 1899, report of March 8, 1928, meeting of Club des Insurgés.

56. The scene in Lyons is described by Auzias, *Mémoires libertaires*, 189.

57. Maurice Wullens, "André Colomer," *Les Humbles*, October 1931, 10.

58. Fernand Fortin, "Parlons d'André Colomer," *La Revue Anarchiste*, February 1932; quotation

from article in same issue by Ganz-Allein, "André Colomer, apôtre de l'action d'art ou l'illusion de l'individualisme lyrique."

59. Maurice Wullens, "André Colomer est mort," *Les Humbles*, December 1931, 25.

60. Arturo Schwarz, *André Breton, Trotsky et l'anarchie* (Paris: Union générale d'éditions, 1974), 94, 95, quotes Breton musing in 1952 about "why surrealism at its beginning took the road of collaboration with the Marxist left, and not the libertarian left. . . . why didn't an organic fusion occur at this moment between anarchist elements properly called and surrealist elements? And 25 years later I'm still asking that of myself."

61. Contre-Attaque, "La patrie et la famille," January 5, 1936, signed Breton, Bataille, Heine, Péret, in Pierre, *Tracts surréalistes*, 1:294.

62. See Richard Wolin, "Left Fascism: Georges Bataille and the German Ideology," in *The Seduction of Unreason* (Princeton: Princeton University Press, 2004). See also Andrew and Ungar, *Popular Front Paris*, 363–65, for a discussion of the tensions underlying Contre-Attaque.

63. André Breton and Diego Rivera, "Pour un art révolutionnaire indépendant," *Les Humbles*, October 1938.

64. "De notre ami V. Serge," *Clé*, January 1939.

65. Leon Trotsky, "Pour la liberté de l'art," *Clé*, February 1939, article dated Coyoacan, December 22, 1938.

66. Durozoi, *Surrealist Movement*, 351, 352.

67. Polizzotti, *Revolution of the Mind*, 486ff.

68. Claude Lévi-Strauss, *Tristes tropiques*, trans. John and Doreen Weightman (New York: Atheneum, 1974), 24.

69. Lévi-Strauss, *Tristes tropiques*, 25.

70. Julian Jackson, *France: The Dark Years, 1940–1944* (Oxford: Oxford University Press, 2001), 500.

Epilogue

1. "The Walls of 1968," in Eugen Weber, *The Western Tradition: From the Renaissance to the Present*, 3rd ed. (Lexington, Mass.: D. C. Heath, 1972), 1006.

2. Greil Marcus, *Lipstick Traces: A Secret History of the Twentieth Century* (Cambridge: Harvard University Press, 1989), 444, 445. The event Marcus described may be seen in the film *Berkeley in the Sixties*, made by a group of veterans of the student movement in 1990.

3. Marcus, *Lipstick Traces*, 18, 19.

4. Sowerwine, *France Since 1870*, 369ff.

5. Daniel and Gabriel Cohn-Bendit, *Obsolete Communism: The Left-Wing Alternative*, trans. Arnold Pomerans (New York: McGraw Hill, 1968), 23. Daniel Cohn-Bendit admits in the preface that he wrote the book in five weeks, responding to numerous publishers' calls for a book by the new celebrity.

6. I culled these names from Jonathan Judaken, "'To Be or Not to Be French': Soixante-Huitard Reflections on 'la Question Juive,'" *Journal of Modern Jewish Studies* 1, no. 1 (2002): 6. Judaken also wrote about "May '68: The Jewish Sub-text," in *Proceedings of the Western Society for French History* 30 (2004): 235–41. See also Judith Friedlander, *Vilna on the Seine: Jewish Intellectuals in France Since 1968* (New Haven: Yale University Press, 1990), and Yaïr Auron, *Les juifs d'extrême gauche en mai 1968: Une génération révolutionnaire marquée par la Shoah*, translated from Hebrew by Katherine Wirchowski (Paris: Albin Michel, 1998).

7. Echoing the phrase applied to Dany Cohn-Bendit, "We are all German Jews," during the trial of Pierre Goldman his supporters cried out, "We are all Polish Jews born in France." On the other hand, a number of young Jewish radicals like Goldman had parents who experienced the Holocaust and, as foreign-born Jews, were much more vulnerable to persecution by the Vichy police.

8. See Jonathan Judaken, "Alain Finkielkraut and the Nouveaux Philosophes: French

Jewish Intellectuals, the Afterlives of May '68, and the Rebirth of the National Icon," *Historical Reflections* 32, no. 1 (2006).

9. The New Philosophy movement emerged just as news was emerging about the horrors of Pol Pot's regime. The French journalist François Hauter has recently written, for example, "Between April 1975 and December 1978, an army of illiterate, indoctrinated children led by depraved intellectuals trained at the Sorbonne caused the deaths of over a million inhabitants of Cambodia's cities; about a fifth of the country's population at that time died" ("Chinese Shadows," *New York Review of Books* 54, no. 15, October 11, 2007). It did not require a Camus to find this revolutionary extremism morally troubling.

10. Krist Novoselic, bass player for the band Nirvana (best known for Kurt Cobain, the charismatic and suicidal lead singer), mused about the gestation of his group's satirically titled hit "Smells Like Teen Spirit:" "We were sitting around the apartment when we were making the record [in 1991], and I was talking about an anarchist high school with, like, black flags, and the cheerleaders have anarchy A's on their shirts, and that whole school spirit, pep spirit. But what if it was, like, anarchy, and it was the school that was espousing it at pep rallies, the whole, like, punk-rock ethos. What kind of world would that be?" "Voices: 1981–1999: The Grunge Invasion," *Newsweek* 133, no. 26 (June 28, 1999): 77.

11. James A. Winders, *European Culture Since 1948: From Modern to Postmodern and Beyond* (New York: Palgrave, 2001), 266ff.

Bibliography

Primary Sources

Archival Sources

Archives nationales (AN), Paris, F7 series, boxes 12865, 13053, 13061, 14790.
Préfecture de police (PPo), Département de la Seine, Paris, series BA, boxes 1583, 1637, 1899, 1900, 2034, 2235.
Internationaal Instituut voor Sociale Geschiedenis (International Institute for Social History), Amsterdam, Humbert Correspondence, microfilm reel #479.

Mainstream French Press

L'Action Française
Le Crapouillot
L'Esprit
Le Figaro
Le Gazette de Tribunaux
L'Humanité
Le Matin
La Nouvelle Revue Française
L'Oeuvre
Le Petit Parisien
La Revue de Paris
Voilà

Anarchist Press

L'Action d'Art
The Egoist
L'En Dehors
Génération Conscient
La Grande Réforme
Les Humbles: Revue Littéraire des Primaires
L'Insurgé
Le Libertaire
Le Néo-Naturien
Plus Loin
La Revue Anarchiste
Le Semeur de Normandie

Artistic and Literary Journals

Action: Cahiers de Philosophie d'Art
Clarté, Bulletin Français de l'Internationale de la Pensée
Clé
Documents
Littérature
La Révolution Surréaliste
Surréalisme

Other Primary Sources

Aragon, Louis. *Libertinage*. Translated as *The Libertine* by Jo Levy. New York: Riverrun, 1987.
Armand, E. *La révolution sexuelle et la camaraderie amoureuse*. Paris: Critique et Raison, 1933.
Armand, E., Vera Livinska, and C. de St.-Hélène. *La camaraderie amoureuse*. Paris and Orléans: Ed. De l'En Dehors, 1930.
Breton, André. *Manifestoes of Surrealism*. Translated by Richard Seaver and Helen Lane. Ann Arbor: University of Michigan Press, 1969.
————. *Ode à Charles Fourier*. Paris: Klinksieck, 1961.
Bulletin des Groupes Féministes de l'Enseignement Laïque, 1924, 1925.
Bureau de recherches surréaliste: Cahier de la permanence, octobre 1924–avril 1925. Archives du surréalisme 1. Paris: Gallimard, 1988.
Cohn-Bendit, Daniel, and Gabriel Cohn-Bendit. *Obsolete Communism: The Left-Wing Alternative*. Translated by Arnold Pomerans. New York: McGraw-Hill, 1968.
Daudet, Léon. *La police politique, ses moyens et ses crimes*. Paris: Denoël et Steele, 1934.
Daudet, Marthe Allard. *La vie et la mort de Philippe*. Paris: Arthème Fayard, 1926.
Desnos, Robert. *Liberté ou l'amour*. Translated as *Liberty or Love!* by Terry Hall. London: Atlas, 1993.
Devaldès, Manuel, *Croître et multiplier, c'est la guerre!* Paris: Mignolet et Storz, 1933.
Duhamel, Georges. *America the Menace: Scenes from the Life of the Future*. Translated by Charles M. Thompson. Boston: Houghton Mifflin, 1931.
Faure, Sébastien, ed. *L'encyclopédie anarchiste*. 4 vols. Paris: Librairie Internationale, 1934.
Fels, Florent. *Voilà*. Paris: Arthème Fayard, 1957.
Fourier, Charles. *Vers la liberté en amour*. Edited by Daniel Guérin. Paris: Gallimard, 1967, 1975.
"Germaine Berton a Suicide." *New York Times*, July 7, 1942.
Goll, Iwan [Yvan]. *Fruit from Saturn*. Brooklyn: Hemispheres, 1946.
————. *Germaine Berton, die rote Jungfrau*. Berlin: Die Schmiede, 1925.
————. *Oeuvres*. Edited by Claire Goll and F. X. Jaujard. Paris: Emile Paul, 1968.
Humbert, Jeanne. *En pleine vie: Roman précurseur*. Paris: Ed. Du Lutèce, 1930.
Jacob, Max. *Lettres à Florent Fels.* Paris: Rougerie, 1990.
Jong, Albert de. *De Roode Maagd: Germaine Berton, geveld, gezag en anarchisme*. Amsterdam: De Fakkel, 1924.
Lafond, André. *Impresssions of America*. Translated by Lawrence Riesner. Paris, New York: Strassburger, 1930.
Lecoin, Louis. *Le cours d'une vie*. Paris: La Liberté, 1965.

Marestan, Jean. *L'émancipation sexuelle en URSS: Impressions de voyage et documents.* Paris: G. Mignolet et Storz, 1936.

Margueritte, Victor. *Ton corps est à toi.* Paris: Flammarion, 1927.

Noguères, Louis. *Le suicide de Philippe Daudet.* Paris: Librairie du Travail, 1926.

Picqueray, May. *May la réfractaire.* Paris: M. Jullian, 1979.

Pierre, José. *Tracts surréalistes et déclarations collectives.* Vol. 1. Paris: Le Terrain Vague, 1980.

——, ed. *Violette Nozières: Poèmes, dessins, correspondance, documents.* Paris: Le Terrain Vague, 1991.

Romier, Lucien. *Qui sera le maître, Europe ou Amérique?* Translated as *Who Will Be the Master, Europe or America?* by Matthew Josephson. New York: Macaulay, 1928.

Ryner, Han. *L'amour plural, roman d'aujourd'hui et de demain.* Paris: Radot, 1927.

——. *Le crime d'obéir.* Conflans-Honorine: Ed. L'Idée Libre, 1925.

Serge, Victor. *Memoirs of a Revolutionary.* Translated by Peter Sedgwick. Iowa City: University of Iowa Press, 2002.

Siegfried, André. *Les Etats-Unis d'aujourd'hui.* Translated as *America Comes of Age* by H. H. and Doris Hemmings. New York: Harcourt Brace, 1927.

Tardieu, André. *Devant l'obstacle: L'Amerique et nous.* Translated as *France and America: Some Experiences in Cooperation.* Boston: Houghton Mifflin, 1927.

Torrès, Henry. *Accusés hors série.* Paris: Gallimard, 1957.

——. *Le procès des pogromes.* Paris: Ed. Du France, 1928.

——. *Souvenir, Souvenir, que me veux-tu?* Paris: Ed. Mondiales, 1964.

Vidal, Georges. *Comment mourut Philippe Daudet.* Paris: Ed. de l'Epi, 1924.

Wullens, Maurice. *Paris, Moscou, Tiflis: Notes et souvenirs d'un voyage à travers la Russie Soviétique.* Paris: Les Humbles, 1927.

Secondary Sources

Accampo, Elinor. *Blessed Motherhood, Bitter Fruit: Nelly Roussel and the Politics of Female Pain.* Baltimore: Johns Hopkins University Press, 2006.

Andrew, Dudley, and Steven Ungar. *Popular Front Paris and the Poetics of Culture.* Cambridge: Harvard University Press, 2005.

Antliff, Allan. *Anarchist Modernism: Art, Politics, and the First American Avant-Garde.* Chicago: University of Chicago Press, 2001.

Antliff, Mark. *Inventing Bergson: Cultural Politics and the Parisian Avant-Garde.* Princeton: Princeton University Press, 1993.

Archer-Shaw, Petrine. *Negrophilia: Avant-Garde Paris and Black Culture.* London: Thames and Hudson, 2000.

Arendt, Hannah. *Eichmann in Jerusalem: A Report on the Banality of Evil.* New York: Viking, 1963.

Auron, Yaïr. *Les juifs d'extrême gauche en mai 1968: Une génération révolutionnaire marquée par la Shoah.* Translated from the Hebrew by Katherine Wirchowski. Paris: Albin Michel, 1998.

Auslander, Leora. "The Gendering of Consuming Practices in Nineteenth-Century France." In *The Sex of Things: Gender and Consumption in Historical Perspective,* edited by Victoria de Grazia and Ellen Furlough, 79–112. Berkeley and Los Angeles: University of California Press, 1996.

Auzias, Claire. *Mémoires libertaires, Lyon, 1919–1939.* Paris: L'Harmattan, 1993.

Barber, Stephen. *Antonin Artaud: Blows and Bombs*. London: Faber and Faber, 1993.

Becker, Jean-Jacques, and Annette Wierviorka. *Les juifs de France: De la Révolution à nos jours*. N.p.: Liana Levi, 1998.

Beecher, Jonathan. *Charles Fourier: The Visionary and His World*. Berkeley and Los Angeles: University of California Press, 1986.

Benbassa, Esther. *Histoire des juifs en France*. Paris: Seuil, 1997.

Benjamin, Walter. "Surrealism: The Last Snapshot of the European Intelligentsia" (1929). Translated by Edmund Jephcott. In *Selected Writings*, vol. 2, *1927–1934*, edited by Michael Jennings, Howard Eiland, and Gary Smith, 207–21. Cambridge: Harvard University Press, 1999.

Bentley, Mott T. *Myron T. Herrick, Friend of France: An Autobiographical Biography*. Garden City, N.Y.: Doubleday, Doran, 1929.

Berenson, Edward. *The Trial of Madame Caillaux*. Berkeley and Los Angeles: University of California Press, 1992.

Berg, A. Scott. *Lindbergh*. New York: Putnam, 1998.

Berry, David. *History of the French Anarchist Movement, 1917–1945*. Westport: Greenwood, 2002.

———. "The Response of the French Anarchist Movement to the Russian Revolution and to the Spanish Civil War." Ph.D. diss., University of Sussex, 1988.

Bertho, Jean. "Autour de la revue *Surréalisme*." *Surréalisme I* (October 1924). Paris: Jean-Michel Place, 2004.

Bonnet, Jean. *Les pouvoirs publique française et l'immigration dans l'entre-deux-guerres*. Lyon: Centre d'histoire économique et sociale de la région lyonnaise, 1976.

Boyarin, Daniel. *Unheroic Conduct: The Rise of Heterosexuality and the Invention of the Jewish Man*. Berkeley and Los Angeles: University of California Press, 1997.

Brandon, Ruth. *Surreal Lives: The Surrealists, 1917–1945*. New York: Grove, 1999.

Brécy, Robert. *Autour de la Muse Rouge, 1901–1939*. Paris: Pirot, 1991.

———. *Florilège de la chanson révolutionnaire, de 1789 au Front Populaire*. Paris: Ed. Ouvrières, 1978.

Breval, René. *Philippe Daudet a bel et bien été assassiné*. Paris: Scorpion, 1959.

Cannistraro, Vincent. "Mussolini, Sacco-Vanzetti, and the Anarchists: The Transatlantic Context." *Journal of Modern History* 68, no. 1 (1996).

Carmody, Francis. *The Poetry of Yvan Goll: A Biographical Study*. Paris: Caractères, 1956.

Carol, Anne. *Histoire de l'eugénisme en France: Les médecins et la procréation, XIXe-XXe siècle*. Paris: Seuil, 1995.

Chevalier, Michele. "*Les Humbles*, 1919–39: En marge du syndicalisme révolutionnaire." Mémoire de maîtrise, Paris I, Centre d'histoire du syndicalisme, 1973–74.

Clemenson, Richard. *Anarchism, Science, and Sex: Eugenics in Eastern Spain, 1900–1937*. Bern: Peter Lang, 2000.

Coquio, Catherine, ed. *Mécislas Golberg, passant de la pensée (1869–1907), une anthropologie politique et poétique au début du siecle*. Paris: Maisonneuve et Larose, 1994.

Costich, Julia. *Antonin Artaud*. Boston: Twayne, 1978.

Crossman, Richard, ed. *The God That Failed*. New York: Harper, 1949.

Day, Hem, ed. *Manuel Devaldès*. Paris-Brussels: Pensée et Action, 1957.

Dean, Carolyn. *Sexuality and Modern Western Culture*. New York: Twayne, 1996.

Devaldès, Manuel. *Han Ryner*. Nice: La Revue des Lettres et des Arts, 1909.

Dijkstra, Bram. *Evil Sisters: The Threat of Female Sexuality in Twentieth-Century Culture*. New York: Henry Holt, 1996.

————. *Idols of Perversity: Fantasies of Feminine Evil in Fin-de-Siècle Culture*. Oxford: Oxford University Press, 1986.

Douglas, Mary. *Purity and Danger: An Analysis of the Concepts of Pollution and Taboo*. London: Routledge, 1966.

Durozoi, Gérard. *A History of the Surrealist Movement*. Translated by Alison Anderson. Chicago: University of Chicago Press, 2002.

Dyer, Colin. *Population and Society in Twentieth-Century France*. New York: Holmes and Meier, 1978.

Eburne, Jonathan. *Surrealism and the Art of Crime*. Ithaca: Cornell University Press, 2008.

Felix, David. *Protest: Sacco-Vanzetti and the Intellectuals*. Bloomington: Indiana University Press, 1965.

La femme et le surréalisme. Nice: Groupe Eluard, 1992.

Friedlander, Judith. *Vilna on the Seine: Jewish Intellectuals in France Since 1968*. New Haven: Yale University Press, 1990.

Friedman, Saul. *Pogromchik: The Assassination of Simon Petlura*. New York: Hart, 1976.

Gourmel, Gérard. *L'ombre double, dits et non dits de l'affaire Papin*. Le Mans: Cénomane, 2000.

Green, Nancy. *The Pletzl of Paris: Jewish Immigrant Workers in the Belle Epoque*. New York: Holmes and Meier, 1986.

Grossmann, Atina. *Reforming Sex: The German Movement for Birth Control and Abortion Reform, 1920–1950*. New York: Oxford University Press, 1995.

Gruber, Helmut. "French Women in the Crossfire of Class, Sex, Maternity, and Citizenship." In *Women and Socialism, Socialism and Women: Europe Between the Two World Wars*, edited by Helmut Gruber and Pamela Graves, 279–347. New York: Berghahn, 1998.

Guerrand, Roger-Henri, and Francis Ronsin. *Jeanne Humbert et la lutte pour le contrôle des naissances*. Paris: Spartacus, 2001.

Halperin, Joan. *Félix Fénéon: Aesthete and Anarchist in Fin-de-Siècle France*. New Haven: Yale University Press, 1989.

Hause, Steven. "More Minerva than Mars: The French Women's Rights Campaign and the First World War." In *Behind the Lines: Gender and the Two World Wars*, edited by Margaret Higonnet et al., 99–113. New Haven: Yale University Press, 1987.

Hauter, François. "Chinese Shadows." *New York Review of Books* 54, no. 15 (October 11, 2007).

Heibling, Mark. "The Meaning of Lindbergh's Flight in France." *Research Studies* 50, no. 2 (1982).

Higonnet, Patrice. *Paris, Capital of the World*. Translated by Arthur Goldhammer. Cambridge: Harvard University Press, 2002.

Humbert, Jeanne. *Eugène Humbert: La vie et l'oeuvre d'un néo-malthusien*. Paris: La Grande Réforme, 1947.

Hunt, Lynn. *The Family Romance of the French Revolution*. Berkeley and Los Angeles: University of California Press, 1992.

Huraut, Alain. *Aragon, prisonnier politique*. Paris: Alain Balland, 1970.

Huss, Marie-Monique. "Pronatalism in the Interwar Period in France." *Journal of Contemporary History* 25 (1990).

Hutton, John. *Neo-Impressionism and the Search for Solid Ground: Art, Science, and Anarchism in Fin-de Siècle France*. Baton Rouge: Louisiana State University Press, 1994.

Jackson, Julian. *France: The Dark Years, 1940–1944*. Oxford: Oxford University Press, 2001.

Jay, Martin. *Downcast Eyes: The Denigration of Vision in Twentieth-Century French Thought*. Berkeley and Los Angeles: University of California Press, 1993.

Johnston, Robert H. *"New Mecca, New Babylon": Paris and the Russian Exiles, 1920–1945*. Montreal: McGill-Queen's University Press, 1988.

Joll, James. *The Anarchists*. New York: Grosset and Dunlap, 1964.

Joughin, G. Louis, and Edmund Morgan. *The Legacy of Sacco and Vanzetti*. New York: Harcourt Brace, 1948.

Judaken, Jonathan. "Alain Finkielkraut and the Nouveaux Philosophes: French Jewish Intellectuals, the Afterlives of May '68 and the Rebirth of the National Icon." *Historical Reflections* 32, no. 1 (2006).

———. "May '68: The Jewish Sub-text." In *Proceedings of the Western Society for French History* 30 (2004).

———. "'To Be or Not to Be French': Soixante-Huitard Reflections on "la Question Juive." *Journal of Modern Jewish Studies* 1, no. 1 (2002).

Kadlec, David. *Mosaic Modernism: Anarchism, Pragmatism, Culture*. Baltimore: Johns Hopkins University Press, 2000.

Kennedy, Sean. "Situating France: The Career of André Siegfried, 1900–1940." *Historical Reflections* 30, no. 2 (2004).

Kline, Wendy. *Building a Better Race: Gender, Sexuality, and Eugenics from the Turn of the Century to the Baby Boom*. Berkeley and Los Angeles: University of California Press, 2001.

Kristeva, Julia. *The Sense and Non-Sense of Revolt*. Translated by Jeanine Herman. New York: Columbia University Press, 2000.

Laloum, Jean. *Les juifs dans la banlieue parisienne des années 20 aux années 50. Montreuil, Bagnolet et Vincennes à l'heure de la "solution finale."* Paris: CNRS, 1998.

Leighten, Patricia. *Reordering the Universe: Picasso and Anarchism, 1897–1914*. Princeton: Princeton University Press, 1989.

Lesure, Michel. "Les réfugiés révolutionnaires russes à Paris: Rapport du Préfet de Police au Président du Conseil 16 décembre 1907." *Cahiers du Monde Russe et Soviétique* 6, no. 3 (1965).

Levenstein, Harvey. *Seductive Journey: American Tourists in France from Jefferson to the Jazz Age*. Chicago: University of Chicago Press, 1998.

Lévi-Strauss, Claude. *Tristes tropiques*. Translated by John and Doreen Weightman. New York: Atheneum, 1974.

Lewis, Helena. *The Politics of Surrealism*. New York: Paragon, 1980.

Löwy, Michael. *Rédemption et utopie: Le Judaïsme libertaire en Europe centrale: Une étude d'affinité elective*. Paris: Presses Universitaires de France, 1988.

Luckett, Perry. *Charles A. Lindbergh: A Bio-Bibliography*. New York: Greenwood Press, 1986.

Lunn, Eugene. *Prophet of Community: The Romantic Socialism of Gustav Landauer*. Berkeley and Los Angeles: University of California Press, 1973.

Magocsi, Paul. *A History of Ukraine*. Seattle: University of Washington Press, 1996.

Maitron, Jean. "De Kibaltchiche à Victor Serge. Le Rétif (1909–1919)." *Mouvement Social* 37 (April–June 1964).

———. *Le mouvement anarchiste en France*. Vol. 2, *De 1914 à nos jours*. Paris: Maspero, 1975.

Maitron, Jean, and Claude Pannetier, eds. *Dictionnaire biographique du mouvement ouvrier français*. Paris: Ed. Ouvrières, 1964– .

Malet, Léo. *La vache enragée*. Paris: Hoëbeke, 1998.

Malinovich, Nadia. *French and Jewish: Culture and the Politics of Identity in Early Twentieth-Century France*. Portland, Ore.: Littman Library of Jewish Civilization, 2008.

Manfredonia, Gaetano, and Francis Ronsin. "E. Armand and *la camaraderie amoureuse:* Revolutionary Sexualism and the Struggle Against Jealousy." In *Free Love and the Labour Movement*. Internationaal Instituut voor Sociale Geschiedenis Research Paper 40. Amsterdam: Internationaal Instituut voor Sociale Geschiedenis, 2001.

Marcus, Greil. *Lipstick Traces: A Secret History of the Twentieth Century*. Cambridge: Harvard University Press, 1989.

Marshall, Bill. *Victor Serge: The Uses of Dissent*. New York: Berg, 1992.

Marshall, Peter. *Demanding the Impossible: A History of Anarchism*. New York: Harper Collins, 1992.

Martin, Benjamin. *The Hypocrisy of Justice in the Belle Epoque*. Baton Rouge: Louisiana State University Press, 1984.

Mauricius. "E. Armand tel que je l'ai connu." In *E. Armand, sa vie, sa pensée, son oeuvre*. Paris: La Ruche Ouvrière, 1964.

McGirr, Lisa. "The Passion of Sacco and Vanzetti: A Global History." *Journal of American History* (March 2007).

McHugh, David. "Book: Lindbergh Had 7 Children with 3 Germans." *Arkansas Democrat Gazette,* June 4, 2005.

McLaren, Angus. *Sexuality and Social Order: The Debate over the Fertility of Women and Workers in France, 1770–1920*. London: Holmes and Meier, 1983.

Melching, Willem. "'A New Morality': Left-Wing Intellectuals on Sexuality in Weimar Germany." *Journal of Contemporary History* 25 (1990).

Merriman, John. *The Dynamite Club: How a Bombing in Fin-de-Siecle Paris Ignited the Age of Modern Terror*. Boston: Houghton Mifflin Harcourt, 2009.

Michaels, Jennifer. *Anarchy and Eros: Otto Gross' Impact on German Expressionist Writers*. New York: Peter Lang, 1983.

Milton, Joyce. *Loss of Eden: A Biography of Charles and Anne Morrow Lindbergh*. New York: HarperCollins, 1993.

Mosse, George. *The Image of Man: The Creation of Modern Masculinity*. Oxford: Oxford University Press, 1996.

Muel-Dreyfus, Francine. *Vichy and the Eternal Feminine*. Translated by Kathleen A. Johnson. Durham: Duke University Press, 2001.

Mulvaney, Marie Marmo. "Sexual Politics in the Career and Legend of Louise Michel." *Signs* 15, no. 2 (1990): 300–322.

Mundy, Jennifer. *Surrealism: Desire Unbound*. Princeton: Princeton University Press, 2001.

Offen, Karen. "Body Politics: Women, Work, and the Politics of Motherhood in France, 1920–1950." In *Maternity and Gender Policies: Women and the Rise of the European Welfare State, 1880s–1950*, edited by Gisela Bock and Pat Thane, 138–59. London: Routledge, 1991.

Ouédraogo, Arouna. "Food and the Purification of Society: Dr. Paul Carton and Vegetarianism in Interwar France." *Social History of Medicine* 14, no. 2 (2001).

Pessin, Alain, and Patrice Terrone, eds. *Littérature et anarchie*. Toulouse: Presses Universitaires du Mirail, 1998.

Pilbeam, Pamela. "Fourier and the Fourierists: A Case of Mistaken Identity." *French History and Civilization: Papers from the George Rudé Seminar* 1 (2005).

Polizzotti, Mark. *Revolution of the Mind: The Life of André Breton*. New York: Farrar, Straus and Giroux, 1995.

Préposiet, Jean. *Histoire de l'anarchie*. Paris: Tallandier, 2002.

Privat, Maurice. *L'énigme Philippe Daudet*. Paris-Neuilly: Les Documents Secrets, 1931.

Quine, Maria Sophia. *Population Politics in Twentieth-Century Europe*. London: Routledge, 1996.

Reshetar, John. *The Ukrainian Revolution, 1917–1920: A Study in Nationalism*. Princeton: Princeton University Press, 1952.

Reynaud Paligot, Carole. *Parcours politique des surréalistes, 1919–1969*. Paris: CNRS Editions, 1995.

Roberts, Mary Louise. *Civilization Without Sexes: Reconstructing Gender in Postwar France, 1917–1927*. Chicago: University of Chicago Press, 1994.

Ronsin, Francis. *La grève des ventres: Propagande néo-malthusienne et baisse de la natalité française, 19e–20e siècles*. Paris: Aubier, 1980.

Ross, Chad. *Naked Germany: Health, Race, and the Nation*. Oxford: Berg, 2005.

Ross, Kristin. *The Conquest of Social Space: Rimbaud and the Commune*. Minneapolis: University of Minnesota Press, 1988.

Roth, Philip. *The Plot Against America*. New York: Houghton Mifflin, 2004.

Sachar, Howard. *Dreamland: Europeans and Jews in the Aftermath of the Great War*. New York: Knopf, 2002.

Salmon, André. *La terreur noire*. Paris: Pauvert, 1959.

Schneider, William. *Quality and Quantity: The Quest for Biological Regeneration in Twentieth-Century France*. Cambridge: Cambridge University Press, 1990.

Sewell, William Jr. *Work and Revolution in France: The Language of Labor from the Old Regime to 1848*. Cambridge: Cambridge University Press, 1980.

Shapiro, Ann-Louise. *Breaking the Codes: Female Criminality in Fin de Siècle Paris*. Stanford: Stanford University Press, 1996.

Shattuck, Roger. "Having Congress: The Shame of the Thirties." In Roger Shattuck, *The Innocent Eye*, 3–31. New York: Farrar, Straus and Giroux, 1984.

Shirer, William. *Twentieth Century Journey*. Vol. 1. Boston: Little, Brown, 1976.

Sohn, Anne-Marie. "Between the Wars in France and England." In *A History of Women in the West*, vol. 5, *Toward a Cultural Identity in the Twentieth Century*, edited by Françoise Thébaud. Cambridge: Harvard University Press, 1994.

Sonn, Richard. *Anarchism*. New York: Twayne, 1992.

———. *Anarchism and Cultural Politics in Fin de Siècle France*. Lincoln: University of Nebraska Press, 1989.

———. "Gender and Political Violence in Nineteenth Century France and Russia." *Proceedings of the Western Society for French History* 28 (2002).

———. "Jews, Manliness, and Political Violence in Interwar France." *Proceedings of the Western Society for French History* 33 (2006).

Sowerwine, Charles. *France Since 1870: Culture, Politics, and Society*. New York: Palgrave, 2001.

———. "The Sexual Contract(s) of the Third Republic." *French History and Civilization: Papers from the George Rudé Seminar* 1 (2005).

Stallybrass, Peter, and Allon White. *The Politics and Poetics of Transgression*. Ithaca: Cornell University Press, 1986.

Stansell, Christine. *American Moderns: Bohemian New York and the Creation of a New Century*. New York: Metropolitan, 2000.

Stovall, Tyler. *Paris Noir: African Americans in the City of Light*. Boston: Houghton Mifflin, 1996.

Strauss, David. *Menace in the West: The Rise of French Anti-Americanism in Modern Times.* Westport: Greenwood, 1978.

Stromberg Childers, Kristen. *Fathers, Families, and the State in France, 1914–1945.* Ithaca: Cornell University Press, 2003.

Temkin, Moshik. *The Sacco-Vanzetti Affair: America on Trial.* New Haven: Yale University Press, 2009.

Thiriot, Franck, and Ronald Creagh. *Sacco et Vanzetti.* Paris: Le Monde Libertaire, 2001.

Tomlinson, Richard. "The 'Disappearance' of France, 1896–1940: French Politics and the Birth Rate." *The Historical Journal* 28, no. 2 (1985).

Vanacker-Frigout, Françoise. "Le mouvement anarchiste à travers *Le Libertaire,* 1934–1939." Mémoire de maîtrise, Université de Paris I, 1971.

Varias, Alexander. *Paris and the Anarchists: Aesthetes and Subversives during the Fin de Siècle.* New York: St. Martin's Press, 1996.

Villepin, Patrick de. *Victor Margueritte: La vie scandaleuse de l'auteur de La Garçonne.* Paris: Francis Bourrin, 1991.

"Voices: 1981–1999, The Grunge Invasion." *Newsweek* 133, no. 26 (June 28, 1999).

Ward, John W. "The Meaning of Lindbergh's Flight." *American Quarterly* 10, no. 1 (1958).

Waroff, Deborah. "When France Embraced a Jewish Avenger." *Forward.com.* October 23, 2008.

Weber, Eugen. *Action Française.* Stanford: Stanford University Press, 1962.

———. *The Western Tradition: From the Renaissance to the Present.* 3rd ed. Lexington, Mass.: D. C. Heath, 1972.

Weinberg, David. *A Community on Trial: The Jews of Paris in the 1930s.* Chicago: University of Chicago Press, 1977.

Weinstock, Nathan. *Le pain de misère, histoire du mouvement ouvrier juif en Europe.* Vol. 3, *L'Europe centrale et occidentale jusqu'en 1945.* Paris: La Découverte, 2002.

Weir, David. *Anarchy and Culture: The Aesthetic Politics of Modernism.* Amherst: University of Massachusetts Press, 1997.

Weissman, Susan. *Victor Serge: The Course Is Set on Hope.* London: Verso, 2001.

Wilson, Nelly. *Bernard-Lazare: Antisemitism and the Problem of Jewish Identity in Late Nineteenth-Century France.* Cambridge: Cambridge University Press, 1978.

Winders, James A. *European Culture Since 1848: From Modern to Postmodern and Beyond.* New York: Palgrave, 2001.

Wohl, Robert. *French Communism in the Making, 1914–1924.* Stanford: Stanford University Press, 1966.

———. *A Passion for Wings: Aviation and the Western Imagination, 1908–1918.* New Haven: Yale University Press, 1994.

———. *The Spectacle of Flight: Aviation and the Western Imagination, 1920–1950.* New Haven: Yale University Press, 2005.

Wolin, Richard. "Left Fascism: Georges Bataille and the German Ideology." In Richard Wolin, *The Seduction of Unreason,* 153–86. Princeton: Princeton University Press, 2004.

Index

CPSIA information can be obtained
at www.ICGtesting.com
Printed in the USA
FSHW010127071218
54295FS